IN THE SHADOW
OF ST PAUL'S
CATHEDRAL

THE CHURCHYARD
THAT SHAPED LONDON

MARGARET WILLES

YALE UNIVERSITY PRESS
NEW HAVEN AND LONDON

For information about this and other Yale University Press publications, please contact:
U.S. Office: sales.press@yale.edu   yalebooks.com
Europe Office: sales@yaleup.co.uk   yalebooks.co.uk

Set in Adobe Garamond Pro by IDSUK (DataConnection) Ltd
Printed in Great Britain by Clays Ltd, Elcograf S.p.A

Library of Congress Control Number: 2023935517

ISBN 978-0-300-24983-5 (hbk)
ISBN 978-0-300-27338-0 (pbk)

A catalogue record for this book is available from the British Library.

10 9 8 7 6 5 4 3 2 1

MIX
Paper from
responsible sources
FSC
www.fsc.org   FSC® C018072

Margaret Willes, formerly publisher at the National Trust, is the author of several books, including *The Curious World of Samuel Pepys and John Evelyn*, *Reading Matters* and *The Gardens of the British Working Class*. She lives in London.

Further praise for *In the Shadow of St Paul's Cathedral*:

'Willes's elegant writing, beautifully illustrated, makes St Paul's present to us once again.'

Alex Fauldy, *Tablet*

'Traces the development of the area around the cathedral from the Anglo-Saxon "Paulesbyrig" to our own day . . . Enlivened by colourful anecdotes.'

Richard Chartres, *Church Times*

'There has long been a need for this book and Willes has fulfilled that need excellently.'

Joe Saunders, *Local Historian*

'St Paul's Cathedral stands at the heart of London, an enduring symbol of the city . . . Margaret Willes tells the full story of the area for possibly the first time.'

Methodist Recorder

'This is a fascinating look at the history of London from a new and different angle.'

Family Tree Magazine

'A revelatory new insight into a part of London that I thought I knew well. I couldn't put it down.'

Adrian Tinniswood, author of *His Invention so Fertile: A Life of Christopher Wren*

'When St Paul's Churchyard was destroyed by the Luftwaffe in December 1940, the "Second Great Fire of London" obliterated centuries of London publishing history overnight. Now Margaret Willes offers us a thrilling and evocative resurrection of the stories buried beneath the ashes.'

Jerry White, author of *The Battle of London, 1939–45*

'Wonderfully evocative . . . Recreates the business and bustle of an area that was the vibrant heart of London for over a millennium and the historic centre of the nation's literary life.'

George Goodwin, author of *Benjamin Franklin in London*

CONTENTS

List of Illustrations vi
Acknowledgements x

Introduction 1
1. Setting the Scene 6
2. The Times Newspaper of the Middle Ages 20
3. The Centre of the Book World 37
4. The Fires of Reformation 62
5. The Children of Paul's 86
6. The Twilight of Old St Paul's 105
7. Resetting the Scene 129
8. Resurgam 150
9. A Place to be Seen 174
10. Literary Circles 198
11. Theatre for London, Britain and the Empire 223
12. Lengthening Shadows 241
Epilogue 269

Notes 277
Bibliography 291
Index 295

ILLUSTRATIONS

Plates

1. One panel of John Gipkyn's diptych, 1616. Society of Antiquaries of London, UK/Bridgeman Images.

2. Detail from the coronation procession of Edward VI, 1547. Society of Antiquaries of London, UK/Bridgeman Images.

3. Henry VIII overthrowing the Pope from *Foxe's Book of Martyrs*. Stationers' Company Library.

4. Latimer and Ridley at the stake in Oxford from *Foxe's Book of Martyrs*. Stationers' Company Library.

5. The title page of the Great Bible, 1539.

6. The title page of the King James Bible, 1611.

7. An illustration of the pageant for the Lord Mayor's Show, 1616. Album/Alamy Stock Photo.

8. Wenceslaus Hollar's engraving of the Cloister and Chapter House of Old St Paul's. © The Trustees of the British Museum, 1850,1109,149.

9. Seventeenth-century woodcut of the Great Fire of London. © Museum of London.

10. Eighteenth-century engraving of Wren's St Paul's Cathedral and Churchyard. Image © London Metropolitan Archives (City of London).

11. Engraving from a late eighteenth-century almanac showing Stationers' Hall. Stationers' Company Archive TSC/1/G/06-02-09.

12.   'A Real Scene in St Paul's Churchyard on a Windy Day'. © The
        Trustees of the British Museum, 1935,0522,1.30.

13.   Photograph of Nicholson's, the drapers, in the Churchyard, 1907.

14.   Watercolour of Paternoster Row by Thomas Colman Dibdin,
        1851. Image © London Metropolitan Archives (City of London).

15.   Funeral procession of Admiral Nelson, 1806. King George III
        Topographical Collection, Maps K. Top. XXIII 35-8, © The
        British Library Board, all rights reserved/Bridgeman Images.

16.   Lithograph of the arrival of the funeral procession of the Duke of
        Wellington, 1852, in St Paul's Churchyard. Image © London
        Metropolitan Archives (City of London).

17.   Drawing by John King of Doctors' Commons, c. 1800. Image
        © London Metropolitan Archives (City of London).

18.   Photograph of the Oxford Arms in Warwick Lane, 1875. Image
        © London Metropolitan Archives (City of London).

19.   Photograph of the bomb damage in Paternoster Row, 1941.
        Image © London Metropolitan Archives (City of London).

20.   Photograph of the total devastation of the Churchyard and
        surrounding streets, 1942. Image © London Metropolitan
        Archives (City of London).

21.   Aerial view of St Paul's Cathedral and Churchyard. Alamy Stock
        Photo.

In text

1.   Old St Paul's and its Churchyard, plate VI, H.W. Brewer   14
        and Herbert Cox, *Old London Illustrated*, 6th edition,
        published by *The Builder*.

2.   The printer's mark of Wynkyn de Worde.   38

3.   The device of John Rastell.   40

4.   The printer's marks of John Day and Reyner Wolfe.   45

5.   Portrait of John Day, 1570. Stationers' Company Archive.   49

6.   James Bainham paying penance, from *Foxe's Book of*   67
        Martyrs. Stationers' Company Library.

7. Skeletons from Queen Elizabeth's Prayer Book, compiled   73
    by Richard Day and printed for the Stationers' Company.
    Stationers' Company Library.

8. Moll Cutpurse, the 'Roaring Girl'.   124

9. Portrait of John Donne on the frontispiece of *Death's*   126
    Duel, 1632. Classic Image/Alamy Stock Photo.
    E192AP (RM).

10. Christopher Wren's plan for rebuilding London, 1666.   131
    Wellcome Library.

11. Sutton Nicholls's engraving of the east end of St Paul's   145
    Cathedral. By permission of the Pepys Library,
    Magdalene College, Cambridge (PL2972, 155).

12. Trade card by Wenceslaus Hollar of a bookseller's sign,   151
    1656. © The Trustees of the British Museum: Heal 17.3.

13. The title page of John Evelyn's *Sylva*, 1664.   155

14. A 'flying mercury' from Marcellus Laroon's *Cryes of*   170
    the City of London Drawne after the Life, 1687. By
    permission of the Pepys Library, Magdalene College,
    Cambridge (PL2973,437).

15. Morocco, the 'wonder horse', from Thomas Corser's   176
    Collectanea Anglo-poetica.

16. Trade card of Phillip Hunt, furniture maker. © The   187
    Trustees of the British Museum: Heal 28.105.

17. Trade card for the Sign of the Sun, linen drapers. © The   193
    Trustees of the British Museum: Heal 70:39.

18. Trade card for Martha Sleepe, fan-maker. © The Trustees   194
    of the British Museum: Heal 60.13.

19. Satirical print of Henry Sacheverell attributed to George   203
    Bickham the Elder, 1709–10. © The Trustees of the British
    Museum: 1868,0808.3427.

20. The 'Coffee-House Mob', frontispiece of part of 'Vulgus   204
    Britannicus: or the British Hudibras', 1710. © The
    Trustees of the British Museum: 1880,0807.301.

21. Trade card of John Newbery, bookseller and dealer in   213
    patent medicine, 1750. © The Trustees of the British
    Museum: Heal 83.24.

22. Engraving attributed to Benjamin Cole of Stationers' 218
Hall, 1756. Stationers' Company Archive,
TSC/1/G/06-02-09.

23. Engraving of statue of Queen Anne, St Paul's Churchyard. 226
Image © London Metropolitan Archives (City of London).

24. Woodcut by T. Batchelor of Queen Caroline's procession 235
to St Paul's Cathedral, 1820. Image © London
Metropolitan Archives (City of London).

25. St Paul's Churchyard in John Tallis's *London Street* 245
Views, 1839.

26. 'Lottery Placard' from Rowlandson's *Characteristic* 248
Sketches of the Lower Orders, published by Samuel
Leigh, 1820.

27. Advertisement for the Cathedral Hotel. © The Trustees 249
of the British Museum: Banks 1.29.

28. The north side of St Paul's Churchyard, an etching 250
by T. Horner, 1822. Image © London Metropolitan
Archives (City of London).

29. Thomas Holmes' bookshop, St Paul's Churchyard, an 255
engraving from 1851. Image © London Metropolitan
Archives (City of London).

30. Exterior of warehouses in St Paul's Churchyard, a 266
photolithograph of 1886. Image © London Metropolitan
Archives (City of London).

Maps

1. St Paul's and its surroundings in the thirteenth century. 7

2. St Paul's Churchyard in 1547. 63

3. The book trades in the neighbourhood of St Paul's in 199
the eighteenth century.

ACKNOWLEDGEMENTS

There are many people to thank because this book covers many fields and many periods of history. Moreover, I have completed it during a pandemic, so the kindness of friends and strangers has been vital. Rather than just provide a list of names, let me try to provide some context to their help.

To my fellow author, George Goodwin, who produced Bishop Francesco Coppini out of his research, convincing me that Paul's Cross really was the Speakers' Corner of its age and setting me on my way. To my sadly late tutor Susan Reynolds and Levi Roach for their help in unravelling some of the mysteries of Anglo-Saxon London, although some remain ravelled. To John Schofield for his masterly knowledge of the archaeology of the cathedral, and to Professor Wall for his excavation of the process of pulpit to press for John Donne's sermon. To Amy Erickson and Sheila O'Connell for the women traders in the Churchyard in the eighteenth century that filled such a lacuna in my knowledge. Charles Sebag-Montefiore told me of the Old Master paintings that hung in the premises of Cook & Son. And Norman Franklin provided an account of the final days of publishing in the Churchyard.

Librarians and archivists have been so generous with help, notably Jeremy Smith at the London Metropolitan Archives, Peter Ross and Jo Wisdom at the Guildhall Library and Ruth Frendo, the archivist of the Stationers' Company. London guides too have shared their knowledge, especially Jill Finch and Sue Jackson. Friends that have provided leads include Gerit Quealy, Fiona Darbyshire, Annie Edge, Deborah Springer, Elizabeth Prochaska and Sally Williams.

The unheralded arrival of Covid made technical help even more vital than in 'normal' times. So thank you to Mike Paterson and Hawk Norton for graphics editing, and Nina-Sophia Miralles for guidance on dealing with images online.

Finally, my publishers, Yale University Press. Thank you to Julian Loose for having faith in my idea for the book, and his editorial team who have helped me through these interesting times. In particular, I want to acknowledge my editor, Rachael Lonsdale, who has been with me through five books now, for her constantly wise guidance.

INTRODUCTION

My first memory of St Paul's Churchyard was when I visited it as a child, most probably in Coronation year, 1953. This was not long after the Second World War, and just over a decade since the area was devastated by bombing. Against all the odds, St Paul's Cathedral survived, along with a handful of other historic buildings nearby, looking like teeth in a wrecked mouth. I remember the tumbleweed pirouetting in the wind that soughed through the mounds of rubble. My whole working career was to be spent in book publishing, so when I became aware that this area had been for centuries the centre of the English book world I resolved one day to write about it. This is the result.

The image of a churchyard is often a rural one, entered by a lychgate with the gravestones of villagers set amid grass and ancient yew trees. St Paul's Churchyard is not, and never has been, remotely like this, nor has it resembled the precincts and closes of any other of England's medieval cathedrals, such as Salisbury or Lincoln, with wide expanses of lawn surrounded by charming residences. First, it was a distinct area known as 'Paulesbyrig'. By the early fourteenth century this had become an enclosed area with walls and gates, a town within the city. In the centuries that followed, more and more buildings were erected, so that by the later Middle Ages it had become a veritable jumble, with stalls and sheds amid larger structures, as shown in the map on p. 7. The City of London has for centuries been short of public open spaces. What open spaces there were, were mostly contained within religious houses until the Reformation, so that St Paul's Churchyard somehow had to combine public space with the functioning of the cathedral.

This book is not a history of St Paul's Cathedral, but rather of the surrounding area, and of the laypeople who lived and worked there, and of those who visited. Inevitably, however, it was the cathedral that shaped what was going on immediately around it. Thus, for example, the Churchyard became the theatre for grand ceremonial, with kings and princes welcomed, and sometimes denounced, for it could also act as a centre for opposition. Thomas Carlyle in the nineteenth century memorably described Paul's Cross, just to the north-east of the cathedral, as '*The Times* Newspaper' for the nation. It was the presence of craftsmen working on the production of manuscript books for the cathedral that drew printers to bring their presses to the area at the beginning of the sixteenth century, and thus it was also a centre for the book trade.

Exactly what constitutes the Churchyard is not always easy to define, as it has changed over the centuries. At one stage, for example, there was a series of churchyards contained within the cathedral precincts, such as the Cross Churchyard and the Pardon Churchyard, but the overall name of St Paul's Churchyard remained. As the metropolitan cathedral of London, St Paul's always played a role in the daily life of the citizens, with buying and selling even taking place in the nave from the fourteenth century onwards. This secular character markedly increased at the Reformation, and the Middle Aisle, as it was known, was where Londoners went to gather news and to be seen. It can be said the Churchyard had invaded the cathedral. Following the Great Fire of 1666, which marked the end of the medieval cathedral, publishers and printers were temporarily obliged to leave the Churchyard and join the bookselling community in the streets to the north, almost up to Smithfield. So it is the *idea* of the Churchyard that forms my theme.

My story begins in AD 604, with the building of the first cathedral on the elevated site in the westernmost part of what had been the Roman city of Londinium. Information about the first centuries of the cathedral and its precinct is all too sparse, but with the arrival of the Norman kings there is much more detail. Covering many centuries of the history of the Churchyard means necessarily that I have had to be selective. For example, rather than describing a long series of the very important sermons preached *en plein air* at Paul's Cross, I have chosen those that reflect the complex religious controversies of the time, put over to the considerable congregations in the Churchyard. Rather than enumerating all the printers, publishers and booksellers who thronged the Churchyard and its environs, I have chosen specific examples that reflect the development of the book and of journals. In the various genres, the Churchyard trade was so often in the vanguard.

There have been books aplenty about the cathedral itself. One in particular, *St Paul's: The Cathedral Church of London, 604–2004*, reflects in its size and scope the massive building that it celebrates. The editors, Derek Keene, Arthur Burns and Andrew Saint, put together over 40 chapters from a series of experts, with rich results. Although comprehensive in its treatment, this inevitably brings with it overlapping and repetition. Thus the area surrounding the cathedral is indeed looked at, but unsurprisingly not in a flowing narrative. It has been invaluable in providing me with much information that I hope provides a narrative that does flow. My approach has been principally chronological, but I have also taken themes, so there is a certain amount of shifting of time.

Paul's Cross as the pre-eminent site for sermons has been the area of study for Mary Morrissey. Her book, *Politics and the Paul's Cross Sermons, 1558–1642*, highlights the close relationship between pulpit and press. She has also contributed to *Sermons at Paul's Cross, 1521–1642,* under the general editorship of Torrance Kirby. The texts of many of the most important sermons of the period are reproduced from the printed versions, enabling us to catch the voices of the preachers at a significant time in England's church history. The plain speaking of the radical Protestant Hugh Latimer during the time of Edward VI contrasts with the ornate style only 30 years later of preachers in the reign of Elizabeth I. These men used complex language and studied repetition that is reminiscent of the style of theatrical dramas of the period. Moreover, there was for a time a theatre within the Churchyard, unusually a 'professional' company permitted within the limits of the City, the Children of Paul's. The first detailed account of this institution was provided by Reavley Gair: *The Children of Paul's: The Story of a Theatre Company, 1553–1608.* The Churchyard, too, played an important role in the drama of the annual Lord Mayor's Show as a pageant station with set pieces by leading playwrights with spectacular sets, as shown in Tracey Hill's *Pageantry and Power: A Cultural History of the Early Modern Lord Mayor's Show 1585–1639*.

The book trade has been extensively studied, notably by Peter Blayney for the sixteenth century, and James Raven for the seventeenth and eighteenth centuries. They have looked principally at the printers and booksellers and their businesses. It is not easy to identify the book purchasers who visited specific shops in the Churchyard, especially in the early period. Jason Scott-Warren, however, has found the book-buying activities of Richard Stonley in the late sixteenth century remarkably well documented through his diary and an inventory of his London house, described in *Shakespeare's First Reader*. By coincidence one of the booksellers patronised by Stonley has been identified as not only supplying publications but also publishing the verses of Isabella Whitney during the early years of the reign of Elizabeth I. Isabella can be regarded as the first published female writer of secular poetry in Britain. She also provides a rare example of a known woman in the Churchyard. Apart from princesses and queens, and women obliged to pay penance at Paul's Cross, the story is very male-orientated, although as shown in *Woman's Labour and the History of the Book in Early Modern England*, edited by Valerie Wayne, right from the early Tudor period women were trading as printers and booksellers, and the female element of the narrative increases as the centuries develop.

Observations by contemporaries have been vital for building up a picture of the people of the Churchyard, beginning in the sixteenth century and growing in range and numbers in the years that followed. Thus the chronicler John Stow offers all kinds of insights into the life of the Churchyard both in his *Survey of London* and in his *Annals*. The correspondence of John Chamberlain gives a first-hand account of walking the Middle Aisle or nave of the cathedral in search of news in the early seventeenth century. Decades later, Samuel Pepys and John Evelyn paint in their diaries a vivid picture of the cathedral and churchyard at one of its times of greatest drama, the Great Fire of London of 1666. The diaries and correspondence of booksellers and writers in the eighteenth century attest to the vibrant sociability of the area, the taverns and coffee houses, and, with developing awareness of the importance of authors, literary gatherings. Alongside these are the diaries and correspond-ence of tourists, with, as so often happens, the most perspicacious coming from visitors from overseas.

Another, perhaps rather surprising, source of information is provided by trade cards, revealing a less well-known aspect of the Churchyard: for centu-ries it was the centre of the book world and an area of luxury shopping. From the late medieval period drapers and mercers not only traded out of Cheapside but in the area around, including the Churchyard itself. The expansion of the

West End, especially after the Great Fire, meant that the Churchyard lay on the principal route from the City through to Fleet Street and beyond. The trade cards produced by the various establishments reflect the wide variety: textiles, yes, but also trunk makers, furniture makers, sellers of mathematical and optical instruments, and grocers and confectioners. An invaluable depiction of the Churchyard is provided by perspectives in John Tallis's *London Street Views* published in the early years of the reign of Queen Victoria, supplemented by the fire insurance maps produced by Charles Goad at the end of the nineteenth century.

Books and journals, side by side with haberdashery and drapery, were the two citadels of the Churchyard and Paternoster Row that continued right through until the Second World War. On the night of 29 December 1940, heavy German bombing devastated the area in what has been described as the Second Great Fire of London. The subsequent story of St Paul's Churchyard is perforce brief, for with this destruction the secular community disappeared, as did the architectural framing of the cathedral. The religious community continues to live here, as it has done for centuries, and by day this is an area for office workers and for tourists.

But this is not quite right, for this book has been completed in a time of pandemic, the consequences of which are still unknown at the time of writing. The future character of the Churchyard and the surrounding streets is in question. What can be said with certainty is that the vibrancy of a secular community, both cultural and social, will not return in the same way. We can, however, look back to those centuries when it was one of the most interesting parts of London, acting as the theatre for a city, a nation, and for a time, an empire, summed up as 'the whole world's map'.

CHAPTER 1

SETTING THE SCENE

The Roman city of Londinium, established in the first century AD, was built on two hills on the north bank of the River Thames. These hills, divided by the Walbrook, had a gravel topping raising them some 15 metres above the marshy ground of the Thames valley. A forum and basilica were constructed on the eastern hill, later known as Cornhill, while the western Ludgate Hill, also overlooking the Fleet River, would seem to have been a 'suburb' of the Roman city, with small houses, pottery kilns and a cremation cemetery. One area of this flat land is now Smithfield, or 'smooth field', and to the south, St Paul's Cathedral and its precinct. The city was in time walled, with a fort in the north-west at Cripplegate.

The first firm reference to the presence of Christianity comes in 314 when Restitutus, Bishop of London, along with bishops from York and Lincoln, attended the Council of Arles called by the Emperor Constantine. No remains of Roman churches, however, have been found in the City, although as one London historian points out, 'non-discovery and non-existence are by no means the same thing', and Restitutus must have had a cathedral church somewhere.[1] In his survey of London, the late sixteenth-century chronicler John Stow recorded a tradition that King Lucius in the second century had founded a cathedral on the site of St Peter Cornhill as the seat of an arch-bishop of London.[2] Stow dismissed the idea, and there is no strong evidence that the church of St Peter has ancient origins. A more likely candidate came to light in the 1990s when traces of a large building on a basilica plan, dating from the later part of the fourth century, were uncovered in the area just north of Tower Hill. This building would seem to resemble a contemporary basilica,

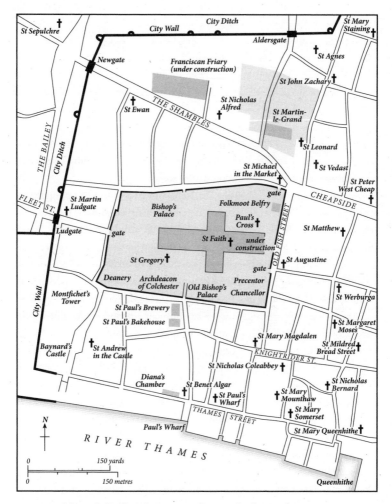

Map 1 St Paul's and its surroundings in the thirteenth century.

St Tecla in Milan, but again the case is not proven for it could have had a secular rather than ecclesiastical use.

When the Romans departed from Britain, the Anglo-Saxons chose at first to settle further to the west, around what is now Covent Garden, with easy access to the Thames. They left the walled Roman city alone, although retaining the road system that led into and through it. The principal west–east route, known by the Anglo-Saxons as Akemannstreet, ran from the Strand, along Fleet Street and up Ludgate Hill. Within the walls, the street passed south of where St Paul's now stands and then through East Cheap and Cannon Street. 'Ceap' or 'Cheap' was the Anglo-Saxon term for market, also retained now in the name Cheapside. This main route was probably joined in the vicinity of St Paul's by two other roads, one north to Aldersgate, and another towards Bishopsgate. The river crossing for the Saxons, as with the Romans, was located close by where London Bridge stands.

By the mid-eighth century the Anglo-Saxons had begun to populate the City, especially the western part, although the early years have yielded few traces. However, Bede, writing around 730, recorded that in 604 'King Ethelbert built a church dedicated to the holy Apostle Paul in the city of London, which he appointed as the episcopal see of Mellitus and his successors'.[3] Pope Gregory had ordered Augustine to re-establish metropolitans in London and York, but Anglo-Saxon politics dictated that the southern archbishopric should be at Canterbury in the Kentish kingdom of Ethelbert who had welcomed Augustine's mission to England.

Unlike many European cathedrals, the site on Ludgate Hill does not appear to have had links with pre-Christian cults, although later legends located a temple of Diana, as recorded by William Camden in *Britannia*, first published in 1596. His friend John Stow, however, when he came to publish his *Survey of London* two years later, also thought there might well have been a temple here, but one dedicated to Jupiter.[4]

London stood on the borders of several kingdoms, and at Ethelbert's death, Mellitus was driven out of the city by the pagan king of the East Saxons. Christianity was only reinstated around 675 with St Erconwald, from the Kentish royal family, who was appointed Bishop of the East Saxons. Legend has it that when he was old and infirm, Erconwald would travel around London on a wooden cart or litter. After his death, probably in 693, this modest form of transport took on miraculous qualities so that splinters were credited with curative powers. The cart was enshrined behind the main altar of the cathedral along with Erconwald's physical remains sealed in a leaden casket.

There were three Anglo-Saxon cathedrals. The first, founded by Ethelbert and Mellitus in 604, was constructed in wood, and destroyed by fire. It was replaced by a structure that could have had some stone component, built by Erconwald between 675 and 685. According to a version of the *Anglo-Saxon Chronicles*, this building was destroyed in a Viking attack in 962, and rebuilt soon thereafter. We have no idea of what these Anglo-Saxon cathedrals looked like, but they would have been aligned west to east, and occupied a part of the site of the later, much more extensive, medieval and baroque cathedrals. Although historians dislike describing the period as 'the Dark Ages', one authority has asserted, 'assessing the Viking impact on the diocese is a nightmare'.[5]

The area emerged, however, from the nightmare in both senses some 20 years later, when fighting between the Anglo-Saxon King Aethelred II and Danish troops led by Canute ended with Aethelred's death in 1016. According to some versions of the *Anglo-Saxon Chronicles*, his son Edmund Ironside was chosen as king by the councillors and citizens (*burhwaru*) of London. But another version of the chronicle had it that the English bishops, abbots and nobles agreed to accept that Canute should succeed to the throne. In the event, Edmund Ironside was defeated at the Battle of Assandun in the autumn of that year, and died shortly afterwards. With Canute as King of England, the attacks from Scandinavia ceased.

Although a period of comparative peace was achieved, London had incurred Canute's disapproval. In 1023 he ordered the body of Archbishop Alphege, murdered at Greenwich by a drunken Viking mob in 1012, to be forcibly removed from St Paul's to Canterbury. Again, versions of the chronicle have different stories. According to one, Canute was obliged to race from his bathtub, clad only in sandals and a cloak, to meet up with the Archbishop of Canterbury at St Paul's and help him to get the body away. The King's housecarls (household bodyguards) then took up position at various sites in the city to create distractions and to counter resistance, for Alphege's cult status was highly lucrative to whoever housed his remains. Fortunately the people of London had the shrine of St Erconwald on which to fall back.

When the third Anglo-Saxon cathedral also succumbed to a fire in 1087 that destroyed a considerable area of the city, work was begun on an imposing building of Caen stone by Maurice, Bishop of London and Chancellor and Chaplain to William I. The Conqueror's son, William Rufus, proved a generous benefactor, and the result was a Romanesque cruciform structure on a grand scale. Maurice had set out to produce one of the largest cathedrals in Europe, and the scale is clearly shown in the engravings that Wenceslaus Hollar produced of the exterior and interior, and reproduced in William Dugdale's *History* of 1658. The Tower of London, built at around the same time, is often described as dominating and intimidating, sending a message to the Anglo-Saxon population of London and of the kingdom as a whole that the Norman kings were here to stay. But St Paul's Cathedral, perched on the hill above the Thames, cast a very considerable shadow over the community that developed around it.

This shadow was to grow even greater when Gothic additions were made in the later thirteenth century, with the choir being extended eastwards in a scheme known as the 'New Work'. A soaring steeple was built atop the crossing tower above the transepts. Stow reckoned it was 260 feet in height, and Christopher Wren concurred with this measurement. His fellow architect Robert Hooke, also a scientist who was fascinated by experiments concerning pressure, came to the conclusion that it was slightly shorter, at 204 feet. Their calculations were perforce estimates, for the spire was struck by lightning and destroyed in 1561, but whichever measurement was correct, this was a very tall structure. We can see the effect of its height in medieval and fifteenth-century illustrations: only in 1964 was a building of equal height erected in the City of London.

Around the great cathedral was a rectangular precinct that developed as a little city within a city, known in Anglo-Saxon times as 'Paulesbyrig'. The concept of a cathedral precinct with wide open space with which we are now familiar is quite unlike the Churchyard of St Paul's in the centuries leading up to the Great Fire of 1666. In a city that was already tightly packed, it, too, was crammed with buildings that only grew more numerous with time. By 1300 it had its own walls and gates that could be locked securely at night.

In the north-west corner was a royal residence until Edward the Confessor decided in the 1040s to move his palace to Westminster, and to rebuild

St Peter's Abbey as a royal burial church. This enabled the bishops of London, whose palace had probably occupied a site in the south part of the precinct, to move into the vacated area. St Paul's was a secular rather than a monastic institution, served by canons, one of nine such medieval cathedrals in England.[6] In time, the cathedral became a major property owner. The Bishop of London, for example, held the manor of Stepney on the east, and on the west, those of Wimbledon and Barnes. Canons also owned many manors not only around London, but in Essex and Hertfordshire.

In the early twelfth century, important changes were made to the constitution of the clerical establishment at St Paul's with the introduction of a dean and chapter. A residence was created for the dean on the south side of the cathedral, answering to the episcopal palace to the north. Before this change, the canons had been able to marry. Now they were to be celibate and to share meals in a common hall, although they lived in individual or shared residences in the north part of the precinct. One interesting effect of this change was the record growth in the number of brothels in the surrounding streets in the 1130s.

Because St Paul's was not a monastic establishment, there was no hospital or extensive dormitory and refectory blocks. However, there was a cloister, a double-galleried quadrangle built in the fourteenth century, tucked into the corner of the nave and south transept of the cathedral. This was designed by William Ramsey, who had already installed a similar cloister at Westminster Abbey, and created the ornate stone screen that divided the nave from the choir within St Paul's. In the centre of the courtyard arose an octagonal chapter house, also of two storeys. An engraving made by Wenceslaus Hollar shows that both the cloister and the chapter house were of advanced Gothic style, looking towards the Flamboyant. This area was rather poetically described as 'the Shrouds' (Plate 8).

The Anglo-Saxons had been restrained in the number of churches that they established in London, but the Vikings, once they had embraced Christianity, were enthusiastic founders of parish churches. It has been estimated that in 1000 there were probably three or four within the city walls, with another two or three in the old settlement to the west. By the 1170s, when William Fitzstephen wrote his description of the city, he claimed there were 126 parish churches, and 13 conventual establishments in London and its suburbs. It is thought that on average a parish covered three acres. Two parish churches fell within St Paul's Churchyard, those of St Gregory and St Faith. Just outside the precinct were four more: St Augustine, St Martin within Ludgate, St Vedast and St Michael le Querne in the Market. The church of St Gregory, first mentioned in 1009, stood by the west door of the cathedral, and survived, more or less, until the outbreak of the Great Fire. Parishioners felt affection and loyalty towards their churches, the place where in life they had bonds both personal and professional, and where in death they could be remembered by their descendants. Thus when St Gregory's was threatened with demolition by Inigo Jones in the 1630s, an outcry ensued. The other Churchyard parish church, St Faith's, was subsumed under the choir of the cathedral with the 'New Work' that extended St Paul's in the late thirteenth and early fourteenth centuries. Its memory is retained in the chapel of St Faith's, in the crypt of the cathedral.

Not all the parish churches had room for a graveyard, so on the north side of the cathedral an area was established where their parishioners might be buried along with the poor of London. St Mary Colechurch, at the east end of Cheapside, was one such parish without a graveyard of its own, so that the parents of St Thomas Becket were buried in the precinct of St Paul's. When Becket was murdered in his cathedral in Canterbury in 1170, his tomb there became one of the great pilgrimage places of Europe. Becket had been a canon of St Paul's, and possibly attended the cathedral school, so that although the people of London may have felt deprived of the presence of his shrine they had the graves of his parents, Gilbert and Matilda, which in time became a significant pilgrimage site. In the fifteenth century the graves were enclosed by a cloister that became known as the Pardon Churchyard in response, it is thought, to the horror of the Black Death. A chapel dedicated to St Thomas was established in the centre of the cloister and a library founded by Walter Sherington, Chancellor of the Duchy of Lancaster, was also installed.

The buildings of the area reflected ecclesiastical developments. Thus in the early thirteenth century, friaries were established nearby: the Franciscans within Newgate on the north side in around 1225, and, half a century later, in 1278, the Dominicans to the south on the site of Baynard's Castle. These mendicant orders brought with them an emphasis upon preaching, which was to become a significant feature of St Paul's Churchyard. In the following century, perhaps prompted by the devastation of the Black Death throughout

Europe, there was a growing consciousness about mortality and the fragility of life, along with the developing concept of purgatory. Chantry colleges arrived in the Churchyard, where priests concentrated on 'obits', prayers for the souls of the departed. St Peter's College was founded for this purpose in 1353 and Holme's College in 1386, while Lancaster College was assigned the role of specifically praying for John of Gaunt, Duke of Lancaster, under the terms of his will at his death in 1399. In addition there were residences for clerical administrators; the Bishop of London's prison for religious offenders in the two western towers; and the school, which was housed at the east end of the cathedral. Key ecclesiastical courts were also held in the cathedral complex so that the Churchyard must have been thronged by people coming to transact Church business.

The complex required a considerable workforce of support. First, there were the cathedral craftsmen, such as marblers, stone carvers and makers of monumental brasses and stained glass, who had their workshops in the Churchyard. Then there were craftsmen who worked on bibles, missals and psalters – illuminators, paper and parchment makers, bookbinders and scriveners. In an age when few could read or write, the scriveners gathered every day in doorways and in the cathedral itself to write contracts and documents for Londoners. Neighbouring the walled area of the actual precinct were other craftsmen and women, such as the makers of rosaries in the aptly named Paternoster Row. In the parish of St Vedast, outside the gate leading from the Churchyard into Cheapside, was the community of embroiderers working on the 'Opus Anglicanum' that was the speciality of the English in the Middle Ages, and exported to all parts of Christendom.

Located by the south gate of the precinct were the bakehouse and brewhouse of the canons, with supplies from their manors coming up from wharves on the Thames. To the west lay the Fleet valley, an industrial area with stone, timber and sea coal landing at its wharves, and lime kilns. These industries were operated by a large workforce that formed part of the St Paul's estate, exempt in the early Middle Ages from customary contributions of labour.

Stimulated by the cathedral's custom, the capital's principal food markets were held in neighbouring streets: corn in Cheapside, meat in Newgate, fish from the riverside streets. Near St Augustine's Gate, in the south-east corner of the Churchyard, a market developed where gardeners from large estates

1. Old St Paul's and its Churchyard viewed from the west, an early twentieth-century reconstruction. Ludgate is in the foreground, with the Churchyard and its many buildings behind.

sold off their surplus fruit and vegetables. In 1345 this was moved south towards Blackfriars. It was declared:

> a nuisance to the priests who are singing Matins and Mass in the church of St Austin and to others, both clerks and laymen, in prayers and orisons there serving God, as also, to other persons passing there both on foot and horseback; as well as to the people dwelling in the houses of reputable persons there, who by the scurrility, clamour, and nuisance of the gardeners and their servants, there selling pulse, cherries, vegetables, and other wares to their trade pertaining are daily disturbed.[7]

St Paul's Churchyard, then, cannot be described as a sea of calm, nor an extensive area of open space. There were two parts of the precinct, however, which provided an outdoor space rare in other locations in the city. The first was in front of the west doors of the cathedral, which became known as the Atrium. Here processions, arriving from the west, up Ludgate Hill, might gather and if appropriate, enter the cathedral.

One example of such a procession was recorded in 1184, when the Archbishop of Cologne and the Count of Flanders arrived in England to offer prayers at Canterbury Cathedral at the site of Thomas Becket's martyrdom 14 years earlier. They were invited by Henry II to London, where the streets and precinct were bedecked for the occasion. As an entertainment for the visitors, citizens performed the 'tripudium', a leaping dance of three steps. This kind of procession became the norm, with the streets specially cleaned and hangings displayed at windows on the route. When Richard I returned from captivity in Germany in 1194, he was received into the City of London at London Bridge and processed to St Paul's Cathedral, and this and similar routes were taken by monarchs throughout the Middle Ages. A watercolour, based on a lost painting of Edward VI processing from the Tower via St Paul's Churchyard to his coronation at Westminster Abbey, gives an idea of how the streets would have looked, albeit of a later period (Plate 2).

In Anglo-Saxon times, the succession of kings rested upon a fluid system, as shown in 1016 at the death of Aethelred II (see p. 9 above). Considerations of dynasty, of continuity, of election and acclamation all might be brought into play. In most cases there was an election followed by consecration, with acclamation considered the right of the citizens of London, and some records suggest that this took place at the folk moot. While the west end of the cathedral looked toward Ludgate Hill and the road to Westminster, the seat of royal government, in the other direction the prospect was Cheapside, the mercantile centre of the city and, by the twelfth century, the Guildhall. In this north-east corner, originally next to the precinct but outside the cathedral's jurisdiction, was the meeting place for the folk moot.

Although the name is clearly Anglo-Saxon, this institution was possibly more ancient, older even than St Paul's itself. In the twelfth century its establishment was attributed, intriguingly, to King Arthur, the legendary Romano-British prince who resisted the Anglo-Saxon invaders. The story of the chivalrous exploits of Arthur had been written earlier in that century by Geoffrey of Monmouth, and it was at this period that the prince's name became associated with the moot, a meeting of all folk summoned by the tolling of the great Jesus Bell that hung in a free-standing belfry.

By the twelfth century the folk moot took place three times a year: at Michaelmas, 29 September, to acknowledge the new sheriff or sheriffs; at Christmas to ensure that the policing duties of the city were being undertaken by the wards; and at Midsummer to highlight fire precautions.[8] These dates reflect the developing system of government of the city. The sheriff was the royal official responsible for a shire: there were two shires for London, the City and Middlesex. In 1130 Henry I had granted a charter to the citizens of London, giving them the right to elect their own sheriffs, and during the reign of King John this key privilege was formally acknowledged. Records of sheriffs at this period show that they had English names, with connections to trade. The ward system was local government at street level, each run by an alderman, with a wardmote (a meeting of the ward's citizens) for maintaining order. The name alderman is derived from ealdorman, the Anglo-Saxon term for a nobleman, translated here into an urban office.

The third date mentioned for the gathering of the folk moot, Midsummer, was the time of celebration around the feast of St John the Baptist, 24 June. It was the custom to carry flowers and plants associated with that saint in procession around the streets, and then to burn them on bonfires to purify communities, probably a pagan tradition that had been adopted by the Church. This must have constituted a hazard in a city that was particularly susceptible to fires, especially as this was a time of 'great drought'. William Fitzstephen in his description of the city noted, 'The only plagues of London are the immoderate drinking of fools and the frequency of fires'.[9] The procession came to be known as the Marching Watch, surviving right through to the sixteenth century with increasingly elaborate features that can be compared to the annual show celebrating the inauguration of the City's lord mayor.

Attendance at the folk moot was compulsory, and those who neglected their duty could face the substantial fine of 40 shillings. In the seventeenth and eighteenth centuries, when parliamentary democracy was much prized, the idea was promoted of the Anglo-Saxons bringing liberal notions of government to Britain, as can still be seen in the landscape garden at Stowe in Buckinghamshire with the Gothic Temple and the British Temple of Worthies. But the folk moot, although perhaps the most democratic institution of the early Middle Ages, was not for 'all folk'. What constituted being a citizen of London at this period, before the term was given a formal definition by the development of the trade guilds, is not entirely clear. Many men, let alone women, were not free, so that it has been estimated that the number eligible to take part in the folk moot was in the hundreds, or possibly low thousands.

This caveat is highlighted by an unusual event that took place in 1196. William Fitz Osbert, known sometimes as 'Longbeard', was apparently a citizen of London who took the Cross, but got no further than Portugal, shipwrecked by a great storm and saved by the miraculous interventions of St Edmund, St Nicholas and St Thomas Becket. Returning to London, he set himself on a revolutionary course, opposing the habit of wealthier citizens of passing on to poorer brethren the main burden of taxes that fell upon the City. Possessed with noted gifts for eloquence, Fitz Osbert decided to champion the cause of the downtrodden, building up a considerable following, which one contemporary, William of Newburgh, inflated to the unlikely total of 52,000. In the spring of 1196 he went to see Richard I in Normandy to emphasise his loyalty to the Crown, probably reminding him that he was a fellow Crusader. But he had aroused the hostility of the King's justiciar, Hubert Walter, Archbishop of Canterbury. When Fitz Osbert returned home, Walter sent two men to arrest him in St Paul's or in the precinct. In the ensuing melee one of the justiciar's men was killed by Fitz Osbert, who took refuge with some supporters in the church of St Mary le Bow. When the tower was set alight,

Fitz Osbert was smoked out, taken to the Tower and then to Smithfield, where he was executed in a grisly manner, no doubt as an example to others. The Smithfield site became a centre of pilgrimage for many travelling to London.

Significantly contemporary chroniclers were not sympathetic, feeling that he had betrayed his own class, for Londoners above all prized economic security. Bede, back in the eighth century, had written how London, on the banks of the Thames, was 'a trading centre for many nations who visit it by land and sea'.[10] The city had seen changes of regime, including a Danish king with Canute, and Norman kings with William the Conqueror and his successors, but the city's mercantile life had continued to prosper along much the same lines, as reflected in the titles and institutions mentioned above. Alongside Cologne, it was Europe's urban phenomenon in the eleventh and twelfth centuries, and as England's largest and richest city, took over from Winchester, the seat of the kings of Wessex, as the capital.

This wealth meant that kings were careful in their dealings with the city. In times of crisis, as for example, during the struggle for power between Henry I's daughter, the Empress Matilda, and her cousin, Stephen, concessions had to be made to the citizens, in return for financial and political support. After the strong government and comparative peace of Henry II's reign, economic insecurity returned with the reign first of Richard I, absent abroad on Crusade and as a prisoner in Germany, and during the disastrous reign of his younger brother, King John. It was Richard who accorded the citizens of London the right to be governed by a mayor. This title, based on French precedents, gave citizens an administrative say in national affairs. The first person with the title of mayor was Henry Fitz Ailwin, who held the role from c. 1191 until his death in 1212. The mayor in 1215, William Hardel, was one of the 'barons' who signed Magna Carta. The modern concept of a mayor, elected annually, followed in the reign of John's son, Henry III, and in the fourteenth century was accorded the title of lord mayor.

By the mid-thirteenth century, the folk moot was in its last days. The population of London was rapidly rising: it reached its peak of 60,000 or even more by 1300 and thus the moot had become an unwieldy institution. Governance at grass roots level was organised in the wardmotes, overseen by aldermen. There were 34 wards within the City until 1394 when Farringdon ward was split into two. These wards were in effect the urban counterpart, in miniature, of the hundreds of shires, with a mixture of judicial, administrative and military functions. The alderman might, for example, be called upon in times of war to protect one of the nearest city gates.

Meanwhile many of the functions of the folk moot had been taken over by the Court of Husting. The term 'husting', still in use at time of elections, is derived from the Scandinavian for house and assembly, suggesting it was held indoors as opposed to the open-air character of the folk moot. The first reference to the husting comes in a document dating from the eleventh century, but it has been argued that the institution existed earlier, to sort out trading questions with the Danes. With the advent of the office of mayor, sheriffs and justices presided over the Husting, and it became part of the administration of the City centred on the Guildhall.

The folk moot may have drifted into memory, but the idea of an outside assembly for Londoners lived on. The location of St Paul's Churchyard, on the main route from Westminster, and the seat of royal government, through to the Guildhall, the seat of city government, made it the ideal theatre for the nation, both in support of the state and the Church, and as an arena for opposition in the years to come.

CHAPTER 2

THE TIMES NEWSPAPER OF THE MIDDLE AGES

In the summer of 1216 a most remarkable event took place in St Paul's Churchyard. The history of England is replete with extraordinary happenings, but this stands out: the offer of the crown to a French prince. Louis, the eldest son and heir of Philip Augustus, King of France, having taken control of the south-east of England, entered London in triumph on 2 June. At St Paul's he was received by the cathedral clergy and cheering crowds of Londoners.

The cause of this event was the regnal career of King John. Despite having enjoyed the support of London in his quarrels with William Longchamp, the governor of the kingdom in the absence of Richard I, John's relations had rapidly soured after his succession to the throne in 1199. The authors of *1066 and All That* singled out John as 'the Awful King', who imposed arbitrary taxes and other payments on his subjects and generally behaved in a despotic fashion.[1] His loss of Normandy in 1204 to Philip Augustus not only spelt economic problems for the merchant citizens of London, but also caused discontent among his leading barons, many of whom held land there and thus now owed homage to the French Crown.

John's dispute with his Archbishop of Canterbury, Stephen Langton, caused Pope Innocent III first to excommunicate the King and then in principle to depose him, authorising Philip Augustus to invade England and take the throne. Philip Augustus decided that this offer should be taken up by his heir, Prince Louis. In a desperate bid to stave off this crisis John chose to throw himself on the mercy of the Pope by officially placing his kingdoms of England and Ireland under papal control. Although Innocent cancelled his order for the French to invade, Philip Augustus was moving towards his goal of taking the crown. In tandem with his son Louis, he inflicted crushing defeats on John first at La-Roche-aux-Moines and then, in one of the few pitched battles of this period, at the Battle of Bouvines in 1214. The chronicler, Matthew Paris wrote: 'The French rejoiced less in the victory at Bouvines than in the defeat inflicted on the king of England by Louis, because they hoped that in him they would have a valiant sovereign who would outshine his father.'[2] This sentiment no doubt was echoed by the leading men of England.

In January 1215 the rebellious barons met John in London, reminding him of the coronation charter of his great-grandfather, Henry I, binding the monarch to uphold ancient laws and liberties, which were now referred to as the Articles of the Barons. Five months later, London opened the gates to the barons, forcing the King to come to terms with them with the signing of Magna Carta at Runnymede on 15 June. When he promptly rescinded this, the barons offered the crown to Louis. St Paul's now became the theatre of opposition to King John. Welcomed by cheering crowds, the prince was received by the canons and solemnly processed into the cathedral where he swore on the holy Gospels to restore the rightful laws and liberties to his new subjects. He then received oaths of faith from the leading baron, Robert FitzWalter, and the Mayor, William Hardel. Versions vary as to where this took place, but one has it in the Churchyard.[3] It seemed only a matter of time before Louis was officially crowned.

But in July 1216 Pope Innocent died. The new Pope, Honorius III, played yet another round in the excommunication game, this time imposing it upon Prince Louis. Although some churches defied the papal order, Westminster Abbey did not, so Louis was obliged to defer his coronation. It is interesting to note that when William Shakespeare came to write his play about King John, the emphasis was upon the interference of the Pope in English affairs rather than the birth of democracy with the signing of Magna Carta by the King and barons. Performances of *King John* in the eighteenth century high-lighted the idea that this was an anti-Catholic play, with the King standing up to papal authority and his excommunication.

The death of King John in October 1216, and a form of crowning of his young son as Henry III at Gloucester organised by William Marshal, spelt the end of this extraordinary adventure, with Louis returning to France. The prospect of a French prince on the English throne had narrowly been averted.[4]

Records of Louis' reception at St Paul's describe speeches being delivered in the Churchyard. The location for these would seem to be St Paul's Cross, although the first proper reference to it comes a quarter of a century later, in 1241. Originally a simple cross was set up in the north-east part of the Churchyard, in the open space close to the bell tower that for centuries had summoned the folk moot. In time a pulpit was installed. It became the place for public announcements and declarations, so that Thomas Carlyle described it as 'a kind of *Times Newspaper*'. In fact he was referring to the Cross in the seventeenth century, adding that it was partly edited by Heaven itself. The description, however, is even more fitting for the Middle Ages and the Tudor period. A more recent description has called it 'the broadcasting house' of the time, and no doubt in the future it will be likened to the source of social media.[5]

Both St Paul's Cross and the place of assembly for the folk moot appear in the annals of the long and often troubled reign of Henry III. The reign had started off well enough, but in 1234 the justiciar Hubert de Burgh was unseated by Peter des Roches, Bishop of Winchester. No respecter of the terms of Magna Carta, des Roches advised the King not to seek counsel from his leading men. When these men protested, Henry backtracked, with the terms of Magna Carta confirmed in 1225. He used St Paul's Cross as his way of presenting 'good news'. Thus in 1241 he 'asked' permission of the people to cross over to Gascony and oppose the King of France, Louis IX, the son of the prince who had so nearly denied him the throne. He repeated this ceremonial leave-taking four years later before an expedition to Wales.

Breaches of Magna Carta continued, however, with the King failing to consult and seek consent, and these, combined with military incompetence and increasing financial problems caused growing opposition. In time this formed around the considerable figure of Simon de Montfort. Simon was not only the Earl of Leicester, with his Midlands power base at Kenilworth Castle, but he also held lands in the southern part of what is now France: his father, also Simon, had conducted here the brutal crusade against the Albigensian heretics. In 1236 Simon married Henry III's sister, Eleanor, a love match which brought happiness along with drawn-out quarrels with the King about her dowry.

Originally the grievances were felt by minor barons, churchmen, rural gentry and tenants rather than by de Montfort and the other great landowners. But Henry's difficult inheritance came not only from his father, King John, but also from his mother, Isabella of Angouleme. She had made a second marriage, to Hugh Lusignan, and the growth in power of their progeny tipped the fragile balance. In April 1258 a confederation of leading magnates swore to confront the King and demand reforms. Henry was forced to submit, agreeing to establish a committee consisting of a balance of royal supporters and baronial representatives, to convene in parliament in Oxford. At this assembly a series of memoranda were drawn up, known as the Provisions of Oxford: these contained radical proposals marking encroachment on the traditional authority of the Crown, to the advantage of local government rather than that of the major barons. This indeed was breaking new ground, even more so than Magna Carta, which in many ways had been a retrospective document focusing on the protection of the interests of the magnates.

Resistance to the Provisions was mounted by the King, who the following year summoned the citizens of London to a folk moot at St Paul's. Here Henry, with the support of his brother Richard, Earl of Cornwall, and son, Prince Edward, required an oath from 'every stripling of twelve yeares of age or upwarde, to bee true to the king and his heyres' (in the words of the sixteenth-century chronicler, John Stow). To ensure that this was carried out, royal guards were set at all the gates of the city. Stow also recorded that in 1262 Henry had a bull obtained from Pope Urban IV read out at the Cross. This absolved him and all those that had sworn to maintain the Provisions.[6] The Mayor, Thomas Fitz Thomas, the first to be elected to the office, and his aldermen were rich men, and natural opponents of the radical terms of the Provisions, but they were alienated not only by the King's actions but also by the subsequent rash behaviour by Prince Edward in breaking into the New Temple and seizing private deposits of treasure to pay his foreign followers.

The situation came to a head in the summer of 1263 when Simon de Montfort returned to England and, recognising the folk moot site as a potential theatre of opposition, rallied his supporters here, a powerful combination of disaffected magnates and London's leading citizens, summoned by the ringing of the Jesus Bell. De Montfort was now in control of the capital. When he prepared to do battle the following year against the King, many Londoners joined his army, having signed up to an oath: 'from this hour forward, we will hold together in all rightful quarrels, and save and maintain our liberties and customs against all those who wish to do us violence'.[7] The names of some of these have been recorded, and show that they were merchants, members of the newly emerging trade guilds: fishmongers, a goldsmith and men associated with the all-important textile trade.[8]

The royal army was overwhelmingly defeated at the Battle of Lewes, with the King, Prince Edward and Richard of Cornwall taken prisoner. In 1265 a Parliament was called first at St Paul's, and then moved to the chapter house and hall at Westminster. Not only were knights summoned to this Parliament, but also townsmen, a new departure. This, however, proved the high point of de Montfort's career. Quarrels soon broke out with his fellow rebel barons, while royal forces were reassembled by Prince Edward who had escaped from captivity. The end came for Simon with his defeat and death at the Battle of Evesham in the same year. This also marked the end of the idea of the folk moot, for when the Prince succeeded his father as Edward I, he closed it down as an institution. Even the site disappeared when the Dean and Chapter of St Paul's enclosed the land within the walls of the precinct. Henceforward it was St Paul's Cross that became the prime site to reinforce the political and religious establishment, and at times to become a theatre of opposition.

Sermons were preached here on a regular basis, for there was no pulpit in the nave of the cathedral, and the choir was shut off behind the great stone screen. Another important and popular outside pulpit was established on the east side of Bishopsgate, at St Mary Spital which had been founded in 1197. Stow described the two preaching venues, both still operating in his day in the late sixteenth century. The custom was to have 'some especiall learned men, by appointment of the Prelates' to preach at St Mary Spital on Good Friday, and three similar clerics preached on Monday, Tuesday and Wednesday of the week following, while another learned man gave a review of these four sermons at St Paul's Cross on Low Sunday. At all these sermons, the lord mayor and aldermen were in attendance.[9]

St Paul's Cross also provided a platform for those who wished to argue their doctrinal point of view. Here, for example, in 1356 and 1357 Richard Fitzralph preached a series of sermons attacking the mendicant orders, and in particular the Franciscans. Fitzralph acquired his preaching skills while studying at Oxford, ironically, perhaps, from the friars at the university. His views radically developed when he became Archbishop of Armagh in 1346 and had to deal at first hand with the matters of his diocese. Not only did he question whether there was a theological basis for the life of poverty adopted by friars, but also that their pastoral work should be exercised outside the parochial structure and thus be exempted from episcopal jurisdiction. His arguments were developed in a treatise, *De Pauperie Salvatoris*.

In the summer of 1356, Fitzralph arrived in London, and the text of his treatise was circulated both in the capital and at Oxford, sparking a vigorous controversy. His friend, Richard Kilvington, Dean of St Paul's, offered him the chance of voicing his position at the Cross. He apparently preached seven or eight sermons at Paul's Cross, but only four survive.[10] Unsurprisingly the friars rose to defend themselves. The Franciscans, who felt especially under attack, gathered the other orders to a meeting at their monastery, Greyfriars, just north of the Churchyard, in March 1357 to organise their defence. Twenty-one errors that they had found in Fitzralph's arguments were listed and delivered to his lodgings by the prior of the Augustinian order in London. The Archbishop's response was a vituperative sermon preached at St Paul's Cross two days later, on 12 March. The friars had the support of the King, Edward III, who forbade Fitzralph to leave the country without royal permission, but he was able to escape to Avignon, where a papal court attempted to adjudicate. His death in 1360 brought this particular religious debate to a close.

Whitsun processions bringing together parishioners from the component elements of the diocese of London represented a major event in the cathedral's year. On three days after Whit Sunday the mayor, aldermen and City officers followed processions to St Paul's of parishioners and their priests. First, the people of the City gathered on the Monday at St Peter Cornhill and went in procession along Cheapside into the north-east part of St Paul's Churchyard and round to the south side of the cathedral. The next day it was the turn of the people of Middlesex, who assembled at the priory of St Bartholomew and entered the City through Newgate, down Old Change and into the Churchyard through St Augustine's Gate. On the Wednesday the people of Essex assembled at St Mary Colechurch, associated with the birthplace of St Thomas Becket, and again took the route along Cheapside. All three processions entered the cathedral through the west doors to hear the *Veni Creator* chanted by the vicars choral. In 1548, among the reforms made by Edward VI's Protestant ministers, these Whitsuntide processions were suppressed and replaced by three solemn sermons.

The Cathedral and its Churchyard were also the venue for civic processions. When the office of mayor was established on a yearly basis, the election took place at Michaelmas. A month later, on the day of the feast of SS Simon and Jude, 28 October, the new lord mayor, accompanied by the aldermen, sheriffs and liverymen of the various craft guilds, would process to Westminster where he would take an oath before the representatives of the Crown at the Exchequer. Returning to the City, and following dinner, the mayor processed with the liverymen of his own company from the site of the birthplace of St Thomas Becket in Cheapside to the Pardon Churchyard just to the north of St Paul's Cathedral, to the graves of Becket's parents where they prayed for all the faithful departed. On seven other days, clustered around Christmas, the Mayor, his household, and the 'good men' of the crafts, attended services in the cathedral.

These were solemn, albeit colourful, occasions, but there were also livelier events. Two dates in the Church calendar were associated with St Paul, the patron saint of the cathedral. These would seem to have survived the Reformation, for John Stow in his survey of London, first published in 1598, says that he had been witness to one such. He explains how in 1274, during the reign of Edward I, an Essex landowner was leased land from the manor belonging to the Dean and Chapter of St Paul's to enclose as part of his hunting park. In return, he undertook

> for ever uppon the Feast daye of the conversion of S. Paule in winter [25 January], give unto them a good Doe, seasonable and sweete, and uppon the Feast of the commemoration of S. Paule in summer [29 June], a good Bucke, and offer the same at the high Altar, the same to bee spent amongst the Canons residentes.

Stow goes on to describe how on 29 June the body of the buck was brought up to the steps of the high altar in the cathedral, and his body was then dispatched for baking, while his head was put on a pole and carried in procession by clerics, wearing chaplets of roses on their heads, out to the Churchyard. Here the keeper who had brought the buck announced its death by blowing his horn, and other trumpeters in the City duly answered him.[11] This exuberant display with its pagan undertones was witnessed back in 1321 by

Edward II, who returned to his palace in Westminster with the fine bread or cakes, known as wastels, that were the speciality of the cathedral, with the image of the saint impressed on them.

The ceremony of the buck has been described as boisterous, and indeed there were activities in the Churchyard at this period which contrasted with the religious solemnity of the cathedral. Wrestling matches, for example, were a regular feature. Robert Braybrooke, Bishop of London from 1382 to 1404, sought to reform the behaviour of both inhabitants and visitors. He complained that birds who nested in the walls of the cathedral were being shot, while the nave was not only used for buying and selling, but as a football pitch, causing great damage to images and to the windows. Attacks on people who passed through the Churchyard are frequently recorded, and quarrels sometimes ended in murder.

Every so often, however, the area could erupt into greater and widespread violence. One such occasion took place in 1326, as the unhappy reign of Edward II neared its end. The overwhelming influence of the King's favourites, the Despensers father and son, had alienated his Queen, Isabelle, 'the she-wolf of France'. Returning from France with her lover, the Marcher Lord Roger Mortimer, she secured the support of the barons. On 28 September the King's proclamation against Mortimer was read to a sullen city, and when Isabelle entered London, the populace rose up, lynching Despensers' men, and setting fire to buildings. One of the buildings chosen for the torch was the palace of the Bishop of London in St Paul's Churchyard. When Bishop Stapledon unwisely returned to dine he was cornered by the north door of the cathedral, knocked off his horse and dragged through the Churchyard out into Cheapside where his head was removed with a bread knife.

Later in the century the volatile London mob again rose in tumult at St Paul's in an incident involving Edward III's son, John of Gaunt, Duke of Lancaster, and the radical theologian, John Wycliffe. Born around 1330, probably in Yorkshire, Wycliffe had studied at Oxford before entering royal service, certainly in 1374, if not earlier. In July of that year he was part of a deputation to Bruges on behalf of Edward III to negotiate a way out of a growing dispute between the King and Pope Gregory XI concerning papal appointments in England. His personal observation of the politics of the papacy during this visit had a profound effect upon him. Horrified by the corruption of the

Church, he began to condemn prayers to saints and pilgrimages, and in particular the simony of the ecclesiastical hierarchy. These views, expressed in sermons and writings, brought him to the attention of John of Gaunt, who became his patron and protector. This was to prove highly valuable, for the Duke of Lancaster was the effective ruler of England during the last years of the reign of his father, when Edward III became gradually incapacitated physically and mentally, and in the first years of the reign of Richard II.

On 19 February 1377, Wycliffe was summoned to appear before the Archbishop of Canterbury, Simon Sudbury, and other bishops in St Paul's Cathedral. He was being charged with seditious preaching, but appeared well supported by representatives of the orders of friars, and also by John of Gaunt and Lord Henry Percy, the Earl Marshal. When Percy ordered Wycliffe to be seated, this was opposed by William Courtenay, the Bishop of London. Gaunt and Courtenay proceeded to have angry words, with the Duke threatening to drag the Bishop from his throne by the hair. This inflamed a riot among the crowd gathered outside the cathedral, furious that the Duke had insulted the Bishop. The situation became far worse the following day, with Gaunt also accused of infringing judicial liberties, at which point he fled with Percy and the meeting was abandoned. Such was the fury of Londoners that a broadside was pinned to the cathedral door accusing the Duke of illegitimacy and, in an age when heraldry was such a conspicuous form of communication, reversing his coat of arms.[12] A few months later, when his young nephew, Richard, ascended the throne on the death of Edward III, Gaunt was able to make his peace with the parliamentary Commons and with the people of London.

Wycliffe's attacks on Church corruption and the papacy found many sympathisers, especially among the secular ruling elite. But another of his teachings was to bring down upon him the strongest condemnation by Church and state alike: the nature of the Eucharist. Transubstantiation had been accorded the stamp of orthodoxy by Pope Innocent III in 1215. Wycliffe, however, rejected this interpretation, arguing that the material of the bread and wine offered in communion remained after consecration, and that therefore the body and blood of Christ are not present in substance, nor physically, but rather figuratively or symbolically. In May 1381 a committee was organised by the chancellor of Oxford University to condemn this view, so that when Wycliffe died three years later, he was condemned as a heretic.

The unpopularity enjoyed by John of Gaunt in 1377 had not endured, and when he died in 1399 and chose to be buried on the north side of the high altar in St Paul's, a special connection developed between the House of Lancaster and the cathedral. His son, Bolingbroke, as he prepared to take the Crown as Henry IV, visited his father's fresh grave, and later had the body of his cousin, Richard II, carried in procession to St Paul's and shown there to prove that he was dead. In 1403, having defeated a rebellion by the Percy family at the Battle of Shrewsbury, he came to St Paul's to give thanks before taking a boat to Westminster.

This was a period dominated by religious dissension created by John Wycliffe's followers, who were known as the Lollards, meaning 'mutterers'. Given John of Gaunt's earlier support for Wycliffe, it is ironical that his heirs were so strongly opposed to Lollardy. Problems had begun even before Wycliffe's death. In 1382 Wycliffe's teachings on the Eucharist were declared heresy at a Council held at Blackfriars. In that same year two Oxford scholars, Nicholas Hereford and Philip Repingdon, nailed *schedulae*, or articles of Wycliffe's teachings, onto the doors of St Paul's Cathedral. This is an interesting precedent to the act of pinning Martin Luther's theses on the doors of the castle church at Wittenberg a century and a half later. According to a chronicler, another set of articles, this time condemning the mendicant orders, was nailed on the doors of St Paul's in 1387 by Peter Potteshull, an Augustinian friar, following a sermon on the theme.[13]

In 1401 a Lollard priest, John Purvey, was put on trial for heresy, and made a full acknowledgement and recantation at St Paul's Cross, reading his list of articles before Bishop Braybrooke. This was one of a whole series of events connected with Lollardy that took place at the Cross. In 1406, William Taylor dared to preach a sermon there condemning clerical possessions. According to the *St Albans Chronicle*, the following day, 21 November, another preacher, Richard Alkerton, refuted his arguments, again at the Cross, declaring all plunderers of church property to be anathema.[14] This sermon pleased the chronicler, who was a Benedictine monk, but won less favour from the congregation. One member, Robert Waterton, sent Alkerton a curry comb, used for grooming horses, to symbolise flattery of prelates. News of this reached the ears of Thomas Arundel, Archbishop of Canterbury, a vigorous opponent of the Lollards, who swore he should pay for the insult. Waterton was a lifelong friend of the King, Henry IV, who intervened to agree that Arundel might be right, but should curb his rage. He persuaded the Archbishop to commute his punishment to private penance, with a servant carrying the offending curry comb and a lighted taper to proceed the procession at St Paul's on certain days.

Not only were the Lollards regarded as heretics for preaching the religious doctrine of John Wycliffe, but also for their desire to be able to read the Scriptures in English. There had been vernacular bibles in Anglo-Saxon England, but these disappeared with the Norman Conquest. Although there is no record of Wycliffe undertaking any actual translation, he was nevertheless denounced for the 'crime' of giving ordinary people the opportunity to be able to consider the Scriptures for themselves. In 1411 Archbishop Arundel wrote to Antipope John XXIII:

This pestilent and wretched John Wyclif, of cursed memory, that son of the old serpent . . . endeavoured to every means to attack the very faith and sacred doctrine of the Holy Church, devising – to fill up the measure of his malice – the expedient of a new translation of the Scriptures into the mother tongue.

A later chronicler echoed this virulent tone, declaring, 'And so the pearl of the Gospel is scattered abroad and trodden underfoot by swine'.[15]

A determined campaign was waged to suppress not only the writings of Wycliffe and the Lollards, but also any Scriptures in English. Remarkably, even the Lancastrian and Yorkist monarchs had copies in their libraries. Although many books were rounded up and burned, about 250 bibles and New Testaments have survived. Some of these are large and beautifully written and decorated, others small and in a comparatively rough hand. The centre for their covert production was the craftsmen who lived and worked in the area north of St Paul's Cathedral. One recorded purchase of a Lollard bible was made by Nicholas Belward of Earsham in Norfolk, who in 1430 paid the substantial sum of £12 6s 8d.[16] This would be roughly the equivalent of two or three years' wages for a skilled artisan, and of course it must have taken the scribe who wrote it out that length of time to complete it.

Persecution of Lollards increased in severity, particularly after the accession of Henry V in 1413. The movement had become associated with social rebellion, despite the fact that many Lollards were drawn from the rural gentry.

While Wycliffe had opposed the Peasants' Revolt in 1381, one of the leaders of that insurrection, John Ball, had preached Lollardy. Recantations and penances undertaken in St Paul's Churchyard were replaced by the burning alive of those found to be guilty of the heresy. One of the first to suffer this terrible fate was John Badby at Smithfield in 1410 after being held in the episcopal prison in one of the towers of the cathedral and tried at Archbishop Arundel's court at St Paul's. John Oldcastle, a friend of Henry V, and possibly the basis for Shakespeare's character of Sir John Falstaff, was brought to trial as a Lollard in 1413. Escaping from the Tower of London, he raised an insurrection, including an attempted kidnapping of the King. When this failed, he was captured and hanged and burnt in St Giles Fields. Lollardy was now associated with treason as well as heresy, and many others suffered his fate over the following century. In 1428 John Wycliffe's bones were dug up from his grave and thrown into the river.

But Lollardy was not the only problem that faced the Crown during the fifteenth century. In the second part of *Henry IV*, Shakespeare has the King declare 'Uneasy lies the head that wears the crown' (Act 3, Scene 1) but this also applied to his son and successor, Henry V, who greatly feared plots to kill him through acts of sorcery. In 1419 Richard Walker, a chaplain from Worcester, appeared at Paul's Cross, having been arrested for the possession of books of magic, beryl stones and other images. Here, subjected to a harangue by John de la Zouche, Bishop of Llandaff, Walker foreswore his magical practices. He was then marched along Cheapside carrying two of his manuscript books, the pages open at illustrations, and on his return to the Cross, they were publicly burnt before him. Walker was lucky to suffer no further punishment.[17]

Another case of alleged sorcery occurred during the reign of Henry VI, this time involving the royal family itself. The King's uncle, Humphrey, Duke of Gloucester, having annulled his first marriage, married his mistress, Eleanor Cobham, a beautiful, clever woman with an interest in astrology. At court, the new Duchess began to exert influence over the young and vulnerable King, who was suffering from what we would now describe as incipient schizophrenia. She also became obsessed with the fact that her husband was the heir apparent, for Henry was unmarried at this stage. Astrologers, including Roger Bolingbroke, Principal of St Andrew's College in Oxford, were consulted to cast the King's horoscope. Very foolishly, the Duchess and her astrologers made public their reading of the King's horoscope, in which they predicted that serious illness would endanger his life in July or August of 1441. News of this quickly spread around London, reaching the royal court, so that Eleanor and Bolingbroke with their associates were examined.

Following her trial for treasonable necromancy and heretical practices, the Duchess was obliged to abjure her errors by penance, walking barefoot and bearing a taper to three London churches on successive market days, before being forcibly divorced and condemned to perpetual imprisonment. A far harsher punishment was meted out to her associates. One, Margaret Jourdemayne, known as 'The Witch of Eye', was burned at Smithfield. Although Bolingbroke made a public confession at Paul's Cross on 23 July 1441, declaring that his actions were not compatible with Christianity and foreswearing his diabolic activities, he was found guilty of treason and hanged, drawn and quartered at Tyburn. Margaret, or Margery, appears in the list of characters in Shakespeare's *Henry VI, Part II*, alongside Eleanor and Bolingbroke, who is described as a conjuror.

Paul's Cross may not have been the primary venue for religious debates over Lollardy, but it remained the most influential pulpit for clergymen to promote their theological doctrine, and as the venue for public penance. Bishop Pecock was to experience both. Although Reginald Pecock, an Oxford-trained scholar, was appointed to the see of St Asaph in 1444, he continued to reside in London, and there is no evidence that he ever visited his Welsh diocese. Three years later he preached a sermon at Paul's Cross in which he defended the practice of absenteeism, arguing that the important role of a prelate was to explain complex points of doctrine, rather than preach to their own flock. This argument caused a furore, and Pecock was summoned before the Archbishop of Canterbury, John Stafford, to answer charges of heresy.

Pecock managed to ride out this crisis, and indeed was given the bishopric of Chichester in 1450, but this elevation brought him to the attention of the household of Henry VI's Queen, Margaret of Anjou. This was a difficult time for Margaret. The King suffered his first bout of insanity in 1453, falling into a catatonic trance for 17 months. In October of the first year of his illness, the Queen gave birth to a healthy son, Edward. Protecting his claim to the throne became her principal interest, in particular against any counter-claim by the King's cousin, Richard, Duke of York. Her steward, Viscount Beaumont, saw an opportunity to boost the future of the Lancastrian dynasty by asserting religious orthodoxy and pressing further heresy charges against the unpopular Pecock.

The bishop had put himself in a vulnerable position not only by defending absenteeism of prelates, but also by writing and circulating books in the vernacular. Back in 1431 Pecock had been appointed master of a college of priests, newly established under the will of the wealthy mercer and Lord Mayor of London, Sir Richard Whittington. As Master of Whittington College, he was also Rector of the city church of St Michael, Paternoster Royal. During his tenure he became familiar with the craftsmen involved with covertly producing Lollard literature. Pecock acquired the writings of Wycliffe and his followers in order to refute their teaching, but recognised the potency of the written word in the vernacular, and thus began to produce his own literature in English. One such work was *The Poore Mennis Myrrour*, a digest of one of his other theological works for those of modest means and education. His desire to communicate directly with such a readership was shared by a friend who developed a scheme for circulating books for 'common-profit'.

These activities, which sound admirable to modern ears, laid Pecock open to prosecution. When Beaumont wrote to King Henry to urge the bishop's prosecution, the Archbishop of Canterbury, now Thomas Bourchier, began to examine his writings in English and Latin. Even though the case was *sub judice*, opposition had been expressed in London, and throughout the Archbishop's diocese. In late 1457, when Pecock appeared before Bourchier and other bishops, he admitted to his heresies and errors, revoking them in a signed statement. As a result he was called to make a public recantation at Paul's Cross, where he consigned his offending books to the flames in front of a huge crowd. He was then stripped of his bishopric and was sent to Thorney Abbey near Peterborough, where he was kept strictly confined, and where he died around the year 1459. Reginald Pecock was the only bishop to lose his see as a heretic in Pre-Reformation England.[18]

The Duke of York did indeed assert his claim to the English throne, thus opening the decades of civil war that we now know as the Wars of the Roses. In the summer of 1460 the leader of the Yorkist faction, Richard Neville, Earl of Warwick, arrived from Calais to London accompanied by the papal legate, Bishop Francesco Coppini, to a tumultuous welcome from the citizens, disgruntled by the economic dislocation resulting from Henry VI's loss of his

French lands. The King was in the Midlands with the Lancastrian forces under the command of his Queen, Margaret of Anjou.

Margaret had made the diplomatic mistake of giving a cold reception to Coppini when he visited the royal court the previous year. He had come to England to seek support for a papal initiative of a crusade to liberate Constantinople from the Ottomans, who had taken the city seven years earlier. In contrast, Coppini was courted by Warwick in Bruges on his return journey. Coppini was 'small of stature and undistinguished in appearance, but he had a strong personality and possessed energy, vivacity and eloquence'.[19] Warwick was charismatic and generous, greatly popular, promising to reform 'the hurts and mischiefs and grievances that reigned in the land', emphasising good lordship rather than ownership of property. Together they made a formidable team.

At a convocation Warwick staged a performance worthy of the theatre, claiming how he and Edward, Earl of March, the heir to the Duke of York, had come to reform government, to remove evil councillors, and thus to aid the King, Henry VI. In St Paul's Cathedral, Warwick, along with the other Yorkist earls, swore allegiance to the King before Almighty God on the Cross of Canterbury. Massed crowds, both inside the cathedral and in the Churchyard, roared their approval. The following day, Coppini posted a message to Henry VI at Paul's Cross. Opening with appropriate courtesies to a reigning monarch, he moved on to make reference to the King's well-known religiosity:

I beg you, for the love of God, for the devotion you have always shown, which served the pious and holy things to the extent of its powers, and out of the pity and compassion you should have for your people and citizens and your duty, to prevent so much bloodshed, now so imminent.

Coppini then proceeded to issue a formidable warning:

You can prevent this if you will, and if you do not you will be guilty in the sight of God in that awful day of judgement in which I also shall stand and require of your hand the English blood if it be spilt.

The original letter had been sent northwards to the King with the demand for a speedy reply 'because the danger is imminent and does not brook delay'.[20]

Weeks later the Lancastrians were routed at the Battle of Northampton, with Henry being taken prisoner by the Yorkists.

Throughout the turbulent years of the Wars of the Roses, one figure of continuity was the Bishop of London, Thomas Kempe. Appointed in the reign of Henry VI, he died in 1489, four years after the Battle of Bosworth Field, when Richard III was killed and the Earl of Richmond became the first Tudor king, Henry VII. At some time during his bishopric, Thomas Kempe built an ornate timber structure to house the pulpit at Paul's Cross, with a domed canopy raised up and reached by a flight of steps. It was probably in place when Canon Ralph Shaa preached a notorious sermon on 23 June 1483. Edward IV had just died, and his younger brother, the Duke of Gloucester, was about to seize the crown as Richard III, with Edward's sons, consigned 'for safety' to the Tower of London, never to be seen again.

Taking the text for his sermon from the Old Testament, '*Spuria vitulamina non agent radices altas*', 'Bastard slips shall not take deep root' (Wisdom 4:3), Shaa pronounced that the children of Edward IV were all illegitimate. His justification for this was that the late King, a famous womaniser, had gone through a form of marriage contract with Lady Eleanor Butler, prior to his marriage to his Queen, Elizabeth Woodville. Not content with this, he suggested that Edward himself was also illegitimate, and not the son of Richard, Duke of York. This was insulting to York's Duchess, Cecily Neville, who was still alive, but made Gloucester the only lawful claimant to the throne.[21] The reception from the audience to this sermon was said to have been sullen silence, and apparently Shaa deeply regretted his action, dying the following year from remorse. This has to be treated with care, for the sources of the story are Sir Thomas More and chroniclers from the Tudor period, and thus hostile to Richard III.

Canon Shaa's brother, Sir Edmund, was the Lord Mayor in 1483. Shakespeare in *Richard III*, taking his information from Thomas More, has Richard's ally, the Duke of Buckingham, describe how, following the ancient tradition, the mayor encouraged the citizens of London to acclaim Richard as king. The response was as sullen as that of the audience for Canon Shaa's sermon, in Buckingham's words, 'mum'.

Yet another incident at this time casts Richard in an unpopular light: the order that Jane Shore should perform public penance. Jane, the daughter of a

London mercer, had been married to a fellow mercer, William Shore, but this was annulled at her petition on the grounds of his impotence. According to Thomas More, she was a witty and well-read woman, who became a mistress of Edward IV. At his death Jane Shore was in need of a new protector, identified as the Lord Chamberlain, William Hastings. The chroniclers record that she was condemned to do public penance 'for the lyfe that she led with the said lord hastyngys and othir grete astatys'. Thomas More for his part described the scene in St Paul's Churchyard:

> He [Richard] caused the Bishop of London to put her in open penance, going before the cross in procession upon a Sunday, with a taper in her hand, in which she went in countenance and pace demure so womanly, and albeit she were out of all array save her kirtle only, yet went she so fair and lovely . . . that her great shame won her much praise.[22]

This theme, the suffering and penitence of a victimised woman, held such resonance that it was taken up by the playwright Nicholas Rowe to produce in 1714 a 'She-Tragedy', with Mrs Siddons making the role famous.

St Paul's Churchyard, with its Cross, had by the end of the fifteenth century become a powerful means of communication, well earning Thomas Carlyle's description of the *Times Newspaper*. But the arrival of new technology into the area around the cathedral was to give the Churchyard an even more powerful role in the century to follow.

CHAPTER 3

THE CENTRE OF THE BOOK WORLD

At the very beginning of the sixteenth century, probably in the year 1500, Londoners would have been treated to the sight of a printing press on the move. Wynkyn de Worde was transferring his business from Westminster to Fleet Street, from the shadow of the Abbey to that of the Cathedral.

Various theories have been put forward as to how Wynkyn got his very appropriate surname. Was he from the Duchy of Lorraine and a town called Wörth, or from the Netherlands, and a town called Woerden?[1] Whatever his origins, he became the assistant of William Caxton who brought printing to England in 1476, a quarter of a century after Gutenberg's invention of moveable type in Mainz. Caxton was a London mercer who had settled in Bruges in the 1450s, becoming Governor of the English Nation there. But it was probably later, in Cologne, that he learned the craft of printing, and subsequently set up a press in either Bruges or Ghent where he produced the first book printed in English, the *Receuil of the Histories of Troy*, a narration of the Trojan wars.

On his return to England, Caxton chose to establish his business in the precincts of Westminster Abbey, realising that there was a market here for books among the members of the royal court and the clergy of the Abbey, as well as the legal world nearby. A Victorian stained-glass window at Stationers' Hall depicts William Caxton showing a printed book to a resplendently dressed Edward IV, 'this sun of York', and his Queen, Elizabeth Woodville. At the bottom of the scene is a young Wynkyn de Worde, preparing an inking ball. De Worde took over the business at Caxton's death in 1492, and produced printed works from the premises, issued under an adaptation of his master's distinctive device or colophon.

2. The printer's mark of Wynkyn de Worde, combining the initials of his master, William Caxton, and the image of the sun.

After nine years in Westminster, de Worde decided to make the move eastwards. Whether he came by river, hauling the printing press and other equipment up from a wharf on the Thames, or trundled them through the streets on carts, his destination was a shop on Fleet Street just west of Shoe Lane, trading under 'the Sign of the Sun'. His premises in Westminster were cramped, but here he had a shop front measuring about 31 feet on Fleet Street, and stretching back at between 40 and 60 feet. This allowed space for his printing press, type cases, a room for the drying of paper and its storage. He was also an importer of books, a binder and a bookseller, so needed plenty of further space for all the copies.[2] Living quarters for his family and servants would have been in the floors above, while a cellar could provide further storage space. Although wider than some premises, it represents a fairly typical layout of booksellers' shops in the centuries that followed.

Two years later, de Worde was joined in Fleet Street by another printer/bookseller, Richard Pynson, from Normandy, who may have also been an assistant to Caxton. Both men were aliens and thus could have been limited in their trade by an act promulgated in 1484 prohibiting imports by foreign merchants. However, it was recognised that printers and booksellers from mainland Europe had the necessary contacts to bring in marketable books. In particular, there was a demand for books of hours, liturgical texts and Latin texts for scholars. A specific proviso was therefore included in the legislation to encourage the development of the trade in London. This aspect of the book business was known as the Latin trade, because the original publishers were outside the 'obedience' of the English Crown.

Pynson was based at the Sign of the George on Fleet Street within Temple Bar, and legal printing was originally the mainstay of his trade. However, he expanded the range of his titles to include grammatical texts, history and chronicles, and verse in the vernacular as well as Latin texts. Likewise de Worde offered a wide remit of titles, such as books for children, works on good manners, marriage, household practice and husbandry, in an equally wide range of prices. Both made use of woodcut illustrations in their books.

Pynson and de Worde, along with other alien booksellers, were shrewd businessmen who recognised that the opportunities for an expanding customer base lay with the City of London. By establishing themselves in Fleet Street, they were also able to link up with the craftsmen who had produced books before the arrival of the printing press: scriveners and limners (painters or illuminators), booksellers and binders, and suppliers of clasps, parchment, pens and paper. These craftsmen had based themselves around St Paul's Cathedral, providing books for the cathedral itself, for the monastic and educational establishments in the Churchyard, and, slightly further afield, the London lawyers of the Temple.

Some of the craftsmen leased their premises from the dominant landlord for the Churchyard, the Bridge House Estates, properties given or bequeathed for the upkeep of London Bridge, administered by the Lord Mayor and the Corporation of London. For example, William de Southflete, a binder, had a shop in Paternoster Row in 1312. The Bridge House records show the expansion of the book trade, with 19 book traders and scriveners in Paternoster Row in the early fifteenth century, rising to 23 by the end of the century.[3] In 1403 a group of these craftsmen formed themselves into a 'Misterie' or company of stationers, approved by the Lord Mayor and aldermen of the City.[4] The term 'stationer' came from the fact that they sold manuscripts and books from 'stations', barrows or stalls in the Churchyard. Why it should be

3. The device of John Rastell with two mermaids.

applied particularly to this trade is not known, but stationers they have been ever since.

The Churchyard had established itself as the heart of the book trade, which is probably why de Worde opened a shop there at the sign of Our Lady of Pity in 1508. This does not, however, seem to have been a commercial success, and he ceased trading from here the following year. The first recorded publisher's device issued from the Churchyard is that of John Rastell, who originally worked from a location to the south of the cathedral. In 1515 he moved to a workshop in the Cross Churchyard, next to the gate leading into Cheapside, and here he traded at the very distinctive Sign of the Mermaid.

Rastell was one of the first generation of native English printers. He was probably born in Coventry in 1475 and moved down to London to study at the Middle Temple in 1502. Sometime soon after he married Elizabeth, the sister of Thomas More. Printing was just one of Rastell's activities: he was also an educationalist, playwright, translator, merchant adventurer, lawyer and member of parliament, and he designed some of the backdrops for the great pageant of the Field of the Cloth of Gold in 1520. He began his printing career with a translation from the Italian of the life of Gianfrancesco Pico by his brother-in-law, Thomas More, and went on to produce a wide range of books. One was a moral play that Rastell had written, *The Nature of the Four Elements*. This included a three-part song that marked the first attempt to print a musical score, with type especially cut for him in northern Europe. In this respect, Rastell joined Richard Pynson and Wynkyn de Worde as a technical pioneer. Pynson would seem to be the first printer in England to adopt Roman or 'white letter', based on ancient Roman inscriptions, as opposed to Gothic type, or 'black letter', the typeface that echoed the hand script of scriveners. De Worde is credited with introducing italic, along with Hebrew, that was part of the humanist curriculum, and Arabic typefaces.

John Rastell was in many ways a man before his time. In *The Nature of the Four Elements* he makes possibly the first reference to the New World, perhaps inspired by More's *Utopia* that had been published in Louvain in 1516. He also has the Messenger in his play encouraging the development of the English language, pointing out that just as Greek and Latin have many words that have to be translated, so likewise English has many words that can be taken in the other direction:

> And the cause that our tong is so plenteouse now
> For we keep our Englyshe continually
> And of other tongis many wordys we borow
> Which now for Englysh we use & occupy;
> These thingis have given corage gretly.[5]

Rastell was also an advocate of the Scriptures in English, courting trouble for his 'Loller' sympathies. This must have put his relationship with More under strain, becoming ever more severe after Rastell's conversion to the reformed faith and his employment by Thomas Cromwell as an agent. By grim coincidence, both men ended up in the Tower of London. Thomas More was executed on Tower Hill in 1535 as a result of his refusal to acknowledge Henry VIII's Royal Supremacy. Imprisoned for his denial of clerical rights to tithe, John Rastell died in the Tower in 1536.

While Rastell never joined the Stationers' Company, de Worde and Pynson did so, becoming the first known printer members. They were followed by others who had learnt their skills in mainland Europe. One such was Reyner or Reginald Wolfe, a Dutchman from Gelderland who settled in Strasbourg where he set up as a printer. He became part of the scholarly Protestant network that brought him to the attention of Thomas Cranmer, who is thought to have invited him to England when he became Archbishop of Canterbury in 1533. Wolfe maintained his connections with mainland Europe, travelling each year to the international book fair that had been established in the city of Frankfurt, using the opportunity to act as an agent for the English government while buying books to import. The proviso that had enabled foreign printers/booksellers to carry out their business in London was withdrawn in 1534, but Wolfe had powerful friends. In 1536, as a result of an application to the authorities of the City of London by Henry VIII's Queen, Anne Boleyn, Wolfe was admitted as a freeman to the Stationers' Company.

The withdrawal of that proviso encouraged the next generation of native printers. One such was John Day, who was probably born in 1522 in Dunwich, then a thriving East Anglian port, now a 'lost town' beneath the waves of the North Sea. Day came to London in the 1540s in the service of a physician-cum-printer, Thomas Raynalde, but then joined the Stringers' Company, the craftsmen who made bowstrings for archers. The only way at this time to be made free of the City of London was via membership of a livery company. This could be achieved by serving an apprenticeship, usually of seven years, but Day was already in his twenties, so unwilling to take this path. As the Stringers were experiencing hard times financially, Day was able to gain entry through payment of a fee.

By the 1540s booksellers and printing shops stretched along a line west to east from St Clement Danes in the Strand to Old Change, just beyond the east end of St Paul's Cathedral. In his magisterial history of the early years of the Stationers' Company, Peter Blayney has analysed this concentration of establishments, showing graphically how they were the heart of England's book trade and remained so for centuries to come. In all there are nearly a hundred premises identified, most of them doubling up as residences for the booksellers and printers. In particular, the Cross Churchyard was dominated by the trade, with 32 establishments, some of them squeezed in the spaces between the buttresses of the cathedral itself, as shown in an early seventeenth-century painting by John Gipkyn (Plate 1).[6]

This was the community that John Day joined by 1549 when he had set up a printing house in the gatehouse of Aldersgate, and he did so at a significant time. The past century and a half had seen controversy over the Scriptures being available to read in the vernacular, as shown in Chapter 2. With the arrival of the printing press, the authorities were faced with the threat of English translations in thousands rather than hundreds. The catalyst for these was the publication in Basel in 1516 of *Novum Instrumentum*. This was a new Latin translation of the New Testament by the humanist scholar Erasmus, with a critical commentary and the original Greek alongside. His Greek text was taken up and translated into English by William Tyndale, an Oxford scholar who was acting as tutor for a family in his native Gloucestershire. Having completed his translation, in the spring of 1523 he sought permission from Cuthbert Tunstall, the Bishop of London, to print an edition. Snubbed by Tunstall, he declared there was no place in England where he might undertake publication, so travelled to mainland Europe. The entire New Testament was printed in Worms in 1525, with copies smuggled down the Rhine and into Britain. Tunstall's response was to round up all copies that he could find, and burn them, along with the numerous publications coming from the pen of Martin Luther, in the Churchyard of St Paul's.

With Henry VIII's break with Rome and his establishment of Royal Supremacy, very different times were fast approaching. Not sufficiently fast, however, to save William Tyndale from a martyr's death, strangled and burnt at the stake at Vilvoorde Castle outside Brussels in 1536. His final, haunting words were 'Lord, open the King of England's eyes', and, in a remarkably short period, this wish was to be fulfilled. In the following year the Protestant scholar John Rogers took Tyndale's New Testament along with work he had done on the Old Testament and amalgamated it with a translation by a former Augustinian friar, Miles Coverdale, using the pseudonym Thomas Matthew after two of Christ's disciples, to create what was called the Matthew Bible. This was produced in Antwerp by two London merchants, Richard Grafton and Edward Whitchurch.

At the foot of the title page of the Matthew Bible was printed 'set forth with the King's most gracious licence', thanks to the support of Henry VIII's chief minister, Thomas Cromwell. He instructed JPs to make parish priests aware of this bible for use in their churches. As there were 9,000 parishes in all, initial printing runs proved inadequate, so Cromwell and Thomas Cranmer decided to produce a revised edition in large folio that could be distributed country-wide. This was the Great Bible, the only one to be officially authorised. Its printing history is complex, beginning in Paris in 1539, with six more editions rapidly following on London presses.

The title page, designed by Hans Holbein, shows the King giving the Scriptures to his people. So dominant is the King that the Bible historian David Daniell wryly pointed out that God had rather a squeeze to get into the top of the page above the King's head.[7] A further irony is that, although the Bible is in English, Henry VIII is depicted handing out 'verbum dei' to Archbishop Cranmer and to Thomas Cromwell, who then pass it on to the common people crowded at the bottom of the page (Plate 5). In fact, conservative clergy and courtiers continued to manifest strong opposition to the idea of the Scriptures in English, and Cromwell's hold on power was slipping. In late 1539 he was accused of introducing and maintaining dangerous heresies, including Lutheranism and Anabaptism, leading to his summary execution. However, his aim that every parish should have a copy of the Great Bible had been secured.[8]

The printing and selling of bibles and other religious publications was highly lucrative, but the outlay was also considerable in terms of materials and labour, and there were dangers attached in these highly charged politico-religious times. The Protestant printers and publishers of the Churchyard were, however, also convinced of the vital importance of the written word. As the Protestant writer John Foxe put it, the technology of printing was part of God's providential design:

> the blessed wisdom and omnipotent power of the Lord began to work for his church; not with sword and target to subdue his exalted adversaries, but with printing, writing and reading: to convince darkness by light, error by truth, ignorance by learning.[9]

Of a reformist persuasion, John Day had been sent to the Tower in 1546 for printing 'naughty books', Calvinist works that continued to be considered heretical. A year later, the succession of Edward VI to the English throne ushered in a regime of strong Protestantism under the government of the boy-king's uncle, Edward Seymour, Duke of Somerset. Now Day could seize the opportunities offered by the new regime, and no fewer than 130 books are attributed to his press during the reign. One of the particularly lucrative areas of printing and bookselling was of catechisms and metrical psalms, with the monopoly of producing them particularly prized, and John Day here found himself in competition with Reyner Wolfe.

4. The marks of John Day and Reyner Wolfe. Day chose a pun upon his name, 'Arise! For it is Day!', while Wolfe took the sign, the brazen serpent, from his shop in the Cross Churchyard.

Wolfe had moved from the Latin trade to establishing his own printing business, setting up his press at the Sign of the Brazen Serpent in the Churchyard. He began with schoolbooks, Latin verse works and in 1544 published the account by Edward Seymour of his military expedition into Scotland, reflecting Wolfe's closeness to the reformist political group. When Edward VI succeeded to the throne, Wolfe's star was in the ascendant, and he became the King's official printer, for Latin, Greek and Hebrew, as well as the royal bookseller and stationer. He was also official printer for Archbishop Thomas Cranmer, printing his refutations of the arguments being produced by leading Catholic theologians.[10] Needing larger premises, in 1549 Wolfe moved into the former charnel house in the Cross Churchyard, disused since the Dissolution of the Monasteries. According to the chronicler John Stow, he cleared over 1,000 cartloads of bones. Along with his other properties, this gave him what has been described as 'a continuous stretch of more than 120 feet of the best bookselling frontage in England'.[11]

However, the worlds of both Wolfe and Day, along with other Protestant printers and booksellers, were yet again turned upside down with the death of Edward VI in July of that year and the accession of the Catholic Mary Tudor.

Day, involved in the production of clandestine literature, found himself once more arrested and briefly imprisoned, so that at his release he kept his head low. Wolfe, apparently a much more diplomatic character, was able to gain the Queen's favour and retain the position of Royal Printer, despite the execution at the stake of his long-time patron, Thomas Cranmer. Wolfe was one of the leading names of printers in the letters of incorporation granted in 1557 by Queen Mary to the Stationers' Company. John Day appears much further down the list.

The royal charter changed dramatically the nature of the Company, by establishing that Stationers were the only men in the City to hold direct responsibility for the book trade, and thus a virtual monopoly on printing in England. Up to this time, it had been possible for men from other companies to print books. Thus the Great Bible had been printed by Richard Grafton, a member of the Grocers' Company, and Edward Whitchurch, a haberdasher. After 1557, apart from certain privileges already granted, or that might in the future be granted by the Crown, the printer had to be a Stationer. These exceptions were indeed made from time to time: the Geneva Bible of 1572, for example, was printed under exclusive privilege by Christopher Barker, a member of the Drapers' Company.

The charter also empowered the Company to regulate its own affairs, and the privileges enshrined in it were reinforced and supported by general legislation. Thus, for example, members would be able to protect their trade by limiting the number of presses and apprentices, but they were also charged with the responsibility of exercising control over the contents of books and other publications. Stationers were expected to seek out unofficial publications, and if these were deemed to be seditious or heretical, then to destroy them and to punish those involved. Herein no doubt lies the Queen's interest in so transforming the Company. With her firm Catholic faith, she was determined to reverse the Protestantism that had been so strongly promoted through the medium of print during the reign of Edward VI. When Mary was succeeded in turn by her half-sister Elizabeth, and the Church of England was re-established, the privileges conferred by the charter remained in place, and the Company continued to protect and develop the trade.

Armed with their royal charter, the Stationers moved into St Peter's, a fourteenth-century chantry college in the south-west part of the Churchyard that had been dissolved in 1548. Here the Company was able to hold its feasts and to maintain the register of copyrights of proposed publications.[12] The Company carried out the eradication of 'naughty books' of a heretical or seditious nature, or a combination of both. The public spectacle of books being burned in the Churchyard had taken place in the reign of Henry VIII, but as was observed at the time, this could be counterproductive for it aroused curiosity among spectators as to what the taste of the forbidden fruit might be. So, during the reign of Elizabeth, it was deemed more politic to incinerate them in the kitchen ovens of the Stationers' headquarters, or in the palace of the Bishop of London nearby.

With the accession of Elizabeth I, the Protestant printers who had lain low during Mary's reign returned to their businesses. John Day celebrated the return of a Protestant monarch by adding to his considerable output the ambitious project of John Foxe's *Actes and Monuments*, more commonly referred to as *Foxe's Book of Martyrs*. The book will be considered in detail in the next chapter, but suffice to say here that it proved a huge success that brought even greater prosperity to John Day as the publisher. However, the one thing that eluded him was a shop in the Churchyard itself. Perhaps he looked with envious eyes at the extensive frontage enjoyed by Reyner Wolfe's printshop.

When Day decided that he wanted a presence in the Churchyard, he found himself a powerful advocate in Matthew Parker, the Archbishop of Canterbury. Writing a letter to Secretary of State William Cecil in December 1572, Parker depicted a sad scene: 'Nowe, sir, daye hath complained to me that selling in a corn^r, and his brotherne envienge him, he cannot utter his bookes wch lie in his hande ij or iij thousand powndes worthe'. The 'corner' was quite a considerable space at Aldersgate, where he claimed he had amassed a large inventory of unsold books, a claim that was probably false. Day's solution was to have a prefabricated shop made up and erected in the Cross Churchyard. But 'envious booksellers' along with the mayor and aldermen would not allow this.

As Peter Blayney has shown in his reconstruction of the story, there was no doubt a subplot with the Cathedral in conflict with the City as to who had the authority to lease the part of the Cross Churchyard that had in former times been the site of the folk moot (see p. 16). But the story also tells us two other things. First, that Day was highly unpopular among his colleagues in the book world. Shortly after this particular incident, in 1573, he was obliged to seek the protection of Robert Dudley, the Queen's great favourite, when he and his family were nearly murdered by 'one Asplin', either an aggrieved apprentice or a rival printer.

Secondly, Parker's letter gives details of the bookshop that Day had ordered to be made. It was 'little and lowe' with a flat roof like a terrace, on which men might stand to watch a pageant. Such shows usually took place in the area known as the Atrium in the western part of the Churchyard, in front of the principal doors of the cathedral, so Day was possibly thinking of dismantling the structure and moving it around the Churchyard. His application for a lease has also survived, and this mentions 'appentices for defence ageinste wether and heat as also ffoldinge Shopp bordes to fall owte warde from the saide Buyldinges with concentient stoopes postes and Steyes to bear the saide Shopp bordes when they be Lett Downe'. These were to be let down on weekdays, but not on the sabbath or on holidays. The details give us an idea of how booksellers were able to display their wares without damage from the weather, with a penthouse or awning to protect the stall, a wooden counter fixed to the wall below windows. At a time before display windows, books could be laid out on the counter to catch the attention of potential buyers. In the event, the opposition to this radical idea was just too great, and this is a bookshop that never existed. Instead, in 1576, Day secured the lease on a 'long shop' near the north-west door of the cathedral, considered one of the prime locations for booksellers.[13]

Day, as might be predicted, was good at marketing his publications, and in the archives of the Stationers' Company is his engraved portrait dating from 1570. This was probably used as part of an advertisement for the sale of his books and could have been pinned or pasted up on walls or the posts of shops to draw the attention of passers-by. With printing had come the need to sell multiple copies. Potential customers could also find out the latest publications from lists and catalogues. In 1548 the Swiss physician and naturalist Conrad Gesner wrote: 'Most printers and booksellers, especially those furnished with the more learned sorts of books, have broadsides and lists of books which they have printed or have for sale, and some of these have actually been printed as book-lets'.[14] Broadsides were fixed on the wall of the bookshop, or behind the counter for the shopman's reference. The idea of the catalogue was developed in Paris in the sixteenth century by the distinguished printer Robert Estienne, to promote books by retail through his own shops, in correspondence with customers who lived a distance from the city, and for wholesale sales to other booksellers.

5. A portrait of John Day, 1570.

No such catalogue was produced in London until 1595 when the *Catalogue of English Printed Bookes* was compiled by the printer and bookseller Andrew Maunsell. He had shops in different parts of the Churchyard in the 1570s and 1580s, including taking over one at the Sign of the Brazen Serpent that had belonged earlier to Reyner Wolfe. Maunsell explained his purpose in the preface: 'Seeing that men desirous of such kind of Bookes, cannot aske for what they have never heard of, and the Booke-seller cannot show that he hath not'. He likened the usefulness of his publication for the bookseller to the dispensary for an apothecary or a dictionary for a schoolmaster.

The triple dedication in the catalogue is to the Queen, to divines 'for some soare so hie that they looke not so low, as on theire owne countrie writers' and to the Stationers' Company. Maunsell set out to collect the titles of books 'either written in our owne tongue, or translated out of any other language' on all manner of subjects that he thought would prove a useful guide to customers as well as to booksellers.[15] The overwhelming proportion of titles are divinity books of the Protestant persuasion. A second part of the catalogue is devoted to 'Mathematics, Physicall and Chirugical', with a wide range of titles including horticulture, dreams, music and the art of war. The originating bookseller, publication history and format are given, but no prices, as it was so difficult to fix standard rates. He intended to write a third section on literature, drama and history, but this never reached fruition.

Another type of catalogue available at this period concentrated on European titles. The great trade fair at Frankfurt was held, and still is, annually. Now it takes place in October, but in the sixteenth century it occurred twice a year, at Lent in spring, and Michaelmas in autumn. Frankfurt enjoyed the status of being an imperial free city, and thus did not have the complicated tolls and regulations that beset so many of the German states, and it offered religious tolerance to both Catholics and Protestants. The first printed catalogue was produced in 1564 by George Willer of Augsburg, 'For the convenience and use of booksellers elsewhere and all students of literature.'[16] Printers would send their lists to Willer to coordinate and put in subject order. Later the city council stepped in and produced an official catalogue. The mystic Dr John Dee, a great book collector, was the first recorded owner of a Frankfurt catalogue in England. To have a book published at the time of the fair could be an advantage. The sensation of the 1587 fair, for instance, was *Historia von D. Johann Fausten*, which was translated into English in 1592 and became the basis for the play by Christopher Marlowe.

One of the principal importers of books from Europe was the Birckmann family from Cologne. As well as importing wholesale, they sold their books at an unidentified shop in the Churchyard. These would arrive at the Port of London in barrels and baskets, to be noted in port books for the purpose of charging petty customs. The 1534 Act mentioned earlier had stipulated that, to protect the English binding industry, imported books should arrive without bindings of board, leather or parchment. The unbound folios would be wrapped in waterproof bales and packed in maunds (baskets) or dryfatts (barrels). The waiters or searchers at the port were concerned not only with securing the customs charges, but also checking for the arrival of seditious literature.

Another major importer into London was the Antwerp printer/publisher Christopher Plantin. In August 1558 the bookseller Nicholas England, returning from the Frankfurt Book Fair, stopped off at Plantin's premises at the Sign of the Golden Compasses in Antwerp, and chose a whole list of classical works to be sent over to his London shop. Many were in small format, with one or two in folio size. The quantity of copies of each title is significant; he ordered, for example, 50 copies of the selected letters of Cicero.[17] Plantin's house and works can still be visited in Antwerp, giving some idea of the premises of the Churchyard booksellers, albeit his were on a much grander scale. His shop, or 'bouticle' was separate from the printing works, and here he sold not only his own products, but those from other publishers, and ran a delivery service to institutions and private individuals. Casks of Rhenish wine and beer were kept on tap to entertain honoured customers and visiting merchants such as Nicholas England.

The identities of customers of the booksellers of St Paul's Churchyard are few and far between for the Tudor period. But one person that we know frequented the Churchyard booksellers and shopped in the neighbouring area is exceptional, for it was a woman, and a published poet, the first Englishwoman to be thus credited. Isabella Whitney was probably born about 1547 in Cheshire, into a minor gentry family, but spent many years in London. At one time she was working as an upper servant in a household. In 1573 she was obliged to return to the family home, unable to support herself, but shortly before her departure she wrote a mock 'Will and Testament' in verse form. This looked at life in the City, including different trades, such as the gold-smiths of Cheapside, the woollen merchants of Watling Street and the linen drapers of Friday Street running between Cheapside and Old Fish Street. Her testament to the book trade ran:

> To all the bookbinders by Paul's,
> because I like their art,
> They every week shall money have,
> when they from books depart.

She then talked of her own publisher:

> Among them all, my printer must
> have somewhat to his share;
> I will my friends these books to buy
> of him, with other ware.

This was Richard Jones, probably a Welshman and thus an alien who was able to pay a small fee for admission to the Stationers' Company and was known as a 'brother'. In the 1560s and 1570s he had both a bookshop adjoining the west door of the cathedral and a printshop nearby in the Churchyard. Although Jones produced a range of books, he specialised in ballads, poetry and drama: later he was to publish Christopher Marlowe's *Tamburlaine*. One book historian who has looked at Isabella's life in London speculates that she gained a haven in Jones's shop, where she could find out about the latest publications. In fact, as a single woman Isabella may have found booksellers in general a sympathetic environment, for there were many women within the trade. Unable to trade independently, they were nevertheless allowed to maintain the membership of their fathers or husbands after their deaths. One of the earliest examples is Elizabeth Pickering Jackson, a widow who married the stationer Robert Redman, a specialist in the printing and publishing of law books. After Redman's death in 1540, she continued the running of his press, sometimes using her maiden name of Pickering as her trademark. When Reyner Wolfe's widow made her will, she referred to 'my printing house at the Brazen Serpent', and the examples of women as proprietors increase with the century.

Jones first published Isabella's poems in *The Copy of a Letter* in 1567, followed by *A Sweet Nosegay* in 1572. Analysis of allusions in her poems indicates an idea of the publications that she might have found in his shop. These include references to classical literature, such as Homer's *Iliad* and Virgil's *Aeneid*, and to Chaucer's *Legend of Good Women*. However, many of these works were not available in English in the 1560s, which suggests that she got her information through a secondary source. In particular, there are resonances in her poems with themes developed by Thomas Underdown in a pamphlet entitled *The Excellent History of Theseus and Ariadne* published by Richard Jones in 1566. Another pamphlet that may well have provided her with sources was a translation by Thomas Preed from Ovid, *The Pleasant Fable of Hermaphroditus and Salmacis*, published the previous year by one of Jones's collaborators, Thomas Colwell.[18] Money was clearly in short supply for Isabella Whitney, but she could have purchased such pamphlets whereas books were outside her price range.

Many years later Richard Jones was to reappear, supplying another book buyer, Richard Stonley, for whom we have an exceptional amount of detail. Stonley was born about 1520 in Bishop's Itchington in Warwickshire, where his father owned a small amount of land. By the late 1540s he was acting as agent for Sir William Petre, the long-standing Secretary of State who managed to walk the tightrope of serving not only Henry VIII but also his three children, Edward VI, Mary and Elizabeth. Through Petre, Stonley secured the office of teller in the Exchequer of Receipts and became his neighbour in Aldersgate Street.

Richard Stonley kept a journal, three sections of which survive.[19] In this he made all kinds of notes, including the wages of his household, some of the sermons that he attended, and purchases of food, drink, clothes and books with the prices paid. In addition to this fascinating account of his daily life, Stonley had the misfortune in old age to be accused of embezzling the very large sum of £13,000 in his role at the Exchequer and was incarcerated in the Fleet Prison in 1597. An inventory was then made of the contents of his Aldersgate house, which provides a picture of his library of around 500 titles.[20]

What is most striking about Stonley's library is the variety. There are expensive books, such as Holinshed's *Chronicles* and *Foxe's Book of Martyrs*, which the inventory makers valued at 20 shillings each, while other publications, such as ballads and pamphlets, were marked down to a few pence. Among the religious titles, which made up approximately one third of the collection, was a variety of bibles, some Catholic works as well as Protestant, and what could be described as 'crossover'. It has been suggested that Stonley was sympathetic to Catholics: not unlikely, as the Petres were a recusant family.

A number of Stonley's books were 'hot off the press', suggesting that he was au fait with what was going on in the publishing world. Aldersgate Street was a short walk from the Churchyard, and he must have strolled down to see his bookseller friends and to talk to them about the latest arrivals. An example of one such book comes in his journal for 12 June 1593, when he noted the purchase for six pence of Shakespeare's poem *Venus and Adonis*. This was a time of plague, with the playhouses closed, so that William Shakespeare may have decided to venture on this, his first published work, printed by another man from Stratford-upon-Avon, Richard Field, on his press in Blackfriars.

The title was registered at Stationers' Hall two months earlier, so Stonley has been called 'Shakespeare's first reader'.[21] At the same time he bought a second book, *The Survey of France*, written by John Eliot, yet another Warwickshire man, as of course was Stonley himself. Was this the connection that prompted him to make these purchases?

No other Shakespeare work appears to have been in Stonley's library. Yet the one bookseller who has the most mentions in his journal, Edward White, was responsible for publishing *Titus Andronicus* in 1594. White's shop was at the Sign of the Gun by the north door of St Paul's Cathedral. Here Stonley came in January 1582 to pay substantial sums for bibles with good bindings and silver clasps. White was also the publisher of Thomas Kyd and Christopher Marlowe, but their robust and at times violent plays were evidently not to Stonley's taste, which may also apply to *Titus Andronicus*. His preferences are reflected in the inventory with references such as 'Enterludes and Commedies', along with literary works by Robert Greene, George Gaiscoigne and, it is thought, Edmund Spenser. Stonley also had works from European authors, such as *La Vida de Lazarillo de Tormes*, attributed to Diego Hurtado de Mendoza and first published in Spain in 1554. This is a picaresque novel of Castilian life through the adventures of a poor squire, which was translated into English by David Rowland of Anglesey in 1586.

The inventory of Aldersgate Street reveals yet more interesting insights. First, there is a copy of Maunsell's *Catalogue of English Printed Bookes*. Stonley would have found this invaluable for identifying books not only for himself, but also for his wife, who had charge of the medical care of the household, and for the family, such as schoolbooks and books of music for his godson and his wards.

There is also mention of portraits for his long gallery, some of which were paintings. A portrait of Queen Elizabeth, costing him 10 shillings, was commissioned from 'John Gipkyn, picture maker at Shordiche'. There were three generations of this family: the first John probably came to London from Holland and sold books in the Churchyard at the Sign of the Spread Eagle, close to St Paul's School. From the date of the portrait, it would seem to have been painted by his son, who could not be sworn into the Stationers' Company because he was deaf and unable to speak. John Gipkin of the third generation worked alongside dramatists such as Ben Jonson and Thomas Middleton to design decorations for annual Lord Mayor's Shows in the early years of the seventeenth century, and painted the diptych of St Paul's Cathedral and Paul's Cross which gives us such a good idea of the appearance of the Churchyard. Stonley also hung in his gallery county maps and prints of distinguished contemporaries, which could have been cut out of books or bought from print shops which operated alongside the booksellers.

Stonley's incarceration in the Fleet Prison was not unduly severe. His journal shows that he was able to take furniture into his lodgings and have his servants with him, to dine with members of the family, and even make visits to the outside world. He continued to make purchases, including books from Richard Jones, who had moved his business westwards.

One book acquired from Jones was Thomas Deloney's tale of Jack of Newbury, which had been registered three months previously at Stationers' Hall. Deloney made a particular speciality of the celebration of the self-advancement of hardworking craftsmen. In this case, he wrote of John Winchcomb, a Berkshire clothier who starts as a weaver and rises to wealth and royal favour. Perhaps Stonley identified this with his own career, though poignantly his fortune had not lasted, and he died in the Fleet Prison in 1599, at the ripe old age of nearly 80.

A second glimpse of the interchange between customer and bookseller at this period comes in the account books of William Cavendish, the future Earl of Devonshire. William was the second and favourite son of the redoubtable Bess of Hardwick, Countess of Shrewsbury. In the 1590s he and his family lived with the Countess at Hardwick New Hall in Derbyshire. A man of cultivation, William was to appoint the philosopher Thomas Hobbes as tutor for his son. His book purchases are to be found in the parts of the accounts headed 'foreign charges', that is, made beyond Derbyshire.[22] Cavendish's book purchases covered a wide range, both in subject and in price. The most expensive was Richard Hakluyt's *Principal Navigations*, published between 1598 and 1600 and costing the substantial sum of £1 2s. His interest in his own country and its history is shown by the purchase of William Camden's *Britannia*, and Richard Carew's *Survey of Cornwall*, both by pioneers of topographical studies.

As befitted a gentleman, Cavendish bought books on etiquette. The accounts refer to the binding up of 'Civil Conversation', probably the 1586 English translation by George Pettie of Stefano Guazzo's *La Civil Conversazione*, that dealt with issues of courtly fashion. He purchased a Latin translation of Baldassare Castiglione's famous *Cortegiano*, published in 1593. A rather cryptic reference to the 'sixth book of Lazarillo deforms in English', shows that, like Stonley, he bought the translation of *La Vida de Lazarillo de Tormes*. Again, like Stonley, Cavendish bought pamphlets, such as an account of the pageant of the Lord Mayor of London, priced at a penny. He purchased five copies of 'the arte of setting the corne' at 3d each. This booklet was written by Hugh Platt, the son of a wealthy London brewer who devoted his life to researches into agriculture and related subjects. The multiple copies may well have been for the farmers on the Cavendish estates.

An entry in the accounts, in 1602, recording the purchase for 6d of a catalogue of books, raises two possibilities. First, that it was Maunsell's 1595 catalogue of English titles, or that it was a Frankfurt Book Fair catalogue, enabling William Cavendish to follow the latest publishing across Europe. Mentioned in the accounts on several occasions is the name of one bookseller, Mr Norton. The Nortons were a considerable publishing family, at one stage setting up the 'Officina Nortonia', an echo of the 'Officina' of the Plantin family of Antwerp. An entry in the accounts next to Norton's name records the payment of 6d to the poor of Ludgate, which suggests that the man in question was John Norton, based in St Paul's Churchyard, rather than his cousin Bonham, principally a printer with premises in Blackfriars. John Norton made regular journeys to the Frankfurt Fair each year and conducted much trade with continental publishing houses. Some of the books noted in the Cavendish accounts were published by the Frankfurt house of Claude Marni and John Aubri, so these may well have come to Cavendish via St Paul's Churchyard. John Norton ran a considerable business at his shop in 'Neere unto Paule's Schoole', on the eastern edge of the Churchyard with a view of Paul's Cross. Like Plantin's shop in Antwerp, Norton's premises had become a social centre for book collectors and literary men, so would have appealed to William Cavendish. In addition it was used as a kind of poste restante, according to a contemporary letter writer.[23]

The accounts also record sending books to the binder, and entries for making hampers to transport them. While Richard Stonley, resident in Aldersgate Street, could make a tour of the bookseller community in the area around the Churchyard, William Cavendish had to do his buying at a distance. It would seem therefore that John Norton was acting as the Cavendish family's agent, gathering the wide range of books and pamphlets from different book-sellers in London, and organising their transport. Other booksellers were probably doing the same for out-of-town customers, using the inns that ringed the Churchyard for dispatch by carrier. Some of Cavendish's purchases would be dispatched up to Derbyshire, but other references make mention of a porter taking them to Holborn, where the London house of the Cavendish family at this time was situated.[24]

These two invaluable accounts of book buying at the end of the sixteenth century indicate that there was now a wide range of publications available in London. In the 1560s, when Isabella Whitney was looking for sources, many had not been available in English, but now William Shakespeare, for example, was able to find a range in Churchyard bookshops. In 1577 Henry Byneman, whose shop at the Sign of Three Wells was located at the north-west door of the cathedral, published Raphael Holinshed's *Chronicles of England, Scotland and Ireland*, providing one of the principal sources for Shakespeare's history plays. For his plays set in classical times, Shakespeare drew on Sir Thomas North's translation of Plutarch's *Lives*, first published in 1579 by Thomas Vautrollier, master of his Stratford friend, Richard Field. Between 1565 and 1567, Arthur Golding worked on his translation of Ovid's *Metamorphoses*, which Shakespeare used both for classical allusions and for legends about the origins of plants, such as laurel, daphne and the narcissus. For the plants themselves, he would have used herbals, and almost certainly that of the London barber surgeon John Gerard, published in 1597. At this time Gerard was curator of the gardens of the College of Physicians in Knightrider Street, just south of the Churchyard, and it is possible that the publisher of the herbal, John Norton, made his acquaintance there. Norton produced this feat of Elizabethan publishing in two large folio volumes, calling upon one of his Frankfurt colleagues to lend him most of the 1,800 woodcuts that illustrate the book.

Shakespeare and his contemporaries, such as Edmund Spenser and Christopher Marlowe, were enriching the English language in an incalculable way. But they in turn owed a debt to the translator of the Bible into English, William Tyndale. As the scholar David Daniell has observed, 'without Tyndale, no Shakespeare'.[25] Tyndale had been a master of seven languages: Hebrew, Greek, Latin, French, Spanish and German, as well as English. Although he aimed for clarity and accuracy, preferring simple syntax, his knowledge of languages enabled him to be supremely flexible in his choice of words. As a result we have a plethora of phrases that have entered the common language such as 'the powers that be' and 'salt of the earth'.

Tyndale was, however, officially a condemned heretic, so his words had throughout the century been hidden in the shadows. As noted earlier, John Rogers amalgamated Tyndale's translation of the New Testament and part of the Old Testament with the work of Miles Coverdale to produce Matthew's Bible, which was then revised as the Great Bible. During the reign of Mary Tudor, Coverdale took refuge in Switzerland and helped to produce what became known as the Geneva Bible, with the New Testament appearing in 1557, followed by the Old Testament in 1560, from the press of the London merchant, Rowland Hall, who had settled in the city.

But Geneva was the city of John Calvin, and the overtones of this bible concerned Elizabeth I's Archbishop of Canterbury, Matthew Parker. He revived a plan that had been mooted 20 years earlier by Archbishop Cranmer, parcelling out parts of the Bible to 12 bishops, including himself, to produce a new version which was to be known as the Bishops' Bible. This was printed in 1568 by Richard Jugge, the Queen's Printer, who had one of the shops between the cathedral buttresses at the appropriate Sign of the Bible. Although Parker ensured that all cathedrals should possess a copy of the Bishops' Bible, and urged all churches to do likewise, this version was not regarded as a great achievement. The bishops involved, unlike William Tyndale, were not necessarily skilled in the translation of the Hebrew and Greek. It was, moreover, a book created by a committee, often a hostage to fortune.

The next enterprise to produce another bible in English was created by the most elaborate series of committees and has enjoyed enduring popular approval: the King James Bible. In 1603 James Stuart inherited the throne of his cousin, Elizabeth Tudor, along with a Church of England divided, under increasing pressure from those of a Puritan persuasion. The following year, James convened a conference at his palace at Hampton Court to try to bring together the parties of the High and Low Churches and to settle some of their differences. The conference failed to do this, with his bishops proving intractable, but out of the proceedings came, more positively, a commission to undertake a new translation of the Bible.

Fifty-four revisers were appointed, drawn from the most distinguished scholars and divines, divided into six companies, based at the universities of Oxford and Cambridge, and at Westminster. Three companies were responsible for the Old Testament, two for the New, and one for the Apocrypha. Richard Bancroft, Bishop of London, worked with James I to draw up specific rules for the translators, including the process of exchanging drafts. One of the rules is of great significance: 'these translations to be used when they agree better with the Text than the Bishops: *Tindoll's, Matthew's, Coverdale's, Whitchurch's* [the London merchant who printed the Great Bible], *Geneva*.'[26] Tyndale's huge contribution to the language of the Bible had at last been officially recognised. It has been estimated that 83 per cent of the final text of the King James Bible was from Tyndale's translations made some 80 years earlier.

With the various sections completed, a meeting was held in 1610 at the hall of the Stationers' Company to discuss and agree the translation. Five years earlier, finding St Peter's College in the Churchyard too small, the Stationers had moved into Abergavenny House on nearby Ave Maria Lane. The Stationers' Company still occupy this site, just to the west of St Paul's Churchyard. Agreement was reached at the meeting, an amazing outcome for such a ponderous editorial structure, and the resulting text was published in 1611 by the King's Printer, Robert Barker at the Tyger's Head in Paternoster Row. It is often described as the 'Authorised Version' but there was no official pronouncement at the time, and the only truly authorised version has been the Great Bible of 1540. Robert had inherited his title as the royal printer from his father Christopher, and it was a lucrative one to hold, but it could have its hazards. An octavo version of the Bible produced in 1631 bearing his imprint was found to be full of errors, not least the arresting variant that 'Thou shall commit adultery' as the seventh commandment. It is now known as the 'Wicked Bible'. Impositions of fines put Barker into serious financial difficulties, and he died in the King's Bench prison in 1645. Sabotage has been suspected.

The large folio format of the King James Bible was one of the most expensive books offered to customers in the early seventeenth century. Alongside it was a range of publications: prayer books, psalters, catechisms, sermons and chapbooks known as 'penny godlies'. These were the meat and drink of the book world in London in the late sixteenth and early seventeenth centuries, even for those not enjoying the official printing privileges. This important point is well made by book historians:

> 'Religious books' in conventional terms are found to have been the single most important component of the publishing trade, comprising around half the total output of the industry, and outweighing political, scientific, practical and fictional works: indeed, fiction had yet to establish its respectable credentials, often disguising itself as edification, or morality.[27]

Study of the libraries of gentlemen in the late sixteenth and early seventeenth centuries shows that the proportion of divinity books was relatively high, even in that of the Cecil family, who were interested in a wide range of subjects. William Cecil, for instance, had numerous bibles, whole and in parts, not only in English, but also in Greek and Latin and in a number of contemporary European languages. He also owned commentaries and other scholarly aids, sets of early Church Fathers, contemporary theological works, sermons and works of instruction. Unsurprising, perhaps, bearing in mind his position as Elizabeth I's Secretary of State, requiring a thorough grounding in the religious controversies of the time. But dominance of religious titles in libraries carries through to many other collections of Elizabethan and Jacobean England.

Details of libraries 'of the common sort' are almost nonexistent. Copies of bibles and of *Foxe's Book of Martyrs* are sometimes mentioned in inventories and wills, but these were books of value, while smaller religious books would have been left unrecorded. Margaret Spufford, however, came upon the notes in the account book of John Tayer, a Gloucestershire shoemaker and glover, made in 1627. Their unique character make them invaluable in casting light on what book collections might have been owned by 'ordinary men' – and it was ordinary men rather than women who were able to read at this period. John Tayer's list contains two bibles and a testament, three psalters and two catechisms.[28]

The dominance in numbers of religious works is reflected by Maunsell: in his catalogue there are five times more of these than books on secular subjects. Moreover, the publishing phenomenon that developed in the last quarter of the century was the production of books of sermons. Until the 1590s, sermon books were customarily printed in black letter which, contrary to modern perception, was easier to read for the comparatively unlettered reader. Usually these publications took up between five and thirteen sheets of paper, selling for a few pence. It has been estimated that 60 sermons preached at the Cross were printed during Elizabeth's reign, and about twice as many under her successor, James I. This was truly a local industry for the booksellers of St Paul's Churchyard, as we shall see in the next chapter.

CHAPTER 4

THE FIRES OF REFORMATION

In May 1521 John Fisher preached for two hours from the pulpit of Paul's Cross before a congregation that included Cardinal Wolsey, Archbishop of York and Henry VIII's most powerful minister, the imperial and papal ambassadors, and many Londoners. The title of his sermon was *Against Pernicious Doctrine*, an attack on Martin Luther. At this time England was firmly attached to the Roman Catholic Church, although protests from Lollards had sometimes been expressed at Paul's Cross. However, the sermon delivered on 12 May 1521 marked the first public assertion of orthodoxy, ushering in a century of further assertions that reflect the troubled religious times in which the nation was embroiled.

The theme developed that day was presented by one of England's most distinguished scholars and churchmen. A friend not only of Erasmus and other humanists, John Fisher was also close to Lady Margaret Beaufort, acting as her chaplain and confessor. At the universities of Cambridge and Oxford, he instituted the Lady Margaret readerships in divinity, and as Chancellor of the former he introduced Greek and Hebrew into the curriculum. In 1504 he was made Bishop of Rochester by Lady Margaret's son, Henry VII.

Fisher was celebrated for his preaching, regarding it as an important function of a bishop. He was, therefore, the ideal person to be asked to speak at Paul's Cross, one of the most influential public venues at this time. And this time was a significant moment in the history of the Church. Less than four years earlier, in October 1517, followers of Martin Luther had posted his handwritten *95 Theses* on the door of the Schlosskirche in Wittenberg. Luther's questioning of Rome's sale of indulgences rapidly evolved

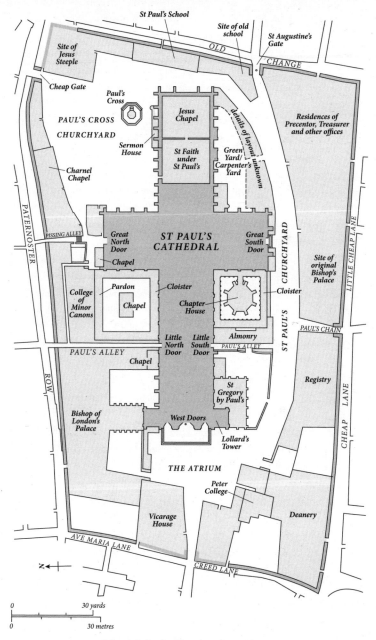

Map 2 St Paul's Churchyard in 1547.

into an argument about papal primacy. At Cardinal Wolsey's suggestion, Henry VIII had developed a written argument concerning indulgences, *Assertio Septem Sacramentorum*, that was to be published after Fisher's sermon by Richard Pynson, acting in his role as the King's Printer. Known as the King's Book, it proved greatly successful, with Pope Leo X bestowing upon him the title *Fidei Defensor*, still held by the British monarchy.

Pope Leo also issued in 1520 a papal bull condemning Luther's writings. In response, Luther not only produced a whole series of further publications, but also burnt the bull in public. Cardinal Wolsey had already attempted to collect up and destroy Luther's books, but was provoked into greater action by a letter from England's ambassador at the Hapsburg court, telling him of Luther's burning of the bull.

This was the rapidly escalating situation when Fisher took to the pulpit. The painting made in the early seventeenth century, known as 'John Gipkyn's diptych' gives some idea of how the scene might have looked. Paul's Cross itself was an octagonal pavilion surmounted by a cupola and cross, raised well above ground level. In the painting, the area immediately around the pulpit has been turned into a kind of box where a chosen few have purchased seats. This was added at the beginning of the seventeenth century, but even in Fisher's day it was laid out like a theatre, with some of the audience on stools and standing, while the very privileged would be accommodated in a gallery leading out from the cathedral.

The cover of the pulpit provided a kind of sounding board, for the preacher had to project his voice to crowds that could be numbered in thousands. They were delivered here every Sunday, although a sermon was given on Good Friday too. The sounds of traffic in Cheapside would have been muted on these occasions, but even so it must have been a feat to reach the furthest edges of the congregation, and for the two hours that was the customary length of the sermons. In 1599, a Swiss visitor to London, Thomas Platter, noted in his journal how the preacher at Paul's Cross 'always has a bottle of wine and some bread behind him near the pulpit, where at his request, he is refreshed with food and drink . . . so that all may hear and understand'. He explained that the reason why these sermons were held outside the cathedral was because the congregation was 'so vast that the aforesaid big church will not hold it'.[1]

John Fisher's style of preaching was based on a form introduced to England by Franciscan friars in the early thirteenth century. It was known as the 'university' style, although it was not offered just to scholastic audiences, but also to lay congregations. As one authority explains:

A text was stated, paraphrased if necessary, or put into its scriptural context, then divided by a word or phrase (*ad verbum*). Alternatively, the paraphrased meaning of the text could be divided according to the ideas to which it referred (*ad rem*). Each division thus formed was expounded separately and the peroration would remind the listeners of each and bring them all to conclusion, reiterating the original text.[2]

Using four 'instructions' Fisher sought to undermine the grounds on which Luther had based his arguments, and to state definitively the validity of papal authority.

At the conclusion of Fisher's sermon, copies of Luther's books that had been rounded up by Cardinal Wolsey were thrown on a fire in the Churchyard as a riposte to Luther's act of burning the papal bull. This echoed the earlier burning of Wycliffe's literature, and provided a dramatic demonstration of Henry VIII's Catholic orthodoxy that had earned him the papal title of defender of the faith.

We know what John Fisher said that day in May 1521 as his text was taken by Wynkyn de Worde and published in English, along with a Latin translation by Richard Pace for dissemination throughout Europe. De Worde had, in fact, been warned by the Bishop of London, Cuthbert Tunstall, for importing Lutheran texts, so he may have been keen to establish his essentials of orthodoxy by printing Fisher's sermon. The English version went through three editions in the 1520s and was republished during the reign of Mary Tudor following England's return to the Church of Rome.

Printers and booksellers were establishing themselves in St Paul's Churchyard and the area around, as shown in Chapter 3. Their close proximity to the Cross created a symbiosis between press and pulpit, so that the sermons preached there were a fruitful area of publishing. The number of Paul's Cross sermons subsequently printed runs into hundreds. The historian Mary Morrissey points out the importance of realising that most of these were not about politics or religious controversy, but rather concerned information about catechetical matters, with exhortations to piety, charity and obedience to superiors. Nevertheless, Paul's Cross was selected by the religious and political authorities as the place for important messages to be delivered.[3]

When Fisher delivered his sermon, the religious reformer William Tyndale was still in England, acting as tutor to a family in his native Gloucestershire. When the Bishop of London refused him permission to print his translation of the New Testament, he left England and published his very influential *Obedience of a Christian Man* in Antwerp. Although this was produced seven years after Fisher's sermon, Tyndale made furious reference to it, underlining the effect that it had made not only on the congregation that heard it at the time in the Churchyard, but on religious debate right across Europe. He objected particularly to Fisher's claim that some things had been given privily by Christ to St Peter and never written down. Papal authority was, of course, claimed as handed down by St Peter. Tyndale had a supreme way with words, as shown by the many phrases taken from his English translation of the Scriptures by the compilers of the King James Bible nearly a century later. In his anger at Fisher's arguments, he made accusations of trickery and other faults: 'Rochester, both abominable and shameless, yea, and stark mad with pure malice, and so adased in the brains with spite, that he cannot overcome the truth that he seeeth not, or rather careth what he saith'.[4]

Church and state in England at this time were adamant that the Scriptures should not be available in the vernacular for all to read, and their determination was ruthless, as can be seen in the case of James Bainham, a law student in London in the 1520s, and a follower of the works of both Luther and Tyndale. In 1531 he purchased the freedom of the City as a Stationer but was arrested on the orders of the Lord Chancellor, Sir Thomas More, and refused under torture to inform on his friends. Nevertheless, ordered by More to pay the substantial fine of £20 to the King, Bainham accepted the chance to recant, doing penance by standing before the preacher at Paul's Cross. A woodcut from *Foxe's Book of Martyrs* shows him dressed in a white shroud, holding a lighted candle and carrying a sheaf of wooden faggots as a warning of his fate should he lapse. But so troubled was Bainham that he subsequently decided to attend Sunday service carrying copies of Tyndale's New Testament and of his *Obedience of a Christian Man*. Inevitably his arrest followed, and he was burned in Smithfield in April 1532 as a heretic.

6. James Bainham, a member of the Stationers' Company, standing in penance before the preacher at Paul's Cross.

At the beginning of his sermon in 1521, Fisher had summoned up the picture of a clear day, with the sun brightly shining, but a 'thyk blacke clowde' appearing 'that darketh the face of the heven', bringing with it 'an hydeous tempest and maketh a great lightning and thundereth terribly'. The image turned out to be all too prophetic, although the thick black cloud in this case was the King's 'Great Matter' which dominated the latter part of the 1520s. Without a legitimate male heir, Henry was determined to divorce his Queen, Catherine of Aragon, and to marry Anne Boleyn. Failing to secure the Pope's blessing, with the help of Thomas Cromwell he asserted his supremacy as Head of the Church of England. One of the vocal opponents to the King's proposed divorce was Bishop Fisher, who, like Sir Thomas More, refused to swear to the Act of Supremacy and was executed in June 1535. Cardinal Wolsey avoided such a fate by dying in 1530.

The drama and uncertainty in both religious and political matters at this period is duly reflected in some of the sermons that were preached at Paul's Cross, described by one historian as 'all England in a little room'.[5] In 1534, Thomas Cromwell, now Henry VIII's most powerful minister, commandeered the Cross and licensed John Hilsey, Fisher's replacement to the see of Rochester, to appoint preachers to give sermons on consecutive Sundays on the subject of the King's supremacy. This was out of the ordinary, for it was the Bishop of London who customarily made the choice of who should preach.

One of the sermons organised by Bishop Hilsey was preached for Lent by Robert Singleton on 2 April 1535. Singleton, Chaplain to Anne Boleyn, now Henry's Queen, was a member of the circle of evangelicals that looked to Thomas Cromwell as their patron. He was therefore a spokesman for Cromwell's legislative programme then moving through Parliament to sever all ties of ecclesiastical jurisdiction with Rome. Paul's allegory of the earthly and heavenly Jerusalem in Chapter 4 of the Epistle to the Galatians was chosen to draw a distinction between the Church visible and invisible. Singleton ended his sermon by calling upon God particularly to preserve the Church of England and the King as supreme head.[6] However, an indication of the uncertainties of the period was that Singleton himself was obliged to recant heresies unnamed at Paul's Cross in 1544, and soon afterwards was sentenced and executed at Tyburn for provoking sedition.

This was a time when men and women were prepared to die for their faith. And it was a time when the twists and turns of Tudor politics made matters ever more hazardous. The career of one theologian shows this in sharp relief: Richard Smyth, who preached at Paul's Cross in May 1547. Smyth had enjoyed a brilliant scholarly career, becoming the 'reader of the Kynges maiestyes lecture in Oxford', or Regius Professor of Divinity, at Christ Church. This was the grand foundation created when the Pope gave Cardinal Wolsey permission to dissolve monastic communities to form Cardinal College. At the Cardinal's death in 1530, the college was reprieved and refounded by Henry VIII as 'King's College', an ecclesiastical rather than an educational establishment. However, in 1546, shortly before his death, the King combined the new cathedral see of Oxford with the college, calling it 'Ecclesia Christi Cathedralis Oxon', or Christ Church College.

The last years of Henry VIII's reign had been particularly difficult, with power oscillating between the traditionalists and evangelicals surrounding a king who was becoming increasingly debilitated. At his death in January 1547 it was the evangelical courtiers that were able to take power in the name of Henry's nine-year-old son, Edward VI, led by the new King's uncle, Edward Seymour, who became Duke of Somerset and Lord Protector. During his time as the Regius Professor at Christ Church Smyth had stoutly adhered to Catholic traditions, but with the accession of Edward, he recognised that a very different religious climate pertained. Therefore, only four months into the new reign, Smyth chose publicly to recant his adherence to Catholicism, and to burn two of the books that he had written in defence of the traditional account that the presence of Christ is truly and substantially contained in the Holy Eucharist, published only the previous year.

Smyth's 'Retraction Sermon' has been described as a masterpiece of equivocation, with an ironical choice of theme: 'Every man is a liar' from Psalm 116, echoed by St Paul in Chapter 3 of his letter to the Romans.[7] It certainly provoked Stephen Gardiner, the quick-tempered and plain-speaking Bishop of Winchester, to write to the Duke of Somerset, to complain:

And when I sawe Doctor Smithes recantacion begin with *Omnis homo mendax* so englished and such a new humility as he woulde make all the doctors of the church liers with him selfe, knowing what oppinions were abrode, it enforced me to write unto your grace for the ease of my conscience.[8]

Somerset's reply did not apply balm to the Bishop's famous sensitivity, for he expressed incredulity at his reaction, instead applauding the sincerity of Smyth.

The 1540s was an age of recantation, scarcely surprising considering the drastic fate that threatened perceived heresy. As noted earlier, one of the areas of debate had been about the publication of the Scriptures in English, and after a statute was issued in 1543 seeking to restrict access to versions in the vernacular, evangelical clergymen were obliged to make public recantations at Paul's Cross. But Richard Smyth carried the practice of recantation to unparalleled heights. Following his 'Retraction Sermon' of May 1547, he withdrew his recantation, forfeiting his Regius professorship and fleeing to Europe, to Catholic Louvain. At the accession of Mary Tudor, he was back in England, elected Chancellor of Oxford, but when the pendulum swung in 1559 with Elizabeth succeeding her half-sister on the throne, he recanted again. Soon after, however, he fled back to Louvain and became Reader of Scripture at the new Catholic University of Douai, where he died in 1563. Smyth has to be the Tudor trimmer par excellence, and unlike so many of his fellow theologians, he died in his bed.

When Edward VI became King, he was hailed by Protestants as the young Josiah, from the reforming King of Judah in the Old Testament, ushering in a very different form of worship. Still earlier, in the reign of his father, when Thomas Cromwell wielded power as Lord Privy Seal, changes had already begun to take place. In the summer of 1538, Charles Wriothesley, a herald who kept a chronicle of contemporary events, noted how 'the Kinge gave a commundement that noe religious persons of the suppressed houses or such other as used to live of the charitie of the people out theyr religious houses should goe abroade in theyr religious habytes'. The Scottish-born poet Alexander Barclay was based at Greyfriars, just to the north of the Churchyard. He had the misfortune to be observed by Cromwell while visiting Reyner Wolfe's bookshop, dressed in his habit. The Lord Privy Seal challenged him: 'will not that cowl of yours be left off yet? An if I hear by one o'clock that this apparel be not changed, thou shalt be hanged immediately, for example to all other.'[9]

St Paul's Churchyard became the place where famous relics were displayed before being destroyed at Cromwell's behest as feigned images that fostered dangerous loyalties. One of the first to be brought here was the phial of Holy

Blood that had been for centuries a magnet for pilgrims to Hailes Abbey in Wiltshire. Charles Wriothesley noted:

> After the 24th day of November [1538], beinge Sunday, the Bishop of Rochester [John Hilsey] preached at Paules Crosse, and there shewed the bloude of Hales and recanted certeine words that he had spoken of the sayd bloude that it was a dukes [duck's] bloude, and now shewed playnely that yt was noe bloude, but hony clarified and coloured with saffron.[10]

Hugh Latimer, the evangelical Bishop of Worcester, told Thomas Cromwell that he had tasted the 'blood', and found it like unctuous gum. While Hilsey preached his sermon, four Dutch Anabaptists were forced to stand by the pulpit of the Cross, carrying their faggots in preparation for being burnt at Smithfield. Anabaptists maintained that adherents should be baptised again as adults, declaring that they were now in the position to make a confession of their faith, which they had not been able to do as infants. Their interpretation of the Scriptures set them at odds with both reformers and traditionalists.

In the same year the Rood of Grace from Boxley Abbey in Kent was displayed at Paul's Cross before being smashed to pieces. This, too, was a famous relic, as the figure on the wooden cross was supposed to move and speak. One of Thomas Cromwell's commissioners during the Dissolution of the Monasteries had found that the relic worked not by miraculous powers, but by a series of levers and wires operated by the monks. The Rood was initially displayed in the marketplace in Maidstone before being sent to St Paul's Churchyard where it was hacked to pieces and burnt while John Hilsey again preached a sermon at the Cross.

Now, with Edward on the throne and his uncle, Edward Seymour, Duke of Somerset, in power, religious images were destroyed in churches all over England. Within St Paul's Cathedral, Somerset was determined to get rid of a series of images. When the great rood screen and imagery were demolished, the felling of the great crucifix killed one workman and injured others. The rood at the north door had drawn particular veneration. According to a fifteenth-century chronicle, King Lucius (see p. 6) had found it in the Thames in the mid-second century, while a later record identified it as the cross that Joseph of Arimathea had set up at Caerleon. It had been thrown into the sea, fetching up at Paul's Wharf. Although the shrine of St Erconwald, close to the high altar, had never attracted the same veneration as that of Thomas Becket at Canterbury, it too had to go. At the end of November 1547, a picture of Christ's resurrection and an image of the Virgin Mary from the cathedral were destroyed after a sermon at Paul's Cross. The cathedral clergy met these acts with a muted response, in contrast to the protests made by citizens when Catholic goods from their parish churches were also brought and destroyed in the Churchyard.

At Somerset's command a famous series of paintings was removed from the cloister of the Pardon Churchyard situated on the north side of the cathedral. According to the chronicler John Stow, these were painted boards commissioned around the year 1430 by John Carpenter. They depicted the Dance of Death, with figures of Death accompanying the mayor, artisans, merchants and nobles in a grim dance, one of the great sights of the City. Carpenter had also commissioned the poet John Lydgate to produce an English version of a poem that had accompanied a Dance Macabre painted on the wall of the Cemetery of the Innocents in Paris. The Pardon Churchyard had been a particular centre of pilgrimage for the citizens of London, as the parents of Thomas Becket were buried there. Now Somerset wanted no reminder of shrines or imagery to survive, nor objects that might attract pilgrims.

Plainness was the order of the day as far as Protestant reformers were concerned. This is reflected in the style of sermons at that time, such as one given by Bishop Hugh Latimer on 18 January 1548. When the weather was inclement, sermons normally preached at Paul's Cross were moved to the undercroft of the Cloister Churchyard, described as 'the Shrouds'. Latimer's 'Sermon in the Shrouds' took as its title 'On the Ploughers' and argued for a programme of religious reform and redress of social and political corruption. The ideal cleric should be like a humble husbandman, ploughman or sower, dedicated to his preaching ministry and not indulging in multiple benefices and the use of curates.

Latimer's language was appropriately homely, so he explained: 'Ye may not be offended with my similitude: in that I compare preachynge to the laboure and worke of ploughing, and the preacher to a plough'. He was at pains to explain another 'similitude' that had been reported, that he had compared the Blessed Virgin Mary to a saffron bag. This must have shocked, particularly as

The Compositor

Leaue setting
thypage: spent
is thineage.

The Presseman.

Let printing
slay: and come
away.

7. Woodcut images from Queen Elizabeth's Prayer Book printed for the Stationers'
Company in 1608. Compositors and printers are shown with the figure of Death, a
reminder of the transitory nature of life. The cloisters of the Pardon Churchyard had
similar reminders with a sequence of Dance of Death paintings.

the Virgin Mary had been placed by so many at the heart of their worship. Latimer sought to deny the allegation:

> It hath bene saied of me, Oh Latimer, nay, as for him I wil never believe hym whyle I lyve, nor never trust him, for he likened our blessed Ladye to a saffrone bagge, where in deede I never used that similitude.

Hoping to retrieve the situation, he also reminded his audience that the precious spice was obtained from the stamens of the saffron crocus, and

> I might have sayed thus, as the saffrone bagge that hath bene full of saffron, or hath had saffron in it, doth ever after savoure and smel of the swete saffron that it conteyned: so oure blessed Ladye which conceived and bare Chryste in her wombe, dyd ever after resemble the maners and vertues of that precious babe which she bare.

He went on to warn that preachers should be circumspect and not give offence to their congregation.[11]

The whole religious situation in England changed again with the death of Edward VI in 1553, and the succession of his Catholic half-sister, Mary Tudor. She seems to have particularly recognised the Churchyard as the stage for her kingdom. When Edward's death was announced, Nicholas Ridley, the Protestant Bishop of London, reminded his flock that both Mary and Elizabeth Tudor were debarred from the succession by the will of Henry VIII, and preached in favour of their cousin, Lady Jane Grey, succeeding to the throne. However, rumblings of discontent against Ridley were heard at Paul's Cross, and when news arrived that Mary had proclaimed herself Queen and was on her way to the capital, huge crowds gathered in the Churchyard. She was duly declared Queen at Cheapside, and a throng led by the Lord Mayor came to the cathedral. Mary also chose to process through the Churchyard on the eve of her coronation, with celebrations that included performances of pageants and a Dutch acrobat disporting himself on the summit of the cathedral steeple.

On 12 November 1553 James Brooks preached a sermon at the Cross. Brooks was Chaplain and Almoner to Stephen Gardiner, who had emerged from the Tower of London having spent the last years of Edward VI's reign there as a prisoner. Brooks, an important figure in the regime's move to restore England to the Roman Catholic Church, began his sermon by appealing to his audience about the fundamental upheavals that had taken place in the previous reign:

> Have not we had chaunge in doctrine, chaunge in bookes, chaunge in tounges, chaunge in aultars, chaunge in placing, chaunge in gesture, chaunge in apparaile, chaunge in breade, chaunge in gevynge, chaunge in receyvying with many changes more, so that we had still chaunge upon chaunge and lyke never to have lefte chaungying til al the hole world had cleane been changed?

He then moved on to his theme, the New Testament story of the resurrected daughter of Jairus. While Mary was described as a second Helen, mother of Constantine, the Roman Emperor who halted the persecution of Christians, Brooks referred to the ill governance of 'certaine wycked rulers', suggesting that Henry VIII and Edward VI might be compared to the likes of Nebuchadnezzar and Herod.[12]

Resistance to the Queen flared in early 1554, with a rebellion led by Sir Thomas Wyatt, son of the poet. He was objecting to Mary's determination to take as her consort Philip of Spain, concerned that England would become a puppet state to the overwhelming power of the Hapsburg Empire. When the rebellion collapsed, Wyatt was executed on Tower Hill, but some of his followers were hanged in St Paul's Churchyard in February 1554. On a happier note, following the marriage of Mary and Philip, the Queen brought her new husband to St Paul's. This time they were entertained by a Dutch acrobat descending by a rope from the top of the chapter house.

England's formal reconciliation with Rome took place in the following December when the Queen's cousin, Cardinal Reginald Pole, absolved the realm at a ceremony in Whitehall. He then processed to the cathedral where he was joined by the Lord Mayor and aldermen, members of the livery companies, representatives from parishes across the diocese and the entire City clergy in their copes. Philip, with an entourage of 400 men, also arrived, to take part in the service of mass. The Cardinal and the Prince then repaired to the balcony overlooking Paul's Cross to hear Stephen Gardiner preach a sermon to a vast assembly, said to number 15,000. In a moment of pure theatre, after Gardiner declared he had been empowered to grant absolution, the entire congregation knelt in silence.

In hindsight, this was the apogee of Mary's popularity, for the years that followed witnessed the terrible scenes of martyrdom when around 300 men and women were burnt alive at the stake. One of the towers of St Paul's Cathedral was used as a prison for those arrested for heresy. Here Edmund Bonner, the Bishop of London who has gone down in history as an enthusiastic burner of Protestants, examined suspects before sending them to the bonfires in nearby Smithfield. The first to suffer this fate was the scholar John Rogers, the creator of the Matthew Bible (see p. 43).

We know about the Protestant martyrs who suffered for their faith from the book that was to be published in 1563, after the death of Mary Tudor and the succession of her half-sister, Elizabeth. The title of the book is *Actes and Monuments*, but it is familiarly known as *Foxe's Book of Martyrs*. John Foxe spent the years of Mary's reign in Europe, collecting the material which was not only to record the persecutions of that reign, but also a history of the English Church from the time of John Wycliffe and the Lollards. The result was published by John Day. Imprisoned in 1554, Day had shared a cell with John Rogers, and may well have been inspired by conversations with him to take on the huge project. Running to over 1,800 pages, the *Book of Martyrs* involved different typefaces, columns and marginal notes, to which Foxe kept on adding as more information became forthcoming. In addition, there were 50 woodcut illustrations, probably produced in the Netherlands, and evidence suggests that they arrived late, generating the nightmare situation that is all too familiar to modern illustrated book publishers. In the event, the book proved the bestselling publication of the sixteenth century, making Day a rich man. It has been estimated that between 1563 and 1616, 28,000 copies were sold of unabridged editions, while thousands more were sold of abridgements, including some, rather terrifyingly, for children.[13]

Among the woodcuts is the illustration of James Bainham making penance at the feet of the preacher at Paul's Cross in 1532 (see p. 67). Another graphic image depicts the bishops Hugh Latimer and Nicholas Ridley at the stake in Oxford on 16 October 1555. On the right hand of the picture another leading figure of the Edwardian Church, Archbishop Thomas Cranmer, is shown at the window of his prison cell, appealing to God to strengthen them. He was burnt at the stake five months later. The scene also shows Richard Smyth, Regius Professor of Divinity at the university and serial recanter, in a nice irony preaching a sermon that urged Ridley and Latimer to recant (Plate 4).

When Elizabeth Tudor succeeded her half-sister Mary in 1558, it was all change again. Only too aware of the extreme religious positions taken by her two predecessors, she would seek to keep to the middle ground, making her Church comprehensive in its theology, so that there would be many mansions for all her subjects. For her the Church was the nation in its religious aspect, with her as the supreme governor. Conformity was very important, but belief was a personal matter and, as she put it, she would not make windows into men's souls.

But this, of course, did not stop her theologians adopting strong positions. A sermon preached at the Cross in November 1559, just one year after Elizabeth's accession to the throne, was delivered by John Jewel, returned from exile in Zurich and Strasbourg to become Bishop of Salisbury. Jewel was a leading humanist scholar, particularly known for his study of the Church Fathers. In his sermon, known as 'the Challenge', he turned to the fraught debate concerning the nature of the Eucharist, and especially the question of sacramental presence.

Jewel aimed to distinguish between the authority of Scripture and patristic tradition as opposed to later scholastic accretion of dogma, and thus seeking to formulate a durable definition of Catholicity. As one historian has put it, 'This triggered extraordinary public sensation with an echoing response elicited in both pulpit and press that was wholly without precedent in both volume and duration'.[14] After John Day printed the sermon, the Dean of St Paul's, Henry Cole, took up Jewel's challenge, leading to an exchange of letters that Day also printed. More sermons and pamphlets followed in an unprecedented flood, stoking up debate right across Europe in what came to be known as 'The Great Controversy'.

One member of the congregation at Jewel's sermon on 26 November was Henry Machyn, a London merchant tailor, who noted: 'ther was grett audyense as [has ever] bene at Paul's Cross', including the Lord Mayor, aldermen and members of the court. Machyn kept a form of diary from 1550 to 1563, when he probably succumbed to plague. Thus he gives fascinating details of a turbulent time, spanning the reigns of Edward, Mary and Elizabeth.

In particular, he shows how attending sermons was such an important part of London life. He noted that the important sermons given to celebrate Easter were at Paul's Cross and at an outdoor pulpit at St Mary Spital, on the other side of the City, and those held at Westminster before the sovereign and the royal court. The customary time for the Paul's Cross sermons was from 10 o'clock to midday on Sunday morning. Machyn records how, having attended the Cross sermon, he moved on to one preached at another London church, a habit that was later to be described as 'sermon gadding'.

Another Londoner, Richard Stonley, recorded his sermon gadding in his diary in the 1580s. His Sundays would begin with morning prayer at home, followed by attendance at a sermon, either at his parish church, St Botolph's Aldersgate, or at Paul's Cross, before returning to his house for dinner and spending the afternoon in reading the Scriptures. On one occasion he talks of hearing a 'rehearsal sermon' at Paul's Cross. This was a summary of the Passion sermon delivered by another preacher on Good Friday, and 'rehearsed' on Low Sunday, the week after Easter.[15]

In the sixteenth century not every church in the City had a preacher, so those keen on hearing a sermon would go beyond their own parish. A later satire shows that the churches within and around St Paul's Churchyard particularly provided a rich source for the sermon gadder:

Let her goe oft to Church, to Paules the huge,
Or to black Fryers, to heare Maister Gowge,
Unto Saint Gregories, Saint Faithes, Sainte Fosters.[16]

Indeed, the custom was sometimes criticised for drawing men and women away from their own parishes, and it was even implied that the desire to find a good sermon might verge on the addictive.

Congregations could be highly responsive, so that in March 1560, when Machyn went to hear the newly installed Bishop of London, Edmund Grindal, at the Cross, he noted 'master Gryndall, in ys rochet and chyminer [vestments]; and after sermon done the pepull dyd syng; and ther was my lord mayre and the althermen, and ther was great audience'.[17] The very location of the Cross, in the open air, made possible incidents of disorderly behaviour. One of the most serious was noted in his diary for 1553 when, just a month after Mary became Queen, her Chaplain, Dr Gilbert Bourne, was attacked by a crowd at the Cross. Men and women, young and old, shouted at his sermon, 'lyke madpepull'.[18] Some flung their caps in the air as Bourne was pulled from the pulpit and a dagger thrown at him by a bystander. He was rescued by the intervention of the Lord Mayor and a courtier.

Another aspect of London life noted in his diary by Machyn is people doing penance at the Cross, sometimes during a sermon. Those made to undertake this humiliating public ritual could be guilty of religious heterodoxy or of a social misdemeanour, and sometimes a combination of the two. In 1554, for example, Elizabeth Croft was punished here for manufacturing a hoax whereby she gave a whistle through a wall that her colleagues then interpreted as messages from a spirit. With the changes in monarch, men and women could suddenly find themselves in trouble. During Mary's reign, priests who had married under the previous regime now had to undergo penance. With Elizabeth on the throne, Henry Machyn recorded in his diary how he too had to recant at the Cross in November 1561. Catholic in his sympathies, he was condemned for slandering a French Protestant preacher Jean Veron by repeating gossip that he had taken 'a wench'.[19]

Machyn may have voiced his accusation by pinning a libel up on or near the pulpit of Paul's Cross. Such libels continued to be posted as part of the local political scene or could be religious in intent; the aim was to create maximum publicity without revealing the identity of the writer. An example of how local politics might intrude came in the 1580s, when a series of libels appeared accusing magistrates of being unduly harsh on the poorer inhabitants of London. As Arnold Hunt has shown in his study of the relationship between preachers and their audiences, here might be the opportunity for the preacher to act as the poor man's lawyer. While the Bishop of London had the right to choose the preachers for the Cross, their fee was provided by the mayor and aldermen, who were careful with their patronage, and this could cause dissension.

The relationship between the ecclesiastical and the civic authorities reached a dramatic low in 1582 when Bishop Aylmer of London delivered a forceful rebuke during a sermon to the Lord Mayor: 'I must then tell you your duty out of my chair, which is the pulpit at Paul's Cross, where you must sit, not as a judge to control, but as a scholar to learn'.[20] How this was received by Sir James Harvey, robed in all his dignity and sitting among his aldermen in the gallery overlooking the Cross, can only too easily be imagined. Four years later a London minister, George Closse, preached a sermon at the Cross in which he accused the Lord Mayor, Sir Wolston Dixie, of fraud and partiality in the administration of justice. When he was ordered to deliver a sermon of recantation, Closse took the opportunity to attack Dixie again, repeating his earlier charges. This particular controversy drew to an unresolved conclusion with the arrival of the sensational news that the conspirators of the Babington plot had been arrested. Antony Babington, a Catholic recusant, had been recruited by a Jesuit priest to take part in a plot to assassinate Queen Elizabeth, and to replace her with Mary Queen of Scots, held in captivity in Chartley Castle in Derbyshire.

Elizabeth I's sensible desire for a middle ground, and not to make windows into men's souls, had received a severe blow when her Catholic cousin, the Scottish Queen, fled to England in 1568. As Mary Stuart had a strong claim to the English throne and thus presented a potent focus of opposition, Elizabeth was given no alternative but to imprison her. In response to this, and to Elizabeth's earlier assumption of the role of supreme governor of the Church of England, Pope Pius V issued a bull in April 1570, 'Reigning on High', that declared her a heretic and released her subjects from their allegiance to her. A well-known London Catholic, John Felton, used the traditional form of protest by nailing a copy of the bull onto the door of the bishop's palace in the Churchyard. Initially, he was condemned to be hanged at Tyburn but, given the location of his offence, he was duly executed in the cathedral precinct. Now Elizabeth, who had thus far tolerated Catholics to worship in private, actively began to persecute them for treason.

A sermon preached at the Cross in January 1580, delivered by James Bisse, focused upon the threat that Catholics now posed to the Queen and her government. His style of preaching presents a complete contrast from the homely language of Hugh Latimer and his contemporaries of 30 years before. The new decade saw a flowering of English drama, both on stage and in the pulpit. Bisse, a fellow of Magdalen College Oxford, employed language that used repetition, witty conceits and verbal elaborations reminiscent of the plays of his contemporary and fellow graduate of the college, John Lyly.

Bisse looked at the heroines of the Old Testament who had confronted and overcome their enemies: 'Sisera by Deborah, a woman, shall have a nayle knockt into his skull, Holofernes by Judith, a woman, shall have his head cut off. Abimelech by a woman, shall have a peece of a milstone breake upon his brainepan'. He then turned to the Queen and the menagerie of her enemies:

> By Elizabeth, a woman, the Goates of Italy. The wolves of Spaine, the cormorantes of Rome. The Irish coltes, and the Foxes of England, that are now in Ireland, and all other her enemies shall so bee brought to shame.[21]

The year following this sermon, new penal laws were passed against Catholics, and the hunting out of Jesuit missionaries was pursued in earnest.

Within the English Church itself a whole range of views were held and expressed. Some objected to what they considered as unnecessary and distracting accoutrements to worship, such as the wearing of surplices by priests, images of the crucifix, 'curious' singing and the playing of the organ. A churchman of this opinion was Alexander Nowell, who served as Dean of St Paul's for over 40 years. As this was almost the entire reign of Elizabeth, it was unfortunate that the two had a difficult relationship. Nowell was one of the leading preachers of his day, but this talent was lost on the Queen. Early in her reign, he urged her during a sermon to marry, and in another given at court, he mentioned she continued to keep a crucifix in her private chapel. On this occasion, Elizabeth called out, 'To your text, Mr Dean – leave that, we have heard enough of that'.[22] Other Protestant churchmen were of a Puritan tendency, attacking the very institution of the episcopacy. To counter these, John Whitgift, who became Archbishop of Canterbury in 1583, preached a sermon at Paul's Cross on Accession Day, 17 November, of that year. He firmly upheld the authority of the episcopacy, stating that the history of bishops as superiors and overseers of clergy could be traced back to the primitive Church.

In the years that followed, Whitgift waged a determined campaign against the followers of Martin Marprelate. The latter was the pseudonym adopted by a Puritan writer who, provoked by Whitgift's campaign, wrote a series of pamphlets in 1588 and 1589 attacking the Protestant Church hierarchy, and in particular the episcopacy. The press upon which the pamphlets were printed was moved around the country, thus eluding the authorities. Marprelate used a combination of a plain style and pungent wit to put over his message. In response John Lyly, along with his fellow dramatist Thomas Nashe, were brought into the fray by the bishops to counter Marprelate's arguments using their theatrical skills. Lyly's *Pappe with an Hatchet* was published in pamphlet form in 1589: it was not a success, for his highly artificial style of writing, as epitomised in his famous play *Euphues*, was no match for the rollicking satire employed by Marprelate.

Richard Bancroft's contribution to the debate was a forceful sermon preached at the Cross in February 1588. A canon of Westminster, Bancroft was close to Whitgift, and was to become Bishop of London in 1597 and in succession to Whitgift, Archbishop of Canterbury. In his 1588 sermon he denounced the Puritan movement in forceful terms, not only seeking to uncover the identity of Marprelate, but also railing against a whole list of what he deemed as heretical groups, such as Arians, Donatists, Papists, Libertines, Anabaptists, the Family of Love, sectaries and atheists. In colourful language he declared them false and hypocritical:

> to trees which have nothing but leaves, bicause they are fruitelesse, and also to the mermaids bicause they hide their errours under their counterfeit and fair speeches . . . to the diseases called the leprosie and the cankar, in that their corruption taketh deepe roote and spreadeth so farre: to the serpent that is lapped up togither, bicause they have many windings and contradictions: to the fish named a Cuttle, for that they infect men with their blacke and slanderous calumniations: to snakes or adders, the poison of aspes being under their lips: to the viper, bicause they regarde not to wound and destroie their mother the church: to tigers and lions, for that they are verie cruell and fierce: and to diverse other such thinges as ought to make them odious to all that love the truth.[23]

Paul's Cross had become not only the arena for religious debate, but also a popular place for the preaching of sermons in observance of political events. The anniversary of Elizabeth I's accession to the throne, 17 November, for example, was marked by a sermon. In attendance on such occasions would be the Lord Mayor, his aldermen, members of livery companies, along with members of the Privy Council, courtiers and citizens of London, amid much pageantry. Phrase books produced for foreign visitors suggest that listening to these sermons was on their itinerary. Claud Hollybrand's *French Schoolemaster* of 1573 has a dialogue for Sunday in which the dignitaries likely to be seated in the gallery of the cathedral overlooking the Cross are named, and a similar text is included in *Spanish Schoolemaster*, compiled by William Stepney in 1591. In 1599 the Swiss traveller Thomas Platter duly recorded in his journal attending a sermon, describing how the Lord Mayor was clad in a scarlet robe, and was preceded by a herald, also finely dressed, carrying a red sword with yellow stripes.[24]

The one person, however, who was not present at these events was the Queen. Never a great enthusiast for preaching in general, she tolerated the sermons preached by Dean Nowell at her court but did not venture to his cathedral. Even in 1588 when the defeat of the Spanish Armada was announced in the Churchyard, and Alexander Nowell preached a sermon of thanksgiving, she did not attend.

Instead, the Queen waited for three months, and then paid her one and only visit, on 24 November 1588, for a celebration of the defeat of the Spanish. She arrived in spectacular style, processing from Somerset House on the Strand. The images that we have from this period show an iconic Queen, in the most elaborate dresses, covered in jewels. Equally elaborate for this occasion was her conveyance. John Stow in his annals described it as

> a chariot-throne, made with foure pillars, behind to have a Canopie, on the toppe whereof was made a Crowne Imperiall, and two lower pillars before, whereon stood a Lyon and a Dragon, supporters of the Armes of Englande, drawne by two white horse.[25]

Accompanying her were members of the Privy Council, the French ambassador, judges and most of her court. When she arrived at Ludgate she was greeted by the Lord Mayor and his aldermen, and at the west door of the cathedral by the Bishop of London, the Dean and about 50 clergymen. The liturgy was duly sung in the choir before the Queen moved to the north transept and into the gallery overlooking Paul's Cross. Here she heard the Bishop of Salisbury preach a sermon, of which no record has survived. For Elizabeth, the important thing was her personal appearance before her people, just as in the famous progresses that she made throughout her reign.

In 1596 a thanksgiving sermon was preached at the Cross to celebrate another defeat of the Spanish, at Cadiz on 21 June. One of the leaders of the naval assault on the city was Robert Devereux, Earl of Essex. Devereux had become Elizabeth's great favourite, but his rash and often arrogant style brought him powerful enemies and made his relationship with the Queen stormy. When it was suggested that a service of national thanksgiving for the taking of Cadiz should be held, the Queen would only permit it to be held in London with William Barlow, Archbishop Whitgift's Chaplain, as the preacher. It is ironical therefore that Barlow should be chosen five years later to preach another sermon at the Cross, this time explaining the rebellion of Essex and his execution.

On 8 February 1601 Essex entered the City with around 200 followers wearing swords and doublets but no armour and carrying few firearms. What precisely was his intention is not at all clear. One historian has suggested that he was not aiming to depose the Queen, but rather to take the political initiative, convinced of his aristocratic right to do so.[26] The 8th was a Sunday, and it is thought that he planned to reach St Paul's Cross at midday, just as the sermon was ending, and he could call upon the crowd gathered there for support. Essex was regarded by many as a charismatic hero. In the event, all hope of support from the citizens of London evaporated, and having retreated to his house on the Strand, Essex was arrested, tried for treason and condemned to be executed before a small audience in the courtyard of the Tower of London on 25 February.

Paul's Cross, having been selected by Essex and his supporters as a rallying point in his rebellion, was used by the authorities to explain their actions to the citizens of London. On the Sunday after the rebellion a sermon was preached by John Hayward, Rector of St Mary Woolnoth. He, along with other preachers, had been instructed by Essex's arch political rival, Robert Cecil, to talk about Devereux's treason with the Irish Earl of Tyrone, and of his religious hypocrisy by having Catholics in his entourage. Unfortunately we do not have Machyn to tell us of the crowd's response, but later Bishop Bancroft reported to Cecil that Hayward's reputation had been damaged because of the sermon. Shortly afterwards, the Privy Council was informed that 600 soldiers had been stationed in the Churchyard, in case of any trouble.

On the Sunday following the Earl's execution, Cecil decided to make another push for the support of Londoners. His first choice of preacher was Essex's Chaplain, Abadias Ashton, but when Ashton refused to accept the poisoned chalice, Cecil turned to William Barlow. Not only had he preached the Cadiz celebration sermon, but he also had heard the Earl's confession before his execution. Written instructions were given to Barlow, with three main messages. First, he should emphasise that mercy could not be shown to Essex as a bloodless coup had been unlikely, especially as some of his supporters were Catholics and thus posed a mortal threat to the Queen. Secondly, he should mention that Essex had initially shown impenitence. And thirdly, the execution should not appear as the reason for the sermon, but rather 'it shalbee fit to speake of this matter as by accident'.[27]

Barlow had been given an impossible task, for the sympathy for the charismatic Earl was strong, and the unpopularity of his message is reflected in a preface that he added to the printed version of the sermon.[28] The poet John Donne, who had accompanied Essex on the Cadiz expedition, included Barlow in his satirical *Courtier's Library*, in a list of fictional titles. He made him the author of *An Encomium on Doctor Shaw, Chaplain to Richard III*. He was harking back to 1483, when Canon Shaw or Shaa preached a sermon at Paul's Cross at the request of Richard. In this he denied the validity of Edward IV's marriage to Elizabeth Woodville, and thus the legitimacy of Edward V. Tradition has it that the Canon could not live with the guilt of his act (see p. 35). Barlow, however, went on preach again at Paul's Cross, as did of course, John Donne himself.

The episode of the Essex rebellion and its aftermath reflects yet once more the importance that the authorities, both ecclesiastical and secular, attached to Paul's Cross for putting over their message. At times this could be extremely effective, at others, as in the case of Hayward and Barlow, the situation backfired on the authorities. As Mary Morrissey points out:

> It would be naïve to say that the early modern authorities could not exert control over Paul's Cross. Yet it would be equally naïve to say that they could exercise a high level of control consistently, week in, week out; or that they behaved with unanimity of purpose with respect to Paul's Cross.[29]

Paul's Cross represented both pulpit and stage, with the area around set out like a theatre, and with dramatic productions frequently being given by the preachers. But it was not the only scene of drama in the Churchyard at the end of the sixteenth century. A theatre also occupied space nearby, as we shall see in the next chapter.

CHAPTER 5

THE CHILDREN OF PAUL'S

At a meeting of Elizabeth I's Privy Council in December 1575, it was reported that 'one of Sebastianes boyes being one of his principall plaiers [was] lately stolen and conveyed from him'.[1] Sebastian Westcott was the Master of the St Paul's choristers, and had recently organised a company of boy actors drawn from among his charges.

Behind this kidnapping, or possibly bribery for the boy to transfer his allegiance elsewhere, lies a fascinating story about a drama company based in the Churchyard, just south of the cathedral. The choristers, ten in all in the 1570s, were drawn from local schools, but sometimes a very promising boy would be 'impressed', forcibly recruited by a privileged regulation given to choirmasters in the major cathedrals. One such recruit in the 1530s had been Thomas Tusser, taken from the chantry college of the castle at Wallingford in Berkshire. Mainly known for his agricultural and gardening advice published in verse form, Tusser also produced a poetic autobiography, in which he described his transfer to St Paul's Cathedral:

> Away of forse, like posting horse
> For sundrie men, had plagards [the right to kidnap] then
> such childe to take.

Luckily for Tusser this proved a good move. Having received harsh treatment at Wallingford, he enjoyed both kindness and good musical training from his master at St Paul's, John Redford:

So found I grace, a certain space, still to remain:
With Redford there, and like no where,
For cunning such and virtue much.[2]

Life must have been extremely busy for the boy actors of the 1570s. Not only did they rehearse and perform their plays, but also sang at the services in the cathedral and attended St Paul's School to further their education. There had been a grammar school in the easternmost part of the Churchyard for centuries, with the masters drawn from the medieval community of canons, dignified with the title of chancellors. It is thought that one of the school's early alumni was Thomas Becket. A merchant's son born in Cheapside about 1120, he had the choice of three grammar schools to attend: St Mary le Bow and St Martin-le-Grand also had schools attached to them. As Becket became a canon of the cathedral before going on to study law at Bologna and Auxerre, it seems likely that he took the short walk from Cheapside to St Paul's. Another possible alumnus is Geoffrey Chaucer, born around 1340, probably in Thames Street, the son of a vintner. Again, he had a choice of grammar schools in the City, but St Paul's School in the mid-fourteenth century received a particularly generous collection of Latin works that Chaucer is known to have used as sources in his writing.

However, by the early sixteenth century the school had declined from its days of pre-eminence. In 1509 John Colet, Dean of St Paul's, described it as one of the 'scholas nullius plane momenti [schools plainly of no worth]', and set about its reformation. He established the largest institution of its kind in England at the time, providing free education for 153 boys 'of all nations and countries indifferently'. The particular number of pupils is said to be based on the number of fish collected in the nets of St Peter in the miraculous draught on the Sea of Galilee, so that scholars still wear a silver fish in their buttonholes.

John Colet replaced the existing timber structure by a stone building at considerable cost on the original site and ensured a good endowment from lands in Buckinghamshire. Moreover, he left the foundation in trust to the wealthy Mercers' Company, of whom he was a freeman, arguing 'that there was no absolute certainty in human affairs, but, for his part, he found less corruption in such a body of citizens than in any other order or degree of mankind'.[3] So, it was the Mercers rather than the cathedral that was responsible for running the school.

The pupils all sat in one large room, with an inscription on the high windows that read '*Aut Doce, Aut Disce, Aut Discede* [Either teach, or study, or leave]'. At one end of the room sat the high master with his assistant, or surmaster at the other end. Colet had travelled to France and Italy in his youth, gaining first-hand knowledge of Florentine neo-Platonism. He was a friend of Erasmus, and thus part of the circle of humanists who brought Renaissance ideas to England. He may have rued the day that he lent Erasmus a Greek manuscript copy of the New Testament that sparked off the publication of *Novum Instrumentum* (see p. 43). As the first high master of the reformed school, Colet selected William Lily, another member of the circle, and St Paul's quickly flourished under his direction, producing generations of distinguished pupils.

Lily, however, is principally remembered for his *Rudimenta*, a Latin syntax in English. In fact, Erasmus and Colet both had a part in its compilation, which was first published in 1513. The book was given the royal prerogative so that it was the sole authorised version for all schools in England, published by the King or Queen's Printer. As a result, Lily's grammar exerted a huge influence on the development of English literature. William's grandson, the dramatist John Lyly, repeated lines from it. Shakespeare has a whole scene in *The Merry Wives of Windsor,* where the Welsh parson, Hugh Evans, questions young William Page on his Latin grammar and on syntax. Finally he dismisses Page with: 'It is *qui, quae, quod*; if you forget your *quis*, your *quaes*, and your *quods*, you must be preeches [your breeches pulled down for a whipping]. Go your ways and play'.[4] No doubt written with unfond memories.

Colet continued a particular tradition of St Paul's, the appointment of a boy bishop. The 'episcopacy' ran from the feast of St Nicholas, 6 December, until the 28th, the festival of the Holy Innocents. The boy was expected to preach a sermon on the last day, a useful way to improve Latin rhetoric, for which he was given a penny by each of the other scholars. The Dean was also keen to promote the development of music, reorganising the Jesus Guild that had been established in 1459 in the crypt of the cathedral. This fraternity was made up largely of laity, who derived their revenue from saying prayers of remembrance for the departed in various dioceses around the country. The guild had run into financial problems, and Colet recognised that here was an opportunity to improve liturgical and musical standards by using their revenue to teach singing to boys, initially eight in number, from the lay community.

Under John Redford, who was the choirmaster and almoner in the 1530s and 1540s, these 'Children of Paul's' became a distinguished group. As Tusser noted in his autobiography, Redford was a skilled and knowledgeable practitioner, 'By whom some part of Musicke art so did I gaine'.[5] He was a composer of organ music, among the first in England to write down his pieces, thus enabling others to develop their skills of the form. He would have taught the boys to play viols, virginals and the organ. Redford was also a playwright: the text for one of his plays survives, dating from around 1534. In *Wyt and Science*, wit/intelligence expresses the desire to marry science/knowledge. It is likely that the parts were played by choristers, for singing was involved, marking an important development in the activities of the choir school.

The title held by Redford, and his successors, is significant: he was the almoner as well as the choirmaster. He acted rather like a housemaster in a public school, accommodating the boys in his house in the Churchyard, and providing them with food, clothing and other necessities . . .

as well convenient and cleane choyce of surpless as also all other manner of apparell as gownes coates capes and dubletts Chaunge of sheetes, hosen shoes, and all other necessaries, holsome and sufficient diet, holsome and cleane beddinge, wth all things nedefull for them and in their sickenes shall see them well looked unto and cherished and procure the advise and helpe of Phisitians or Surgians if neede so requier.

The grammar school of St Paul's provided their general education, where they represented a small addition to the 153 'silver fish'. Although drawn up in the 1580s, the instructions given to the almoner/choirmaster would have applied to earlier generations of his charges. It was stipulated that the boys should 'resorte to paules schole' for two hours in the morning and one in the afternoon, each year from the feast of the annunciation of the Blessed Virgin (25 March) until the feast of St Michael the Archangel (29 September). Apart from the hours spent at divine service, they should learn the principles of grammar and study the catechism, first in English and then in Latin. They should use the 'good books' taught in the school. These books in 1559 for the lower school included the works of Terence and Aesop's fables. For the upper school, they would have included the epistles of Cicero and Virgil's *Bucolics*. Greek became part of the curriculum in the 1560s.

However, being a member of the cathedral community set this small group of boys apart from the other pupils at the school. The almoner had to:

> teach or cause to be taught the said Children as well in the principles and groundes of Christian religion, conteyned in the little Cathechisme ... and in writing, as also in the arte and knowledge of musicke, that they may be able, thereby to serve as Quiristers in the said Churche.[6]

At Redford's death in 1547, he was succeeded in the role of choirmaster and almoner by Sebastian Westcott, one of the cathedral's lay singing men, known as vicars choral. This was the year that saw the death of Henry VIII and the accession to the throne of Edward VI, ushering in a period of fundamental religious reform. The Chantries Act passed in 1548 abolished the trust funds that had been established before the Reformation for the singing of 'obits', prayers for the souls of the departed. This legislation and the imposition of an attenuated liturgy reduced the income of the choristers and their participation in church services. Westcott appears to have been a man of diplomacy, for he was a convinced Catholic and thus could have found himself at odds with the new regime. He was also an entrepreneur, so that he used the opportunity of the boys' extra time to find new venues where they might perform. For example, Sir William Petre, who shared Westcott's religious beliefs and his ability to cope with the different Tudor regimes, had the boys entertaining guests at his London home in Aldersgate Street. They also performed at the feasts of City livery companies, such as that of the Merchant Taylors.

Christmas 1551 proved an important date for the boys of Paul's. Westcott and his musician colleague, John Heywood, mounted a play for the boys in the presence of Princess Elizabeth at Hatfield Palace in Hertfordshire. The boys returned to act before her at Hatfield in April 1557, and her pleasure at their performance must have inspired the Earl of Arundel to invite them to Nonesuch Palace in Surrey while she was on one of her progresses in her first year as Queen. Thereafter, Westcott and the 'Children of Paul's' became a regular fixture during the winter season at Elizabeth's court. They were not the only company of boys to be honoured in this way, but they were the most frequent in their appearances.

The kind of entertainment that they presented at court is contained within the accounts of the Office of Revels. At this time, the Office, which came under the Lord Chamberlain, was located at the former hospital of St John of Jerusalem in Blackfriars. Its remit was to organise the court festivities and keep account of payments to performers and craftsmen. For the season from Christmas to Shrovetide 1567–8, Sebastian Westcott received from the Office the substantial sum of £13 6s 8d:

> For seven playes, the firste namede as playne as Canne be, The second for the paynfull pillgrimage; The thirde Iacke and Iyll, The forthe six fooles, The fyvethe callede witte and will. The sixte called prodigallitie, The sevoeneth of Orestes and a Tragedie of the kinge of Scottes.

In fact, eight plays are listed. The texts for these have not come down to us, and the genre of *As Plain as Can Be* is unknown. Three can be identified as morality plays – *The Painful Pilgrimage; Wit and Will; Prodigality* or *The Contention between Liberality and Prodigality*. One is a classical tragedy, *Orestes*, another a historical tragedy, *King of Scots*, and two are comedies, *Jack and Jill* and *The Six Fools*.[7] Westcott could have been the author of these plays, for he certainly produced a new version of John Redford's *Wyt and Science*. It also seems very likely that vocal and instrumental music were part of the entertainment.

The organisation required in sending the boys to the royal court is vividly shown in the accounts of the Office of Revels for the Shrovetide entertainments of 1574. First, the children were boarded out so that they could learn their parts and gestures 'meete for the Mask in which ix of them did serve at hampton court'. As Shrovetide approached, so a six-oared barge and two tilt wherries were hired to take the frames and painted cloths of the scenery and costumes, along with the boys, upstream to Hampton Court. Not only were the boys thus conveyed, but also their teachers, an Italian woman 'to dresse their heades', tailors, haberdashers and men to organise the props. Although the Queen may have been an enduring patron of the boys of Paul's, she could also be whimsical, and on this occasion she was unable to decide whether she wanted to see the play, or masque as it is described. The company and its entourage were therefore lodged with Mother Sparrow at Kingston-upon-Thames while a barber was summoned to trim their hair. After waiting for some days, the play was not called for, so the children were returned to London, with a payment made to Thomas Totnall of 6s 6d for 'ffyer and vittells for the Children when they Landed sum of them being sick and colde and hungry'.[8]

Elizabeth may not have been an easy taskmistress, but her support for Westcott was important, and indeed at times vital with his maintenance of his Catholic faith. In 1564 he had been ejected from his benefice of vicar choral by Bishop Grindal for declining Protestant communion and refusing to subscribe to the royal supremacy. Robert Dudley, Earl of Leicester, intervened on the Queen's behalf, and Westcott was allowed to retain his appointment as master of the choristers. In 1578 he was imprisoned for 11 weeks in the Marshalsea in Southwark 'for papistry', but once more was rescued by his royal patron. These incidents are reminiscent of the Queen's toleration of the musician William Byrd, who likewise maintained his Catholic faith: indeed, William may have been a pupil of Sebastian Westcott, for he certainly taught his two brothers, and was the friend of Byrd's patron, Sir William Petre.

Given the royal seal of approval, Westcott decided at some time around 1575 to open a theatre to the public in the Churchyard. Seasons of plays were now being presented at some of the major inns in London. To the north-west of the cathedral, off Ludgate Hill, was one such, the Belle Sauvage. Its exotic name conjures up Rousseau's concept of the noble savage, but the derivation is more prosaic – the inn, the Bell and Hoop, was owned in the fifteenth century by a man called William Savage. Galleries around its large courtyard made it ideal both for bear-baiting and for theatrical performances. The famous comedian Richard Tarleton, who also kept an 'ordinary' or dining establishment in Paternoster Row, played here. Performers, however, were seeking to find more permanent premises under their own control. The 1572 Vagabonds Act was part of a series of poor laws, but it also empowered justices of the peace to license 'comon players in Enterludes, Mynstrels, Iuglers . . . [who] wander abroade'.[9] James Burbage, whose troupe of players had the Earl of Leicester as their patron, was given just such a licence and in 1576 built the Theatre in Shoreditch, north of the City, London's first purpose-built playhouse. Before any plays could be performed, the theatre manager had to get this approval from the Lord Mayor and aldermen as to their content. Although Westcott in his turn failed to get this approval from the City authorities, the canons of the cathedral supported him in his venture.

Where exactly Westcott's theatre was located has been the subject of some speculation. Reavley Gair in his book about the Children of Paul's proposed that the theatre was located within the chapter house precinct on the south side of the cathedral. The undercroft around the chapter house was used for preaching when it was too cold or wet for the sermon at Paul's Cross, and was known as 'the Shrouds' (p. 72). The cloisters were double-storeyed, so, noting lines from some of the plays performed by the boys that give some indication of the composition of the stage, he suggested that three of the cloister arches made a central door and two side entrances, with a gallery on the upper storey where musicians might be housed.[10]

This ingenious theory has, however, been rejected by more recent historians after careful perusal of leases and the physical dimensions of that area of the Churchyard. It is now thought that the theatre was accommodated within the Almoner's House, where the boys lodged with their master. This building was located between the south door of the cathedral and the cloister of the chapter house. Roger Bowers has suggested that the timber-framed house resembled late medieval hall houses, with two wings and a large central room on the first floor. Here the boys could perform their plays, with the stage erected at the screen's passage end and the passage itself serving as both back stage and tiring house for the troupe of up to 12 players. This was not as large a space as might be had in the purpose-built theatres that were being constructed in the late sixteenth century, so could only accommodate an audience of a few dozen. Members of the public going to a play would take the narrow lane known as Paul's Alley that led up to the cathedral from the south, and turn right into the house, where they paid an entrance fee before climbing up to the first floor.[11]

When Sebastian Westcott died in 1582, Thomas Gyles was given a probationary period as his successor. No doubt feeling that his first priority was to concentrate on the singing of his choristers, he agreed with the dramatist John Lyly to link up with the other children's acting company in London, that of the Chapel Royal at Blackfriars. Since 1576 these children had been staging plays in the refectory of the former Dominican monastery, close by the part occupied by the Office of Revels. The combined company were known as Oxford's Boys, because the Earl of Oxford was Lyly's patron.

Lyly had made his literary reputation through the publication of *Euphues*, a prose romance in two parts, the first appearing in 1578, and the second two years later. A slender plot formed the peg on which Lyly hung his combination of courtly compliment, classical learning and witty dialogue: the term 'euphu-istic', a high-flown stylistic expression, is derived from his play. For the joint boys' company, Lyly devised two plays to be performed at the royal court: *Campaspe*, on New Year's Day 1584, and *Sappho and Phaon*, for Shrove Tuesday of that year. But the combined company was short-lived. Lyly and the manager of the boys' theatre, a scrivener called Henry Evans, had employed a certain amount of legal chicanery to rent their space in the warren of different residences that made up Blackfriars, so that the lease was declared void in June 1584.

Thomas Gyles, whose probationary period had ended, was now officially appointed master of the choristers, and he broke up the agreement with Lyly and Evans so that the St Paul's boys became again a separate entity. He also was granted by Royal Commission the right of impressment that had been enjoyed by Westcott along with other masters of choristers in major cathe-drals. The warrant ran:

> to take upp suche apte and meete children, as most fit to be instructed and framed in the arte and science of musicke and singing, as they may be had and founde oute with in anie place of this our Realme of England or Wales.[12]

This was extraordinarily draconian in practice, for the boys could be as young as six or seven, and their parents were denied the right of refusal. Talented boys who had been well trained in both their singing and their letters were valuable properties and thus vulnerable to seizure or to being persuaded away by bribery. As noted at the beginning of this chapter, Westcott had lost one of his boys in this way in 1575, possibly to the Blackfriars company, which was being set up at the time.

A fascinating case has been uncovered of the abduction of Thomas Clifton, a 13-year-old London merchant's son, ordered by Henry Evans for the Blackfriars company in 1600. According to the court report, men seized him on his way to school near St Paul's 'with greate force & violence . . . to the greate terror and hurte of him'. Evans then presented the child 'in a moste disdaynfull & dispight-full manner a scrolle of paper, conteyning parte of one of theire sayd playes or enterludes, & comaunded [him] to learne the same by hart'. He was threatened with whipping if he did not comply. Fortunately for Thomas, his father, Henry Clifton, was able to track him down. Evans claimed that he had the right of impressment, but this was not so, for it applied to masters of choristers, not to theatre managers. Thomas was reunited with his family.[13]

Henry Evans would appear to have been a tricky individual, who found it politic to leave the country soon after the Clifton incident. After a year he returned, attracting various lawsuits concerning his use of boy players. William Shakespeare is thought to have taken his surname for the Welsh parson, Sir Hugh Evans, in *The Merry Wives of Windsor*. Shakespeare himself was not keen on the concept of companies of boy players, preferring to have formal apprenticeships for child actors, trained up by the shareholders of the company. In *Hamlet* he has Rosencrantz describing how boy actors had taken over the stage at the Danish court:

> There is, sir, an aery of children, little eyasses [untrained hawks] that cry out
> on the top of the question, and are most tyrannically clapped for't: these are
> now the fashion, and so be-rattle the common stages . . . that many wearing
> rapiers are afraid of goose-quills, and dare scarce come thither.[14]

Shakespeare suggests in these lines that the boys were not very well trained. He also may have been concerned about the vulnerability of the boys at the hands of adults in charge of them. In *A Midsummer Night's Dream*, where there are a number of parts for children, he introduces the quarrel between Titania and Oberon over a changeling boy that carries rather sinister overtones.

Shakespeare's lukewarm attitude towards boy actors contrasts with the view of Ben Jonson about one of the boys who had begun his acting career at St Paul's and then moved to Blackfriars. In some lines composed on the death of Solomon Pavy at the age of 13, Jonson makes clear his particular skill in playing old men:

> Yeeres he numbred scares thirteene
> When Fates turn'd cruell,
> Yet three fill'd Zodiackes had he beene

The stages iewell;

And did act (what now we mone)

Old men so duely,

As, sooth, the Parcae [female personifications of destiny] thought him
one[15]

The interconnection between St Paul's and Blackfriars was a complex one.
Nathaniel Field was a student at St Paul's School when he was impressed into
the Blackfriars company. He remained there until he was in his mid-twenties,
when he joined an adult company and became a distinguished playwright.

John Lyly continued to work with St Paul's boys at their theatre in the
Churchyard, in 1587 putting on two of his plays, *Endymion* and *Midas*. But
the indication is that these were not proving a hit with the paying public.
When he produced *Sappho and Phao* in 1584, he had included a note of regret
in the prologue that his plays were not being appreciated:

Where the Bee can suck no honney, she leaveth her stinge behinde, and
where the Beare cannot finde *Origanum* to heale his griefe, he blasteth all
other leaves with his breath. Wee feare it is like to fare so with us, that
seeing you cannot draw from our labours sweete content, you leave behind
you a sowre mislike, and with open reproach blame our good meanings:
because you cannot reap your wonted mirthes.

The problem was that Lyly's allusive allegorical style was difficult to follow.
The public were now enjoying the beginning of a flourishing of English drama
with good storylines, strong characterisations and plenty of humour in the
adult theatres of the capital.

However, the first closure of the theatre in St Paul's Churchyard resulted
from a rather different cause. As noted in the previous chapter, John Lyly,
along with the playwright Thomas Nashe, had been drawn into the Marprelate
debate (see pp. 81–2), invited by the bishops to counter the criticisms
levelled by Puritans. In his pamphlet, *Pappe with an Hatchet*, Lyly suggested
that if the witty lines composed by the mysterious 'Martin' were played out on
the stage, then he would be unmasked. It is not known whether actual plays

by Lyly or others were written on the debate and publicly performed, but the Church authorities were concerned by the threat that serious political and religious issues such as the status of the episcopacy should be shown in this way by the boy actors. Once the press producing the Marprelate tracts was captured in August 1589, the Privy Council decided to suppress all aspects of the controversy, and playing at St Paul's duly ceased some time between Twelfth Night 1590 when the children performed Lyly's *Endymion* at Richmond Palace, and October 1591, when the play was entered in the register at Stationers' Hall.

The 1590s were not a good time for the boys of Paul's. After their theatre closed, they are known to have performed just once, at a private evening for the household of Archbishop Whitgift. Meanwhile an unseemly quarrel developed among the canons of the cathedral, who lived in houses on Paternoster Row. The two senior minor canons were known as cardinals, a pre-Reformation tradition associated with their college. In 1590 Hugh Andrews became Sub-Dean under Alexander Nowell, followed soon after by the promotion of Ambrose Goulding to the position of Senior Cardinal. William Maicocke hoped that he would then step into the position of Junior Cardinal but was thwarted by the opposition of Goulding. The boys of Paul's were directly affected by the developing hostilities, for Goulding was Rector of St Gregory, their parish church that stood just across Paul's Alley from the Almoner's House, and the two cardinal canons were responsible for their spiritual welfare.

The actors in this real-life drama make an unattractive cast. Goulding was contentious and turbulent, known for his violence both physical and verbal. At one point he accused Maicocke of suffering from French pox, calling him a range of names, including Barking Cur and Goodman Red Scabbe. His ally was Hugh Andrews, the Sub-Dean, and his wife, who had a reputation as drinkers, with 'Continuall runninge to the taverne wth wine potts until ten of the Clocke' which they paid for by embezzlement of the minor canons' plate. Maicocke found an ally in a family called Slegg. The father, Edward, taught his daughters to shout insults at the children of the minor canons. These included 'preests chitts, preests bastardes . . . preests dingdongs'. Jane Goulding and Mary Maicocke also quarrelled, coming to blows, and encouraging the chorister actors to throw stones and issue insults.[16] Dean Nowell does seem to have tried to control his Sub-Dean, but to no great effect. He may have been too unworldly for the task, and his fraught relations with the Queen suggest that he was not always politically shrewd. As he was probably born in 1518, he was now in his seventies, a mighty age at this time.

Unsurprisingly the quarrel became a notorious scandal throughout London. It was also just one of a series of problems concerning the cathedral and its Churchyard that prompted the Bishop of London, Richard Bancroft, to undertake visitations in 1598, the year after his installation. Bancroft already had close associations with the cathedral as its treasurer and a senior prebendary, but nevertheless the revelation of the drunkenness and brawling were disturbing. It was reported that some of the women of the Churchyard were even performing masques of their own, dancing first in the house of Edward Slegg in Paternoster Row, then coming down and dancing in the Churchyard itself. Gyles, along with the masters of St Paul's School, would appear to have been lax in their supervision of their charges 'suffereinge their Children to plaie in the Churches yard whereby the windows are broken, and well disposed people in the churche disquieted at the time of divine service'.[17] The children were forbidden to frequent bear-baiting, bowling alleys or tumbling shows, but the fact that these were specifically mentioned suggests that they did indeed do so.

Bancroft's investigation into the activities of the quarrelling cardinals eventually stirred Dean Nowell into activity to protect the choristers. A new master was appointed, Edward Pearce, described as a gentleman of the City of London, although Thomas Gyles was not dismissed. Why Gyles was allowed to continue to draw his stipend and to live in the Almoner's House is unknown, but the Bishop and the Dean may have been trying to avoid further scandals.

Without payment for his services, Pearce had to find a way of making money, so decided to reopen the theatre. Ambrose Goulding combined his role as Senior Cardinal and Rector of St Gregory in the Churchyard with the curacy of Serjeant's Inn in Fleet Street, adjacent to the Inner and Middle Temple. This may have provided the contact with a potential author of plays for the St Paul's repertoire, albeit a potentially risky one. John Marston, a resident of the Middle Temple, enjoyed such a reputation as a satirist that in 1599 two of his plays were burnt by the common hangman after being declared offensive by Archbishop Whitgift and Bishop Bancroft.

Despite this ecclesiastical reprimand, Marston began to work with the boys of Paul's from the time of the reopening of their theatre. He helped to renovate the stage area, and provided the first play, *Antonio and Mellida*. This had an elaborate beginning, with an 'induction', followed by a prologue and the first act, which took advantage of the fact that the players were totally inexperienced because of the 10-year closure. The eight boys began by learning their parts, without stage apparel or make up. As the play proceeded, so they developed their musical skills and appeared costumed. As Marston's mother was Italian, a distinctive theme imbued the later acts, with the two principals, Antonio and Mellida, exchanging their lines in Italian. In the final scene, portraits were brought onto the stage: one was of William Stanley, Sixth Earl of Derby, who was also a playwright and seems to have invested some money in the theatre; the second was of Marston himself. He was thus making a strong statement about his connection with the theatre of St Paul's Churchyard.

Ben Jonson attacked *Antonio and Mellida*, criticising it for the affectation of the dialogue, dismissing it as an outward sign of vacuity of mind. Marston, unsurprisingly, was irritated by Jonson's assuming the role of judge of supreme literary quality. This marked the opening salvo in what has been described as the Poets' War or Poetomachia. The theatrical scene in London had greatly expanded in the past few years. A second theatre in Shoreditch, The Curtain, had opened in 1577, and in time was used by the Lord Chamberlain's Men for their plays, including some by Shakespeare. However, the centre of theatrical gravity moved in 1596 when James Burbage purchased the former boy players' house at Blackfriars and began to install two galleries in the substantial space for use as a public theatre. Once again, a dispute arose over the legality of this use, and the Privy Council forbade any performing there. Instead, the indefatigable Henry Evans took it over as a private theatre for performances of what he now called the Children of the Chapel.

When James Burbage died in 1597, the owner of the Shoreditch site refused to renew the lease because, with his Puritan views, he strongly disapproved of playhouses. James's two sons, Richard and Cuthbert, dismantled the building under cover of night with the assistance of their troupe, and carried the materials first to a warehouse at the Bridewell and then across the river to Bankside in Southwark. Here they built a new theatre, the Globe, next to the Rose and Swan theatres. With the new century, Richard Burbage linked up with John Marston at St Paul's to provide a combination of dramas for adult actors and for the boy players. This was in response to the Children of the Chapel at Blackfriars where Ben Jonson was now the principal dramatist.

Although presenting themselves as the chief protagonists of this 'war', Jonson and Marston were alike in some ways. Both used the weapon of satire, albeit in very different styles. Both were highly contentious characters: Jonson notoriously killing a fellow actor, only escaping the death penalty by claiming clerical status and being branded on the thumb for his offence. For his part, Marston was notorious for his gratuitous rudeness, and presented himself as a castrated dog, 'W. Kinsayder', alluding to the dog-like barking of his satire which could fawn and flatter as well as be rough and cynical. Jonson later claimed that he had many quarrels with Marston, on one occasion beating him and taking his pistol from him. On the stage, Jonson attacked Marston in two plays performed by the Children of the Chapel at Blackfriars. In *Cynthia's Revels* in 1600, he characterised him as the voluptuous courtier Hedon, and with graphic savagery followed this up in *Poetaster* as the effeminate Crispinus, forced to vomit up a number of pretentiously complex words known to be favoured by Marston.

Fellow playwright Thomas Dekker was also satirised in *Poetaster*. As a riposte he wrote *Satiromastix*, a history play set in the eleventh century in the reign of William Rufus. This was performed in 1602 by both the Lord Chamberlain's Men at the Globe and the boys of Paul's. The subtitle of *Satiromastix* was 'The Untrussing of the Humorous Poet': this untrussing revealed Jonson's characteristics of irritability, anger and perversity, and poked fun at his old clothes and eccentric personality. Characters from *Poetaster* made their reappearance: Crispinus (Marston), Demetrius Fannius (Dekker) and Horace (Jonson). A lot of sound and fury was expressed in these quarrels, but it is thought that some of this was put on, possibly for publicity purposes. John Marston and Ben Jonson were very conscious of each other's work, comparing, contrasting, and sometimes admiring.

The link up between the Globe and the Children of Paul's produced an interesting combination of two plays from the same sources, but very different in their content: Shakespeare's *Hamlet* and John Marston's *Antonio's Revenge*. There has been speculation about the sequence of their composition, but it is generally agreed that Shakespeare wrote his first version in 1599 and it was performed at the Globe in 1601. He probably used as his source a play, now lost, by Thomas Kyd, *Ur-Hamlet*, based on Norse legend. John Marston, meanwhile, wrote *Antonio's Revenge* as a sequel to *Antonio and Mellida*, performed by the boys of Paul's in their Churchyard theatre in 1600. It is interesting that Shakespeare made his comments about boy actors in *Hamlet*: did he amend his text as a result of seeing *Antonio's Revenge*? Both plays are centred around the concept of revenge, and have similar plot devices. In *Antonio's Revenge,* Piero is murdered by poison administered by his rival in love, and a vengeful ghost duly makes his appearance.

In his plays, Marston makes specific reference to the small playing area with which the boys had to contend. In *Antonio and Mellida*, for example, he has the line: 'The room's too scant: boyes, stand in there close'. In a follow-up play, *Endymion*, one actor declares, 'Let's place ourselves within the curtains for, good faith, the stage is so very little we shall wrong the generall eye else very much'.[18]

Not only was the stage small and the number of players limited to around 10 or 12, but also the audience that could be accommodated was similarly restricted. The entrance fee seems to have varied between twopence and sixpence, a modest amount. A note from one dramatist in a copy of his play script gives us an idea of timing of performances. He instructs the master of the children of Paul's that if his

Pastoralls and Comoedeyes shall but over reach in length (the children not
to begin before foure, after prayers, and the gates of Pawles shutting at sixe)
the tyme of supper, that then in tyme and place convenient, you do let
passe some of the songs, and make the consort the shorter.[19]

The music used to accompany the songs would be strings, as suggested by the reference to a consort, and cornets rather than the louder trumpets often used in larger theatres.

Despite the limited space and audience, the theatre flourished after the dip in popularity suggested by John Lyly. No doubt Edward Pearce recognised that courtly plays would not suit, and chose a broad-based repertoire of modern fashionable drama. St Paul's Churchyard enjoyed a series of advantages as a location for a theatre. The parishes around the Churchyard were the home of some of the wealthiest merchants of London: for example, the goldsmiths and mercers of Cheapside. In addition there were the printers and booksellers from the Churchyard itself, and young craftsmen drawn to the city. It has been estimated that the possible audience from these surrounding parishes offered around 500 households of people who could afford the admission fee. Nearby were the legal establishments of Doctors' Commons and, over the Fleet, the various Inns of Court.

St Paul's Cathedral was, moreover, the great gathering place for the fashionable. The Royal Exchange, established by Sir Thomas Gresham in the 1560s at the eastern end of Cheapside, had hived off the gathering for financial business, but the Churchyard offered a centre for pleasure, right in the middle of a shopping area, drawing customers from both the City and the developing West End. For the gallants who met up in the Middle Aisle of the cathedral, there was not only the opportunity to show off their fashionable credentials, but also to take in a play in the afternoon. It was cheaper and more convenient to visit the Churchyard theatre than to travel to the Globe and other attractions on Bankside which involved making one's way across the notoriously congested London Bridge, or paying a fee to a boatman. The Churchyard audience provided business for local comfit makers, bakers, sellers of ale and other vendors. The dramatist's note mentioned above indicates that the plays were about two hours in duration, and thus would have been more convenient for working men and women with constraints on their time.

It is possible to identify a few of the individuals who attended the theatre. The accounts of the Darrell family of Littlecote House in Wiltshire record that in 1589, when Sir William was staying in lodgings in Warwick Lane, his servant, James More, was sent to a play at the cost of sixpence.[20] We also know that in 1603 two local tradesmen, John Flaskett, a bookbinder resident in Knightrider Street, and John Howe, a barber surgeon who lived close to St Gregory's in the Churchyard, attended a play at the theatre. They were accompanied by Edward Brompton, servant to Dr John Milward, the preacher at Christchurch, Newgate Street.

Remarkably, John Flaskett invited the dramatist George Chapman to write a play, *The Old Joiner of Aldgate*, that parodied a local scandal. This centred on

Howe's dowry negotiations with several suitors, including Flaskett, for the hand of his daughter, Agnes, the recipient of a generous bequest from her aunt. Concerned about the number of suitors, Howe sought the advice of the preacher at his local church, John Milward, who promptly married Agnes himself with the connivance of her mother, but unbeknown to her father. Even more remarkable, when Howe and Flaskett went to see the play, they could not recognise themselves, despite the fact that Chapman had written the play at Flaskett's invitation. The play has not survived, but some of the details have been reconstructed from the court proceedings that followed. In the end, none of the parties was convicted due to lack of evidence.

Another play with a local theme was Thomas Middleton's *The Puritaine, or the Widdow of Watling Street*, performed by the boys of Paul's. John Marston had ceased being their principal playwright in 1604, moving to Blackfriars, and instead various dramatists worked with the boys. Two, however emerged as regular providers of plays. One was William Percy from the prominent Catholic family of the Earls of Northumberland. His brother Henry, the Ninth Earl, known to posterity as the 'Wizard Earl', was imprisoned in 1605 for alleged complicity in the Gunpowder Plot. His dramatist brother, William, steered a safer course with his choice of plays, and stayed out of trouble.

The second playwright, Thomas Middleton, pursued a more controversial line. His family life was dominated by legal arguments, following his mother's second, unhappy, marriage and her determined attempts to protect her children's inheritance from her new husband. In one play, *A Game of Chess*, he wrote of a 'law-tossed world'. Brought up in a Calvinist parish, Middleton particularly disliked the more radical wing of the Church, as represented by the Brownist and Arminian sects. This dislike was personalised when the brother of his sister's husband, a fervent Brownist, attempted to defraud her in the first weeks of her widowhood. In *The Puritaine*, performed by the boys of Paul's either very late in 1607 or in the first weeks of 1608, Middleton targeted what he considered the mercenary hypocrisy of separatists. The play is set in nearby Watling Street, in the parish of St Antling, which was at the time particularly Puritan in persuasion.

On Valentine's Day 1608, the Puritan divine William Crawshawe preached a sermon at Paul's Cross. He began by generally inveighing against the theatre:

The ungodly Playes and Enterludes so rife in this nation; what are they but a bastard of Babylon, a daughter of error and confusion, a hellish device, (the divels owne recreation to mock at holy things) by him delivered to the Heathen, from them to the Papists, and from them to us?

But his specific target was the master and boys of Paul's for performing Middleton's play. Crawshawe found it particularly offensive that the parishioners and their minister of St Antling were depicted in the play as drunkards, liars and hypocrites. In his final onslaught he described the boys of Paul's as 'children of Babylon that will not be healed; nay, they grow worse, for now they bring religion and holy things upon the stage'.[21]

James I had already been riled by the play *Eastward Ho!* performed at Blackfriars in 1605, which contained lines poking fun at the Scottish courtiers who had come south with him at his accession the previous year. Two of the authors of the play, Ben Jonson and George Chapman, were imprisoned but the third, John Marston, escaped this fate. Although the two playwrights were released at the intercession of powerful friends, the problem was greatly exacerbated by the performance of a play now lost, *The Silver Mine*, which very unwisely depicted King James as a verbally incontinent drunkard. Crawshawe's sermon in 1608 proved the final straw, and the stage went dark for the Children of Paul's along with the Children of the Chapel at Blackfriars. This time there was to be no renaissance.

CHAPTER 6

THE TWILIGHT OF OLD ST PAUL'S

The dramatic role long played by St Paul's Churchyard was demonstrated yet again when it was chosen in 1606 as the site for the execution of five men implicated in the Gunpowder Plot. The plot was a daring attempt by a group of Roman Catholics to assassinate James I and his entire government during the state opening of Parliament. It was foiled by a search of the House of Lords at midnight on 4 November 1605, when Guy Fawkes was found with 36 barrels of gunpowder. The next day, the inhabitants of London were encouraged to light bonfires in celebration of the King's providential deliverance.

After their trials, four of the conspirators, including Guy Fawkes, were hanged, drawn and quartered in the Old Palace Yard at Westminster, just across from the Parliament building that they had planned to blow up. The previous day, 30 January 1606, four of the other conspirators – Sir Everard Digby, Robert Winter, John Grant and Thomas Bates – met a similarly grim fate in St Paul's Churchyard. This was an exceptional decision, for although the Churchyard had been the site of punishments such as penance and the public burning of books, it had rarely been the scene of an execution.[1] As the conspirators had planned not only to kill the King and his Privy Council, but also the leading figures of the English Church, the location near the palace of the Bishop of London may have played a part.

The courtier Sir Arthur Gorges probably reflected the concern of others when he wrote to Robert Cecil, now Earl of Salisbury, to protest at this use of space 'under the eaves of the most famous church of our kingdom', recalling it as a 'place of happy memory' where Queen Elizabeth had celebrated the defeat of the Spanish Armada.[2] Such objections were ignored, but the decision to make a public spectacle of the execution of Catholics could backfire, and indeed did so when Father Henry Garnet, a Jesuit priest, met the same fate on 3 May 1606 for upholding the confidentiality of the confessional and not revealing the plot to the authorities. A stand was erected in the Churchyard by the west door of the cathedral, and one witness noted how it cost the sum of one shilling to gain a place to watch the terrible spectacle. But a sympathetic crowd ensured that Garnet was dead before he was cut down from the gallows and disembowelled.

Every 5 November thereafter, the lord mayor and City dignitaries assembled at Paul's Cross to hear a sermon of thanksgiving and deliverance. The Gunpowder Plot Sermon of 1614 was delivered by William Goodwin, Dean of Christ Church, Oxford. He combined the occasion of the political anniversary with a Jeremiad, or lamentation, a familiar type of Paul's Cross sermon, exhorting the community to strive for greater godliness while reminding them of the story of the captivity of the Israelites in Babylon as a parallel to God's protection of Protestant kings:

> I say this day this fifth day of the 11th month, it was a day of great danger, a more pernitious plot, and a more traitorous designe then all the days that the sun ever looked upon, here was no difference, *King, Queen, Prince, Nobles,* no respect of honour, person, degree, sex, condition, guilty, innocent, Crows, Doves, Ravens, Eagles, must all be confused together in one furnace, this was the day, even this same day, the *King of Babilon set himself against Jerusalem.* . . .

Goodwin's theme was remorselessly anti-Catholic, describing it as 'a religion of treason, and a religion of conspiracy'. Condemning the popular sympathy that had been shown to Father Garnet at his execution in the Churchyard eight years before, he declared him 'the great and Arch Traytor in this Gunpowder Treason how he is excused, nay how he is canonized and sainted among them, because under the seale of confession he was content to conceale so heinous a plot'.[3]

The presence of the lord mayor and the dignitaries of the City at the Gunpowder Plot Sermons reflected the vital role played by St Paul's in the civic life of London. Thus, for example, the Churchyard was a venue for one of its major traditions, the annual Lord Mayor's Show. From the mid-fifteenth century the participants in the Show had taken to the water, with the new mayor processing from the Guildhall on 28 October down to the Thames, and thence by river to Westminster to take the oath. On his return, his barge, accompanied by those of the livery companies, would usually land at Paul's Stairs, move up to St Paul's Churchyard and return to the Guildhall along Cheapside. After a formal banquet in the Guildhall the lord mayor returned to St Paul's to listen to a sermon marking the inauguration.

By the second half of the sixteenth century the Show had become a high-profile affair, marked with all kinds of features, including tableaux, music and dancing, with one of the pageant stations located in the Churchyard. A record made by a French visitor to London in 1578 gives an idea of the scale:

> It is customary to make a most magnificent portable theatre, completely covered with gold or silver leaf, in the shape of a mountain, which is commonly called the 'Pageant' or mystery. On top and across the front of it are several maidens most lavishly bedecked, representing several virtues such as Justice, Truth, Charity, Prudence and others similar. Also carried are figures of several wild and strange beasts such as elephants, unicorns, leopards, griffons, camels, sirens and other such animals which are most wonderful to behold.

He explained that a firework display had been added to the proceedings, consisting of 72 pipes charged with gunpowder arranged in the Churchyard and set alight as the new mayor approached. The result was 'such a song that it seems as if the great church of St. Paul's might fall to the ground, and there is not a house even in the outermost surroundings which does not shake vigorously'.[4]

In the early seventeenth century, London's leading playwrights were commissioned to provide texts for the mayoral 'triumphs'. Thomas Middleton was selected in 1613 to write *The Triumphs of Truth* to celebrate the inauguration of the lord mayor who happened to share his name. This Thomas Middleton was from the wealthy livery company of Grocers, and no expense was spared in the pageant's production. One of the artists who helped to produce some of the tableaux was John Gipkyn of the third generation of that family (see pp. 54–5).

As the text was subsequently published in printed form, we have a detailed account of how Truth prevailed over Error. The dramatic action began with Truth's Angel and Zeal accompanying the lord mayor up from the river to Paul's Chain on the south side of the Churchyard. Five islands had been set up within the Churchyard itself, each carrying one of the Senses, with a float in the form of a ship bringing the King and Queen of the Moors to dry land. The playwright made use of the comparatively large space south of St Paul's Cathedral to lay on a battle between Error, in a chariot, and Envy, mounted on a rhinoceros, fighting against Truth, again in a chariot, and Zeal.[5] At one stage the King of the Moors, who had purportedly been converted to Christianity by English merchants, gestured towards the cathedral, describing it as a 'faire temple'. The pageant then moved on to Cheapside for the next part of the performance.[6] This was clearly a great success, for Middleton went on to write another six triumphs for lord mayors.

Remarkably, images of the 1616 Show have been preserved. Anthony Munday was chosen to devise the pageant *Chrysanaleia*, 'The Golden Fishing', for the lord mayor that year was Sir John Leman, a member of the Fishmongers' Company. Munday introduced into his text William Walworth, Fishmonger and Lord Mayor of London in the fourteenth century. In the summer of 1381 Walworth had accompanied the young Richard II when he met the leader of the Peasants' Revolt, Wat Tyler, at Smithfield. When Tyler apparently insulted the King, Walworth stabbed him to death, and as a result was regarded as a civic hero on a par with the mercer Sir Richard Whittington. In a drawing, William Walworth is depicted in his bower at the pageant station in the Churchyard. At the approach of the new lord mayor, he rises from a table to deliver a congratulatory address in verse form (Plate 7).[7] Again, Gipkyn was involved with the tableaux, so may even have been responsible for this drawing.

Such pageants sought to emphasise the harmony between the Crown, the Church and the City, but the interests of the three could diverge, as we have already seen in Chapter 4. The anti-Catholic vehemence of Goodwin's sermon of 1614 contrasts with the attitude of the King in his foreign policy. Despite the threat on his life posed by the Gunpowder Plot, James maintained the position that he had initiated at the beginning of his reign, to harmonise relations with Catholic Spain, and thereby encourage international trade. His elder son, Henry, was more overtly militant in his Protestantism, supporting the marriage of his sister, Princess Elizabeth, to Frederick V, the Elector Palatine. This marriage took place in February 1613, just three months after Henry's sudden death. A few months later, Philip III of Spain sent as his ambassador the scholarly Count of Gondomar, who was to enjoy a good relationship with James.

James's wish to be even-handed in his dealings with European powers was severely compromised when in 1619 his son-in-law Frederick rashly accepted the Crown of Bohemia, following a revolt against the rule of the Holy Roman Emperor, Ferdinand II. Frederick had set himself up as the leader of the German Protestants, challenging the power of the Catholic Hapsburgs. Ferdinand's response was to crush his forces at the Battle of White Mountain in December 1620, ousting him from Bohemia: Frederick and Elizabeth were forced into exile in The Hague. James meanwhile had been pursuing a marriage for his surviving son, Charles, with a princess from the Spanish branch of the Hapsburgs.

The following year John Donne was appointed Dean of St Paul's. He had been born in Bread Street, just down the road from the cathedral, in 1572, the son of a prosperous ironmonger and a mother from a devout Catholic family who claimed kinship with Sir Thomas More. In his youth, Donne enjoyed the reputation of being a 'great visitor of the ladies', and an adventurer who sailed with the Earl of Essex to sack Cadiz and with Sir Walter Raleigh to hunt Spanish treasure ships off the Azores. He published poems and satires, becoming part of a literary circle along with the dramatist Ben Jonson, the architect Inigo Jones and the travel writer, Thomas Coryat, the 'Right Generous, Ioviall and Mercurial Sirenaicks', that met at the Mermaid Tavern in Bread Street.[8] In 1601 he secretly married Ann More, 'the most remarkable error of his life' according to his biographer, Izaak Walton, which caused him to lose his job as secretary to Keeper Egerton, and plunged him into financial difficulties that lasted for many years as his family grew in size.

In 1614, however, John Donne decided to become a priest, urged on by the King himself. Although Donne had maintained the Roman Catholic faith in his youth, he came to regard the Catholic Church in England as no longer universal, but rather a religious splinter group that wasted lives for lost causes and threatened the security of the kingdom. There was a personal edge to this, for his younger brother had died in prison in 1593 after being arrested for harbouring a Catholic priest.

Donne took holy orders on 23 January 1615, ordained by the Bishop of London, John King, at his palace on the north-west side of the cathedral, and preached his first sermon at Paul's Cross in 1617. He quickly earned a reputation as a fine preacher, giving sermons in various London churches as well as at Lincoln's Inn. Izaak Walton, a young linen draper with a shop on Fleet Street, attended several of Donne's sermons, and described his preaching:

> as shewed his own heart was possessed with those very thoughts and joys that he laboured to distil into others: a preacher in earnest; weeping sometimes for his auditory, sometimes with them; always preaching to himself, like an angel from a cloud, but in none.

Walton likened his delivery to a courtship, wooing his audience: he was, after all, one of the greatest exponents of love poetry. He also highlighted Donne's dramatic style, which was also noted by Thomas Crosfield, a clergyman with an interest in theatrical performances. In his diary he described his control of 'gestur and Rhetoriquall expression'.[9]

James I, unlike his cousin Queen Elizabeth, was particularly interested in sermons, considering himself somewhat a connoisseur of the art, so Donne's preaching skills must have been a factor in the decision to make him the Dean of St Pauls. Another was that Donne's patron, George Villiers, the Duke of Buckingham, was now firmly established as the King's favourite. According to Isaak Walton, the King personally broke the news to John Donne:

> When his Majesty was sat down, before he had eat any meat, he said after his pleasant manner, 'Dr. Donne, I have invited you to dinner; and though you sit not down with me, yet I will carve to you of a dish that I know you love well; for, knowing you love London, I do therefore make you Dean of St Paul's; and when I have dined, then do you take your beloved dish home to your study, say grace there to yourself and much good may it do you'.[10]

Donne, now a widower, moved with his mother into the deanery in the Churchyard.

His appointment as Dean did not pass without some comment. Richard Corbett, also a poet, was now the Dean of Christ Church College, Oxford, so John Chamberlain quoted one wag who pointed out that if Ben Jonson be made Dean of Westminster, then we 'should be furnished with three very pleasant poeticall deanes'.[11] On other occasions, he expressed reservation that John Donne should continue to write poetry after becoming Dean, considering this an inappropriate levity. Chamberlain was a man of independent means who lived at various locations near the Churchyard and used it and the cathedral as his way of news gathering. Most of his letters were to Sir Dudley Carleton, abroad for long periods on business, and provide a picture of London life during the first quarter of the seventeenth century that is both vivid and shrewd in its observation.

In 1622 James set his Dean the really difficult task of preaching a sermon at Paul's Cross to put across to the congregation, and thus to the nation, the series of *Directions Concerning Preaching and Preachers* that had been issued through a letter from the Archbishop of Canterbury, George Abbott. The directions set out to restrict discussion of political, religious and doctrinal subjects to certain ranks of preachers and of pulpits. Low-level preachers like vicars and curates were commanded to confine themselves to the basic subjects of the catechism, and only bishops and deans were to debate key areas of doctrinal Protestant controversy, such as predestination. There was to be no discussion whatsoever on the prerogative powers of the monarch, and no meddling with matters of state. A significant direction banned criticism of Roman Catholics or Puritans, unless they should attack Anglican doctrine. All parish lecturers were to be licensed to ensure that these measures were observed. *Directions Concerning Preaching and Preachers* was promulgated on 4 August, two days after a formal suspension of laws against Catholic recusants. The two announcements were intended to send a signal to the Spanish court that, despite the plight of his daughter Elizabeth and the Elector Palatine, King James was determined to appease the Hapsburgs and to ease the path for the Prince of Wales to wed the Infanta.

Such stipulations were very unpopular with the Protestant community, presenting Dean Donne with a major challenge when he climbed up to the pulpit at Paul's Cross on 15 September of that year. His strategy was to emphasise the positive aspects of the directions, seeking to reassure his audience that sermons based on the catechism and homilies would be encouraged and there would be no reduction in their number. The reason for excluding some subjects, he explained, was that they were too abstruse or 'high soaring', rather than that messages considered by the government as seditious and dangerous were being censored.

The King was delighted by the content, ordering the text to be printed, the first of Donne's sermons to be published. However, John Chamberlain makes plain that some in the audience were not convinced by the arguments. He remarked that the sermon was 'somwhat a straunge text for such a business, and how he made yt hold together I know not, but he gave no great satisfaction, or as some say spake as yf himself were not so well satisfied'.[12]

Two months later, John Donne delivered the Gunpowder Plot Sermon at Paul's Cross, in which he sought to counter the opposition to the directions that was being expressed by the citizens of London. He looked to the kings of the Bible for his argument, insisting that subjects should trust and obey their monarch, regardless of those kings' qualities, with Zedekiah as a representative of a 'bad king', and Josiah of a 'good king'. Catholics had fallen into the error of refusing to accept subjection to the monarch. As this was rather tricky ground, anticipating the idea of the divine right of kings, Donne was quick to identify James with Josiah, just as preachers in the previous century had hailed Edward VI as a modern Josiah.

Two versions of this sermon have survived. The first consists of a manuscript drafted by a professional scribe at the request of James I, now in the collection of the British Library; this version also contains corrections and additions in Donne's own hand. The second appears in a printed collection of Donne's sermons entitled *Fifty Sermons* and published in 1644. The printed version includes the prayer delivered by Donne before starting his sermon, as well as a few additions to the text. John Wall, who has been working on a 'virtual performance' of the sermon, thinks that these versions represent only two stages in Donne's work on it. He hypothesises that Donne first prepared a set of elaborate notes which he took with him into the pulpit as the basis of the sermon delivered. Wall believes that Donne, at the request of the King, then wrote out a copy of what he remembered preaching, or wished he had preached, that was given to the scribe to put in fair hand. Revising it slightly, Donne then sent this to James. Further minor editing also took place before the sermon appeared in print in 1644.

The different stages that Donne went through produce a concept more complicated than just 'Donne's sermon for Gunpowder Day 1622'. No doubt sermons by other preachers went through a gradual process from pulpit to press, albeit in a simpler form. Our consideration of what Donne actually said in that sermon must also take into account the physical setting, including the challenges in delivery. Donne, like all the preachers at the Cross, had to contend with the distracting sounds of birds flying above, by horses and dogs who accompanied members of the congregation, the bells of London churches, and especially the clock bell of St Paul's.[13]

John Donne at this time was not only seeking to shore up the religious and political policies of King James, but he was also involved in the consideration of the very state of St Paul's Cathedral and its Churchyard. The cathedral and churchyard played such a familiar part of the daily life of London that they were referred to by Chamberlain and other contemporaries not as 'St Paul's', but rather as 'Paul's', 'Powles' and so on. Here was the largest public space in a tightly packed city. Part of it was open to the skies in the form of the Churchyard, and part under cover in the form of the nave of the cathedral. From medieval times the nave became a location for all kinds of secular activities, bringing the Churchyard, as it were, into the cathedral. In the early twelfth century, one of the canons, Algar, had a foot length inscribed on a pier base of the recently built nave. Algar was from a family of money dealers, and it is suggested that he himself was a dealer. The 'foot of Algar' was the standard measurement of length used for many years until superseded by the royal standard lodged at Guildhall. By the late fourteenth century, traders gathered daily in the cathedral and its doorways, with 12 scriveners assigned places in the nave where they might write contracts and other legal documents for Londoners.

Although in time the Guildhall took over measures of governance, and financial trading moved eastwards with the opening of Gresham's bourse or Royal Exchange in 1567, the nave of St Paul's continued to be a centre for many activities. The area around the font became particularly associated with formal conduct of legal business, while there was a 'serving man's pillar' where domestic staff might be hired. Sir John Falstaff declared that he had 'bought' Bardolph 'in Paules' in the second part of Shakespeare's *Henry IV.* The *Si Quis* ('if anyone') door at the west end of the north aisle was used as a location for advertising. Here bills could be posted, with those interested writing a suggested time and place for meeting at the bottom. Paul's Alley, linking Paternoster Row to the north with Carter Lane in the south, had been established by the fifteenth century as a public thoroughfare, passing straight through the cathedral.

With the Reformation, the secularisation of the nave became yet more marked. In 1549 Nicholas Ridley, as Bishop of London during Edward VI's reign, undertook a radical rearrangement of the worship at St Paul's. At Ridley's trial during the reign of Mary Tudor, another bishop reproached him for setting 'an Oyster table' in the place of an altar. Ridley went further, moving this table from the high altar to the upper choir and blocking sight of the communion bread with veils, and even brick screens, to prevent adoration. Some citizens mourned these measures, others supported them with characteristic robustness.

During both the reigns of Mary and Elizabeth, proclamations were issued to try to reduce the use of the cathedral for secular purposes. In an Act of the Common Council of London, in the joint names of Mary Tudor and her husband King Philip, issued in 1554, it was stated that the 'material temples of God were first ordained for the lawful and devout assembly of people', not to be used as markets. It went on to complain that many were accustomed

> to make their common carriage of great vessels of ale or beer, great baskets full of bread fish, flesh and fruit, fardels [bundles] of stuff, and other gross wares, through the cathedral church of S.Paul's, and some in leading mules, horses, and other beasts irreverently to the great dishonour and displeasure of Almighty God.

Fines were to be imposed for the first and second offence, and imprisonment for the third.

Elizabeth followed this up seven years later with another proclamation:

> if any person shall make any fray, or draw or put out his hand to any weapon for that purpose, or shoot any hand-gun or dagg within the cathedral church of S.Paul's, or churchyard adjoining thereto . . . they shall suffer imprisonment for two months. Any of her Majesty's subjects who

shall walk up and down, or spend the time in the same, in making any bargain or other profane cause, and make any kind of disturbance during the time of preaching, lecturing or other divine service, shall incur the pain of imprisonment and fine, the fine to go to the repair of the church.[14]

Such threats do not appear to have had much effect, so that in 1598 the Bishop of London, Richard Bancroft, undertook a series of visitations. Some of them were concerned with the care and behaviour of the choristers and boy actors, and with the domestic strife among the clergy, as described in Chapter 5. Others concentrated on unease about profanation and the way that the cathedral was being used.

The visitation reports make for painful and odoriferous reading, describing how the cathedral was being polluted by smoke and smells from the chimneys of sheds erected, in particular in the Cross Churchyard. Such was the popularity of the sermons at Paul's Cross that shops were being opened on a Sunday to cater to the crowds by selling them tobacco, beer and ale. Schoolchildren playing in the Churchyard were breaking windows, while some living in the houses between the cathedral buttresses were gaining access to the roof and damaging the leads. Too many citizens had keys to the cathedral, enabling them to throw open its door 'at unlawfull times in the night'. Some of the vaults were leased by carpenters, while the crypt and cloister to the south of the cathedral were occupied by trunk makers. A chapel had been let to a glazier, and his cartwheels had damaged the step to the south door; another was used on occasion for a schoolroom.[15]

Having a public thoroughfare running right through the cathedral meant that even while church services were being conducted in the choir, tradesmen continued to pass through with their pack animals. Beggars and drunkards abounded with 'Idle and masterless people' who reclined and slept in the pews and 'aboute ye quire dores . . . where they doe verie often tymes leave all yt is within them verye loathsome to behold'. The lack of sanitary facilities prevailed throughout the area around the cathedral. Lavatories for the relief of the students at St Paul's School and local inhabitants had been lost when the booksellers took over valuable space in the Cross Churchyard, 'whereby the Churche yard nere about the Crosse lyeth more like a laystall than a churche yarde'.[16] The nickname for Paul's Walk was tellingly Pissing Alley.

Some efforts were made for reform, but these proved desultory. Thirty years after Bancroft's reports, a new broom was demanding that the chaotic state of the nave of St Paul's be tackled. This broom was William Laud, Charles I's favoured prelate who became Bishop of London in 1628. Donne was already only too aware of the dire situation: in a sermon preached in January the previous year he complained to his congregation:

> You meet below, and there make your bargaines, for biting, for devouring Usury, and then you come up hither for prayers, and so make God your Broker. You rob, and spoil, and eat his people as bread, by Extortion, and bribery, and deceitfull waights and measures, and eluding oaths in buying and selling, and then come hither, and so make God your Receiver, and his house a den of Thieves.[17]

The comparison with the biblical den of thieves was taken up by others. The satirist John Earle, who became Bishop of Salisbury, described Paul's Walk in vivid terms:

> The noise in it is like that of bees, a strange humming or buzz mixed of walking, tongues and feet: it is a kind of still roar or loud whisper. It is the great exchange of all discourse, and no business whatsoever but is here stirring and a-foot. . . . The best sign of a temple in it is, that it is the thieves sanctuary, which rob more safely in the crowd than a wilderness. . . . It is the other expence of the day, after plays, tavern and a bawdy-House. . . . It is the ear's brothel, and satisfies their lust and itch.

Earle also adjudged the walk 'the land's epitome . . . the lesser isle of Great Britain. It is more than this, the whole world's map'.[18] The desire for reform was coming up against the fact that this was one of the most popular gathering places in London. Francis Osborne later recalled that

> It was the fashion of those times, and did so continue till these [1650s] . . . for the principall Gentry, Lords, Courtiers, and men of all professions not meerely Mechanick, to meet in Paul's Church by eleven, and walk in the middle Ile till twelve, and after dinner from three, to six; during which

time some discoursed of businesse, others of Newes. Now, in regard of the universall commerce, there happened little that did not first or last arrive here; . . . And those newes-mongers, as they called them, did not only take the boldness to weigh the public but most intrinsick actions of the State, which some courtier or other did betray to this Society.[19]

Those not able to afford dinner would gather around the tomb thought to be of Humphrey, Duke of Gloucester, brother of Henry V, hence the saying, 'dining with Duke Humphrey'.

Paul's Walk appears constantly as a location in contemporary dramas. Jonson, for example, set one of his scenes there in *Every Man Out of His Humour*, first performed at the Globe Theatre in 1599, featuring Sir Fastidious Brisk as an affected courtier devoted to fashion. Thomas Middleton in *Michaelmas Terme* and Thomas Dekker and John Webster in *Westward Hoe* also set scenes here: these plays were part of the repertoire of the Children of Pauls. In his ironic commentary on social manners, *The Gull's Horne Book*, Dekker satirises the fashionable gallant:

He that would therefore strive to fashion his legs to his silk stockings, and his proud gait to his broad garters, let him whiff down these observations; for, if he once get to walk by the book . . . Paul's may be proud of him.[20]

While the satirists poked fun at the gallants of Paul's Walk, these gentlemen also came under more severe attack from the pulpit at Paul's Cross. In 1612 Thomas Adams preached a sermon that was later printed as *The Gallants Burden*:

Are not the alleys in this Temple often fuller of Walkers, then the Quire of Petitioners? Conference with profane ostentation of Clothes; perhaps plots of mischief, as frequent, as suits to God: (making it little less than a den of Thieves): If men stumble into the Church, as company, custom, recreation or (perchance) sleep invites many, they feed their eyes with vanities.

The gallants, who had possibly bought their ostentatious clothes from drapers and mercers near St Paul's, could now go out into the Churchyard and purchase the satires and sermons that were so critical of them. There were even Paul's Cross sermons that complained about book browsers within the Churchyard, further creating a dramatic intercourse.[21]

One devotee of Paul's Walk, John Chamberlain, would not appear to have gone there to display or to observe the latest fashions, but rather to gather news. His letters suggest that he resorted to the Churchyard and cathedral on a daily basis when in London. On one occasion he wrote to his friend Carleton, 'for want of other newes I do only tell you what is said in Powles', and on another described an attempt to curb the numbers in Paul's Walk, 'a new devised order to shut the upper doores in Powles in service time, whereby the old entercourse is cleane changed and the traffic of newes much decayed'. He calls himself and other newsgatherers 'verbes' and 'novellants'.[22]

The booksellers in the Churchyard began to produce 'corantos' or news-books, an idea imported from the Netherlands in response to the Thirty Years War. The first newsbook in English was published in 1620, and two years later Nathaniel Butter, a bookseller at the Sign of the Pied Bull in the south-eastern part of the Churchyard, by St Augustine's Gate, formed a syndicate for supplying news serials.[23] But these could never provide the daily domestic news that was so keenly sought. Ben Jonson, in his play *The Staple of News*, first performed in 1626, parodies this demand for news, and his description of 'a fine-paced gentleman' may have applied to Chamberlain.

Contemporaries sometimes made a link between the moral and physical deterioration of St Paul's. For example, Dekker in *The Deade Terme* used the truncated cathedral tower as a mouthpiece to express dismay at the behaviour of the gallants of the Middle Aisle:

> What swearing is there; yea, what swaggering, what facing and out-facing? What shuffling, what shouldering, what jostling, what jeering, what byting of thumbs to beget quarrels, what holding up of fingers to remember drunken meetings, what braving with feathers, what bearding with mustachoes, what casting open cloakes to publish new clothes.[24]

The steeple of wood covered with lead that stood atop the tower, dominating the skyline of London, had been struck and destroyed by lightning in the summer of 1561. This disaster was taken as a sign of divine wrath by both Protestants and Catholics, with a sermon preached at Paul's Cross warning of greater plagues if Londoners did not amend their lives.

Queen Elizabeth, not known for her generosity with her privy purse, contributed £6,000 towards the repair of the roof of the cathedral damaged in the fire, but this only patched things up, and she expressed displeasure that it was not repaired. Despite a call for funds, money was not forthcoming to replace the steeple, and the tower remained a forlorn sight. One of the perpetual problems for St Paul's was that Londoners tended to be more generous to their parish churches.

Early in his reign, James I wrote to the Lord Mayor and to the Bishop of London, Thomas Ravis, urging them 'to remove the scandal that hath long lien open our city of London especially, but in a manner upon the whole realm, for the neglect of the repairing of the steeple of St Paul's Church'.[25] Offering generous help towards the repair, he noted that the nave and tran-septs were in danger of ruin, and ordered a survey and estimate of the costs of such repairs. When the estimate was produced, it was proposed that the belfry stage of the crossing tower should be rebuilt, and a design by Inigo Jones dating from around 1608 shows that rather than the steeple be reinstated, an elaborate crown be added. Jones had spent some years in Italy in the entou-rage of the Earl of Arundel, and his suggested design, which blends Gothic and classical motifs, reflects some of the ideas that he had seen during his travels. With its domes and obelisks, his drawing takes on a fantastical oriental feel.[26]

In the event, nothing happened. The King's finances were in crisis, while the man who probably commissioned Jones's design, Robert Cecil, Earl of Salisbury, died in 1612. But the problem was not going to go away. In 1616 Henry Farley, a scrivener, published a poetic monologue, *The Complaint of Paules to all Christian Soules*, adopting the voice of the building and pleading for repair. It opens:

I Poore Paules dejected and distressed, yet being in the best prospect, and taller than all my fellowes, doe see, or at least may see, (if my windowes be eyes) many stately monuments, houses, and other things builded, and done within these few yeeres, some for Honour, some for profit, some for

Beautie, some for pleasure, some for health and recreation, some for Royall entertainments and sports, and many for charitable use: And I have seene the Globe burnt, and quickly made a Phoenix. Q But who sees me? A Who sees thee not?

This cry may eventually have prompted James to make his one and only visit to hear a sermon preached at Paul's Cross, on 26 March 1620. John Chamberlain, in a letter to Dudley Carleton, described the build-up to the occasion:

Here is great speech and expectation of the Kings coming to Paules Crosse on Sonday next, where the bishop of London [John King] should preach his court-sermon in the afternoon: some surmise that the King will there deliver somewhat touching the matters of Bohemia, others, concerning the intended match with Spaine, but yf yt so fall out that he come I rather believe yt is about the repairing of Paules which indeed growes very ruinous.[27]

Twelve days later Chamberlain wrote again to Carleton, telling him that Bishop King had given 'a patheticall speech for the repairing of Powles'. The preaching of a sermon is one of the subjects of a diptych that had been commissioned earlier by Henry Farley from John Gipkyn. The 'cover' of this remarkable painting shows James I with his Queen, Anne of Denmark, and his son, Charles, Prince of Wales, in procession from St Saviour's Church in Southwark, across London Bridge and making their way along to St Paul's. This was Farley's 'dream' of how the King might process: in fact, he arrived in 1620 in the opposite direction, and the Queen had died the previous year. The first half of the diptych shows James sitting in the 'sermon house' with the Queen and the Prince of Wales, and the Lord Mayor and City dignitaries resplendent in their scarlet ceremonial robes, watching the preacher in the pulpit of Paul's Cross (Plate 1). The second half shows Farley's vision of a rebuilt tower for the cathedral, complete with statues of the royal family.[28]

After the sermon James attended a banquet at the bishop's palace in the Churchyard, where 'he moved the Lord Maior and aldermen to undertake the works, protesting (as the Bishop had touched in his sermon) that he could be content to fast with bread and water to see yt don'. The King then went back into the cathedral and met the Dean, Valentine Cary, who

> made a short speech in Latin that he was come to visit an old man whose head was bald with age, his shoulders bowing, and his legges fayling so that without helpe of such a physician to restore him he would not long last.[29]

A royal commission was then established to assess what repairs were required and how the funds were to be raised. John Chamberlain, appointed as one of the 70 commissioners, kept Carleton abreast of developments. He reported how 'The King has allotted £1,000 per annum for certaine years' with Prince Charles pledging £500, the Duke of Buckingham 200 marks, and so on, 'to the perfecting of that worke'. But he had shrewdly pointed out that the King was calling upon the City, nobles and the clergy also to help with the Elector Palatine's efforts to win back his kingdom in Bohemia and that 'the motion for Powles comes not very opurtunly, for yt cannot be but these contributions coming together must needes crosse one another'. As the commission began to identify houses and other buildings around the Churchyard that should be demolished before work could be done, so resistance developed. Chamberlain noted:

> but the people either do or will not seeme to believe yt, nor do not remove nor avoide, but some make jests as yf yt were not meant in earnest, and one in knaverie wrote upon his doore *stet quaeso candid lector* [Let it stand, gentle reader].[30]

The King was the man trying to push forward this major project, but his health was failing and his finances were in a dire state. Neither the Bishop of London, nor the Dean of St Paul's, by 1622 the 'poeticall' John Donne, appear to have had the will to take on the burden. Indeed, some of the Portland stone that had been purchased to carry out the repairs was taken by the Duke of Buckingham to build the water gate for his London residence, York House by Charing Cross. This sleight of hand may well have been undertaken by his protégé, Dean Donne. In his biography of Donne, John Stubbs interestingly likens him to his cathedral, an incongruous mixture of the secular and the sacred.[31]

The necessary impetus came with a new monarch, Charles I, and his assumption of personal rule in 1629, together with the appointment of William Laud as Bishop of London. The two men set out not only to restore uniformity of worship, but also to provide 'beauty of holiness' to services and the buildings in which they were held. Again a commission was established to secure the funds necessary for the repair of the cathedral, to be carried out by the City of London. At the first meeting of the commission in 1631 proceedings were agreed for the acquisition and demolition of Churchyard buildings that encroached on the cathedral.

Unfortunately, John Chamberlain's extant correspondence ends in 1627, so we do not get invaluable details from a contemporary commentator. However, it is clear from records that Laud met resistance from Churchyard residents and owners, for he was giving them notice to quit without compensation, and they pleaded difficulty in finding new premises, delaying the work of demolition for several years. A list of 19 booksellers contributing to the repairs has survived, with sums ranging from £6 up to £40, but whether these are voluntary gifts or enforced assessments is not clear.[32]

Inigo Jones was appointed the King's Surveyor and began to identify the parts of the structure most in need of repair. The south side was found to be particularly dangerous, a fact supported by a letter written 30 years earlier by Chamberlain in which he wrote how 'a peece of the south battlements of Powles fell downe lately and kild a carman's horse without doing more harme'.[33] Much of the work was repair to the structure and refurbishing of the interior decoration, but Jones designed and built a new west portico, paid for by the King from his privy purse. It is interesting that Charles chose to expend a substantial sum on this, rather than in the restoration of the spire over the central crossing. In so doing, he was no doubt persuaded by Inigo Jones that it was the fashion in European church architecture to emphasise the main entrance. This portico was in classical style, a marked departure from the Gothic of the rest of the cathedral, with giant Corinthian columns. An inscription on the frieze announced the King's munificence, and above were set statues of Charles and his father, James. This was a declaration, in no uncertain terms, of the Stuart monarchy.

From the outset of the Stuart regime, the royal government sought to use St Paul's Churchyard as the means to display authority. Recantation of Catholic clerics continued as under Elizabeth I, but the softening of attitude towards the Church of Rome dictated by James I's foreign policy made these rare occurrences. Counterintuitively, however, there was an increase in the burning of 'popish books'. While the government of Elizabeth preferred for such literature to be burnt discreetly in the ovens of Stationers' Hall (see p. 47), the destruction of books in the Cross Churchyard is often mentioned by Chamberlain in his letters.

Another area of government crackdown was upon social misconduct, with penance at Paul's Cross imposed by the High Commission, the prerogative court dealing with ecclesiastical matters. John Chamberlain gives two particularly dramatic examples that took place in February 1612. The first concerned Sir Pexall Brocas who entertained and abused 'a younge mignon' in his household since she was 12 years of age. Dressed in a white sheet and carrying a stick, he performed the penance not only for the abuse of his maid, but also for 'secret and notorious adulteries with divers women'.

This was closely followed by the penance of Moll Cutpurse, 'a notorious baggage', whose pranks are recorded in a somewhat idealised form in *The Roaring Girl* by Middleton and Dekker, and Nathan Field's *Amends for Ladies*. Her misdemeanour on this particular occasion was to appear in Paul's Walk on Christmas Night, 'with her petticoat tucked up about her in the fashion of a man' and challenging 'the field of divers gallants'. When Moll was brought to the Cross, Chamberlain described how 'she wept bitterly and seemed very penitent, but yt is since doubted she was maudeline druncke, being discovered to have tipled of three quartes of sacke before she came to her penaunce'. The event descended into farce because the preacher who was presiding over the penance was a young clergyman:

the daintiest preacher or ghostly father that ever I saw in pulpit, one Ratcliffe of Brazen Nose at Oxford, a likelier man to have lead the revels in some ynne of court then to be where he was, but the best is he did extreem badly, and so wearied the audience that the best part went away, and the rest tarried rather to hear Mall [sic] Cutpurse than him.

While the audience watched the absurd scene, associates of Moll relieved some of their purses.[34]

8. Moll Cutpurse, the 'Roaring Girl', in her male garb.

When Laud became Bishop of London, he sought to maintain a firm grip on the sermons that were preached at the Cross, requiring all preachers to submit their text before preaching. The result was a dramatic decline in the popularity of the Paul's Cross sermons, and in the level of preachers chosen. Many of them were young university divines, regarded as 'safe pairs of hands'. This is reflected by the one visit of Charles I to hear a Paul's Cross sermon, on 30 May 1630, the day after his first son and heir, the future Charles II, was born. In stark contrast to the visits of Elizabeth I and of James I, which had been organised as events that would help their public image, he arrived at 8 o'clock in the morning by coach. There is no record of a procession or of the King being formally received by the dean and chapter. We are only told that the sermon was preached by a Suffolk man, whose turn to preach, it would seem, had arrived that day. Having heard the sermon, which was never published, Charles I departed back to St James's Palace, trusting neither the congregation that had gathered at Paul's Cross nor the printing press that might have recorded the theme of that day.

This was a far cry from the heights of preaching that had been developed over the decades. The following year a last trump was delivered by John Donne at his final sermon for Lent at court before Charles on 25 February. He was by this time desperately ill, emaciated, almost skeletal in appearance. Yet he produced possibly his most dramatic sermon: 'Wee have a winding sheete in our Mothers wombe, which grows with us from our conception, and we come into the world, wound up in that winding sheet, for wee come to seeke a grave'.[35]

Shortly after, Donne summoned an artist to the deanery to make a sketch. Izaak Walton records this extraordinary scene:

Several charcoal fires being first made in his large study, he brought with him into that place his winding-sheet in his hand, and having put off all his clothes, had this sheet put on him, and so tied with knots at his head and feet, and his hands so placed, as dead bodies are usually fitted to be shrowded and put into their coffin, or grave.[36]

Donne was so pleased with the drawing that he had it placed by his bedside, where he died on the last day of March 1631. The sculptor Nicholas Stone used the image to carve Donne's statue in white marble, showing him standing in his shroud, rising from a funeral urn. The striking monument was placed just within the choir on the south side of the cathedral. It was one of the very few to survive the Great Fire, and is now to be seen in the ambulatory of Wren's cathedral. The image also appeared on the title page of Donne's *Devotions*, an epitaph to the great era of sermons, many of which had been given at the Cross.

Although many of the buildings demolished in the Churchyard at this period were to clear ground for the repairs and refurbishment of the cathedral, the dismantling of the pulpit of Paul's Cross seems to have been undertaken because of the falling attendance at the sermons. When exactly it was demolished is not certain, but it took place between 1634 and 1635, and it is a sign of the times that no protest was raised at its passing. Instead, sermons were preached inside the cathedral, at the east end by the Lady Chapel and choir. Despite the fact that the outside pulpit was no longer extant, these sermons were described as being preached at Paul's Cross. One of the last was given in May 1642 by a

Corporis hæc Animæ fit Syndon Syndon Jesu
Amen.
Martin (R) scup. And are to be sould by R.R and Ben. ffisher

9. Portrait of John Donne on the frontispiece of his last sermon, *Death's Duel*,
published in 1632.

fellow of Pembroke College, Cambridge, Mark Frank. He chose as his text the story of the faithful obedience of Jehonadab's descendants. This laid emphasis upon loyalty in troubled times, for Charles I had departed from London at the beginning of the year and forces in support and opposing the King were gathering ready for war. Frank offered an appeal for obedience to Charles, but was preaching to an increasingly embattled audience, many of whom were not likely to have listened with a sympathetic ear: London was firmly for Parliament.

The noxious chaos of St Paul's returned with interest in the period during the Civil War and the Commonwealth. At a time when even the survival of

England's cathedrals came into question, St Paul's was not only used as a shopping precinct and gathering place, but also to provide stabling for the horses of the Parliamentary forces and quarters for the horse guards. On one occasion the font was mocked by the baptism of a new born foal. Woodwork of every kind – pews, stalls from the choir, the organ loft – were torn out and used for firewood. Stained glass was smashed and pillars were blackened with smoke. Inigo Jones's new portico again accommodated shops, and now a nine-pin alley. Once a republic had been declared, the statues of Charles I and James I were knocked off the portico and smashed. Monuments inside the cathedral were also defaced, but the arresting statue of John Donne was left untouched – stayed by the power of his poetry, perhaps, or the power of Nicholas Stone's image. The huge stores of valuable material that had been brought in to repair the building were sold, and only the timber scaffolding around the central tower was left because nobody dared to take it down, recognising the fragility of the stonework.

The end of the republic came suddenly with the death of Oliver Cromwell in September 1658, apparently at the height of his power. Richard, his son, was named as his successor, but he lacked the will and the ability to hold the balance of power among the conflicting forces. A winter of riots and protests followed, and in St Paul's Churchyard a snowman was built with 'one eye in his heade and with an old face and haulter or rope about his neck, many old shewes lying around by him, a horne on his head'.[37] A year later, Charles II was restored to his throne, and entered London in triumph. John Evelyn described the scene in ecstatic terms:

> This day came in his Majestie Charles the 2d to London after a sad, & long Exile and Calamitous Suffering both of the King & the Church . . . The Wayes straw'd with flowers, the bells ringing, the Mayor, Aldermen, all the Companies in their liver(ie)s, Chaines of Gold, banners; Lords & nobles, Cloth of Silver, gold & velvet every body clad in, the window & balconies all set with Ladys, Trumpets, Musick & myriads of people flocking the streets.[38]

But not everybody rejoiced. In January 1661 a group, around 50 strong, of Fifth Monarchists led by Colonel Venner stormed St Paul's Churchyard. These men, described by Pepys in his diary as 'Fanatiques', had declared war in the name of Christ the King to bring salvation to the nation. Yet again the Churchyard became a theatre of dissent, with a bookshop raided for the keys to enter the cathedral. Although Venner and his men were driven out, they returned three days later and after a fight with overwhelming numbers of City troops, several were killed and their leaders captured.

As the capital returned to some kind of normality, attention turned to the dire state of St Paul's Cathedral. Yet another commission was established in 1663 to investigate the repair and refurbishment. This included three architects, Christopher Wren, Hugh May and Roger Pratt. Pratt and May had experience of designing country houses, and two striking houses in Piccadilly: Clarendon House by Pratt and Berkeley House by May. However, Wren, the brilliant young Gresham Professor of Astronomy, had barely begun his architectural career, with only the chapel of Pembroke College, Cambridge, and the Sheldonian Theatre in Oxford to his name. In the late summer of 1666 Wren presented his plans for what could be done to prevent the cathedral's collapse after yet more years of neglect and vandalism. The decision back in 1631 to spend money on a new west front rather than sorting out the problem of the tower had proved unfortunate, for during the Interregnum part had collapsed.

Now Wren was proposing that a dome should be built over the crossing. John Evelyn, who had recently been appointed to the commission as surveyor of the repairs, noted in his diary that such a dome was 'a form of church-building not as yet known in England, but of wonderful grace'.[39] While Evelyn backed Wren's idea of a dome, Roger Pratt was strongly opposed to it, no doubt feeling that his was the experienced voice. In one way he had a point, for St Paul's with the mixture of Gothic and classical could have resembled a mythological hybrid creature such as the sphinx or the chimera.

However, this debate turned out to be academic, for only a week later, in the early hours of 2 September 1666, fire broke out in a baker's shop in Pudding Lane, just north of London Bridge. At first it seemed so small that the lord mayor unwisely dismissed it, saying that a woman could piss it out. Fanned by exceptionally strong winds from the east, however, the flames spread rapidly over the next few days, gradually moving across the City. The Great Fire of London was to sound the death knell not only for Old St Paul's Cathedral, but also for its Churchyard.

CHAPTER 7

RESETTING THE SCENE

As the Great Fire moved inexorably towards St Paul's, the booksellers of the Churchyard hastened to protect their stock. Stationers' Hall in Ave Maria Lane, Christchurch in Newgate Street, and the chapel of St Faith in the crypt of St Paul's Cathedral were chosen as places of safety. The last, affectionately known as 'the baby in the womb', had been a parish church subsumed into the cathedral when the choir was extended in medieval times, and served as the church of the Stationers' Company. The desperate booksellers believed that the thick stone walls of the cathedral would provide effective protection. But the flames took hold of all kinds of debris in the area around the cathedral and climbed up the timber scaffolding that encased the tower in preparation for its repair. From here, as they spread along the roof of the choir the flames melted the lead that poured down into the interior of the cathedral, causing everything below to explode like a huge bonfire.

The scale of the destruction of Old St Paul's is reflected in contemporary accounts. So intense was the light from the burning cathedral that a Westminster schoolboy, William Taswell, recorded how he was able 'to read very clearly a 16mo. [the smallest format] edition of Terence which I carried in my pocket'. Fanned by the exceptionally strong winds, half-burned leaves of books from the crypt were swept westwards. Some were seen by the Nonconformist divine Richard Baxter, at his home in Acton, eight miles away, and some even reached Windsor, a distance of 24 miles. The philosopher John Locke recorded how in Oxford he was able to detect an 'unusual colour of the air, which without a cloud appearing made the sunbeams a strange red, dim light'.[1]

The fire that had rampaged across London for four days began to die down when the strong winds abated. By the night of 6 September 1666 the worst was over, and shocked Londoners could survey the damage. Nearly 400 acres had been burned within the city walls, and a further 63 acres beyond to the west, across the Fleet River. Eighty-seven churches had been destroyed, together with 44 livery halls and 13,200 houses. Only the area in the north and easternmost parts of the city had escaped the flames, along with London Bridge where a firebreak had been created by an earlier conflagration.

Samuel Pepys, born in 1633 in a house on Salisbury Square, just off Fleet Street, had spent much of his childhood in the shadow of the cathedral, and had attended St Paul's School. His account of the Great Fire therefore carries particular poignancy, for the disaster had destroyed many of the places of his youth. On the morning of 7 September he climbed up from Paul's Wharf on the Thames

and saw all the town burned, and a miserable sight of Pauls church [the cathedral] with all the roofs fallen and the body of the Quire fallen into St Fayths – Paul's school also – Ludgate – Fleet street – my father's house and the church [St Bride's], and a good part of the Temple the like.

On that same day fellow diarist John Evelyn also went to see what remained of St Paul's. He found that Inigo Jones's portico had survived remarkably unscathed, although the intense heat had 'in a manner Calcin'd, so as all the ornaments, Columns, freezes, Capitels & proje(c)tures of massie Portland stone flew off, even to the very roofe'. He ended, 'Thus lay in ashes that most venerab(le) Church, one of the (antientiest) Pieces of early Piety in the Christian World'.[2]

Official figures suggest that only nine deaths occurred as a result of the fire, but there were almost certainly others. William Taswell, exploring around the cathedral, was horrified to find not only the carcasses of dogs 'stiff as a plank, the skin being tough like leather' but also the body of a woman who had taken shelter by the walls, with 'every limb reduced to a coal'.[3] Thousands had lost their homes and were camped out on any open ground around the capital, including members of the Churchyard community.

Once the fire was completely extinguished, Charles II and his Parliament were eager to begin the rebuilding of the city. A number of plans were speedily

10. Detail from Christopher Wren's plan submitted to Charles II, showing how the City might be rebuilt. He proposed that the new Churchyard should be a triangular space.

presented as to how the new London might be organised, casting aside the centuries of haphazard arrangements, and recalling the grid system of Roman Londinium. One such plan was proffered just a week after the fire by John Evelyn, who for many years had been critical of the state of the capital, with its 'streets . . . so narrow and incommodious in the very Center, and busiest places of Intercourse'. In his scheme St Paul's Churchyard would act as a hub of the city, oval in shape, with the cathedral at the centre, the school, a library, deanery and booksellers' shops gathered around it. Thoroughfares of varying widths would cut through the layout, linking the cathedral to other key buildings, such as the Guildhall, with visual breathing spaces for 'breakings, and enlargements into piazzas'.[4]

Despite his celerity, Evelyn was pipped to the post by Christopher Wren, who got his plan to the King at Whitehall on 11 September. In many ways his scheme resembled that of Evelyn, with a series of wide straight streets radiating from central points. Unsurprisingly, given his architectural experience, Wren's was much more professional. In the end neither of these projects was adopted, nor were several others, for these were desperate days: not only was

131

the capital in ruins, but England was at war with both the Dutch and the French. It was recognised that practical measures overrode ideal solutions. As one member of parliament noted in his diary:

It was the general opinion of the whole House that if some speedy way of rebuilding the City was not agreed upon that the City would be in danger never to be built, for if the citizens found a difficulty in it, and that things were not speedily provided for, the merchants and the wealthiest citizens would alter their course of life and trade and remove themselves and estates into other countries and so the City would remain miserable for ever.[5]

The King therefore ruled that rebuilding should take place on previously occupied sites, although some streets should be widened and houses should be constructed in brick and stone. Upset by this decision of compromise, Evelyn unfairly wrote in his commonplace book:

London since the Conflagration might so have been made the most beautiful, uniforme and usefull and stately Citty in Europe, had K. Chas II taken any care about it; But the Women and his love of ease broke up all his Thoughts; so he minded nothing.[6]

At the beginning of October Charles and the Lord Mayor agreed to form a commission of experts to advise on the rebuilding. Three commissioners were nominated by the King to meet weekly with three city surveyors. Their task was to formulate a new shape for the City, oversee a survey and deliver proposals. The King's nominees were the three architects from the commission formed three years earlier to decide how to repair St Paul's Cathedral: Roger Pratt, Hugh May and Christopher Wren (see p. 128). The Mayor in turn nominated two men experienced in building in London: Peter Mills, the City's General Surveyor, and Edward Jerman, a carpenter by training who had also worked as a builder. Their third choice was Robert Hooke, the brilliant scientist and Professor of Geometry at Gresham College.

Within the Churchyard and the surrounding area three kinds of rebuilding were planned, very different in scale both in respect of size and of time: private

1. Part of the diptych painted by John Gipkyn in 1616, showing a sermon being preached at Paul's Cross in the presence of King James I, Queen Anne and the Prince of Wales seated in the 'sermon house' in the east end of the cathedral. Shops, possibly of booksellers, can be seen between buttresses of the north transept.

2. The procession of Edward VI in 1547 on the day before his coronation. The houses along Cheapside are decorated with wall hangings as the cavalcade makes its way towards St Paul's. For centuries such processions were part of the ceremonial associated with the Churchyard.

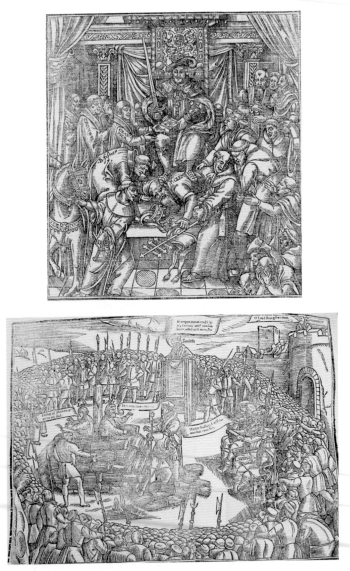

3 & 4. Two woodcut images from *Foxe's Book of Martyrs*, first published in 1563. (Above) Henry VIII is shown throwing down Pope Clement and John Fisher, Bishop of Rochester, in this graphic depiction of the Reformation of the English Church, with the assistance of his chief minister, Thomas Cromwell, and Archbishop Thomas Cranmer. (Below) Although this scene is set in Oxford in October 1555, the principal players all took part in the religious drama played out in St Paul's Churchyard. The Protestant bishops, Ridley and Latimer, at their stakes are being urged to recant by the arch recanter, Richard Smyth, while Archbishop Cranmer calls from his cell on the right for the Lord to strengthen their resolve.

5. The title page designed by Holbein for the Great Bible of 1539, with God squeezing in with difficulty above the head of Henry VIII. Cromwell and Cranmer hand down the Word of God, ironically in Latin, to the people.

6. The title page of the King James Bible, printed in 1611 by the King's printer, Robert Barker, at the Sign of the Tyger's Head in Paternoster Row. Neither the King nor his subjects appear as in the Great Bible, but regal authority is nevertheless present.

7. A drawing of one of the pageant stations established in the Churchyard for the Lord Mayor's Show in 1616, part of a play written by Anthony Munday in celebration of the new mayor, a member of the Fishmongers' Company. William Walworth, a famous fishmonger and lord mayor, is shown in a garden bower preparing to greet the procession.

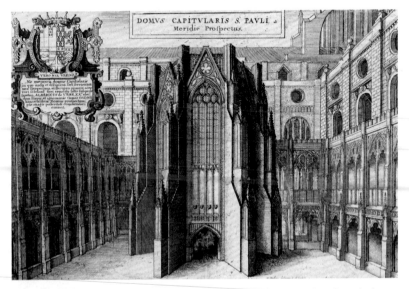

8. Wenceslaus Hollar's engraving of the octagonal chapter house and its surrounding cloister built in the fifteenth century on the south side of the cathedral. It was reproduced in Sir William Dugdale's history of Old St Paul's, published in 1658.

9. Detail from a seventeenth-century woodcut showing the Great Fire of London of September 1666. Viewed from Southwark, it shows the City engulfed in flames, including St Paul's Cathedral.

10. Wren's St Paul's Cathedral, a coloured engraving from the eighteenth century. The cathedral, with the statue of Queen Anne at its west end, is enclosed by the cast iron railings that caused the aged architect so much grief.

11. Stationers' Hall in 1781, appropriately from one of the almanacs that were the source of much profit through the Company's English Stock scheme. Such almanacs were stored in warehouses in the courtyard behind the dining hall.

12 & 13. The retailing 'citadels' of St Paul's Churchyard were booksellers and the drapery trade. The eighteenth-century coloured engraving features fashionable shoppers caught by a gust as they pass the windows of the printshop of the Bowles family. The print, naturally, was sold by Carrington Bowles. The photograph taken in 1907 shows crowds thronging the pavements to view the spring fashions on display at Nicholson's.

14. Paternoster Row in 1851 from a watercolour by Thomas Colman Dibdin. The narrow street was packed with the premises of booksellers, offering not only books but also journals, magazines and tracts.

15 & 16. The funeral processions of Lord Viscount Nelson in 1806 and of the Duke of Wellington in 1852. On both occasions the Churchyard was packed with onlookers, but in the half century between the two the buildings around had increased in height and grandeur as department stores took over from traditional shops.

17. Pen and wash drawing of Doctors' Commons, *c.* 1800, looking into the entrance from St Paul's Churchyard. Dickens was to describe it as a 'cozy, dozy, old-fashioned, time-forgotten, sleepy-headed little family party'.

18. The Oxford Arms in Warwick Lane, one of the principal coaching inns of the Churchyard. This photograph was taken in 1875 when it had fallen into a dilapidated state. At the time memories were evoked of its rich history, including its use as a theatre in Elizabethan times: its destruction proved a landmark in the development of the movement to preserve historic buildings.

19. The devastation of the German air raid on the night of 29 December 1940 can be seen in this photograph taken of part of Paternoster Row with Wren's Chapter House.

20. Many buildings in the Churchyard and surrounding streets were demolished after they were deemed unsafe. This photograph taken from the Golden Gallery of the cathedral shows circular water dams marking the junction of Paternoster Row and Ivy Lane.

21. St Paul's Cathedral and Churchyard today. The only survival of the former oval shape of the Churchyard before its destruction in the Second World War can be seen at the top of the photograph, at the cathedral's west end leading onto Ludgate Hill. The monument marking the site of Paul's Cross stands in the middle of gardens at the bottom of the photograph.

residences; institutional buildings and parish churches; and the cathedral. The first priority was to get people back into their houses, which would be rebuilt whenever possible on previously occupied sites. It was stipulated that the buildings should be of brick and stone: two storeys for by-lanes, three for streets and lanes of note, four storeys for high streets and 'mansion houses for citizens of extraordinary quality'.[7] For the houses on main streets, there should be iron balconies at first floor level.

A basic survey of burned neighbourhoods was drawn up by Hooke and his fellow surveyors. This was a simplified document enabling street-widening schemes: no way was to be less than 16 feet, enabling a cart to pass through. Detailed plans of individual properties were then recorded in the surveyors' books, along with the names of neighbouring plots. Disputes, which inevitably arose, were handled by Fire Courts held in Clifford's Inn in Holborn, following a Parliamentary act in 1667 'for erecting a judicature for determination of differences touching houses burned or demolished by reason of the late fire'. The efficiency of Hooke and his fellow surveyors is extraordinary to perceive. The turmoil must have been huge, and the demand for labour and supplies intense. Yet within three years, it is estimated that 1,200 families had been rehoused, and that within six years the burnt-out area was largely rebuilt.

In some parts of the City, a substantial number of the residents did not return to the site of their former homes, but the area around St Paul's Cathedral retained a high proportion of the pre-Fire population, a phenomenon known as 'residential persistence'.[8] These residents were living in one of the most economically and socially important areas of the capital. One example of speedy persistence is James Allestree, a bookseller based in the Churchyard. The inventory taken at his death in 1670 shows that his house and bookshop had been completed, and he and his family had moved back in from temporary lodgings in Duck Lane. We do not know the appearance of the residences of the Churchyard and Paternoster Row, but an idea of what they might have looked like can be seen in Amen Corner, just off Ave Maria Lane. Three residences there have survived. They are of three storeys above a basement, built for the residentiary canons of St Paul's by Edward Woodroffe, Wren's assistant on the rebuilding of the cathedral.

Not only was it vital for residents to get back into their rebuilt homes and continue their businesses, but also for the institutions of the City to be able to function again. Among the livery halls rebuilt was that of the Stationers on the site of Abergavenny House, on Ave Maria Lane. It is not known who was responsible for its design, but its interior resembles in many ways the hall of the Company of Apothecaries in Blackfriars, built to the designs of Edward Jerman. The Apothecaries moved into their hall in 1672, with the Stationers following a year later. These two halls are now the oldest in London, having largely escaped bombing in the Second World War.

Edward Jerman also worked on the halls of seven other livery companies and drew up the designs for the rebuilding of St Paul's School which reopened in 1670. The latter was demolished in the nineteenth century, but images show it to have been an imposing classical building. Other institutional buildings neighbouring the Churchyard included the Royal College of Physicians, which had moved in the early seventeenth century to premises at Amen Corner on Paternoster Row leased to them by the Dean and Chapter of St Paul's. The physicians' new home after the Fire was in nearby Warwick Lane, designed for them by Robert Hooke. He provided for them an octagonal gatehouse crowned by a dome which housed the anatomical theatre. So noteworthy was his building that it became a regular venue for visitors, with guidebooks recommending that the payment of at least threepence should be paid to the person who showed them round.

A pre-Fire neighbour in Paternoster Row had been the Doctors' Commons, established at the very end of the fifteenth century. This was the home of the advocates of civil and ecclesiastical, as opposed to common, law. Following the Reformation they trained in Roman law at the universities of Oxford and Cambridge, and were familiarly known as 'civilians'. After the Fire they moved to Knightrider Street, just south of the Churchyard, where they lived in lodgings apparently more intimate than those of the Inns of Court (Plate 17).

Before the Fire there had been 87 parish churches in the City, a huge number to sustain, so it was decided to amalgamate some parishes. An initial suggestion of pruning the number to 39 caused an outcry, and as a result in 1670 it was amended to 51. St Gregory's, which for centuries had stood like a sentinel at the west end of St Paul's Cathedral, was one of the parishes to disappear. The new manifestation of the Churchyard thus contained no parish churches. Instead they formed a circle at some distance from the cathedral: St Martin within Ludgate to the west; Christchurch in Newgate Street to the north; St Mary Magdalene in Knightrider Street; and to the east, just outside the Churchyard's perimeter, St Augustine in Watling Street, to which was added the parish of St Faith's, the chapel of which had been in the crypt of the old cathedral. Again, these churches were mostly built upon their old footprint, requiring considerable architectural ingenuity. The 51 City churches produced in the years that followed are often referred to as 'Wren churches', but he was working in a creative partnership with Robert Hooke and, in the 1680s, with Nicholas Hawksmoor on the towers, lanterns, cupolas and spires which gave London its distinctive skyline.

The landscape of St Paul's Churchyard was going to be very different from its medieval predecessor, when it had been filled with a disconcerting number of buildings, many of them religious in function. Now there was to be one great religious building, that of the cathedral itself. But who would be its architect? It might have seemed at the time that Roger Pratt was the most obvious choice, and he certainly had views about its form and appearance, as shown in 1663 when refurbishment of the old cathedral had been under discussion. In 1667, however, Pratt's star was suddenly in the descendant as a result of the fall from power of his patron, Lord Clarendon. In June of that year the Dutch arrived in the River Medway, burnt the English fleet which had been laid up there to save money, and towed away the *Royal Charles*. A terrified London, already reeling from the Great Fire, waited to see what the Dutch would do next. Fortunately, along with their French allies, they wanted peace on reasonable terms, resulting in the Treaty of Breda. But Clarendon, as the King's chief minister, was held responsible for the mismanagement of the war. On the very day that news reached London of the Dutch breaking of the boom on the Medway, a mob had cut down trees outside Clarendon House in Piccadilly, thrown stones through the windows and painted a gibbet on the gate. When Clarendon was impeached and driven into exile, Pratt decided to retire to his Norfolk estate.

By this time, Hugh May was busy acting as the Surveyor of the King's Works during the long indisposition of Sir John Denham. Those with the most influence were now looking in a different direction. The Dean of St Paul's, William Sancroft, had been impressed by Wren's proposals for the old cathedral and felt that the plans for the new building should be entrusted to him alone. In this matter, he was supported by Gilbert Sheldon, the Archbishop of Canterbury, who had commissioned Wren to build the Sheldonian Theatre in Oxford, and not least, by the King himself. Therefore it was Wren, the least experienced of the three architects, who was now charged with the challenge of producing a design for the new St Paul's.

Challenge, indeed it was, for this was the first cathedral to be built in Britain since the Reformation, and Wren was going to have to satisfy the requirements for worship of the Anglican Church. This could go against the design instincts of the architect, as shown in the one possible precedent in London: the church of St Paul's in Covent Garden, designed by Inigo Jones and completed in 1633. William Laud as Bishop of London had ruled that the altar should be given its traditional place against the east wall, so that the main entrance facing the piazza of Covent Garden could not be used.

Significantly, Wren was to write that the most important element in a new church was:

> that all who are present can both hear and see. The Romanists, indeed, may build larger Churches, it is enough if they hear the murmur of the Mass, and see the elevation of the host, but ours are to be fitted for auditories.[9]

Both the Catholic and the Reformed Churches ran from west to east, facing the altar. In addition, Wren needed to answer the Anglican need for ceremony, for processing up to the altar, and for the preacher to be heard by his congregation. In 1669 he was working on his initial design, known as the First Model, when he was made Surveyor General of the King's Works due to the personal favour of Charles II. The First Model consisted of a rectangular block, modest in dimension, 70 feet in width and 180 feet long, with no transepts and no distinction between nave and choir. Wren needed the royal favour that had been bestowed upon him, for when the scheme was presented for approval by a commission of clergy and courtiers, the response was not good. As he explained, 'it seemed in vain in any new designs, to propose an edifice too large and costly', and ironically the commission found it too modest.[10] Pratt, in London from his Norfolk fastness, was predictably critical.

Wren promptly moved on to a more ambitious scheme, taking the form of a Greek cross. The round central space measured over 120 feet in diameter, with four short arms, and a monumental dome supported on a ring of eight pillars. But this was simply too radical for the dignitaries of the Church of England 'who thought it deviated too much from the old Gothick form of Cathedral Churches, which they had been used to'.[11] In 1673 a Royal Commission for the Rebuilding of the Cathedral Church of St Paul's was finally instituted, replacing the more informal group. It consisted of a panel of churchmen, privy councillors and city officials. This was going to be a tough group of people to please, and so it proved when Wren presented his third set of plans, later known as the Great Model. This retained the Greek cross design, but with a long nave. Wren had a model made in oak of the design, 20 feet in length, large enough for visitors to enter and savour the effect. The care lavished on this model was remarkable. The dome was plastered by the King's master plasterer, John Grove, while the floor below was constructed so that it could be lowered by lines on brass enabling visitors to stand inside. Richard Cleare, the carver, made nearly one thousand ornaments, including pilasters for the exterior, festoons and cartouches, cherubims' heads and a figure of St Paul. The Sergeant-Painter, Robert Streater, painted the walls stone colour inside and out, and coloured the roof to simulate lead, gilding the detail.

In February 1674, when Robert Hooke walked through the bare bones of the model in the Convocation House, it was impressive, and by the summer it was nearing completion, protected from the sun by calico curtains specially made for the purpose. In October the Great Model was finished, providing one of the exciting sights of London. The King liked the design, and Wren later considered it one of the best of his entire career: quite a feat when one considers the huge number of architectural designs he produced. But the churchmen on the commission felt it was too Roman in concept, and it was turned down, apparently reducing Wren to tears. A tourist to London in the early eighteenth century, observing the Great Model, described it as rejected for being too like a pagan temple.[12] The city officials were also concerned that the funds available for rebuilding St Paul's, from the tax on imported coal, would prove insufficient, leaving a half-completed structure in the midst of London.

Overwhelmed by disappointment, Wren fell out with the King, whom he felt had betrayed him. But this rupture proved short-lived, for in November

1673 he was rewarded with a knighthood, and returned to the drawing board. In 1675 he produced what became known as the Warrant Design. This retained the long cruciform plan, but consisted of a strange mixture of styles, harking back in some ways to the designs that Inigo Jones had produced in the 1630s, with a dome surmounted by an elongated spire that resembled an oriental pagoda. This time, the commission gave their full approval. With the coal tax dues in mind, the commission declared 'we found it very artificial, proper, and useful; as because it was so ordered as it might be built in parts'.[13] The King gave his warrant on 14 May 1675.

We have an inkling of what was going through Wren's mind when he received the royal warrant, for he wrote that he would 'make no more Models, or publickly expose his drawings, which, (as he found by experience,) did but lose time, and subjected his Business many times, to incompetent Judges'. This may have been an exasperated response to the six years of trying to please the various interests, but more probably it was a cover for a plan to develop a scheme to his own liking. For Charles had told his surveyor that he could 'make some variations, rather ornamental, than essential, as from time to time he sees proper'.[14]

Nearly nine years had passed since the Great Fire. In that time, the Churchyard had very quickly become a demolition site. First, the sheds and lean-tos that had cluttered the area around the cathedral, and which had contributed to the spread of the fire, were swept away. This was an easy task, but the remains of the old cathedral were another matter. Wren decided to retain Inigo Jones's western portico which had suffered comparatively less damage than the rest of the building. However, even in the badly damaged parts of the structure there remained a considerable amount of stonework, hardly surprising given that the medieval building had been so massive. A Dutch artist, Thomas Wyck, showed the formidable challenge presented by the ruins in a drawing made in 1670.

One of the problems facing Wren and his team of workmen was that the Churchyard was a main thoroughfare for traffic passing from west to east. With the City being rebuilt, carts were constantly bringing through stone, brick and timber in addition to all the normal traffic of horses and carriages. People too were passing through and inevitably paused to watch the proceedings. In the autumn of 1668 Pepys was on his way from his home in Seething Lane to the Temple

> and stopped, viewing the Exchange and Paul's and St.Fayth's; where strange how the very sight of the stones falling from the top of the steeple doth make me sea-sick. But no hurt, I hear hath happened in all this work of the steeple – which is very much.

In fact, there was plenty of opportunity for hurt, and two days later he recorded how a workman had been killed by falling from the roof at the east end.[15]

In particular, the massive columns of the central crossing posed a problem. At first the workmen used battering rams along with pickaxes and hammers, but these proved ineffectual. Wren decided therefore to blow them up with gunpowder, in 1672 bringing in a gunner from the Tower of London. The result was spectacularly successful, but the disruption to life in the Churchyard was intense with thunderings like earthquakes. Wren's son, in his account of his father's life, *Parentalia*, recounted an incident when Edward Woodroffe, left in charge, overestimated the amount of gunpowder required. A large explosion ensued, with stones shooting in all directions, one of which crashed into the iron balcony on the first floor of a booksellers' shop and penetrated the room where some women sat at work. This proved the last straw, and while carpenters were dispatched to make repairs, the commissioners ruled that further explosions were off the agenda.

With the signing of the royal warrant, the Churchyard could move from demolition to building site. The late Gothic chapter house on the south side of the cathedral, which at the Reformation became the Convocation House, had lost its roof in the fire, but was otherwise serviceable as a headquarters for Wren and his team, and for discussions with the Dean. Once the roof had been reinstated, the upper room was furnished with a mantelpiece, a table with drawers, wall hangings and a large map of London hung over the chimney.[16] To protect the workmen from the elements, sheds were constructed nearby.

Apart from Woodroffe, who had lodgings in the Churchyard, Wren's team lived elsewhere. Robert Hooke had managed to hold on to his rooms in

Gresham College in Bishopsgate, despite the fact that all the other professors had given up theirs. After the Royal Exchange was consumed by the fire, the activities of the main trading floor of the City had been transferred to the college. Hooke was spared because of his invaluable City connections. Although he had official lodgings at Scotland Yard in Whitehall, Wren is believed to have taken a house on the Thames front in Southwark so that he could watch across the river the progress of the work at St Paul's. Today the Cardinal's Cap, just to the east of the Globe Theatre, is pointed out as Wren's house, but in fact dates from after his time. A residence further west on Bankside is a stronger possibility.

Many of the workmen probably lived in the more modest riverside parishes. The core group, numbering between 20 and 30, were required to arrive at the site at six o'clock in the morning in summer, having checked in at a call booth that is thought to have stood on the south side of Cannon Street. A large hour-glass marked out the hours, with dinner taken on site at midday, and work ending at six in the evening with the ringing of a bell that had been rescued from the rubble and set up on a frame.[17] A tavern still standing on the corner of Watling Street and Bow Lane, Ye Olde Watling, is said to have been built on Wren's orders as a place where his workmen might have victuals and possibly to provide some accommodation. The long and important association that the architect had with the area is also demonstrated by the theory that he was respon-sible in 1717 for the founding of the first Grand Lodge of Freemasonry in England, at the Goose and Gridiron tavern in St Paul's Churchyard (see p. 181).

As the old foundations of the cathedral were dug up, so archaeological remains came to light. This was a time of growing consciousness of the nation's early history. Wren was a Fellow of the Royal Society, and so familiar with the reports presented by John Aubrey and Walter Charleton about their research of the prehistoric site at Avebury in Wiltshire. So, when a succession of nine wells in a row came to light, beneath the Gothic choir of the old cathedral, Wren speculated that a very early Roman Christian church might have occu-pied the site. He was also keen to discover whether there was any evidence to support the theories of the Tudor chroniclers: William Camden had thought it the site of a temple to Diana; John Stow that one dedicated to Jupiter might have been located here (see p. 8). Wren was helped in his archaeological inves-tigations by Edward Stillingfleet, a residentiary canon of St Paul's and Rector of St Andrew's Holborn, who was interested in the early history of the Church. When no oxheads, antlers or boar's heads, which would have supported Stow's Jupiter theory, were found, the two men rejected that theory. Instead, a figurine of Diana was found further south towards the Thames, between Blackfriars and the new deanery built for Sancroft by Wren.

Wren carefully noted the finds that were unearthed in the 10 years from 1675 to 1685 as the workmen worked on the site of the cathedral. He came to the conclusion that he was finding an area of buildings that were domestic rather than religious in nature:

> The most remarkable Roman urns, lamps, lacrymatories, and fragments of sacrificeing-vessels, etc were found deep in the ground towards the north-east corner of St Paul's Church, near Cheapside; these were generally well-wrought, and embossed with various figures and devices, of the colour of the modern Portugal ware, some brighter like coral, and of a hardness equal to China ware, and as well glazed.

One piece that particularly interested him was a basin fragment, showing Charon the ferryman of Hades, greeting a naked ghost.[18]

Some of the pieces unearthed in the north-east area in the 1670s were recorded by John Conyers, an apothecary living in Fleet Street. Although he was never a Fellow of the Royal Society, he attended many of the meetings as the guest of leading members, including Robert Hooke and Jonathan Goddard, the Professor of Physic at Gresham College. Conyers made the important observation of stratigraphy when noting the remains. A small number of coloured stones were found at the depth of 15 feet, but even lower was Roman pottery:

> which tells me this laying so low & the Roman pott 6 or 8 or 10 feet deeper that as tyme passed awaye I might see the epochs or beginning of things & in these various height of ground point & and show with my finger the Romans concernes lay deepest, than higher those of more recent or fresher concerne.

Conyers amassed a collection of antiquities excavated from sites as the City was rebuilt, which he put on public display. This collection was dispersed, but his memorandum book, containing his notes, along with drawings of Roman pots and glass beakers, and of a kiln, on the cathedral site, is now in the British Library.[19]

On 21 June 1675 the first stone of the new cathedral was laid. Wren and his master mason, Thomas Strong, began to set out the dimensions of the new cathedral on the ground. The appearance of an 'archaeological find' was taken as a good omen. In Wren's words:

a common labourer was ordered to bring a flat stone from the heaps of rubbish (such as should first come to hand) to be laid for a mark and direction to the masons; the stone, which was immediately brought down for the purpose, happened to be a piece of a grave stone, with nothing remaining of the inscription but this single word in large capitals, RESURGAM – I will arise.[20]

The Churchyard at this time has been memorably likened to a great ship.[21] Near the ruins of St Gregory's Church, a sawmill was established, turning out poles for scaffolding and planking. The scaffolding was built up high above the surrounding streets, lashed together like rigging with ropes and struts. Cranes operated from capstan houses raised the stones, with the larger blocks carried up by reinforced ropes between two masts braced by lintels of strong timber. The white Portland stone was worked by carvers before being put in place, or balanced precariously on planks strung between the scaffolding poles.

The workmen clocking in each morning became more varied in their skills: plumbers and carvers, bricklayers and painters. Some came from Wren's stable of the craftsmen employed in the different projects for rebuilding the City. Others were outsiders, attracted to London by the immense amount of available work and able to claim the same rights and privileges as the freemen of the City, thanks to the relaxing of regulations in the 1667 Rebuilding Act. Women's names begin to appear in the accounts: Sarah Freeman, Plumber; Widow Pearce, Painter; Anne Brooks, Smith.

Busy with all his many architectural commitments, Wren took time to visit the site three times each week. He would then repair to a coffee house, often in the company of Robert Hooke. The first coffee house in London had been established in St Michael's Alley just off Cornhill in 1652, sparking a tremendous fashion for coffee drinking with dozens of establishments being opened across the City and the West End. Wren and Hooke had a choice of two close by: the Chapter Coffee House in Paternoster Row, and Child's in Warwick Lane. The latter was right by the Royal College of Physicians, so that it became a second home for some of the Fellows of the Royal Society. Hooke's diaries from this period note meetings there where scientific theories were discussed, and fraught Royal Society politics aired.[22]

The building materials for the cathedral were of considerable value, for demand was exceeding supply throughout the City, especially of timber and lead. First, a wall was built of loose stones from the old cathedral to keep out intruders, with spikes and tenterhooks installed above the gateways. Watchkeepers were employed during the night hours, aided by mastiffs. A rather different threat was a letter found within the worksite warning of an insurrection by Catholics and promising a riot as destructive as the Great Fire. In 1678 the uneasy equilibrium of the country was thrown into turmoil by the revelation of the Popish Plot. Two unsavoury characters, Israel Tonge, a cleric specialising in the discovery of Jesuit conspiracies, and Titus Oates, a former Jesuit priest who made his living by swearing testimony to bring culprits to justice, claimed evidence of a Catholic conspiracy to murder the King and supplant him with his brother, James, Duke of York, who had a few years earlier converted to the Roman Church. Had the choice of the Churchyard as the place for a provocative letter been made as a reminder of earlier incidents, such as the posting of John Felton's bill on the doors of the cathedral in the reign of Elizabeth?

The following year, distracted by the political situation, Parliament failed to renew the Licensing Act, thus freeing restrictions on all printed material. This resulted in highly radical material of every persuasion being produced, especially in the printshops in the neighbourhood of St Paul's Churchyard. One author of extremely virulent anti-Catholic material was Stephen College, a skilled carpenter whose fine screen for the hall of the Stationers' Company can still be seen. The 'Protestant joiner' as he was known, not only wrote satires against James, Duke of York, but more seriously spoke threateningly against the King and advocated resistance. In 1681 he was tried for high treason and condemned to be hanged, drawn and quartered in Oxford, becoming one of the last Protestant martyrs of that city.

By the 1680s, leading artists were being employed upon features for the cathedral's interior. Some of the most distinguished came from Continental Europe. John Evelyn claimed that he discovered Grinling Gibbons, born of English parents in Holland, working in a cottage in Deptford. The exquisite quality of Gibbons's work, a wooden model of Tintoretto's Crucifixion, prompted Evelyn to introduce him to Charles II, and work on both wood and stone followed in royal palaces, the City churches, and for St Paul's the carving of the wooden choir stalls. While he was working on the carvings for the cathedral, Gibbons had lodgings in the newly rebuilt Belle Sauvage Inn. The design of the organ was the specific charge of a German, Bernard Schmidt, known also as Father Smith. He worked in Holland before arriving in London and becoming the King's organ maker.

The decision in 1685 by Louis XIV to revoke the Edict of Nantes, thus forbidding the exercise of the reformed religion, caused tumult among some of the finest craftsmen in his kingdom who were Protestants and a 'brain drain' followed. One of these Huguenot artist craftsmen was the ironsmith Jean Tijou. He enjoyed the patronage of William and Mary when he arrived in England and made some magnificent gates for their palace at Hampton Court. Wren commissioned him in 1691 to work on the cathedral, creating immense frames for the plain glass windows that enabled the interior to be flooded with light. Tijou's masterpiece for the cathedral was the screen gates on either side of the high altar.

In 1686 Wren had decided that the west portico of Inigo Jones would have to be demolished, as it was impossible to link it up satisfactorily with his new nave. The work proceeded slowly, so that even ten years later there was no roof on the nave, the west front was without a facade and there was a great hole over the crossing. During these years the public was naturally fascinated by what was gradually taking shape before their eyes. Wren, however, wanted to keep details of his new cathedral away from prying eyes, so wickerwork screens were erected. An example of these, surrounding the north transept, can be seen in an engraving made by Sutton Nicholls. In 1695, however, the scaffolding was struck from the choir, revealing this first instalment of the new St Paul's, and crowds flocked to see it.

Two years later, despite the unfinished state of the cathedral, a thanksgiving service was held in the choir on 5 December 1697 to celebrate the signing of the Treaty of Ryswick that ended the long war between France

11. Sutton Nicholls's engraving of 1695 showing Wren's new cathedral under construction, with the east end almost complete, but with screens to keep the curious away from the middle part of the building.

and England, with Louis XIV at last recognising William III as king. Crowds lined the streets as a formal procession led by the lord mayor and aldermen, marching companies of the City and grandees from Westminster made their way up to the newly completed west front. Only the King himself was absent: William, now widowed, was notoriously shy of such occasions, and remained in his palace at Hampton Court. When the procession arrived at the west end, the organist of St Paul's, John Blow, played an anthem specially composed for the occasion. John Evelyn was among the congregation for the morning service, noting in his diary how it 'was the first Sonday, St Paules had had any service in (it) since it was consumed at the Conflagration of the Citty, 1666: which I myself saw, and now (w)as likewise myself there'.

Henry Compton, Bishop of London, preached from the new pulpit that Gibbons had carved. His sermon, appropriate for the occasion, was based on Psalm 122, 'I was glad when they said unto me: Let us go into the house of the Lord'. He intended that the cathedral should unite the nation, reviving the concept of anniversary services and sermons that had been such a feature of Elizabethan and early Stuart times. But now these were to take place inside the cathedral, rather than at the pulpit of Paul's Cross in the Churchyard. One such anniversary was the double deliverance on 5 November, the discovery of the Gunpowder Plot in 1605 and the arrival, thanks to the Protestant wind, of William of Orange to rid the nation of its Catholic King, James II, in 1688.

John Evelyn wanted also to attend the afternoon service, but 'the presse of people was so greate that I durst not venture'.[23] Instead, he listened to a sermon in St Martin Ludgate, although he did mingle with the crowds in the Churchyard. He was delighted to learn from some of Wren's workmen that they had been making use of his translation of Fréart's *Parallèle de L'Architecture Antique et de la Moderne*. So impressed was he by the new St Paul's that he resolved to write a preface to a new edition of the book. In his characteristically flowery style, he paid tribute to Wren, declaring:

> the great Esteem I have ever had of Your Virtues and Accomplishments, not only in the Art of Building, but thro' all the learned Cycle of the most Usefull Knowledge and Abstruser Sciences, as well as of the most Polite and Shining. . .; if the whole Art of Building were lost, it might be Recover'd and found again in St Paul's, the Historical Pillar.

He also declared rather more succinctly in a letter to Wren that 'the Phoenix is Risen'.[24]

But in 1697 the cathedral was still lacking its crowning feature. Wren had from the very beginning intended that the new St Paul's should have a dome at the crossing. Indeed, back in 1666, with John Evelyn's support, he had argued for a dome for Old St Paul's. It was going to be this part of the cathedral that departed radically from the Warrant Design of 1675. Instead of the rather modest dome topped by a tall spire, Wren was planning a much more monumental structure to rise in magnificence over London's skyline. However, such a structure would be too lofty when seen from the inside. His solution was to build a brick cone in support of the lantern that was to be surmounted by a ball and cross. Over this cone he built the outer dome, 60 feet taller.

Wren was a young man in his early thirties when he began to work on St Paul's. It was literally a life's work, taking many decades, but this was a rapid timespan compared to other cathedrals, and the first to be the work of one architect. On 26 October 1708, just after his 76th birthday, Wren watched as his son, also called Christopher, was hauled up to the dome along with Edward Strong, the son of Wren's first master mason, Thomas. The two men were to place the copper cross and ball on the lantern. In the words of James Wright, a poet who penned many verses on the progress of the building of the cathedral:

The Cupola, that mighty Orb of stone,
Piercing the clouds in figure of a crown,
A diadem that crowns not Paul's alone
But the whole Isle, placed on her head-town.[25]

This was a moment of triumph, but times were changing. Serious differences developed between the ageing architect and the commission, and in particular with the new Dean who was appointed in 1707. Henry Godolphin was determined to have his say in the final touches to the cathedral and the Churchyard, and considered Wren to be too possessive, and his workmen not sufficiently deferential. He was encouraged in this stance by one of his residentiary canons, Francis Hare, who had been Chaplain-General of Marlborough's army. Both men had powerful Whig political connections, for Queen Anne's leading minister, Francis Godolphin, was the Dean's cousin, while Wren's long-term supporters, Archbishop Sancroft and Bishop Compton, were growing increasingly infirm. One dispute concerned the decoration of the interior of the dome. Wren wanted to use mosaics, but Dean Godolphin was determined on paintings, choosing James Thornhill to create a series of scenes of the life of St Paul.

A second dispute developed over the style of the Churchyard. Wren's original vision had been to create a cloistered piazza with terraced houses, five storeys in height, decorated by a giant order of Corinthian pilasters, and shops on the ground floor beneath arcades. In the centre of the forecourt he wanted to build a small, circular chapter house surmounted by a dome. This grand scheme was rendered impossible because of the swift rebuilding after the Fire, and the existing blocks of houses were there to stay. In place of the chapter house a statue group by the sculptor Francis Bird was installed, featuring Queen Anne and figures representing her realm (see p. 226).

To the south of the cathedral the road was a main thoroughfare, so to protect the building from the continual and heavy flow of traffic it was agreed that it should be fenced off. Wren's plan was to have wrought iron railings made by the master smith Thomas Robinson, but the Dean insisted on cast iron to be installed by his nominee, Richard Jones. The latter would seem to have been a somewhat shady character, convicted for manslaughter during an anti-Catholic demonstration. Wren also did not consider that his work was up to standard, but in this he may have been wrong. The railings, made at great expense at Lamberhurst in Kent and installed in 1714, are still standing today, one of the earliest examples of cast iron in Britain.[26]

This unedifying quarrel came at the end of half a century of exciting developments in the creation of a new cathedral:

> it was thought strange by most People, that after Sr Chr had completed so noble a Fabrick with universal Applause, the Direction of so small a Circumstance as a Fence to encompass it, should be peremptorily and obstinately denied him.[27]

This pertinent observation was made during a pamphlet war which began with a provocative attack in 1712 on Wren's workmen by Francis Hare entitled *Frauds and Abuses at St Paul's*. The ensuing claims and counterclaims were to keep the local printshops busy.

The Committee became ever more obstructive, refusing to pay Wren the balance of money due to him, arguing that the cathedral was not finished. In 1711 Wren had successfully resorted to Parliament: this was a case of good timing, for the Whigs had suddenly fallen from power and the incoming Tory government declared that St Paul's was indeed complete. Yet, as accusations and counter-accusations were made, the new iron fence remained incomplete and unpainted, while the booksellers and their customers complained that the footway on the north side of the Churchyard was still unpaved. But in 1713 a chapter house was built just to the north of the cathedral, one of the few buildings of the era that has survived. Seven windows wide, of red brick with stone dressings, the facade is articulated by a slightly projecting central bay and two pedimented doorways at either end.

With the succession of George I to the throne and the return of the Whigs to power, Wren probably felt he was fighting a losing battle, rarely attending meetings of the commission. When court intrigue deprived him of his office as Surveyor-General to the King, he retreated to his house on the green at Hampton Court, occasionally visiting his cathedral incognito. This was indeed a sad conclusion to such an exceptional career. However, when he died in February 1723 his body was brought to St Paul's for burial in the crypt. His son Christopher composed an epitaph in Latin that poignantly summed up his achievement. In translation it reads: 'Below is laid the builder of this Church and City, Christopher Wren, who lived above ninety years, not for himself but for the public good. Reader, if you seek a monument, look about you.'

The reader might look around the interior of the great cathedral, but in addition, from all parts of London he or she could take in the skyline that over the decades Wren had created with his team. The long shadow cast by the spire of the medieval cathedral was now cast by the dome with its distinctive gold cross and ball. A century later, in *Bleak House*, Charles Dickens evoked an image familiar to all Londoners, and the polluted atmosphere that so often accompanied it. Jo, the tragic crossing sweeper, looks up at 'the great Cross on the summit of St Paul's Cathedral, glittering above a red and violet-tinted cloud of smoke . . . the crowning confusion of the great, confused city'.[28]

CHAPTER 8

RESURGAM

In 1667, Samuel Pepys recorded in his diary the death of one of his favourite booksellers, Joshua Kirton, adding, 'I believe, of grief for his losses by the fire'. In happier times, he had noted visiting Kirton's shop at the Sign of the King's Arms by Paul's Cross in the easternmost part of the Churchyard. In 1663, he wrote, 'I did here sit two or three hours, calling for twenty books to lay this money [£2 to £3] out upon; and found myself at a great loss where to choose'. Kirton had brought to him all kinds of titles: literature such as works by Chaucer and Shakespeare; nonfiction, such as William Dugdale's history of St Paul's Cathedral, Stow's chronicles of London and Conrad Gesner's study of natural history; and Samuel Butler's satirical *Hudibras*, which Pepys described as 'in greatest Fashion for drollery, though I Cannot confess, see enough where the wit lies'.[1]

The range of titles listed reflects how the London book trade had moved on from its slow beginnings in the sixteenth century, and the political upheavals of the mid-seventeenth century did not interrupt this. One of the major publishing ventures of the 1650s was the production of the Polyglot Bible. Unlike the King James Bible, this was not intended for use in parish churches, but rather for scholars to be able to make a comparative study of the Scriptures. There had been earlier polyglots, the first issued in Alcalá de Henares in Spain in the early sixteenth century, followed by a version printed by Christopher Plantin in Antwerp and another in Paris in 1645. These were all produced at the behest of Catholic monarchs, but the London Polyglot was organised by a Protestant academic, Brian Walton, who, having been ejected from Oxford for his royalist views, joined members of his family in the capital.

Post Tenebras Splendet

Iohn Allen *at the Rising Sunne neare S.t Pauls*

12. A signboard for the bookseller John Allen 'at the Rising Sunne neare St Pauls', 1656. The etching, attributed to Wenceslaus Hollar, includes the medieval cathedral, shorn of its spire.

Walton's plan was magnificently ambitious, to reproduce the Old and New Testaments, along with the Apocrypha, in nine ancient languages: Greek, Hebrew, Arabic, Persian, Syriac, Chaldee, Ethiopic and Samaritan – each with their own Latin translations. A team of distinguished linguists and leading biblical scholars was recruited from across the country, some of them having lost their academic posts like Walton. The project not only required this exceptional scholarly input, but also technical skill. Type for Latin, Greek and Hebrew was already available, but for the other six languages, faces had to be specially cut by craftsmen. Production of the six large folios began in 1653, taking three years to complete using two presses. The printshop of Thomas Roycroft was located in Bartholomew Close, just off Little Britain, an area to the north of St Paul's Churchyard with an established community involved in the manufacture and selling of books. The first run of copies carried the portrait of Walton as the organiser of the huge enterprise, along with a preface thanking the Lord Protector, Oliver Cromwell, for his support, probably through the good offices of his Latin Secretary, John Milton. With a second run, it was Charles II who was hailed as benefactor, and Brian Walton became Bishop of Chester.

A second ambitious publishing project dating from the 1650s was the history of St Paul's Cathedral that Pepys was offered by his bookseller. Alarmed at the threat to England's cathedrals posed by the Commonwealth government, the Herald and antiquary Sir William Dugdale resolved to produce a definitive history of St Paul's. A chance meeting between Dugdale and the chairman of the Parliamentary Committee responsible for former cathedral lands enabled him to borrow a considerable number of deeds and other documents connected with St Paul's. Not only was he able to draw on this rich historical resource, but also to commission the Bohemian artist Wenceslaus Hollar to produce the illustrations, some based on drawings by William Sedgwick. These depicted both the exterior and interior, along with what Dugdale considered the most important tombs. Romanesque, Gothic and the classical additions made in the 1630s by Inigo Jones are all to be seen in these fine illustrations. Dugdale had instituted a subscription system for earlier projects, so it is probable that he did the same for this work, which was printed in 1658 by Thomas Warren, a business partner of Joshua Kirton. Not only was it an expensive and brave venture, but it turned out also to be an extremely fortuitous one, for within eight years the medieval cathedral of St Paul's was destroyed by the Great Fire, leaving Dugdale's book as an invaluable record.

At the other end of the scale at this time came an increase in publications disseminating current news. Eagerness to keep up with the political turmoil taking place in Europe during the Thirty Years War had resulted in corantos and newsbooks being produced in the Churchyard (see p. 118). At first these came in the form of half sheets, but in time they grew into quarto publications. Following England's withdrawal from European conflicts and the outbreak of the Civil War, there was a concentration on domestic affairs: the first, *The heads of several proceedings in this present Parliament*, was published on 29 November 1641. News of the state was considered the property of the state, enforced by the Star Chamber, who in 1637 attempted to tighten control on the right to print, but with government in retreat, this control began to evaporate. The production values of these publications, costing a penny or a halfpenny, were minimal, for the currency of the news was the vital factor. The titles often used the terms 'true', 'faithful' and 'perfect'. During the Civil War, some were produced by Royalists, such as *Mercurius Aulicus*, printed in Oxford, others by Parliamentarians, such as *Mercurius Britannicus*, printed in London. The proliferation in the production of periodicals at this period is phenomenal: in 1649, the year of Charles I's execution, 54 different newsbooks were published.

Charles II attempted to regain control at the Restoration: in 1662 an 'Act for preventing the frequent abuses in printing seditious, treasonable and unlicensed books and pamphlets, and for regulating of printing and printing presses' was promulgated. The following year Sir Roger L'Estrange, who has been memorably described as 'an unreconstructed Cavalier', assumed the role of the Crown's enforcer.[2] His office was located above the shop of his bookseller, Henry Brome, first in Ivy Lane, then Little Britain, and finally at the Sign of the Gun, in Ludgate Street, just to the west of the Churchyard.

The first official newsbooks emanating from L'Estrange's authoritarian pen were the *Intelligencer*, which appeared on Mondays, and the *News* on Thursdays, both priced at half a penny. The entry in Pepys's diary for 4 September 1663 records 'by water to White-hall and Westminster-hall, and there bought the first newsbooks of Lestrange's writing, he beginning this week; and makes methink but a simple beginning'. This suggests that Pepys was less than impressed, for when the *Oxford Gazette* in half-sheet format was introduced two years later, he compared it favourably with L'Estrange's work: 'This day the first of the *Oxford Gazettes* came out, which is very pretty, full of news, and no folly in it – wrote by Williamson'.[3] Joseph Williamson was secretary to one of the King's chief ministers, Lord Arlington, and probably provided the material that was then written up by Henry Muddiman. In time, 'Oxford' was replaced by 'London' in its title.

Early runs of newspapers and newsbooks were collected by George Thomason, along with printed pamphlets and tracts. Thomason was a bookseller whose business was based first at the Rose and from 1643 at the Rose and Crown, both in St Paul's Churchyard. His speciality as a bookseller was imported books from Europe, regularly attending the Frankfurt Book Fair. But from 1641 he built up a systematic collection of political and religious tracts, 'acquiring either by purchase or occasionally by presentation, every book, pamphlet and newspaper issued in London, and as many as he could obtain from the provinces or abroad'.[4] The resulting collection of around 22,000 items is now in the British Library. It is remarkable not only for its size, but also for the invaluable note made by Thomason of dates of publication on the title pages. Such publications are ephemeral by nature, so their survival is exceptional, on a par with the collection of ballads and chapbooks built up by Samuel Pepys in the 1680s and now in his library at Magdalene College, Cambridge.

Periodicals of a more specialised nature began to be published at the Restoration. Arguably the most distinguished of these was the *Philosophical Transactions* issued by the Royal Society. Originating as a series of informal meetings in London and Oxford in the 1640s, the Society was given its charter by Charles II in 1662 and amplified its name to the Royal Society of London for the Promotion of Natural Knowledge the following year. Its chosen motto was *Nullius in Verba*, 'Take nobody's word for it', from the Epistles of Horace, reflecting the Society's primary motive of knowledge through practical experimentation. Among the founding fellows were Christopher Wren and John Evelyn. Regular meetings and practical demonstrations were held at Gresham College in Bishopsgate, often carried out by the Curator of Experiments, Robert Hooke.

Recognising the importance of disseminating the results of experiments in a credible manner, the fellows also devoted time to the receipt and reading of written papers. Many of these were published in journal form in *Philosophical Transactions*, launched by the Society's Secretary Henry Oldenburg in 1665, and still being published today. Such was the distinction of the fellows that their publishers, the Churchyard booksellers John Martin and James Allestree, were able to sell their works in the English language in Europe and in North America – the Latin trade in reverse. The Royal Society also was permitted by the terms of the royal charter to license books, a way of freeing the work of fellows from potential censorship by the Church. The first of these, published in 1664, was *Sylva, or a Discourse of Forest-trees and the Propagation of Timber* by John Evelyn. His book arose from a report written and read to the Society two years earlier, in response to questions posed by the principal officers and commissioners of the navy concerned about the shortage of timber for His Majesty's ships.

Sylva became a great publishing success, for it moved beyond the confines of naval sources of timber to aesthetic considerations of the cultivation of

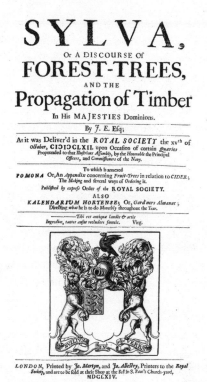

SYLVA,

Or A DISCOURSE Of

FOREST-TREES,

AND THE

Propagation of Timber

In His MAJESTIES Dominions.

By J. E. Esq;

As it was Deliver'd in the ROYAL SOCIETY the xv^th of *October*, CIↃIↃCLXII. upon Occasion of certain *Queries* Propounded to that *Illustrious Assembly*, by the *Honorable* the Principal *Officers*, and *Commissioners* of the Navy.

To which is annexed

POMONA Or, An *Appendix* concerning *Fruit-Trees* in relation to CIDER; The *Making* and several ways of *Ordering* it.

Published by express Order of the ROYAL SOCIETY.

ALSO

KALENDARIUM HORTENSE; Or, *Gardners Almanac* ; Directing what he is to do Monethly throughout the Year.

——— *Tibi res antiquæ laudis & artis* *Ingredior, tantos ausus recludere fonteis.* Virg.

LONDON, Printed by *Jo. Martyn*, and *Ja. Allestry*, Printers to the *Royal Society*, and are to be sold at their Shop at the *Bell* in S. *Paul's Church-yard*, MDCLXIV.

13. The title page of John Evelyn's *Sylva*. The author designed the layout of the page, including the Royal Society's coat of arms and motto.

trees, becoming the horticultural must-have for the library of any propertied gentleman. The following year another ground breaking book was published by Allestree and Martin with the Royal Society imprimatur: Robert Hooke's *Micrographia*. Its subtitle explained how it 'provided physiological descriptions of minute bodies made by magnifying glasses with observations and inquiries thereupon'. Beautiful engravings from drawings by Hooke accompanied the text, so that readers could for the first time see details of tiny creatures such as fleas, gnats and bugs, along with the snowflake, the sting of the nettle and mould on blue cheese that resembled the ranunculus flower.

Samuel Pepys, who was elected a Fellow of the Royal Society in the year of Hooke's publication, 1665, noted in his diary going to Joshua Kirton's shop in the Churchyard, and seeing the new book, finding it 'so pretty that I presently bespoke it'. He had to wait three weeks while it was bound, but when he collected it, declared it 'a most excellent piece of which I am very proud'. He was so excited by his acquisition that he sat up reading it until two in the morning. Not only did he read about potential images, but with the help of instrument-maker friends rigged up his own microscope and wrote triumphantly how 'most excellently things appeared indeed beyond imagination'.[5]

Only a few weeks after Pepys wrote this last entry, the innovative growth in publishing was dramatically checked by the destruction of the Great Fire. As noted in the previous chapter, the booksellers had put their stocks of books into the crypt of St Paul's Cathedral and Christchurch Newgate Street in the misplaced confidence that the stone of the buildings would protect them from the flames. Pepys reckoned that £150,000 worth of booksellers' stock had gone up in flames, while his fellow diarist, John Evelyn, put the figure even higher, at £200,000. Whatever the figure, it was a devastating blow, and it is thought that booksellers suffered more than any of the other City trades, losing not only their stock but also their intellectual property.

First, the booksellers, printers and engravers of the Churchyard and Paternoster Row had to find temporary quarters elsewhere. Two booksellers immediately wrote to the great Antwerp publisher, Balthasar Moretus, great-grandson of Christopher Plantin, describing to him the 'terrible desolation' of London,

> among others, the Church of St Paul's and with it almost all the book-shops. Which is why we, John Crooke and Thomas Dicas, having set up our shop in the area called Little Britain, request the books listed here for our Company, that is to say the two of us. For which we promise just and good payment in the normal time. Asking you to put everything at your best price and at the best discount you can . . . Awaiting the honour of your response by the first post to know if we could expect these or not, since winter is coming on.[6]

In the event, the Fire marked the end of the long trading relationship between the London book trade and the Officina Plantiniana (pp. 50–1), for Moretus stipulated payment in advance and this proved too much capital outlay for the two traders.

However, other booksellers were able to move their businesses northwards to Little Britain and Duck Lane, which had escaped the flames of the Great Fire. This area became particularly well known for the sale of second-hand books. One Duck Lane bookseller who enjoyed the custom of Pepys, a collector of early printed books, was William Shrewsbury. He was drawn not only to the fine books on sale but also to Shrewsbury's handsome wife. In April 1668 he noted: 'So to . . . Duck-lane and there kissed the bookseller's wife and bought *Legend* – 14s'. The book was *The Golden Legend*, the most popular collection of lives of saints of the late Middle Ages, compiled by Jacques de Voragine, a thirteenth-century Dominican. This version was probably published in English by Wynkyn de Worde in 1527. After several visits to the shop, Pepys's final reference to both books and Mrs Shrewsbury comes in the autumn of 1668 when, finding her pregnant, he adopted the curious language that denoted his sexual exploits, and ungallantly pointed out that 'ella is so big-bellied that ella is not worth seeing'.[7]

Inventories show that these were not large premises: a shop and back room on the ground floor and living rooms above. The American author Washington Irving lived in Little Britain in the early nineteenth century and wrote a pen portrait in his sketches of English life. 'Over this little territory . . . the great dome of St Paul's swelling above the intervening houses of Paternoster Row, Amen Corner, and Ave Maria Lane, looks down with an air of motherly protection.' He described how some of the half-timbered pre-Fire houses were 'magnificently enriched with old oaken carvings of hideous faces, unknown birds, beasts and fishes; and fruit and flowers which it would perplex a naturalist to classify'.[8]

Picturesque these houses may have been to more modern eyes, but the Churchyard booksellers were no doubt relieved to get back to their new premises of brick and stone. They did so remarkably quickly. As noted in the previous chapter, James Allestree, for example, had moved back from Duck Lane to the Churchyard by the time of his death in December 1670. He had been comparatively lucky, for he was able to rebuild his business through the lucrative publishing of the sermons of his cousin, Richard Allestree, Dean of Christ Church College, Oxford. He was also, with John Martin, the Royal Society's official printer and publisher. The inventory taken at the time of Allestree's death reflects a rather commodious dwelling, with a ground floor dedicated to business, and living quarters above that were richly furnished with hangings of gilt leather. A counting house was located at the back of the shop which was furnished with presses and shelves. A double arch with two doors in a decorative partition gave Allestree an inner sanctum where he could entertain prospective authors, prestigious customers and members of the Royal Society.

Not everybody returned to the Churchyard. Allestree's partner, John Martin, for example, moved westwards to Temple Bar on Fleet Street. When Pepys visited his shop in January 1668, Martin described to him in some detail how the fire had spread across the Churchyard, and that the books were burnt that had been stored in the crypt of the cathedral apart from one warehouse. He also explained that

> most of the booksellers do design to fall a-building again the next year; but he says that the Bishop of London doth use them most basely, worse than any other landlords, and says he will be paid to this day the rent, or else he will not come to treat with them for the time to come.[9]

The Bishop, Humphrey Henchman, was said to have been equally harsh with the booksellers and the mercers of Paternoster Row.

Not only did the booksellers have to cope with episcopal intransigence, but it has to be remembered that those who did rebuild their businesses in the area immediately around the cathedral were going to be trading in the midst of a building site. Nonetheless they did so, living up to the declaration '*Resurgam*' (I shall rise again) that was to be incorporated in the pediment of the south door of Wren's new cathedral along with a representation of the phoenix.

The priority of getting back to business is shown by the response of the Stationers' Company. Even before they rebuilt their hall on Ave Maria Lane, a warehouse was erected within the courtyard in order to store their English stock. This was a co-operative joint holding scheme that had been established in 1603, involving books such as psalters, almanacs, school primers and legal texts. The company held the sole licence for producing these books, which in practice meant enjoying a monopoly, although masked by the creation of the joint-stock scheme. The more powerful the status of members within the Company, the more shares they were able to hold of these valuable titles.[10] Although there is a possibility that some of the stock escaped destruction because it had been kept in the house of the Company's treasurer George Sawbridge in Clerkenwell, most of it perished.

George Tokefield, the clerk of the Stationers' Company, realising that the flames were approaching St Paul's Churchyard, had bundled the Company's registers and court books into a barrow and wheeled them to his residence in Gray's Inn. Thus, when the Stationers were preparing themselves for their renaissance, a note was duly made in a ledger:

> After the sadd and never to be forgotten Judgment of the Ffire which upon the 2nd, 3rd 4th and 5th days of September 1666 destroyed the greatest part of this City, and in the comon Calamity of Hall, Warehouses and Stock of Bookes and other goodes therein.

This was followed by a list of books printed 'for beginning a Stock again', which begins with psalters, followed by primers and almanacs. The print runs are considerable, 5,000 psalters and 12,000 primers. However, these are modest in comparison with the total number of almanacs, annual publications that listed a set of events forthcoming in the year ahead, such as weather forecasts and the planting dates for farmers. These were compiled by different editors, so that the list includes the popular Poor Robin, 20,000, Andrew's (*News from the Stars*), 10,000, Wings, 40,000, and Lilly's (*Merlini Anglici*), 14,500. In total, the order is for a quarter of a million copies, showing just how lucrative the monopoly of printing almanacs was for the Stationers.

A second list follows, of books supplied by the university press at Cambridge. The relationship between the universities and the Company had been fraught, with the Stationers fighting to maintain their valuable monopolies. While Oxford University Press accepted a monetary annual 'covenant of forebearance' not to produce specific categories, Cambridge was more aggressive, securing concessions that included certain sizes of bibles, versions of the psalms and the venerable Latin grammar of William Lyly. Thus the university printer was now able to supply the Stationers with publications such as Aesop's *Fables*, the works of Ovid, adages for children, and Edmund Coote's primer, *The English Schoolmaster*.[11] The Company's records show that these were supplied to the treasurer George Sawbridge, possibly as a way again of avoiding charges of monopoly. The considerable stock was soon accommodated at Stationers' Hall. The warehouse, which still stands in the garden, looks like a terrace of cottages, next to the more formal buildings of the Hall. It now houses the Company's archives in the Tokefield Centre, to commemorate the quick thinking of the clerk.

One way that booksellers could finance expensive new projects was by subscription, as had been employed by both William Dugdale and Brian Walton. In the case of the Polyglot Bible, subscribers were invited to make gifts, or to advance money that would be repaid by copies at £10 per set. A list of the subscribers is printed in the front of the bible. Top of the list comes James I's grandson, Karl Ludwig, Elector Palatine and leader of the European Protestants. This is significant, for although both sides of the English Civil War conflict are represented in the roll call of subscribers, they are Protestants rather than Catholics. Those who did subscribe found their investment paid off handsomely, for Pepys noted in his diary that many sets had perished in the printer's warehouse in the Great Fire, and it was reckoned that surviving copies would now be worth £40.

Subscription publishing was to be used increasingly after the Restoration, especially for projects requiring illustrations. One bookseller who specialised in high quality illustrated works was John Ogilby, a particularly colourful figure in the London book world. He was a man of many parts – dancing master, theatre owner, poet, translator, publisher. After the Great Fire, he became one of the assistant surveyors working with Christopher Wren and Robert Hooke and produced a post-Fire map of the City through securing subscriptions. He repeated this means when he conceived the idea of a series of atlases covering the world. These were compilations of accounts of continents such as Africa and America, and countries such as Japan and China, which appeared at regular intervals in the early 1670s, and only ceased with his death in 1676.

Ogilby also used lotteries for funding. The lottery centre of London was located in St Paul's Churchyard, reflecting the role of the cathedral in the civic life of the capital. The practice of holding lotteries began when Elizabeth I's chief minister, William Cecil, needed to find money for the repair of England's harbours. He got the idea from the Low Countries, where the mercantile cities had raised funds for military and municipal projects. Having overcome the Queen's initial reluctance, a royal proclamation was published in 1567, announcing 'a very rich lotterie generall without any blanckes'. Posters advertising ticket prices and trumpeting the prizes were put up on walls and doors around the City. One has survived, showing the royal arms and a panorama of 'Civitas Londinium' dominated by St Paul's Cathedral topped by its soaring spire, although this had been destroyed a few years earlier, and alluring images of plate and piles of coins. This first lottery was drawn two years later in a temporary timber and board house near the west door of the cathedral, but did not prove a success, with low ticket sales. However, the idea was revived in 1585, again in a temporary building in the Churchyard, and this proved sufficiently encouraging for the Virginia Company to decide to overcome their financial problems by holding a lottery in 1612. This time a more permanent house was built, and the prizes, including 'fair plate' were displayed there. According to John Aubrey in his *Brief Lives*, John Ogilby rescued his father from debtor's prison by participating in the lottery. Although just 12 years old at the time, he scraped enough money together to buy some of the sixpenny tickets, one of which was a winner, and his father was duly released.

Maybe that was why Ogilby took lotteries up with such enthusiasm in the 1660s. In his diary for 19 February 1666, six months before the Great Fire, Pepys records attending a book lottery where he acquired two of Ogilby's books. One was a translation of Aesop's *Fables*, with illustrations by David Loggan. The second was Ogilby's own account of the coronation of Charles II, with engravings by Wenceslaus Hollar. The books were expensive, so that tickets cost a considerable 40 shillings each, and there was only one blank for each. By this means Ogilby was able to offer 500 copies of Aesop and 225 of the coronation. Pepys avoided both blanks, and triumphantly returned home with the books in their white vellum bindings.

The lottery for Ogilby's volume on Asia was noted by Robert Hooke in his diary for 1673. He regularly included entries on his book acquisitions, although in very terse terms, which do not give us the rich detail of Pepys's entries. In this case he just notes, 'Ogylby's lottery began'.[12] These lotteries were advertised in newspapers. One such held in 1668 was announced in the *London Gazette*:

> Mr Ogilby's lottery of books opens on Monday, the 25th instant, at the Old Theatre between Lincoln's Inn Fields and Vere Street, where all persons concerned may repair on Monday, May 18, and see the volumes, and put in their money.

Newspaper advertisements were also used in another area of marketing for books, the conduct of auctions. The first identified use in England of an auction specifically for books came in 1676 when the London bookseller William Cooper sold the library of Dr Lazarus Seaman, former Master of Peterhouse, Cambridge. The sale proved highly successful, as Cooper noted in the catalogue of his next sale, 'to the great content and satisfaction to the Gentlemen who were buyers'.[13] The sale was conducted by outcry, going to the highest bidder, a method imported from the Netherlands that was to provide the pattern for future sales. So, too, was Cooper's placing of advertisements in the *London Gazette* and his production of a catalogue.

Where William Cooper led, others swiftly followed, provoking the Churchyard bookseller Robert Clavell to complain that they were misleading people who could get the books cheaper in shops, and that this was a way of clearing out rubbish and inferior editions. Clavell, as shall be seen, was no slouch at protecting his own interests, and his protests went unheeded. The auctions often involved the libraries of university scholars, who did not have families to whom they could bequeath their books, and whose colleges already had similar collections. These sales took place in coffee houses, especially in the neighbourhood of the Churchyard. In some cases the establishment became better known for its auctions than its coffee. For example, Nathaniel Rolls originally set out to advertise his coffee house in Petty Canons Lane by the north door of St Paul's Cathedral, but by the mid-1690s he was describing it as an auction house.

Clearly, buying books at auction had become a common practice. Robert Hooke, for example, listed no fewer than 57 auctions and catalogues between

August 1686 and the same month in 1689, although he apparently went to even more than this tally. One of his favourite booksellers was Robert Littlebury, whose shop was in Little Britain. He was a major importer of second-hand books, and Hooke went to him particularly for scientific works. Samuel Pepys also bought from Littlebury's auctions. He had abandoned his wonderfully informative first diary in 1669, but some of his letters show his book-buying thereafter. Suffering from increasingly poor health, he made use of agents, including the very knowledgeable John Bagford. A letter from 1697 records Pepys's request to him to acquire a Latin work at one of Littlebury's auctions:

> I commission you to secure it for me upon the easiest terms you can: letting me know, in the meantime, by a line or two, as soon as you may, whether I may expect to be supplied herewith from thence or no, that I may be at liberty to look out for it elsewhere.[14]

One of the major book auctions of the late seventeenth century took place in May 1690, marking the dispersal of the library of John Maitland, Duke of Lauderdale. He had been a leading minister of Charles II's government, the 'L' of his Cabal, and his library was one of the finest in London. The advertisement inserted in the *London Gazette* ran:

> The late Duke of Lauderdale's French, Italian and Spanish Books, which consist chiefly in History, Antiquity, Architecture, Geography, &c, being very curiously bound, will be sold by Auction on Wednesday the 14th instant, at Sam's Coffee-house in Ave-Mary-lane. Catalogues are given at Mr Partridge's near Charing-Cross, Mr Hensman's in Westminster-hall, Mr. Bateman's in Holborn, Mr Swalle's in St-Paul's Churchyard, Mr Eddowes under the Royal Exchange, Booksellers, and also at Mr. Hall's, Printer at the theatre in Oxford, and at Mr Dawson's Bookseller in Cambridge.[15]

The listing of booksellers reflects the geography of the book trade at this time: St Paul's Churchyard, other shops in the City and West End, along with the two universities.

This was a grand auction, but they could be much more informal affairs. One of the leading practitioners of the art was Edward Millington. He not only conducted auctions at his bookshop in Little Britain, but also went out to fairs, including the annual one held on Stourbridge Common, just outside Cambridge. The 'London Spy', Ned Ward, cleverly parodied Millington's style, so that his voice echoes across the centuries. He opens with a description of one of his second-hand books:

Here's an Old Author for you, Gentlemen, you may Judge by his Antiquity by the Fashion of his Leather-jacket; herein is contain'd for the Benefit of you Scholars, the Knowledge of every thing Written by that Famous Author, who thro' his Profound Wisdom, very luckily discover'd that he knew nothing. For your Encouragement, Gentlemen, I'll put him up at Two Shillings, advance three Pence; Two Shillings once: What, no Body Bid?

Millington then brings down his gavel, perhaps as the result of a gesture by an unsuspecting member of the audience.

Knock, and now you've bought him, Sir, I must tell you you'll find Learning enough within him to puzzle both Universities. And thus much, I promise you further, Sir, when you have Read him Seven Year, if you don't like him, bring him to me again, in Little Brittain, and I'll help you to a Man shall give you a Shilling for him to cover Band-Boxes.[16]

So famous was Edward Millington that an elegy was composed in his memory in 1703:

Mourn, mourn, you Booksellers, for cruel Death
Has robb'd the famous *Auctioneer* of Breath:
He's gone, he's gone! ah! the great Loss deplore,
Great *Millington*, alas! he is no more:
No more will he now at your Service stand
Behind the Desk, with Mallet in his Hand.
No more the Value of your Books set forth,

And sell 'em by his Art for twice their Worth.
Methinks I see him still with smiling Look
Amidst the Crowd, and in his Hand a Book,
Then in a fine facetious pleasing Way,
The Author's Genius and his Wit display . . .[17]

Another form of auction was employed by the leading booksellers in order to preserve their control over the market, and in particular the distribution of titles in popular genres. This elite group was known as 'congers', possibly derived from the conger eel that swallows up smaller fry. They met regularly in the 1690s at the Chapter Coffee House in Paternoster Row, a favourite haunt of the book trade. Here they held private auctions at which books were sold wholesale. Another form of private auction was the trade sale in copyrights, which at this time were invariably held by the publisher rather than the author.

The development of book auctions led to the production of special catalogues for each sale, but in addition to these, from 1668 booksellers began to produce catalogues of their published and forthcoming titles. These came to be known as 'term catalogues' because they were issued to coincide with the legal terms of the year, Michaelmas, Hilary and Trinity. One of the first producers of term catalogues was Robert Clavell who traded at the Sign of the Peacock in Paul's Churchyard. He also ingeniously found another way of exploiting the provincial book market by sending out title pages of books that were about to be published: not only his own, but at a fee for other London booksellers. Clavell had been a clerk serving in the Post Office under Lord Arlington after the Great Fire. In this capacity he was able to collect from local postmasters all over the country the names and addresses of provincial booksellers, and thereby furnish them with the title pages. He justified sending these free of charge on the grounds that they would ultimately increase the revenue of the Post Office.

Unsurprisingly this practice was challenged. A rival bookseller, John Starkey, pointed out that 'Country Booksellers usually write by their Carryers, and post masters do not much concern themselves with Bookes'. Starkey published a newspaper, *Mercurius Librarius*, at Michaelmas 1668, priced at sixpence per copy, in which he included advertisements from booksellers, but did not charge them. Clavell recognised the threat, for a single sheet paper was far more convenient to send by post than a parcel of title pages. He appealed through Lord Arlington to the licensor Sir Roger L'Estrange, who diplomatically proposed that Clavell and Starkey should run *Mercurius Librarius* in partnership, and the edition that appeared at Easter 1669 carried both names. Nevertheless, given the commercial potential of the countrywide market, the quarrel between the two rumbled on for many years.[18]

Booksellers had long enjoyed a close relationship with their regular customers: John Chamberlain used Norton's shop as a kind of poste restante in the early seventeenth century, and later Samuel Pepys clearly valued the advice of Joshua Kirton. Chamberlain and Pepys both lived in London, so their demands were not wide-ranging. However, the correspondence of one gentleman with his booksellers at the end of the seventeenth century contains some surprising requests. Sir William Boothby resided at Ashbourne Hall in Derbyshire, about 150 miles from London, a journey on horseback of four or five days. He was an avid purchaser, writing to one friend, 'Books are the Great Joy of my Life.'

Several booksellers supplied Boothby. The closest to Ashbourne was Michael Johnson, who had been apprenticed to a Churchyard bookseller, but had set up shop in Lichfield: he was the father of the great eighteenth-century literary figure Samuel Johnson. A variety of establishments in London had Boothby's custom, some from the City, others from the expanding trade westward, but his principal source was Richard Chiswell at the Rose and Crown in St Paul's Churchyard. In a letter to Chiswell dated 21 May 1684, Boothby wrote:

> We do not come up to London as we designed (at present). I have returned you some moneys from [name illegible], so soon as it comes to your hands, let me hear. I hope you receipt my last letter sent with the bookes by the carrier ... May send me the last terme catalogue and continue the pamphlets with care (which I take much delight in). Pray buy me a quarter of pound of tee of the best, though deare, for I cannot drinke bad.

Significantly the letter is signed 'Your friend'. The request for tea was not an unusual one. Chiswell was also expected to undertake money broking and to find cheap lodgings for Boothby in Lincoln's Inn for his trips to London.

By late 1688, Boothby had moved on to another Churchyard bookseller as his principal supplier, Joseph Watts at the Sign of the Angel. James II had fled the country, and the throne was taken by his elder daughter Mary and her consort, William of Orange. Feeling out of touch in these tumultuous times, Boothby complained to Watts,

> I believe you are in great disorder and disturbance in London, as we are in the Country, many great men, and others being up. But my Allegiance and Religion According to ye principles of the Church of England keeps me Joyning with them..

Two months later, his desire for news and for every kind of current newsletter, pamphlet and proclamation burst out in another complaint to Watts: 'you have omitted sending the weekely Intelligences . . . the above are in most Gentlemens hands and in Coffy Houses Long Ago', and he furnished the unfortunate bookseller with a list of missing issues.[19]

St Paul's Churchyard had become a dispatch centre for books to all parts of the country, and to markets overseas, including the English colonies in North America and the West Indies. Some of these consignments were packed into barrels and taken down to the Thames-side wharves to be loaded on ships. More often, they were sent off to carriers at the various inns in the neighbourhood of the Churchyard. The Goose and Gridiron was located in London House Yard, next to the former site of the Bishop of London's palace at the west end of the cathedral. Before the Great Fire, the inn was called the Mitre, but on rebuilding in grand style was given its curious title, which is thought to be a perversion of the swan and lyre, the crest and charge on the arms of the Company of Musicians, for musical entertainments were often held here. At the top of Ludgate Hill was the Belle Sauvage (see p. 92), and further north, the Oxford Arms in Warwick Lane. This last survived the Great Fire, right through to the late nineteenth century, when it was photographed before demolition. The striking images show a galleried building around a courtyard, with the dome and towers of St Paul's rising up behind (Plate 18). Books and periodicals would have been loaded up on carriers' carts in the courtyards of these establishments and dispatched across the country to provincial booksellers and to private clients.

Contemporary accounts bring to life the book trade in these vibrant times. Two very different portraits were painted in words at the outset of the eighteenth century. The first was produced by Ned Ward, who took his cue from Samuel Butler's *Hudibras* (see p. 150), writing a series of satirical sketches of London life from 1698 to 1709 under the title of 'The London Spy'. Among these are perambulations around St Paul's Churchyard, introducing the sights and sounds. He describes the second-hand booksellers in the northern part of the Churchyard:

> where booksellers were as plenty as pedlars at a fair; and parsons in their shops as busily searching after the venerable conceits of our worm-eaten ancestors, as if they came thither for want of brains, or a library, to patch up a seasonable discourse for the following Sunday.

In another walk to the west of the cathedral he turns his satirical eye upon

> a picture-seller's shop, where as many smutty prints were staring the church in the face as a learned debauchee ever found in Aretino's *Postures*. I observed there were more people gazing at these loose fancies of some lecherous engraver than I could see reading sermons at the stalls of all the neighbouring booksellers.[20]

Just like the later cartoons of Thomas Rowlandson and James Gillray, these are satires, or drolleries as Pepys would have them. A very different kind of picture, more like a group portrait, is provided by the pen of the bookseller John Dunton. He was a pioneer in two ways. First, he made the perilous voyage across the Atlantic to Boston, where he established a bookstore and warehouse: among his customers was one of the fellows and some of the students at Harvard College. Secondly, he published his autobiography, *The Life and Errors of John Dunton*, in 1705. In it he provided sketches of the characters of his bookseller colleagues, along with printers, binders, engravers and even a list of his own customers.

At the top of his list of booksellers appears Richard Chiswell, the Churchyard bookseller who coped with the demanding Sir William Boothby. Dunton describes him in glowing terms, deserving the Title of Metropolitan Bookseller of England, if not of all the World. His NAME at the bottom of a Title Page, does sufficiently recommend the Book. *He has not been known to print either a Bad Book, or on bad paper.*

Of William Shrewsbury, the veteran Little Britain bookseller whose wife had attracted the attention of Samuel Pepys, Dunton wrote:

The Morning of his Life was clear and calm, and ever since his whole Life has been a continu'd Series of Honesty. He merits the Name of *Universal Bookseller*, and is familiarly acquainted with all the books that are extant in any Language – He keeps his Stock in excellent Order, and you will find a Book as ready as I can find a Word in the *Dictionary*.

John Dunton was not complimentary in all his 'portraits'. John Salusbury is memorably described as

a desperate Hypergorgonick *Welchman* – He wou'd dress as it were in Print, only to have the Ladies say, *Look what a delicate Shape and Foot that Gentleman has* – He was a Silly, Empty, Morose Fellow – He had as much Conceit, and as little Reason for it, as any Man that I ever knew.

The reason for this animosity probably lies in the fact that Salusbury started up a periodical, *The Flying Post*, in direct competition with Dunton's own *Athenian Mercury*.[21]

Among the booksellers and printers described in Dunton's survey are several women. It has been estimated that around 320 women worked in the London book trade between 1550 and 1700, of whom three-quarters were the wives or widows of stationers.[22] By the mid-seventeenth century it was also possible in theory for women to be admitted to the freedom of the Stationers' Company in their own right through the traditional routes of apprenticeship, patrimony or redemption. The first to do so, as an apprentice, was Joanna Nye, the daughter of an Essex clergyman, who was bound to Thomas Minshall, an engraver, in 1666.

Perhaps the most striking woman listed by Dunton is Elinor, the wife of Thomas James, a journeyman printer in the parish of Silver Street, near

14. A 'flying mercury' offering copies of the *London Gazette*.

Aldersgate. John Dunton describes Thomas as competent and well-read, but as 'something better known for being husband to that She-State Politician, Mrs. Elianor James'.[23] Elinor earned her name of 'She-State Politician' as a result of a series of extraordinary broadsides and pamphlets, more than 90 in number, that she wrote, printed and distributed between 1681 and 1716. In these she addressed a whole range of political, religious and commercial issues. Three monarchs were brought to book in written 'interviews': Charles II for 'sins of the flesh'; James II for promoting Catholicism; and William III for taking James's crown. And to make no mistake as to who was speaking, Elinor put her name in large letters at the beginning of her texts. One example was *Mrs James's Vindication of the Church of England*, produced in 1687. Unsurprisingly, Elinor James was arrested, tried and fined for distributing scandalous papers but this appears not to have deflected her in her political activism. In her own time she was dubbed 'London City Godmother'. A portrait of the redoubtable lady shows her holding a copy of her *Vindication*.[24]

Mrs James was an exceptional woman for the age, but Dunton gives several other examples, and it is clear that he admired and valued his first wife, whom he refers to as Iris. He mourned her death not only for her companionship but also her business acumen, recognising a downturn in his fortunes thereafter. In addition to the named female printers and booksellers, Dunton alludes to the 'Worshipfull Society of Mercury Women'. These were the women who sold newspapers and ballads on the streets and in the marketplace. Sometimes known as 'flying mercuries', they feature in Marcellus Laroon's *Cryes of London Drawne After the Life*, published in 1687, and would have been a familiar sight and sound in St Paul's Churchyard. Copies of Dunton's own newspaper, *The Athenian Mercury*, were carried by them.

Not all booksellers flourished, and Dunton mentions several who failed in their businesses. Perhaps the most spectacular was Moses Pitt, who had been apprenticed to the Little Britain bookseller Robert Littlebury before setting up on his own account nearby at the Sign of the White Hart in 1667. A few years later, when the Churchyard shops had been rebuilt, he moved to the Sign of the Angel there and printed and published for members of the Royal Society, including the eminent scientists Robert Boyle and Robert Hooke. With the support of fellows of the Society, including Christopher Wren, he produced proposals for a huge project, an atlas of the world in 12 volumes. Four were published, but then Pitt was struck by every eventuality that could afflict a bookseller at that time. In the mid-1670s he was in dispute with a predatory neighbour in the Churchyard, and was obliged to move to smaller quarters nearer the cathedral, with his stock 'much dampnified . . . by the breaking spoyling and disordering of his goods & books & by being forced for some time to discontinue his trade'.[25] He managed to get tangled up in a property deal with the notorious Judge Jeffreys, and then was thrown into the Fleet Prison for debt, where he remained for at least seven years. In 1691 he published *The Cry of the Oppressed*, a vivid appeal on behalf of prisoners of debt across the country, as well as a detailed account of his own tragedy. Dunton had no doubts about his integrity, describing his as 'an honest man every inch and thought of him; and had his "Atlas" succeeded . . . had died worth Twenty Thousand Pounds'.[26]

Publishing and bookselling were, and still are, risky businesses. Yet the majority of the practitioners of the book trade were prospering. As their trade expanded, guides were produced that provided advice on where customers might track down their book quarries. One German customer used as his guide Edward Chamberlayne's *Angliae Notitiae, or, the Present State of England* that had been published in 1669. Zacharias Conrad von Uffenbach, a wealthy collector from Frankfurt, spent five months in England in 1710, buying books and manuscripts. Visiting the bookshop of Mr Badman at the Corner House on Paternoster Row, he wrote how:

> he is the most eminent man in London – nay, the whole of England – who deals in old bound volumes and also in Latin books and what one does see is like a store of rough volumes. But Badman had two great shops full, in such quantities that they lie in great confusion in heaps on the ground. I found among them many splendid books, but so terribly dear that I bought some English Histories and only one single Latin book, namely Mabillon *de Re diplomatica*.

Von Uffenbach was a canny purchaser, knowledgeable about the various European markets. He makes the point that although London booksellers imported in numbers, the export market was still underdeveloped:

It should always be borne in mind that it is very foolish to buy Latin books in England, for one gets them much cheaper in Holland. But English books, namely those written in that language, one has to buy, because they are not sent out of England, and, when I began to learn English, I could find nothing in Frankfurt but a Bible.

Later he visited Little Britain,

where many 'antiquarii' or booksellers live, who deal in nothing but old books. I bought 30 guineas' worth . . . many chorographic or topographic descriptions of England, such as Plots *Oxon*, [Robert Plot's survey of Oxfordshire] for there is no shire or region of which a most elegant description has not been written.[27]

Macky's *Journey through England*, published in 1714, also directed book buyers to the various centres in London. They were told that 'divinity and classicks' were to be found on the north side of St Paul's Churchyard, and 'antient books in all languages' were to be had in Little Britain and Paternoster Row. But an indication of how the book trade was also moving into the developing West End was that Macky advised for history and plays to go to Temple Bar, the traditional centre for legal books, and to the Strand for titles in French.

It has been estimated that the trade in books doubled between 1600 and 1700, a truly remarkable achievement when the dire situation following the Great Fire is remembered. Moreover, St Paul's Churchyard, totally destroyed in 1666, had so recovered just 30 years later that it continued to be the heart of Britain's book world. Just as Hatton Garden was to become identified with the diamond trade, Savile Row for men's tailoring and Fleet Street for newspapers, so the Churchyard stood for books, even if some booksellers had premises elsewhere. As the book historian, James Raven, has put it:

For coaching inn or coffee-house readers in the country towns, the world of books was constructed from these names: St Paul's Churchyard, the Great (or Little) North Door, Pater-noster Row, Ave Maria Lane, Ivy Lane, Carter Lane, the Chapter Coffee house, and (much loved by the unlicensed) Pissing Alley.[28]

CHAPTER 9

A PLACE TO BE SEEN

In November 1666, Samuel Pepys visited the cathedral ruins in the aftermath of the Great Fire. He went to the yard of the Convocation House, the former chapter house, to view the corpse of Robert Braybrooke, Bishop of London in the early fifteenth century. He recorded how the body had fallen

> in his tomb out of the great church into St Fayths this late Fire, and is here seen his Skeleton with the flesh on; but all tough and dry like a spongy dry leather or Touchwood all upon his bones. . . . A great man in his time, and Lord Chancellor – and now exposed to be handled and derided by some, though admired for its duration by others. Many flocking to see it.[1]

Although a rather ghoulish example, this fits into the long tradition of tourism at St Paul's. John Chamberlain, in one of his letters written at the very beginning of the seventeenth century, described how Queen Elizabeth had dispatched her courtier, Sir Walter Raleigh, to take the Flemish ambassador on a tour of the capital: 'He . . . carries him up and downe to see sights and rarities hereabout. He hath had him at Powles, at Westminster, at Whitehall, and where not?'[2]

There have been many different kinds of visitors and tourists to St Paul's Cathedral and its Churchyard over the centuries. Perhaps the earliest were pilgrims, drawn to the tomb of the late seventh-century Bishop of London, St Erconwald. At his death around the year 693, his remains were originally sealed in a lead casket fashioned in the form of a gabled house, and then in a silver shrine located near the high altar. The colour blue was associated with him, so that gifts to his shrine included a sapphire and a blue girdle. As blue was considered the colour of wisdom and short-sightedness, and students of law were regarded as both clever and myopic, so St Erconwald became particularly connected to the profession. In the early sixteenth century, successful lawyers, having gained nomination as serjeants at law, would walk to St Paul's to venerate the shrine.[3]

The cult of St Erconwald never achieved the astonishing dimension of that of St Thomas Becket, and no associated pilgrim badges have been found. However, the connection between St Paul's and the murdered Archbishop was well recognised by Londoners, who made their way to the Pardon Cloister to the north of the cathedral to visit the graves of Becket's parents, Gilbert and Matilda, and from the fifteenth century, the chapel there dedicated to St Thomas. At the Reformation, such cults disappeared, with Protector Somerset ensuring total destruction of the Pardon Churchyard chapel during the reign of Edward VI, along with the shrine of St Erconwald behind the high altar in the cathedral.

But the cathedral and surrounding precinct drew visitors from all over Europe. The height of the tower proved a great attraction, with records of acrobats descending by rope into the Churchyard below. In 1601 the magician William Banks climbed up the tower with his wonder horse, Morocco. How he did it is a mystery, but John Chamberlain in one of his letters mentions how somebody 'caried up a horse and rode upon him on the top of Powles steeple'.[4] So famous was Morocco that dramatists mentioned him in their plays: John Marston, for example, included a reference in *Jacke Drumes Entertainment*, that was performed by the Children of Paul's. More usual was ascent by human feet, with visitors paying a penny to the wives of the bell-ringers. In September 1599 the Swiss traveller Thomas Platter attended a service in the cathedral and then

> climbed three hundred steps to the church roof, which is broad and covered with lead, so that one may walk there, indeed every Sunday many men and women stroll together on this roof. Up there I had a splendid view of the entire city of London, of how long and narrow it is.[5]

It was reported that visitors to the tower made whooping noises when they reached the top, dropping stones into the garden of the minor canons and onto people walking within the cathedral itself.

15. A woodcut showing the 'wonder horse' Morocco with the magician Banks.

When James I's brother-in-law, Christian IV of Denmark, paid his boisterous state visit to London in 1606, he was duly taken to St Paul's and up the
tower by Edward Soper, the keeper of the steeple. After he had enjoyed the
view of the city, the Danish King was invited to be part of the St Paul's hall of
fame by having the shape of his foot cut out in the lead with Soper's knife.
According to the chronicler who continued Stow:

> The said Soper, within few days after, made the Kinges Character in
> gilded copper, and fixed it in the middest of the print of the Kings
> foote, which was no sooner done, but some rustie minds of this yron
> age, thinking all gold that glistred, with violent instruments attempted to
> steale it. . . .[6]

Three years later, the playwright Thomas Dekker published his satirical book of manners, *The Gull's Horne Book*, parodying the courtesy books of the period. As noted earlier, his particular target was the fops and gallants of London who daily promenaded in the nave of the cathedral, instructing them on making themselves conspicuous. He suggested they should pay the fee to climb the steeple, where they should

> draw your knife, and graue your name, (or for want of a name, the marke which you clap on your sheep) in great Caracters vpon the leades . . . and so you shall be sure to haue your name lye in a coffin of lead when your selfe shall be wrapt in a winding-sheete: and indeed the top of Powles contains more names then Stowes Cronicle.[7]

The Great Fire of 1666 provided all kinds of new opportunities for visiting St Paul's. Disasters always attract onlookers, and the entry from Pepys's diary quoted at the head of this chapter shows that many flocked to see the tombs that had been rescued from the burnt-out cathedral and could be viewed in the Convocation House. Pepys was a Fellow of the Royal Society, drawn by curiosity to see the remains of Bishop Braybrooke. Other fellows went even further in their curiosity, adhering to the tenets of the Society that emphasised practical experimentation. John Aubrey noted in his biographical sketch of John Colet, Dean of St Paul's at the beginning of the sixteenth century, and refounder of the School:

> After the Conflagration (his Monument being broken) somebody made a little hole towards the upper edge of his Coffin, which was closed like the coffin of a Pye and was full of a Liquour which conserved the body. Mr. Wyld and Ralph Greatorex tasted it and 'twas of a kind of insipid tast, something of an Ironish tast. The Coffin was of Lead, and layd in the Wall about 2 foot ½ above the surface of the Floore.
>
> This was a strange rare way of conserving a Corps: perhaps it was a Pickle, as for Beefe, whose Saltness in so many years the Lead might sweeten and render insipid. The body flet, to the probe of a stick when they thrust into a chinke, like boyld Brawne.[8]

The men undertaking this extraordinary and potentially hazardous experiment were Edmund Wyld or Wild, and Ralph Greatorex. Wild was a wealthy amateur inventor and horticultural innovator who often assisted Robert Hooke with his experiments. While Wild was a Fellow of the Royal Society, Greatorex was not, but attended many meetings and introduced Pepys to Gresham College. Although a skilled scientific instrument maker, Greatorex was regarded, or perhaps regarded himself, as a craftsman rather than a scholar able to be invited to take up a fellowship.

The eternal interest in building sites manifested itself, so that Christopher Wren was obliged to erect spiked fences, and later tall screens, to keep out the curious and the light-fingered (see p. 145). However, once St Paul's Cathedral was revealed in all its new, Baroque glory, the crowds were encouraged to visit and to admire. From the very moment that the dome was completed, visitors could pay a fee to climb up. The German bibliophile Zacharias Conrad von Uffenbach, arriving in the summer of 1710, found that previous visitors had already continued the practice of inscribing their names that had been such a feature of the steeple of the medieval cathedral. He noted in his diary; 'Right at the top of the tower we found countless names written in chalk or scratched on stone, so we had ours done also by our man'. Once back on the ground floor of the cathedral, he was thrilled by the magnificence of Wren's work, but noted, 'It is easier to make it out from the drawings and engravings that we bought than to describe it in words'.[9]

Where exactly von Uffenbach obtained his prints and drawings is not recorded. There was a range for him to choose from, but their authenticity was often in doubt. Printmakers were thwarted by the fact that Wren was altering details as he proceeded with the building of the cathedral, and especially the form of the dome. Thus when in 1682 William Morgan produced a wall map of 'London &c. Actually Survey'd', he was obliged to apologise for his inaccurate representation of St Paul's: 'For so much as is built is taken from the work itself: the rest is added according to the best information we could get, hoping it may not be very unlike when finished'.

Recognising the demand for images, Wren in 1698 decided to produce his own, applying to William III for a licence, and obtaining the exclusive right of printing and publishing for 15 years. A proof of one of his prints is held in the Guildhall Library. It shows a section from the west to the east ends with the dome over the central crossing, with instructions to the engraver in the hand of Wren's assistant, Nicholas Hawksmoor. Three more approved engravings appeared in the early eighteenth century with the imprimatur 'Ex Autographer Architecti'. These were the work of the French engraver, Simon Gribelin, who had helped Wren with his drawings to work out the final details of the cathedral.

These official images, however, did not prevent other prints being produced. At the beginning of 1703 Thomas Bowles advertised for sale three engravings by William Emmet, with the claim that they had been 'examined and revised by some of the best Architectors, and approved by other Ingenious Persons'. His economy with the truth is shown by the fact that his 'South Prospect' was a reversed copy of the authorised 'North Prospect'. Custom nevertheless was good, for Emmet went on to produce more images under his own name. The commissioners of St Paul's also officially engaged Robert Trevitt to produce five prints that showed the architecture, and one of the ceremonial thanks-giving following the Duke of Marlborough's victory at Ramillies in 1706 (see p. 224).[10] These various prints were offered for sale in shops in the Churchyard, and in particular in the Great Picture Shop of Thomas Bowles, situated next door to the chapter house (Plate 12). This establishment may well have been the shop satirised in Ned Ward's 'London Spy'.

It was the dome of St Paul's that proved the popular experience, with visitors climbing up to the Whispering Gallery to enjoy the acoustic effect, and on up to see the golden orb and cross. A young lawyer, Dudley Ryder, managed to gain entry to view the series of paintings of the life of St Paul within the dome, being executed by the artist James Thornhill. As he noted in his diary, he visited St Paul's on 28 August 1716, 'to view the City from the top of it. It was a fine sight, but I had a great curiosity to see the inside of the scaffolding of the Dome.' The key holder told him nobody ever went up there because Thornhill would not allow it, but nevertheless showed him the door. A servant let him in, and he explained:

> I had a great curiosity to see so extraordinary a piece of painting as that of the Dome of St Paul's, and begged the favour of being allowed the liberty which he did not usually allow to anybody, because if it was people would come in so great crowds that they would interrupt him in his study and painting.

Thornhill relented, thinking him an expert, and explained how the architecture was finished, and only the gilding and enriching still to be done. Ryder goes into detail in his diary about the paintings and columns, and explains that he had managed to be evasive about his expertise, giving the servant a shilling for letting him in.[11]

Georg Christoph Lichtenberg from Oberramstadt near Darmstadt in Hanover paid two visits to England, in 1770 and in 1774–5. His letters provide a vivid picture of London life of the time. In one, to his professor at Gottingen University, he declared:

> At seven o'clock on the morning of 6 October [1774] I climbed to the summit of St Paul's Church and drank your health and that of your dearest wife. With my glass in my hand I called out the names of all my friends which occurred to me, on the pinnacle of the second place of worship in the world, above a dome 420 feet in circumference and raised 350 feet higher than the tallest house in immeasurable London, below me the Thames with its three bridges, of which the highest cost two million thalers, ships, human beings, coaches, and countless houses.[12]

A constant theme among visitors to St Paul's Churchyard was the polluted atmosphere caused by the ubiquitous burning of sea coal. A Russian traveller, Nikolai Karamazin, visiting in the late eighteenth century, lamented in a letter that 'London's eternal smoke has not spared the great dome and has blackened it from the bottom to the golden sphere that serves as its crown'. Urged on by a French lady, he agreed to go up into the dome, and was enthralled by the result:

> We climbed up virtually to the cross itself: finally – *nec plus ultra!* We stopped and forgot our fatigue. A marvellous view! The entire city and all its surrounding before our eyes! London looked like the shining shell of a tortoise: innumerable ships on the Thames were like reeds on a rivulet: groves and parks covered with thick heather.[13]

The cathedral was obviously a huge draw through the centuries, but the Churchyard could also offer all kinds of attractions. As described in Chapter

5, the Children of Paul's performed plays in the Almoner's House, and the courtyard of the Belle Sauvage Inn was used as a theatre as well as for bear-baiting. Another of the coaching inns, the Mitre, was home to a museum of curiosities. This was put together by Robert Hubert, who published 'A Catalogue of many Natural Rarities with Great Industry, Cost and Thirty Years travel in Foreign Countries; daily to be seen at the place called the Musick House at the Miter, near the West end of St Paul's Church', which was printed for him in 1664. The catalogue shows that most of the objects on display were of natural history – birds, fish, vegetables, minerals – although the star of the show would surely have been 'A *Mummy*, intire and adorned with Hieroglyphicks, that shew both the Antiquity, and eminent Nobility of the Person, whose Corps it is, taken out of one of the Egyptian Pyramids'.

The museum was probably like the Ark, the collection of the gardening John Tradescants, father and son, displayed in South Lambeth, which was to form the basis of the Ashmolean Museum in Oxford. Hubert provided a list of the eminent people 'whose Love of Vertue, Learning and of the admirable works of God in Naturall Rarities has been shewed by their Bountiful adding of something to the increase of the forementioned collection'. This list is headed by Charles I and Charles II, along with various members of European royal families, including the keen horticulturalist Gaston d'Orléans. Sir Thomas Roe, England's Ambassador to the Great Mogul in India, must have been a generous donor. Thomas Povey, treasurer to the Duke of York, is recorded as presenting 'A *Phenocopter* or *Passoflamingo*' which was noted for its good meat, and 'was much esteemed by the delicate-mouthed *Romans*'.[14] Such an attraction reflects the great curiosity of this period, as shown by the interests of the fellows of the Royal Society sampling the liquid contents of a coffin.

The Great Fire destroyed both the Mitre Inn and its museum. When the inn was rebuilt, it was first named the Lyre, and later became the Goose and Gridiron, both indicating its association with the Musicians' Company. Musical entertainments of some kind were held here, and the area became known for its shops selling music and instruments. Ned Ward in his peram-bulations around the Churchyard wrote:

We . . . came amongst the music-shops, in one of which were so many dancing-masters' apprentices fiddling and piping of borees and minuets, that the crowd at the door could no more forbear dancing into the shop than the merry stones of Thebes could refuse capering into the walls, when conjured from confusion into order by the power of Amphion's harmony. Amongst 'em stood a little red-faced blade, beating time upon his counter, with as much formality as if a Bartholomew Fair consort, with the assistance of a Jack-pudding, had been ridiculing an Italian Sonnet in the balcony to draw people into the booth, for he was as prodigally pert in giving his instruction to the rest as a young pedagogue tutoring a disciple in the hearing of his father.[15]

The 'red-faced blade' could have been John Young, whose musical instrument shop was at the Dolphin and Crown at the west end of the cathedral. A catch about John Young and his son included in a collection of songs published in 1726, suggests that the shop was often full of noise:

You Scrapers that want a Fiddle well Strung,
you must go to the Man that is Old while he's YOUNG.
But if this same Fiddle you fain would play bold,
you must go to his Son, who'll be YOUNG when he's old.
There's old YOUNG and young YOUNG,
both men of Renown,
Old sells, and Young
Plays the best FIDDLE in Town.
Young and Old live together, and may they live long;
Young to play an Old Fiddle, Old to sell a New Song.[16]

The bookseller Thomas Bowles, who sold prints of the cathedral, also began to produce helpful information for visitors to the area. His *New Guide to London: or, Directions to Strangers* was adapted from a late seventeenth-century guidebook, *Guide de Londres*, by François Colsoni, with the original French text side by side with an English translation. The introduction to this edition claimed that it was the prerequisite for 'all those who come to this great Metropolis' and wished to visit its curiosities and antiquities. A single circuit of the capital was offered so that the visitor could begin and end their tour as it best suited them. The section on St Paul's begins: 'for Amplitude,

Splendor, Solidity, Figure, and curious Architecture, [it] is esteemed the first in all the Universe'. The visitor was recommended to climb up to the Whispering Gallery and cupola, for which a fee of sixpence was charged.

The guidebook also recommends Cheapside and all the streets from Charing Cross, promising that 'the great Concourse of People, the Magnificence of the Shops and Merchandises, will Surprise and Charm you'.[17] One of the great attractions of the Churchyard was as a shopping centre for all kinds of luxury goods. In the sixteenth century, as in other parts of the City, there were groupings of trade, here most notably booksellers. This trade not only involved ink and paper, but also craftsmen expert in metal engraving. In the late sixteenth century Humfray Cole established a shop in the Churchyard, and was employed as an engraver: for example, in 1572 he engraved a map for the Bishops' Bible. But he also made and sold navigational and mathematical instruments, numbering explorers like Martin Frobisher among his clients. Some of his beautiful products are to be seen in the British Museum.

For those who wanted to buy a pair of spurs, Creed Lane, also known as Spurrier Row, on the south-west corner of St Paul's Churchyard, was the place to go. The Elizabethan or Jacobean fashionable gallant could buy a handsome pair that he might then show off in Paul's Walk, but he had to take care, for this was a fineable offence. Thomas Dekker advised in his *Gull's Horne Book*:

Never be seene to mount the steppes into the quire, but upon a high Festivall day, to proferre the fashion of your doublet, and especially if the singing boyes seem to take note of you: for they are able to buzze your praises, above their *Anthems* if their Voyces have not lost their maiden-heads, but be sure your silver spurres dogge your heels, and then the Boyes will swarme about you like so many white butter-flyes when you in the Open *Quire* shall drawe forth a perfum'd embrodred purse . . . and quoyt Silver into the Boyes hands, that it may bee heard above the first lesson.[18]

The choristers could claim the goodly sum of one shilling 'spur money' for the gallant's misdemeanour.

Further opportunities for purchasing ostentatious goods were above all provided by Cheapside, which originally had been almost monopolised by goldsmiths and the mercers who dealt in luxury textiles such as silk, velvets and fine woollen cloth. By the 1620s, it was noted that milliners and book-sellers among other tradesmen were moving into the street, and Charles I ordered the Lord Mayor to close their shops and to instruct the goldsmiths to return. This proved too late, however, and the mixture of establishments prevailed both here and in St Paul's Churchyard and Paternoster Row.

These early seventeenth-century shops were tall and narrow, with the living quarters on the upper floors. Workshops, requiring the maximum light, were often located on the top floor. The shop itself had an open window with a hinged counter that could be let down onto the street. By the end of the century the open window might be replaced by glass of small panes, and the counter and business dealings moved inside. Some stock could be displayed in the glazed windows, with shop hours depending on the light: from six in the morning in summer, eight in winter, until eight or nine in summer and dusk in winter. Often the shopkeeper, his wife or an apprentice stood outside, drawing in customers.

An apprentice features in *The English Rogue*. This was an early form of a novel, written by Richard Head, calling himself Meriton Latroon, and self-published in 1665, for he was also a bookseller:

> My master was not only a tailor but kept a broker's shop wherein he sold all sorts of clothes, new and old. He lived in one of the principallest streets in the City and was in good esteem with his neighbours who were all persons of some quality, not of the meaner sort but substantial tradesmen, as goldsmiths, grocers, drugsters, scriveners, stationers, etc. And I, being now well fitted with clothes and having my pockets well lined with money, which I had still kept by me, was a fit and welcome companion to the best sort of apprentices.[19]

As this passage suggests, a good advertisement for drapers and mercers was to dress up their apprentices. Ned Ward echoes this in his satirical perambulation of the southern part of the Churchyard:

> We . . . crossed a dirty kennel to take a view of a parcel of cleanly beau apprentices, who were walking in their masters' shops with their periwigs just combed out of buckle, well dredged with the barber's powdering puff, the extravagant use of which made them appear so particoloured that their

upper parts looked like millers. And their coats, from the waist downwards, hung in as many folds as a waterman's doublet, to show they had more cloth in the skirts of one tunic than any of their ancestors wore in a whole suit. But this much may be said in excuse of 'em, they might the better afford it because they were woollen-drapers.[20]

Samuel Pepys visited the Churchyard and Paternoster Row in the early 1660s to acquire various articles of clothing, sometimes accompanied by his wife Elizabeth. In November 1660 he noted in his diary, 'This morning my wife and I went to Paternoster-rowe and there we bought some greene watered Moyre for a morning wastcote'. In 1663, on the advice of Lady Sandwich, the wife of his patron, Pepys went to the Row to buy Elizabeth a new petticoat of striped silk. 'With Mr Creed's help; a very fine rich one, the best I did see there and much better then she desires or expects.'

The south side of the Churchyard was traditionally known as a centre for woollen drapers, one of whom was Sir William Turner, Pepys's relative by marriage and a leading member of the Mercers' Company. In 1664 Pepys noted in his diary:

up Sir W Turners and there bought me cloth, coloured for a suit and cloak, to line with plush the cloak – which will cost me money, but I find that I must go handsomely, whatever it costs me; and the charge will be made up in the fruits it brings.

Two years later, just as the Plague of London was diminishing in its terrible effect, he travelled with Elizabeth

to Bennetts in Paternoster-row (few shops their being yet open,), and there bought velvet for a coat and Camelott for a cloak for myself. And thence to a place to look for some fine counterfeit damasks to hang my wife's closet, and pitched upon one . . .[21]

Pepys could not have imagined that the shopkeepers of St Paul's Churchyard and Paternoster Row would in a few months' time suffer an even more devastating blow, the total destruction of their properties in the Great Fire.

Yet, just as the booksellers returned remarkably quickly to their rebuilt premises, so these traders in cloth and clothes were back in new shops within a few years. Sir William Turner, for example, reopened his shop in the early 1670s. There were others, however, who moved westwards. The early eighteenth-century chronicler John Strype noted of Paternoster Row:

> This Street, before the Fire of London, was taken up by eminent Mercers, Silk-men, and Lacemen; and their Shops were so resorted unto by the Nobility and Gentry, in their Coaches, that oft times the Street was so stop'd up, that there was no passage for Foot Passengers. But since the said Fire, those eminent Tradesmen have settled themselves in several other Parts; especially in Covent Garden, in Bedford Street, Henrietta Street and King Street. And the Inhabitants in this Street are now a mixture of Trades People and chiefly Tire-Women; for the Sale of Commodes, Topknots, and the like Dressings for the Females. There are also many Shops of Mercers and Silk-men; and at the upper end some Stationers, and large Warehouses for Booksellers; well situated for learned and studious Mens access thither; being more retired and private.[22]

Many small businesses specialising in luxury goods had traded from the galleries of the Royal Exchange, the bourse founded in Elizabeth I's reign by Sir Thomas Gresham, and of the New Exchange in the Strand established in the early seventeenth century by Robert Cecil, Earl of Salisbury. The Royal Exchange was destroyed in the Great Fire, while the New Exchange declined in popularity as traders preferred to operate from shops rather than the tightly packed boutiques. Some of these businesses probably moved into the Churchyard and the surrounding area.

The woollen drapers grouped in the south of the Churchyard were joined by workshops and shops offering fine furniture and furnishings, with convenient access to the Thameside wharves. One such firm was that of Coxed and Woster, cabinetmakers, who traded from the Sign of the White Swan near the south gate of the Churchyard from the beginning of the eighteenth century. Mahogany and kingwood, the very fashionable timbers from South America, along with walnut from New England, were inlaid with lines of pewter in the Boulle technique introduced by the royal cabinetmaker, Gerrit Jensen. The

Cabenetts, Looking Glasses, Tables and stannss Scretor
Chests of Drawers, And Curious inlaid Figures
for any worke made and sold By Phillip Hunt
at y Looking Glas & Cabenet at East end of
S:t Pauls Church y:d

16. Trade card of one of the shops selling fine furniture in the eighteenth-century Churchyard. Phillip Hunt's advertisement dating from 1720 shows samples of his work: a looking glass and a cabinet.

earliest examples, bureaux and secretaire cabinets dating from the reign of Queen Anne, have labels pasted into them announcing 'John Coxed. At the Swan in St Paul's Churchyard, London, makes Book Cases, Chests of Drawers, Scrutoires and Looking-glasses of all sorts'. Labels from the 1730s show that the firm had expanded its range, with Dutch and Indian tea tables, large sconces, dressing sets and wainscot work 'of all sorts, at Reasonable Rates, Old Glasses New polished and Made up fashionable'. These rates may have been reasonable, but this was high-end furniture, so that Richard Hoare of the banking family paid the substantial sum of £9 12s 6d for a 'strong wainscot table' and a 'large wainscot press' in 1735.

Related trades were located alongside. John Hutton at the Golden Lion 'over against the south east iron gate in St Paul's Churchyard' made and sold gilt leather for wall hangings and screens. Such leather hangings were made by cord-wainers, working in Cordoba goatskin leather, and their hall was situated in the gardens by St Paul's Cathedral. The iron gate was part of the railings that surrounded the cathedral, and which had afforded Wren such grief (p. 148). Cordwainers also made fine leather shoes, and Chaucer in the fourteenth century described how these were cut to look like the windows of Old St Paul's.[23]

Also south of the Churchyard were upholsterers or upholders, as they sometimes termed themselves. One such was the establishment of John Brown, who occupied a site near St Paul's School from 1728 to 1744. His sign was 'Three Cover'd Chairs & Walnut Tree' and his trade card announces that he

makes and sells all sorts of the best & most fashionable chairs, either Cover'd, Matted or Can'd. Likewise all Sorts of Cabinet-Work, with Sconces, Pier & Chimney-Glasses, Mohogany and other Tables: Blinds for Windows made & Curiously Painted on Canvas, Silk, or Wire.

Another upholsterer was Jonathan Fall at the Blue Curtain, offering 'all sorts of Beds and Bedding, Mohair Silk worsted and mix'd Damask, And all kind of Upholder's goods. Great Choice of English French and Turkey Carpets, Screens of every kind . . .'.

These two upholsterers had signs appropriate to their trade, but often there was no connection. John Hutton, for example, probably inherited the Sign of the Golden Lion from a previous incumbent who may have pursued a completely different trade. There was also the possibility of doubling up of images on the same street. By the 1730s the number of retail establishments in London had greatly increased, numbering thousands, and identification of addresses caused not only confusion, but also physical hazards, as the simple device set over the shop door grew into elaborate signs, painted boards hung on iron brackets. Such was the number of these in Cheapside that they were likened to the picture galleries of the Medici. In narrow streets the signs could meet overhead, and their weight posed a threat to the supporting walls, and to pedestrians passing beneath, with one fatal accident caused by a falling sign in 1718. Although a commission was set up soon after, nothing happened until

1762 when legislation was passed to replace signage by street numbering. Many businesses, nevertheless, retained the name of their sign for years to come.

The devices used on the signs are to be found in the trade cards that were commissioned by proprietors, and which have survived in collections. Sophia Bankes, the sister of the botanist and explorer Josiah, made such a collection in the early nineteenth century, and Ambrose Heal, from the furniture-making family, amassed an even larger collection a century later.[24] These cards were produced by engravers and printers in the area. The artist William Hogarth, who began his career as an apprentice to a silversmith, drew and engraved the design for the card of his sisters, Mary and Ann, who sold a wide variety of fabrics as well as ready-to-wear clothes. Their premises were in Little Britain, and their card shows the interior of a shop, with a little boy trying on a coat. Possibly he was a Bluecoat pupil at nearby Christ's Hospital.

Such trade cards were used like modern business cards. Printed on sheets of paper, or on cards cut to size, they might be distributed to potential customers. Sometimes they formed the reverse side of a bill. They were useful to those who were purchasing from outside London, through a local agent, or through personal contacts in the capital, so the wording would have been carefully chosen. Having moved premises, Mary and Ann Hogarth, explained precisely their location: 'From the old Frock-shop the corner of the Long Walk facing the Cloysters, Removed to ye Kings Arms joyning to ye Little Britain-gate, near Long Walk.' They then made a catalogue of the goods on offer:

> ye best and most Fashionable Ready Made Frocks, sutes of Fustian, Ticken & Holland, stript Dimmity & Flanel, Wastcoats, blue & canvas Frocks, & bluecoat Boys Drar's [uniforms]. Likewise Fustians, Tickens, Hollands, white stript Dimitys, white & stript Flanels in ye piece; by Wholesale or Retale at Reasonable Rates.

Their brother was hard put to fit all this in. Other traders laid emphasis upon the exotic nature of their goods, such as the Dutch and Indian tea tables of Coxed and Woster, or the French and Turkey carpets of Jonathan Fall. As the export opportunities increased, so some cards would state that they supplied the colonies, in North America and the Caribbean.

The survival of these cards, along with eighteenth-century trade directories, gives us a picture of the establishments around St Paul's that made it such a centre for luxury shopping. As the population and wealth of London moved westwards, so the Churchyard became the city's 'hinge', lying on the important east–west axis that ran from the Royal Exchange and Cheapside through to Fleet Street and the Strand. The first London trade directory, produced in 1677, concentrated on establishments that offered banking facilities, but more general directories followed. In 1763 Mr Mortimer produced the first edition of *The Universal Director*. His intended audience is made clear on the title page: 'the Nobleman and Gentleman's True Guide' with the establishments contained within described as being 'the Masters and Professors of the Liberal and Polite Arts and Science and of the Mechanic Arts, Manufacturers and Trades established in London, Westminster and their Environs'. The tradesmen of St Paul's Churchyard are well represented.

We have a rare glimpse of the customers who purchased these goods in the Churchyard from the correspondence of the Purefoy family, mother Elizabeth and son Henry, who lived at Shalstone Manor in Buckinghamshire. Elizabeth was widowed early, in 1704, at the age of 32, and died, over 90 years of age, in 1765. She comes over as a strong character, and the editor of her letters considers she would have made a good lawyer, for she does not hesitate to argue with her suppliers. Her son Henry, a scholarly collector of books, was a gentleman of independent means who made occasional visits to Oxford and London. His requests to their London agents for the purchase of furniture and clothes show that he wished to obtain the latest fashion.

The cabinetmaker from whom the Purefoys purchased their furniture was John Belchier at the Sign of the Sun on the south side of St Paul's Churchyard. In February 1743, Elizabeth wrote:

This desires Mr. Belchier to send mee a round neat light mahogany folding table with four legs, two of them to draw out to hold the folds. It must be four foot two inches wide. Send it (with the price thereof) by Mr. Zachary Meads, the Bucks carrier who sets out of London on Monday nights and Friday nights [from the Oxford Arms in Warwick Lane]. This will oblige.

Although houses often had 'eating rooms', a permanent dining table was rarely a feature. Folding tables of the kind ordered by Elizabeth Purefoy were kept against the wall of the room or in a corridor, to be set up when required. Six years later, after Henry Purefoy bought a desk or writing table from Belchier he asked for an explanation about how to open it. Subsequent correspondence showed that damp was the problem.[25]

Two other, very different, Churchyard shops supplied the Purefoys with goods. The first was the optician George Sterrop. A cluster of opticians was based in the west side of the Churchyard and at the top of Ludgate Hill. They may have established themselves here because of the proximity of the Royal College of Physicians, and of course, there were short-sighted lawyers as customers. These businesses, however, dealt not only with spectacles, but also with scientific instruments. One shop in the Churchyard, that of James Mann, traded at the Sign of Sir Isaac Newton and Two Pairs of Golden Spectacles. In the summer of 1752 Henry Purefoy was in communication with George Sterrop for a barometer. He had seen one advertised in a newspaper, but Sterrop had not specified whether it was portable, for taking on journeys, or for setting up in the house: 'I don't care how plain my Barometer is so as it be strong & durable because it is for travelling'. He asked Sterrop to let the carrier know its fragility lest it was broken or shaken too much on the journey to Shalstone.

After Sterrop's death, the workshop and showroom, now described as 59 St Paul's Churchyard, were taken over by Peter Dollond, the founder of the firm of Dollond and Aitchison, whose skill with scientific instruments earned him the title of Father of Practical Optics. Scientists had been frustrated in their study of distant objects by the appearance of blurring and coloured fringes, but Dollond was able to overcome this problem by developing the achromatic telescope. He made instruments for Captain Cooke's voyages, and for English aristocrats who took an amateur interest in science, so that in 1774 he delivered a Dollond achromatic telescope to the country home of the Earl of Sandwich.

Different problems beset the purchase of groceries by Elizabeth Purefoy from Mr Wilson at the Three Sugar Loaves, again at the west end of St Paul's. In medieval times grocers specialised in selling exotic spices 'by the gross' and were members of one of the most powerful City companies, second only to the mercers in precedence. Cloves imported from the East Indies are featured on the Grocers' coat of arms, while symbols of camels still march through its hall. By the eighteenth century an important part of grocers' business was the import of three exotic beverages: coffee, tea and chocolate. In 1747 Elizabeth ordered from Wilson one pound of best bohea tea, half a pound of best green tea, two pounds of coffee berries, along with mace, nutmegs, sugar, Poland starch and rice. She pointed out, however:

> The last Bohea Tea was so ordinary I could not drink it, my neighbours had as good for six shillings a pound. The last hundredweight of Raisins were so bad they spoiled the Liquor they were made on. I hope you will send no more Bad Goods.[26]

Some of Elizabeth Purefoy's letters are addressed to Mrs Wilson, and it is striking how many women were involved in or ran the enterprises of the Churchyard and surrounding streets in the eighteenth century.[27] Under the English rule of coverture, any business of a wife belonged legally to the husband. This convention is shown in the trade card of a shop selling lace and fine fabrics at the Sign of the Sun on the north side of St Paul's Churchyard. Two assistants are serving customers in the interior of the shop, but the name on the card is that of Benjamin Cole, who was a printer and engraver, and no doubt responsible for designing and producing it. The business was that of his wife.

As shown in earlier chapters, women were involved in the trades connected with the rebuilding of St Paul's Cathedral, and in printing and publishing enterprises. The range of retail businesses run by them in the eighteenth century was wide. For example, Jonathan Fall's successor in the upholstery business at the Blue Curtain was Elizabeth Hutt, trading in partnership with her son, a member of the Clothworkers' Company. The two of them trained up a succession of apprentices, girls as well as boys. When one of the apprentices, John Iliffe, took over the business in 1760, his card described him as 'successor to Mrs Elizabeth Hutt'. For 39 of the 60 years of its life, the distinguished firm of cabinetmakers at the White Swan, Coxed and Woster, traded under a female name. Grace Mayo set up here in 1704, and when her husband died, took his former apprentice, John Coxed as her business partner and husband. When in turn John died, she went into partnership with Thomas Woster. Later, the firm was run by Elizabeth Bell trading in partnership with her son.

Benjamin Cole
at the Sun in S.ᵗ Pauls-Church-Yard
LONDON.
Imports & Sells all sorts of Cambricks,
Lawn, Macklin & English Lace, & Edgin,
Where all Merchants, Dealers &
Others may be Furnish'd, Wholesale or
Retail at Reasonable Rates.

17. Trade card for the linen drapers at the Sign of the Sun, 1720. Customers are shown choosing their purchases, which might be checked at a cheval glass in the room beyond.

At the corner of St Paul's Churchyard and Cheapside was the shop of George Willdey, a member of the Company of Spectacle Makers, and one of the leading eighteenth-century makers and sellers of expensive trinkets, known as toys. More than half of his 15 apprentices were women, including Susannah Passavant, from a Huguenot family of jewellers. From 1737 Susannah was the manager of Willdey's shop, and then went on to open her own, on Ludgate Hill, at the Sign of the Plume of Feathers. Her trade card describes her business in both English and French, wishing no doubt to emphasise elite status.

One of her customers was Martha Washington, who in 1759 bought through her London agent a garnet necklace, now on display at Mount Vernon.

Two shops of trunk makers, also situated in St Paul's Churchyard by Cheapside, were run by women. Sarah Rands traded at the Sign of the Golden Cup and Two Trunks, while Rachel Bryant continued the business at the Trunk and Bucket that she had shared with her husband at his death in 1780. The range offered for sale from these businesses was wide: from large shipping trunks, through portmanteau trunks for travelling on horseback, and sumpter trunks for packhorses, to peruke boxes for wigs, and cases for musical instruments. Leather fire buckets were also part of the trade as Bryant's trade sign indicates.

The mother of the author Fanny Burney was Esther Sleepe, from a City family that combined music – her father is believed to have been the leader of the lord mayor's band – with fan making, the trade of her mother. Sleepe's daughters took the freedom of the Musicians' Company by right of patri-

18. Martha Sleepe, the aunt of the novelist Fanny Burney, had her fan shop on the north side of the Churchyard at the appropriate Sign of the Golden Fan and Seven Stars. This card dates from *c.* 1750.

mony. While Esther married the musician and musicologist Charles Burney and turned to bringing up a family, her sister Martha remained single, setting up her own shop making and selling fans in St Paul's Churchyard. The fans often had elaborate painted scenes, which would have been assembled with other components in a workshop on an upper floor. Sometimes the subjects of the scenes chosen for the fans had to be registered at Stationers' Hall, conveniently close at hand.

Fanny was therefore familiar with the shopping establishments of Cheapside and the Churchyard, and she drew on these when she wrote her epistolary novel *Evelina*, that was published in 1778. Evelina, who has come to London to be introduced into society by Mrs Mirvan, reports in a letter:

> We are to go this evening to a private ball, given by Mrs Stanley, a very fashionable Lady of Mrs. Mirvan's acquaintance.
>
> We have been *a-shopping* as Mrs. Mirvan calls it, all this morning, to buy silks, caps, gauzes, and so forth.
>
> The shops are really very entertaining, especially the mercers; there seem to be six or seven men belonging to each shop; and every one took care, by bowing and smirking, to be noticed. We were conducted from one to another, and carried from room to room with so much ceremony, that at first I was almost afraid to go on.
>
> I thought I should never have chosen a silk: for they produced so many, I knew not which to fix upon; and they recommended them all so strongly, that I fancy they thought I only wanted persuasion to buy every thing they showed me. And indeed they took so much trouble, that I was almost ashamed I could not.
>
> At the milliners, the ladies we met were so much dressed. That I should rather have imagined they were making visits than purchases. But what diverted me was that we were more frequently served by men than by women; and such men! so finical, so affected! they seemed to understand every part of a woman's dress better than we do ourselves; and they recommended caps and ribans with an air of so much importance, that I wished to ask them how long they had left off wearing them.
>
> The despatch with which they work in these great shops is amazing, for they have promised me a complete suit of linen against the evening.[28]

Burney wittily indicates how shop assistants, both male and female, were used like mannequins to attract customers, echoing Ned Ward's point about the dressing up of apprentices.

Glazing had been introduced into shops in London in the late seventeenth century, and subsequent developments in the manufacture of glass had made possible the enlargement of the panes. By the eighteenth century panes of plate glass could be up to two feet high, with thin brass bars in between. The brilliant effect of such windows illuminated by candlelight is described by the German traveller Georg Lichtenberg just after Christmas in 1774 as he passed from Cheapside through the south part of St Paul's Churchyard and on to Fleet Street. He was on his way from the house in Cheapside belonging to the printseller and engraver John Boydell to his lodgings at eight in the evening:

On both sides tall houses with plate-glass windows. The lower floors consist of shops and seem to be made entirely of glass; many thousand candles light up silverware, engravings, books, clocks, glass, pewter, paintings, women's finery, modish and otherwise, gold precious stones, steelwork, and endless coffee-rooms and lottery offices.

The street looks as though it were illuminated for some festivity: the apothecaries and druggists display glasses filled with gay-coloured spirits . . . they suffuse many a wide space with a purple, yellow, Verdigris-green, or azure light. The confectioners dazzle your eyes with their candelabra and tickle your nose with their wares, for no more trouble and expense than that of taking both their establishments.

He, too, noticed how the shop assistants were used to attract customers:

In these [confectioners] hang festoons of Spanish grapes, alternating with pineapples, and pyramids of apples and oranges, among which hover attendant white-armed nymphs with silk caps and little silk trains, who are often (here's the devil to pay) too little attended. Their masters wisely associate them with the cakes and tarts to make the mouth of even the most replete water, and to strip the poor purse of its last shilling but one; for to entice the hungry and rich, the cakes and their brilliant surroundings would suffice.

The hubbub of the area is brilliantly evoked:

In the middle of the street roll chaises, carriages and drays in an unending stream. Above this din and the hum and clatter of thousands of tongues and feet one hears the chimes from church towers, the bells of the postmen, the organs, fiddle, hurdy-gurdies, and tambourines of English mounte-banks, and the cries of those who sell hot and cold viands in the open at the street corners.[29]

This was a major assault on all Lichtenberg's senses, as he contrasted the experience with the calm of the streets of Gottingen. He felt the whole crowd was rushing along, as if being summoned to a death bed. The editors of his correspondence point out that the scene painted is like the engravings of William Hogarth, with which he was familiar: he was to publish explanations of the artist's scenes for the German audience. But the vividness of his words is reminiscent of those of Charles Dickens, whose evocations of London life were to appear more than half a century later. And clearly, in the eighteenth century, St Paul's Churchyard represented the vibrant heart of London, where there was all to see, and for many, the importance of being seen.

CHAPTER 10

LITERARY CIRCLES

At some time around 1750 a raid was made upon a publisher's Paternoster Row premises to seize copies of a work pronounced pornographic, John Cleland's *Memoirs of a Woman of Pleasure*, known more widely as *Fanny Hill*.[1]

The unlikely publisher in question was Ralph Griffiths, a pillar of the Nonconformist community and founder of a serious journal, *The Monthly Review.* Griffiths escaped prosecution by having all the offending copies bundled out of the back door as the warrant was in process of being served. Chutzpah was clearly one of Griffiths' qualities, for he had promoted *Fanny Hill* in *The Monthly Review* as being on a par with Henry Fielding's *Tom Jones*, while paying Cleland the modest sum of 20 guineas for the publishing rights, and then making thousands in profit. His escapade on this particular occasion was spectacular, but also touches upon different aspects of the literary scene in the Churchyard in the eighteenth century.

The question of copyright was a source of considerable debate, and of friction within the trade. As James Raven explains:

> The fundamental division among the booksellers of the [cathedral] precinct . . . was between those who invested and dealt in the ownership of the copyright to publication, and those who either printed, sold or distributed books for the copyholders or who traded entirely outside the bounds of the copyright materials.[2]

The more powerful booksellers, the congers, had come together to split the cost, risk and profit on new copyrights, or to purchase in auctions part shares in existing copyrights.

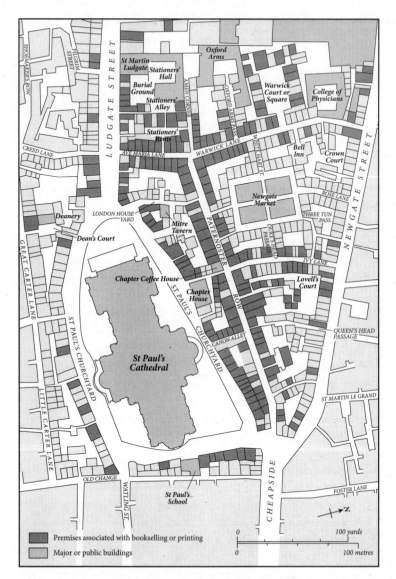

Map 3 The book trades in the neighbourhood of St Paul's in the eighteenth century.

The 1710 Statute of Queen Anne, known as the Copyright Act, was introduced 'for the encouragement of Learning by vesting the Copies of printed Books in the Authors or Purchase of such copies during the Times therein received'. It explained that

> printers, booksellers, and other persons have of late frequently taken the liberty of printing, reprinting, and publishing . . . books and other writings, without the consent of the authors or proprietors of such books and writings, to their very great detriment, and too often to the ruin of them and their families.

The Act set out to prevent such practices in the future, and 'for the encouragement of learned men to compose and write useful books'.

The Act stipulated that copyright should be given to authors for 14 years, renewable for a further 14 if that author was still alive, and then passed to the public domain. It also attempted to limit the congers' hold on particularly valuable perpetual copyrights, such as those on Shakespeare and other 'canonical classics'. Griffiths' very low payment outright to Cleland indicates one way that publishers could exploit their authors. And publishers sought through court injunctions to maintain their copyright on classics, a protection of their valuable assets but also resulting in a form of cultural exclusivity.

Although the range of books and publications produced in London had widened during the seventeenth century, religious books still represented a large proportion of the output, and indeed proved extremely lucrative for their publishers. One of the enduring bestsellers of the period was a guide to religious conduct, *The Whole Duty of Man*, first published in 1658, at the very end of the Interregnum. For political reasons no author was declared at the time, but it is now generally accepted that the book was written by Richard Allestree, a High Church of England clergyman who was active during the Civil War in support of Charles I, and expelled from Oxford when Parliamentary troops arrived in the city. Although Richard's cousin was a bookseller, James Allestree (see p. 158), the book was published by another member of the Churchyard community, Timothy Garthwaite, who carried out his business at the little north door of the medieval cathedral. The title of the book is taken from Ecclesiastes 12:13: 'Let us hear the conclusions of the whole matter. Fear God, and keep his commandments: for this is the whole duty of man.' The title page explains that the manual concerns the practice of Christian grace, laid down in a plain and familiar way for the use of all, but especially the meanest reader. It is divided into 17 chapters, to be read every Sunday, three times a year.

Garthwaite claimed that he paid the author 'a valuable consideration' for the copyright. This turned out to be an exceptionally wise investment, for the book was a publishing sensation, and he was obliged to take steps to prevent the appearance of pirate editions. At the Restoration of Charles II, Allestree became a powerful figure in the Established Church and at Oxford as the Regius Professor of Divinity. However, he never revealed that he was the author of *The Whole Duty*.

By the end of the seventeenth century, it has been estimated that the book was purchased by one in ten households, and it became a symbol of a good and sensible life. The close and intense friendship between Queen Anne and Sarah, Duchess of Marlborough, was by 1709 reaching breaking point, with Anne taking Abigail Masham as her bosom companion. At this point the furious Sarah wrote:

> I immediately set myself to draw up a long narrative of a series of faithful services for about twenty-six years past. And knowing how great a respect her Majesty had for the writings of certain eminent divines, I added to my narrative the directions of the author of The Whole Duty of Man with relation to friendship.[3]

In 1684, three years after Richard Allestree's death, his friend John Fell produced a folio collection of religious guidebooks which he claimed were all from the author of *The Whole Duty*. These included *The Gentleman's Calling*, *The Ladies' Calling*, *The Young Man's Calling* and even a version appropriate for a criminal to read on his or her way to the gallows.

Although he did not benefit from his cousin's bestseller, James Allestree was able to recover his business after the devastation of the Churchyard from the Great Fire by issuing some of his sermons. The business of sermon publication was a highly lucrative one, and never more so than when the text contained political controversy. On 5 November 1709, at the invitation of the newly elected Lord Mayor, Sir Samuel Garrard, the traditional Gunpowder Plot Sermon was delivered by an Oxford scholar, Henry Sacheverell. The original site of these sermons had been Paul's Cross, but since its demolition in the mid-seventeenth century they were delivered within the cathedral.

Sacheverell was zealously High Church, and a Tory. By the mid-1670s, two political factions had begun to emerge, occasioned by the revelation that James, Duke of York, Charles II's brother, and heir to the throne, had converted to Roman Catholicism. The two parties were given terms of abuse: Whig from the Scottish Gaelic for horse thief, and Tory from the Irish for an outlaw. The Whigs claimed the power to exclude James from the throne, while the Tories supported his hereditary right, despite his religious faith. James did succeed his brother in 1685, but the birth of a male heir to his Catholic Queen three years later sparked what became known as the Glorious Revolution, with the King fleeing the country after the invasion by his son-in-law, William of Orange. Nonetheless, the debate between the Whigs and the Tories continued, with both political and religious connotations.

Sacheverell took as the title of his sermon 'The Perils of False Brethren Both in Church and State', and used the opportunity to accuse the Whigs of imperilling the Anglican Church by siding with Nonconformists. He pulled no punches, declaring his determination

to open the Eyes of the Deluded People in this our Great Metropolis; being conscious of what prodigious importance it is to the welfare of the Whole Nation to have its Rich and Powerful Citizens set right in their Notions of Government, both in Church and State.

He then proceeded to accuse Whig ministers of being 'vipers in our bosom':

These false brethren in our government do not singly and in private spread their poyson, but (what is lamentable to be spoken) are suffer'd to combine into bodies, and seminaries, wherein atheism, deism, tritheism, socinianism, with all the hellish principles of fanaticism, regicide, and anarchy, are openly profess'd and taught, to corrupt and debauch the youth of the nation.[4]

Preaching within the cathedral may have meant a smaller congregation than the open-air sermons of earlier times, but the opportunity to print could bring the sermon to a greatly increased audience. Against the advice of his supporters, Sacheverell not only got his sermon into print, but also claimed that it was authorised by the lord mayor: whether this was true or not has never been established. For the bookseller Henry Clements at the Half Moon in St Paul's Churchyard an initial print run of 50,000 copies was produced, 1,000 in quarto format selling for one shilling, and the rest in octavo at twopence. Even this very large run was not sufficient for the avid public, with reprints and pirated editions following. It is thought that a quarter of a million copies were circulated, which would equate to the entire electorate of the nation at the time.

19. A Whig pamphlet published in the Sacheverell debate.

20. 'The Coffee-House Mob', showing men quarrelling over Henry Sacheverell's provocative Gunpowder Plot Sermon.

A pamphlet war ensued. One print from the Whig presses, headed 'the High Church Champion', shows Sacheverell flanked by two seconds, the Devil and the Pope. The accompanying verse reminded readers that once again there was no direct Protestant heir to the English throne, despite Queen Anne's many pregnancies, and that her half-brother, James II's Catholic son, the Pretender, in exile in France presented a constant threat. At the bottom of the print, a note enjoins the reader that the emblem (message) may be short but, 'since you bought the Sermon, buy the print'.

When the Tories did well in the forthcoming general election, the Whig response was to have Sacheverell impeached for preaching sedition. He had a group of vociferous supporters, so that his coach was surrounded by cheering crowds as he drove to Westminster Hall for his trial. This lasted for three weeks, attended each day by the Queen, with the crowds calling upon her to support Sacheverell. In private she told Gilbert Burnet, the Bishop of Salisbury, that the sermon had been a bad one, and he deserved to be punished. Unaware of this, the Duchess of Marlborough, firmly Whig in her views, assumed that Anne was for the doctor, and this precipitated the final break-up of their friendship. In the event, Sacheverell was found guilty, but his sentence, a three-year suspension from preaching and the public burning of the offending sermon, was so lenient that it was considered a victory for the Tories. Many verdicts were delivered on the whole affair, but perhaps the most succinctly memorable was that the sermon was more a 'Billingsgate Auditory than a Cathedral Harmony'.[5]

If there was a lack of harmony in St Paul's Cathedral, this could also be applied to its Churchyard. Some of the booksellers were flourishing through the monopolies that had been established early in the seventeenth century with the systems of Stationers' stock, in particular English stock (see pp. 158–9). In addition, the confused copyright system was giving the powerful booksellers, the congers, a valuable asset not enjoyed by others. A year after the 1710 Copyright Act, Charles Rivington bought the premises and business of Richard Chiswell, changing the sign from the Rose and Crown to the Bible and Crown, and when he subsequently moved to a site in the north part of the Churchyard, he retained this. Not all booksellers' signs were appropriate, but this certainly was, for the Rivingtons were staunch supporters of the Anglican Church and became the leading theological publishers in the City. Charles's eldest son, John, played out this role in his private life, being described as 'of dignified and gentlemanly address, going with gold-headed cane and nosegay twice a day to service at St Paul's . . . and breakfasting every alternate Monday with Bishop Secker at Lambeth [Palace]'.[6] On occasion he was known to complete his dress in the cathedral because of the early hour of the service.

Charles had established the dynasty of Rivington publishers that was to last for nearly two centuries. Another long-standing publishing dynasty founded at this time was that of the Longman family, which survived as an independent house right through to the mid-twentieth century.[7] In 1724

Thomas Longman took over the business of William Taylor, the publisher of Defoe's *Robinson Crusoe*, at the Sign of the Ship in Paternoster Row. With Rivington he became a leading shareholder in the Stationers' English stock, buying up many shares in copyrights. In 1728 he was a member of the consortium that published the influential work of reference *The Cyclopaedia of Arts and Sciences* compiled by Ephraim Chambers, and he was later to participate in another important reference work, the *Dictionary of the English Language*, compiled by Samuel Johnson. Described as the greatest wholesaler of the eighteenth century, Thomas rapidly built up a major export business to the North American colonies, particularly with the leading New England bookseller, Daniel Henchman.

Inevitably disputes arose between the Rivingtons and Nonconformists like Ralph Griffiths. But they were also capable of quarrelling among themselves. John Rivington may have displayed dignified behaviour, but his brother James was of a more volatile disposition, taking risks and seeking quick profits. After dissolving their partnership in 1756 James was accused of cheating John and other members of the trade by pirating their books. Gambling debts and unwise investments drove him to emigrate to New York, where he opened a bookstore in Hanover Square, and later stores in Boston and Philadelphia. During the American War of Independence, although he edited a loyalist newspaper, he was suspected of being a spy for George Washington. James Rivington died in poverty in New York in 1802.

John Rivington, meanwhile, maintained a flourishing bookselling and publishing business in the Churchyard. Much of the output of the Rivingtons were works of theology, and in 1760 John was appointed publisher to the Society for Promoting Christian Knowledge: the family was to retain this relationship for over 70 years. However, his father Charles, had been responsible for the composition and publishing of a work of a very different genre, Samuel Richardson's *Pamela, or Virtue Rewarded*.

Like Charles Rivington, the printer Samuel Richardson hailed from Derbyshire, and the two men were close friends. Richardson was the son of a joiner who prefigured Tom in William Hogarth's modern moral series, 'The Industrious Apprentice', moving from the margins of his trade to marry his master's daughter and become Master of the Stationers' Company. One of his earlier publications was *The Apprentice's Vade Mecum*, a book of advice on morals and conduct. Aged 13, he penned letters for young lovers, providing him with plenty of material when Rivington, in association with the Paternoster Row bookseller John Osborn, encouraged him to write on the concerns of everyday life. These letters grew into *Pamela*, the first part of which was published in 1740, and the second following the next year.

In the role of editor, developing the story with six correspondents, Richardson relates the life of Pamela Andrews, an unusually literate servant girl aged 15 who endures all kinds of misfortunes, including attempted rape and mock marriage, before winning over her seducer through her goodness. She then accepts his hand in a genuine marriage. The second part of the novel, *Letters to and for Particular Friends*, carries a heavy dose of moralising, as Richardson relates Pamela's life as a perfect wife.

Pamela enjoyed considerable acclaim, with Richardson hailed as 'a salutary angel' in Sodom, and clergymen preaching sermons that extolled the theme set out on the title page, a story designed 'to cultivate the principles of religion and virtue in the minds of the youth of both sexes'. It also proved popular for, like today's soap operas, his audience often merged fiction with reality. Thus the church bells in Slough were rung to celebrate Pamela's wedding at the moment the village blacksmith reached that particular part of the story in his public readings. A series of 12 paintings produced by the artist Joseph Highmore showing scenes from *Pamela* further heightened the sense of reality and was widely distributed as a set of prints. The novel became an international bestseller, with North American editions appearing in New York, Philadelphia and Boston, and translations into French, Italian, Dutch, German, Swedish, Russian, Spanish and Portuguese.

Richardson's book was by no means the first of what might be described as a novel. Pepys was familiar with Samuel Butler's satirical *Hudibras*, that he described as 'drollery' (p. 150), and in his diary he recorded his wife Elizabeth reading romances by the French author, Madeleine de Scudéry. In 1719 Daniel Defoe's *Life and Strange Adventures of Robinson Crusoe* was published. It was based on the true-life experiences of Alexander Selkirk, set on an uninhabited island during a privateering expedition. Another of Defoe's works of fiction, *The Fortunes and Misfortunes of Moll Flanders*, published in 1722, purported to be the autobiography of the daughter of a woman transported to Virginia for theft soon after the birth of her child. This may well have served as a model for John Cleland's racy account of the adventures of Fanny Hill, although his development of his 'heroine' is much less effective. Richardson himself claimed that by using the vehicle of letters in *Pamela* he had hit upon a new species of writing. Although here too there were precedents, he raised the form to a new, higher level.

Claiming the moral high ground inevitably incurred mockery. The Rivington family was satirised by other members of the bookselling community. John, for example, was described in a poem by the bookseller Henry Dell as a hypocrite with a 'weak, dishonest, rotten heart'.[8] Likewise *Pamela* met with ridicule in certain quarters. Even as the second part was issued, a parody appeared, entitled *An Apology for the Life of Mrs Shamela Andrews*, by 'Conny Keyber'. This was almost certainly the writer Henry Fielding, who went on to deride *Pamela* openly in his novel *The History of Joseph Andrews*, chronicling the adventures of Pamela's equally virtuous brother, a footman who resists the advances not only of the housekeeper, but also of the mistress of the house. Richardson was deeply upset by Fielding's actions, and never forgave him. Nevertheless, his first excursion into fiction had been hugely successful, and helped towards a burgeoning of the novel as a literary form.

This burgeoning coincided with the development of review journals. One of the first reviews of an English book was written at the publication of the third edition of John Evelyn's *Sylva* in 1679. It appeared in the 'Domestic Improvements' section of a London newspaper, *The True Domestic Intelligence*, and not only mentioned *Sylva*, but also two of Evelyn's other publications.[9] The bookseller John Dunton (see p. 169) was the proprietor in the 1690s of an innovative journal, the *Athenian Mercury*. He included literary pieces, such as the early verse of Jonathan Swift, that proved successful with both male and female readers, and paved the way for similar content in two influential journals, Richard Steele's *Tatler*, launched in 1709, and two years later, *The Spectator*, edited jointly by Steele and his school friend, Joseph Addison.

These last two publications focused on notices of plays, but the baton of book reviewing was taken up by Edward Cave, the publisher of the *Gentleman's Magazine*. The first issue was produced in 1731 from his printshop in the gateway of the former priory of St John of Jerusalem in Clerkenwell, with a reproduction of the building featured on the title page. In his early career Cave had worked first as a sorter and then as an inspector of franks in the Post Office's inland office in Lombard Street. As a result, he was able to gain excellent and cheap distribution of his magazine throughout Britain and North America, to the consternation of his competitors. He carried abridgements of recently published books and pamphlets which escaped legal action by various means, including printing letters from readers claiming to have bought the whole book as a result of reading extracts. A review of Samuel Richardson's second novel, *Clarissa*, appeared in the magazine in June 1749, with the claim that it was a translation from the Dutch by Albrecht von Haller. As Richardson's text ran to over a million words and had only just been published in its completed form, the Dutch reviewer may well have been a ploy to avoid legal action, especially as the name is identical with that of an eminent German botanist.

Where Cave and the *Gentleman's Magazine* led, others followed. Ralph Griffiths began *The Monthly Review* in 1749, originally from his premises in the Churchyard, and later from Paternoster Row. Running such a journal may have been time-consuming, but also a useful vehicle for a book publisher. Other publishers' books could be included, but it also ensured in-depth reviews of Griffiths' own titles, and the added bonus of damaging reviews for a threatening rival. As noted earlier, Griffiths used the journal to promote *Fanny Hill*, riding upon the enthusiastic welcome that had just been given to Henry Fielding's novel *Tom Jones*.

The Monthly Review carried a few long book reviews plus a fairly comprehensive list of other new novels, making 16 printed pages in octavo. Many of Griffiths' reviewers lived outside London, and worked hard for their fees, which, like those offered to authors, were far from generous. Although the reviews were anonymous, it is possible to work out the names of the contributors during Griffiths' editorship, as he made a note of their initials. He called upon a network of dissenters, with his pre-eminent reviewer from 1778 to 1786 being Samuel Badcock, a Nonconformist minister based in Devon. Badcock wrote notices for over one hundred novels. Griffiths himself wrote reviews, and his wife, who strove to keep their finances on track, contributed articles. From 1756 competition was provided by *The Critical Review*, established by Archibald Hamilton in conjunction with the author Tobias Smollett. Quickly prospering, he became a leading journal publisher, also producing the *Lady's Magazine* and the *Town and Country Magazine*.

The title of these last two periodicals is significant, for here was a readership particularly keen on the novels that were emerging from the printing presses in ever-increasing numbers. And running parallel, or rather intertwining with the development of fictional publishing, came that of circulating libraries. Such libraries began in Fleet Street, on the fashionable shopping route from Cheapside through to the Strand, as noted in the previous chapter. The first was opened by the Rev. Samuel Fancourt at around the time that the first part of Richardson's *Pamela* emerged from St Paul's Churchyard in 1740.

Fancourt offered primarily theological and technical books, but soon ran into financial trouble. However, other libraries concentrated on more popular publications, and these flourished, such as that of the Noble brothers, Francis and John, in St Martin's Court in Leicester Fields. Skilled at publicity, they produced engravings of the elegant interiors of their library. Their catalogue, priced at sixpence sewn, one shilling bound, offered several thousand volumes in English, French and Latin, with a subscription fee of 12 shillings per annum or four shillings per quarter. Their opening hours were generous, 8 a.m. to 8 p.m. (but no longer, the catalogue warned). Two books at a time might be borrowed, and there were fines for keeping books over time. An engraving of one of the first circulating libraries shows lady subscribers being given direct access to the shelves, rather than obtaining their books through a librarian.[10]

Circulating libraries were not only located in bookshops, but also in taverns and in coffee houses. The Irish traveller Dr Thomas Campbell wrote in his diary for 21 March 1775:

> Strolled into the Chapter Coffeehouse, Ave Mary Lane, which I had heared [sic] was remarkable for a large collection of books, & a reading Society &c – I subscribed a shilling for the right of a years reading, & found all the new publications I sought, & I believe what I am told that all the new books are laid in.[11]

The development of circulating libraries, however, was not to everybody's satisfaction: a chorus of disapproval, growing ever louder, met the idea of reading novels for pleasure, especially when those readers were women. An early shot in this debate came from a Scottish clergyman, Rev. Robert Wodrow, former librarian of Glasgow University, who wrote of 'all the villainous profane and obscene books and playes printed at London . . . and lent out, for an easy price, to young boyes, servant weeman of the better sort, and gentlemen, and vice and obscenity dreadfully propagated'. Others followed suit, such as the author of *Village Memoirs*, first published in 1765, who declared that 'turnpike-roads and circulating libraries are the great inlets of vice and debauchery – the ladies will say this remark is quite Gothic, but their husbands feel the thrust of it too forcibly'.[12]

The identification of women, be they the servant or the lady of the house, as readers of novels and thus prey to moral degeneration, was a common one. As early as 1736, William Hogarth included in his engravings of a seduction scene, *Before and After*, a book inscribed 'Novels' in the open drawer of the desk of an endangered lady, signifying the corrupt imagination that would lead to her downfall. In his play of 1775, *The Rivals*, Richard Brinsley Sheridan had Sir Anthony Absolute warning Mrs Malaprop of the twin dangers of novels and circulating libraries. He describes them as the 'ever-green tree, of diabolical knowledge, blossoming through the year', and warning that 'they who are so fond of handling the leaves, will long for the fruit at last'. As a counterpoint he recommended *The Whole Duty of Man* as reading matter, especially for ladies.

Less controversially, younger members of the family were also being catered for by the booksellers of London. For teaching Latin grammar, the primer composed by William Lily at St Paul's School in the sixteenth century still held sway (see p. 88). Primers for teaching children to read English, notably the one written by Edmund Coote, formed part of the English stock jealously guarded by the Stationers' Company and presenting sober fare to modern eyes. One of the more attractive surviving examples is *A Guide for the Child and Youth* published in 1723, which includes a pictorial alphabet of woodcuts. 'K' refers to 'King Charles the Good, No Man of Blood', indicating that originally this was probably produced some time after the Restoration.[13]

It was in the 1740s that the style of children's book publishing changed dramatically, thanks to two booksellers. The first, Thomas Boreman, who had a shop on Ludgate Hill, and another retail outlet 'near the Two Giants [Gog and Magog] in Guild-hall', produced 'Gigantick Histories'. These were miniature books, often with pictures of London, that entertained children as well as teaching them. He rejected the idea of fairy stories, that had been the standard fare of chapbooks, declaring:

> Tom Thumb shall now be thrown away
> And Jack who did the Giants slay;
> Such ill connected artless lyes
> Our British Youth shall now despise:
> In thy Gigantick works they'll find
> Something to please and form the mind.[14]

Boreman cleverly introduced a subscription scheme, so that children could see their name listed in the front of his books. The second innovator was Mary Cooper, the widow of a prolific pamphlet publisher, who traded at the Globe in Paternoster Row. She published the first collection of nursery rhymes, *Tommy Thumb's Pretty Song-Book*, around the year 1744.

Boreman probably died in 1743, while Mary Cooper published a whole range of other books, but it is thought that they inspired John Newbery to put children's books on the map. His shop was at the Bible and Sun at the west end of the Churchyard, looking at the principal door of the cathedral. His Juvenile Library was made up of a series of tiny books bound in flowered and gilt Dutch paper in the style of Boreman's 'Gigantick Histories'. Perhaps the most famous is *The History of Little Goody Two Shoes*, that may have been written anonymously by Oliver Goldsmith, with woodcuts by 'Michael Angelo'. In this story the heroine's father dies because he could not obtain Dr James's Fever Powder. Booksellers often offered for sale patent medicines as well as their publications, and John Newbery was particularly keen on Dr James's product, prominently displaying it in advertisements. After his death, when his heirs transferred the business to a new building in the Churchyard, they had an inscription placed in large letters on the facade, 'The only Warehouse of Dr James's Powder'. Henry Dell, in his poem on booksellers, presents this portrait of Newbery:

> Bookseller, author and quack doctor too;
> Renown'd for all – He knowledge can supply,
> To lisping babes and babes of six feet high.[15]

The range of books for children published by Newbery was very wide, from simple picture books to the far from simple Tom Telescope's *Newtonian*

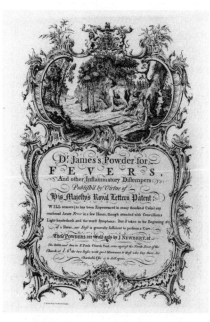

21. Although John Newbery was the leading publisher of books for children, his trade card concentrates on the lucrative sale of Dr James's Fever Powders.

System of Philosophy. He even published illustrated versions for children of the leading novels of the time: Richardson's *Pamela*, *Clarissa* and *Sir Charles Grandison*, and Fielding's *Joseph Andrews* and *Tom Jones*. He also launched a periodical for children, *The Lilliputian Magazine*, referring on the title page to a society of juvenile subscribers, using a marketing ploy similar to Boreman's. The magazine, however, did not prosper and soon folded.

Although children's publishing represented a considerable proportion of Newbery's business, he also produced two 'adult' journals, *The Christian Magazine*, edited by Dr William Dodd, who subsequently was executed for forgery, and *The British Magazine*. The latter contained pieces written anonymously by friends of Newbery, including Tobias Smollett, Samuel Johnson and Oliver Goldsmith. He was clearly a sociable man, attested by two affectionate pen portraits. Samuel Johnson in *The Idler* nicknamed him 'Jack Whirler', a bundle of energy:

when you call at his house, his clerk tells you, that Mr Whirler has just stept out, but will be at home exactly at two; you wait at a coffee house till two, and then find that he has been at home and is gone out again, but left word that he should be at the Half-moon tavern at seven, where he hopes to meet you. Jack's cheerfulness and civility rank him among those whose presence never gives pain.[16]

Oliver Goldsmith included a similar description of Newbery, a little man with a 'red-pimpled face' in his novel, *The Vicar of Wakefield*, published in 1768:

The philanthropic bookseller in Saint Pauls Churchyard has written so many little books for children: he called himself their friend: but he was the friend of all mankind. He was no sooner alighted, but he was in haste to be gone: for he was ever on business of 'utmost importance'.[17]

Close by St Paul's Cathedral with its clerical community was a group of intellectual institutions, Doctors' Commons, the Royal College of Physicians and the Royal Society, now established at Crane Court off Fleet Street. The Churchyard was also, of course, the centre of London's book trade, the community of booksellers, printers and of some of their writers. It was natural, therefore, that the neighbourhood taverns and coffee houses should be the venues for clubs and related social activities. One of the first was located in Dolly's Chophouse in Queen's Head Passage, just north of Paternoster Row. Here met publishers, clergymen and writers, such as Daniel Defoe, Alexander Pope and Samuel Johnson, who were served beefsteaks and ale by attractive waitresses.

The famously clubbable Johnson had cut his literary teeth on contributions and reviews in Edward Cave's *Gentleman's Magazine* in the late 1730s. As he indicated in *The Idler*, he would meet up with John Newbery at the Half Moon, a tavern in Aldersgate Street. Another of his favoured hostelries was the King's Head in Ivy Lane, just by Paternoster Row and an easy journey from his lodgings first off Fleet Street, and then in more style in Gough Square. In Ivy Lane in the 1740s he founded a literary and social club, the members of which were a diverse group: the bookseller John Payne, authors, including his first biographer, Sir John Hawkins, physicians, the Archdeacon of Norwich and the theatre manager David Garrick. Three decades on Johnson, now famous for his dictionary among other literary triumphs, met up with his intimates at the Queen's Arms in St Paul's Churchyard. His dislike of Whig politics made him stipulate that the club should include no patriots.

Rather different in political persuasion was the Club of Honest Whigs, although their name suggests that they were sceptical of the current government's integrity.[18] They met in the London Coffee House in the Churchyard, with as their moving spirit the experimental philosopher and master of a dissenting academy in Spitalfields, John Canton. Among the members was Benjamin Franklin, in London as agent for the Pennsylvania Assembly. He had become friends with Canton as a result of his work on electricity and magnetism. Other members included the dissenting ministers Joseph Priestley and Richard Price, and William Rose, a schoolmaster and critic who wrote regularly for Griffiths' *Monthly Review*. We have some details both of the social flavour of the club, and of their political stance, from James Boswell, an occasional member:

> Some of us smoke a pipe, conversation goes on pretty formally, sometimes
> sensibly and sometimes furiously. At nine there is a side-board with Welsh
> Rabbits and Apple Puffs, Porter and Beer. Our reckoning is about 18d per
> Head. Much was said this night against Parliament. I said that, as it seems
> to be agreed that all Members of Parliament became corrupted, it was
> better to chuse men already bad and so save good men.[19]

At the Chapter Coffee House, on the south side of Paternoster Row by Ave Maria Lane, publishing congers met to auction copyrights and to sort out their shares of ventures such as the production of Dr Johnson's dictionary, which required major financial outlay and was commissioned by five publishers. The Chapter Coffee House was characterised in the first number of the *Connoisseur*:

> It is frequented by those encouragers of learning, the booksellers . . . Their
> criticisms are somewhat singular. When they say a good book, they do not
> mean to praise the style or sentiment, but the quick and extensive sale of it.[20]

A box or booth in the north-east part of the principal room of the coffee house was known as the Witenagemot, set aside for the exclusive use of a club. In Anglo-Saxon times the folk moot had been held nearby (pp. 16ff) but that was a very different institution from the Witenagemot, an assembly of wise men who advised the King, and was regarded in the eighteenth century as a precursor of parliamentary democracy. One group of the club took possession of the box early in the morning, and from their custom of acquiring papers fresh from the news vendors were known as the Wet Paper Club. In the afternoon a second group gathered here. One regular visitor was Dr William Buchan, author of the standard treatise *Domestic Medicine, or The Family Physician*. Despite being an avowed Tory, he acted as moderator of meetings, where the newspapers were studied and politics discussed.

Another club that met, fortnightly, at the Chapter Coffee House in the early 1780s was the Philosophical Society. The purpose of this group, as set out in their minutes, was 'that the Conversation of this Society shall be confined to Natural Philosophy in its most extensive significance'.[21] The membership was a diverse group of experimental scientists, medical practitioners and instrument makers, who exchanged scientific information, discussed experiments and considered industrial improvements. Priestley was a member, along with Josiah Wedgwood and William Nicholson, a chemist who worked with the pioneering potter in his development of materials.

Child's Coffee House in Warwick Lane had been the meeting place for Sir Christopher Wren and his team during the rebuilding of London after the Great Fire, and for members of the Royal Society. In the early eighteenth century it became the favourite venue for the clergy and for proctors from Doctors' Commons. Joseph Addison came here to listen in on conversations as copy for the *Spectator*, on one occasion relating the confusion of a country gentleman who mistook the scarves worn by the proctors as being those of doctors of divinity: a forerunner of the Bateman cartoons.

Not all were flourishing in this environment. Hack writers, nicknamed Grub Street writers after the thoroughfare south of Smithfield, lived in penury in garrets high above bookshops, making a precarious living by contributing to the growing number of journals. Oliver Goldsmith kept himself just above the breadline by writing reviews and biographies, translations and abridgements, rescued at one stage from being thrown into prison for debt by his friend Dr Johnson, who sold the manuscript of *The Vicar of Wakefield* to John Newbery. Another writer, the poet Thomas Chatterton, used the Chapter Coffee House to compose his poems and to dispatch his letters trying to drum up work before finishing his tragically short life, aged 18, in 1770 in his lodgings by taking arsenic.

As the 1760s drew to a close, so the conversation among the booksellers in these coffee houses must have revolved around the hot topic of copyright. As noted earlier, the passing of the 1710 Act failed in practice to loosen the hold on perpetual copyright by the powerful booksellers of the Stationers' Company. At the auctions held in the Chapter Coffee House, interlopers were not welcome and were ejected on the occasions that they gained access. Copyright was not often sold in entirety, and sometimes the shares could be as little as a hundredth. In 1766, when Richardson's widow sold off some of her shares of his novels, a sixteenth share in *Pamela* fetched £18, and a twenty-fourth of the more recently published *Clarissa* went for £25. The 'classics' went for even more: Shakespeare was calculated at £1,800, while Alexander Pope's *Works* was valued at the huge sum of £4,400.[22]

Into this closed shop came Alexander Donaldson, an Edinburgh bookseller, who established himself in the Churchyard in 1769. In Scotland the courts had upheld the provisions of the 1710 Act, rejecting the concept of perpetual copyright, and the booksellers north of the border had long been a thorn in the side of their English counterparts. Donaldson boasted of selling books at 30 to 50 per cent cheaper than the usual London prices. His assault came at the very time that the House of Lords was ruling on copyright interpretation. The London booksellers responded to the Scotsman's challenge with suits in the court of Chancery, but in 1774 perpetual copyright was declared invalid by the House of Lords in the case of *Donaldson v Beckett*. John Murray, founder of yet another great publishing dynasty, pronounced the decision the Magna Carta for booksellers.

The ruling not only enabled booksellers to share in the profits of publishing cheap editions of canonical classics, such as the works of Chaucer, Shakespeare and Milton, but also for a much wider audience to be able to buy them. The bookseller John Bell, for example, produced between 1777 and 1782 no less than 109 volumes in his series, *Poets of Great Britain from Chaucer to Churchill*, each priced at 1s 6d. He had refused to join the conger of London publishers

Stationers' Hall, near Paternoster Row.

22. The entrance to Stationers' Hall, from Ave Maria Lane, with the dining hall facing and the Stock Room, where booksellers and printers came to register their titles, on the right. This engraving from 1756 is attributed to Benjamin Cole, see p.193.

who financed a similar series with prefaces by Samuel Johnson. Although Johnson's *Lives of the Poets* represents a height of English literary criticism, the series failed commercially while Bell's proved a triumph. Interestingly Johnson was sceptical of the idea of cheap editions, comparing their publishers with Robin Hood, robbing the rich to give to the poor.

Meanwhile the monopoly enjoyed by the Stationers' Company for the extremely valuable production of almanacs was being challenged by Thomas Carnan, the stepson of John Newbery. In 1779 a bill brought to Parliament by the Company to legalise this monopoly was thrown out, this time by the House of Commons. On hearing the news, Carnan drove his phaeton and pair in triumph repeatedly around St Paul's Churchyard and through Paternoster Row, pointedly past the entrance to Stationers' Hall.

The convivial life offered by the City taverns and coffee houses was almost exclusively male.[23] However, by the late eighteenth century there were a growing number of female novelists and poets. One of their early supporters was Ralph Griffiths, who employed the poet Elizabeth Moody to write for him in *The Monthly Review*. In 1798, while writing a review of her *Poetic Trifles,* he noted:

> The polished period in which we live may be justly denominated the Age of ingenious and learned Ladies; who have excelled so much in the more elegant branches of literature, that we need not to hesitate in concluding that the long agitated dispute between the two sexes is at length determined; and that it is no longer a question, - whether woman *is* or is *not* inferior to man in natural ability, or less capable of excelling in mental accomplishments.[24]

Two publishers – George Robinson and Joseph Johnson – remedied the lack of social opportunities for their female authors by hosting literary dinners. According to the obituary that appeared in the *Gentleman's Magazine* in 1801, George Robinson was regarded as the most important publisher in England in the late eighteenth century. He became part publisher with Archibald Hamilton of the *Critical Review,* the *Town and Country Magazine* and the *Lady's Magazine,* and was involved in several newspapers, including the Whig *Political Herald and Review,* which was edited by William Godwin. His strongly held political views got him into trouble in 1793 when he was fined for selling copies of Thomas Paine's *Rights of Man*.

Robinson was generous towards his authors, male and female. William Godwin was paid 700 guineas for his *Political Justice*, with a further 300 guineas after the sale of the first 3,000 copies. For her Gothic novel, *The Mysteries of Udolpho*, Anne Radcliffe was given what was considered the sensational sum of 500 guineas. Along with 'the wits and critics of the day', Mrs Radcliffe was entertained at the Sign of Addison's Head in Paternoster Row. Other literary ladies enjoying Robinson's hospitality included Dr Johnson's great friend, Hester Lynch Thrale, and the novelist and dramatist, Elizabeth Inchbald. Tall and affable, Robinson was clearly able to take his drink: 'a most social companion . . . said to be a six bottle man, sometimes knocking up, as it was termed, some of his Irish and Scotch friends.'[25]

His 'invariable and confidential friend', Joseph Johnson, was providing similar largesse and stimulating company, around the corner in St Paul's Churchyard.[26] Born in 1738 into a Baptist dissenting family in Everton, just north of Liverpool, Johnson was apprenticed to the bookseller George Keith in Gracechurch Street, close to London Bridge. With his proximity to Guy's and St Thomas' hospitals in Southwark, Keith specialised in medical books. When Johnson set up on his own account in Paternoster Row, however, he launched into a wide range of publications, including works of science, travel narratives, children's books and poetry, and, after 1774, he took advantage of the decision in the Donaldson case to publish the 'canonical classics'. A regular visitor to the Chapter Coffee House, he met up with all the leading booksellers, making particular friends with John Murray, then based in Fleet Street.

In 1770 after Johnson's shop was destroyed in a fire, he moved to 72 St Paul's Churchyard, a corner site, looking towards the west doors of the cathedral. As he never married, Johnson treated his stable of authors as his family. And what a stable it was: scientists Joseph Priestley and Erasmus Darwin, poets William Wordsworth and William Cowper, the statistician Thomas Malthus, novelists Charlotte Smith and Maria Edgeworth among many more. He was patron of the Swiss artist, Henry Fuseli, and of William Blake, displaying the latter's engravings in his shop.

In 1786, knowing that Johnson had a special interest in educational works, John Hewlett, a schoolmaster in Hackney, introduced him to Mary Wollstonecraft. He agreed to publish her *Thoughts on the Education of Daughters*, and after she was sacked from her post as a governess to an aristocratic family in Ireland, he employed her to write on a regular basis for the journal, the *Analytical Review*, that he was about to launch with Thomas Christie. At first he gave her shelter in 72 St Paul's Churchyard, and then found her lodgings just south of Blackfriars Bridge, within easy walking distance. Wollstonecraft nicknamed him 'little Johnson' in contrast to the considerable bulk of his namesake, Samuel, and wrote how she loved him like a father.

Joseph Johnson initiated three o'clock gatherings in the dining room that looked out over the Churchyard. These were described by Thomas Campbell as 'a sort of Menagerie of Live Authors'. The 'menagerie' was treated to a dinner, imagined by Marilyn Gaull as consisting of 'boiled cod, veal, vegetables, rice pudding, and wine, served under the brooding image of Fuseli's

"The Nightmare"'.[27] It was at one of these dinners that Mary Wollstonecraft first met William Godwin in November 1791. Godwin had come to hear the celebrated Thomas Paine talk about *The Rights of Man*, but instead found himself listening to Wollstonecraft all evening. He thought her strident, and they parted 'mutually displeased with each other' according to the entry in his diary for that day.[28] The following year Mary published with Johnson her most famous work, *A Vindication of the Rights of Women*. And, rather like Beatrice and Benedict in Shakespeare's *Much Ado About Nothing*, having begun their relationship so unfavourably, Mary and Godwin married in 1797. This marriage was cut tragically short when she died shortly after the birth of their daughter Mary. Mary was to become the wife of the poet Shelley and the creator of the Gothic masterpiece *Frankenstein*, which she described as coming to her in a half-waking nightmare.

Johnson worked closely with his authors giving them feedback, sometimes to their surprise, suggesting that this was not the usual practice of the time. A good example of his editorial skills was his advice to Maria Edgeworth. He was the publisher of her novels, but he also worked with her on *The Parent's Assistant or Stories for Children* that she wrote with her father, Richard Lovell Edgeworth, helping her to tailor her language for young readers. The notice of the book in *The Monthly Review* applauded her for making the book 'adapted with peculiar felicity to the understandings of children' and that the 'language is varied in its degrees of simplicity, to suit the pieces to different ages'.[29] The stories were illustrated with engravings by William Blake.

From the 1760s, Johnson had been working with Benjamin Franklin and became particularly active in publishing works related to the American Revolution by authors such as Richard Price and Samuel Adams. In 1791 he initially offered to publish Thomas Paine's *Rights of Man*, but let it go to another bookseller, recognising that he was being identified with radical movements and the dangers involved therein. As revolution convulsed Paris, the Prime Minister, William Pitt the Younger, began to introduce increasingly repressive measures. The house and laboratory of Johnson's friend and author, Joseph Priestley, was destroyed by a Birmingham mob on the second anniversary of Bastille Day, and he eventually emigrated to the safer environment of the United States. Although Johnson considered doing the same, he decided to stay in London. In 1798 he was arrested and put on trial, with the indictment that he was 'a malicious, seditious and ill-disposed person and being greatly disaffected to our said Lord the King'. Found guilty, he was sentenced to confinement in the King's Bench Prison, in fairly comfortable accommodation thanks to his ability to pay. Here he entertained his authors in rather different circumstances from his literary dinners. William Godwin, for example, took tea with him. After three months, he was released on surety of good behaviour.

Johnson returned to St Paul's Churchyard and continued his publishing, but ceased his more controversial political activities. The *Analytical Review* had been closed down shortly after he was found guilty, to the delight of the right-wing *Anti-Jacobin Review.* Johnson is often described as radical, but the editor of his correspondence points out that he published a wide spectrum of works, and that the uniting theme was that they represented the spirit of free enquiry.[30] At his death in 1809, his business was inherited by his great-nephews Rowland Hunter and John Miles, who continued the tradition of his literary gatherings in St Paul's Churchyard with authors of the next generation.

As far as St Paul's and its environs were concerned, the eighteenth century had been a golden age of book and periodical publishing. A book published in 1834, looking back, declared:

> It was calculated . . . that few books were published in England besides those that were printed and published in London; and that most of them were issued to the public from this narrow, inconvenient street [Paternoster Row], and its adjoining ways of Warwick-lane, Ave-Maria-lane, Stationers'- court and particularly the north side of St Paul's church-yard.[31]

But the Churchyard itself was also the setting for events on a national, indeed an international scale, as Britain became an imperial power, as will be seen in the next chapter.

CHAPTER 11

THEATRE FOR LONDON, BRITAIN AND THE EMPIRE

When Sir Christopher Wren came to design the new St Paul's Cathedral following the Great Fire, he wanted to provide the building with an impressive approach and forecourt. His plan submitted to Charles II in the immediate aftermath proposed a triangular piazza leading up to the west end of the cathedral. That scheme was rendered redundant when it was decided not to go for a wholesale replanning of the City (see p. 131). Expense intervened yet again when the design of the new cathedral was approved in 1675. Substantial brick houses now lined Ludgate Hill, and so, beyond slightly widening the street, Wren was obliged to work with an irregular layout and the cathedral aligned at an angle. However, he was able to provide a generous space immediately in front of the west doors. In the Middle Ages this area was known as the Atrium, a theatrical stage for great events, and the idea was repeated in the new Churchyard.

The great events began even while the cathedral was under construction. As noted in Chapter 7, a thanksgiving service was held at St Paul's in December 1697 to mark the signing of the Treaty of Ryswick and the end of war between France and England. The procession that wound its way up from Westminster, along the Strand and Fleet Street, and finally up Ludgate Hill, was led by the lord mayor and his aldermen, followed by leading ministers and militia bands. Crowds lined the Churchyard as the procession entered it and climbed the steps into the cathedral. This was a formula that was to be repeated again and again in the years that followed.

In 1697, the one notable absentee was William III, who stayed upriver in his palace at Hampton Court: the City with its polluted atmosphere exacerbated his asthma and the King had become reclusive following the death of Queen Mary. But St Paul's was a favourite place for his successor, Anne, and from 1702 onwards there were royal visits for thanksgiving services to mark victories over the French when England once more became embroiled in Louis XIV's determination to dominate Europe in the War of the Spanish Succession. The first of the services took place in the autumn of that year, commemorating the military gains of John Churchill, Duke of Marlborough, in the Low Countries and Admiral Rook's destruction of the Spanish fleet at Vigo Bay. The procession began at St James's Palace, with the lord mayor presenting the Queen with a sword at the Temple Bar in the Strand, and then making its way up to the cathedral.

Two years later, the thanksgiving for Marlborough's famous victory at Blenheim was even more splendid, with the surrounding streets railed off and hung with blue cloth. The roofs and windows of the houses lining the route and around St Paul's Churchyard were hung with oriental carpets and tapestries. As victory followed victory – Ramillies, Oudenarde, Malplaquet – so the processions revisited the Churchyard. On 31 December 1706, William Nicolson, Bishop of Carlisle, noted in his diary attending the Queen for the thanksgiving service marking Marlborough's victory at Ramillies, and how cheering crowds surrounded the Queen's carriage as it climbed Ludgate Hill and she made her way into the cathedral.[1] These occasions, however, cannot have brought unalloyed joy to Anne, whose health was deteriorating at the same time that the rift was deepening with the Duchess of Marlborough, her Mistress of the Robes. On 23 August 1708, the day of thanksgiving for success at Oudenarde, the Duchess realised that the Queen wore no jewels, despite the fact that she had laid them out for her. As the royal coach approached the cathedral, a bitter quarrel broke out, with the Duchess accusing the Queen of showing disrespect to Marlborough. The Queen never forgave Sarah and after this Abigail Masham became her main friend and confidante.

The Oudenarde thanksgiving was also the occasion of a so-called plot. There had been many hatched over the centuries in St Paul's Churchyard, but this has to figure as one of the more bizarre. It was named the Screw-Plot, and was supposed to have been the work of Whigs, who were accused of removing the screws and bolts of part of the cathedral roof so that it would fall upon the Queen and her Tory ministers. Poems appeared on the subject such as a ballad, 'Plot upon Plot':

Some of your Machi'villian Crew
From heavy roof of Paul,
Most trait'rously stole every screw,
To make that fabric fall;
And so to catch her Majesty,
And all her friends beguile
As birds are trapt by boys most sly
In pitfall with a tile.[2]

The previous year, on 1 May 1707, the kingdoms of England and Scotland were united to become Great Britain. A collect that had been especially commissioned for that day was read in St Paul's Cathedral. It noted 'all the signal providences by which the Union of this island [is] brought to a happy conclusion: so that as we were before under one head, so are we now become one people'. The preacher at this service was William Talbot, Bishop of Oxford, who spoke of creating 'a hearty Union' from which prosperity would follow. Nigel Aston makes the point that a distinctively British culture would not be created overnight, but that the recently built cathedral could play a part in fostering this.[3]

The union was soon given corporeal form in a statue group sculpted in white marble by Francis Bird and placed in front of the western doors in 1712 to mark the completion of the cathedral. Queen Anne is shown in her coronation robes, holding a sceptre and orb, with four emblematic female figures at her feet. These represent what was regarded at the time as the British Empire: Britannia, for Great Britain which now had the united kingdoms of England and Scotland, holding a trident, an allusion to naval power; France, a reminder that England had laid claim to the French Crown ever since the fourteenth century; America, with feathered head-dress and skirt, her foot on a man's severed head; and Ireland, carrying a harp. When yet another thanksgiving service was held at the cathedral to mark the signing of the Treaty of Utrecht in 1713, the hoarding around the statue group was removed. But the Queen herself was not present: ill, and bowed down by sorrow, she remained at St James's Palace. A year later she was dead, and her distant cousin George, Elector of Hanover, was the next, Protestant, monarch. An unkind epigram was written about the statue, which is usually attributed to the Jacobites, who had urged Anne to name her half-brother, James Stuart, as her successor:

The Statue of HER MAIESTY &c Erected at the West End of S.T PAULS Ann 1713

23. The statue of Queen Anne erected at the west end of St Paul's to mark the cathedral's completion in 1713.

Brandy Nan, Brandy Nan. Left in the lurch,
Her face to the gin shop, her back to the church.

An alternative reading is that the Queen is looking towards the gin shop at the south-east corner of St Paul's Churchyard as a symbol of Protestantism, for the drink had been made popular with the arrival of the Dutchman, William III, while brandy symbolised France and Catholicism. Whatever the interpretation, Queen Anne was known to have turned to both for solace, racked as she was by gout and dropsy.

The 1713 celebration for the Treaty of Utrecht also witnessed the first appearance of charity children. *The Post Boy* reported how

> near four thousand Charity Children, boys and girls, being new clothed, were placed upon a machine extended in length 620 feet, which had in breadth eight ranges of seats one above another. During the whole procession which lasted near three hours, they sung and repeated hymns which were prepared upon her Majesty's Royal Presence.[4]

The Queen's presence was in fact lacking, as recorded by the Poet Laureate Nahum Tate, in *The Triumph of Peace*:

> See! Britain's Peers and senate move in state,
> For whose appearance gazing millions wait . . .
> tis true, we see our Peers and Senate come,
> In state advancing to the sacred dome;
> That glorious sight affords no small relief;
> But still the QUEEN is absent . . . That's the Grief.

Charity schools had enjoyed a long history: Eton College began life as a foundation for poor scholars, while Dean Colet stipulated that 153 boys should be provided with free education when refounding St Paul's School. From the sixteenth century poor boys at Christ's Hospital in Newgate, just north of the Churchyard, were known as Bluecoats because of their uniform. But a significant marked expansion in charity schools for both boys and girls came about through the efforts of a clergyman, Thomas Bray. This is associated with the founding of the Society for Promoting Christian Knowledge (SPCK) in 1698. Bray, with a small group of friends, met up at Lincoln's Inn, concerned by what they perceived as the growth in vice and immorality owing to a fundamental ignorance of the principles of the Christian religion. Their intention was to meet regularly to devise strategies whereby they could increase knowledge of Anglican Christianity by publishing and distributing literature, and by encouraging education at all levels. Charity schools for poor children aged between seven and eleven were established along with libraries.

One man prominent in the activities of the SPCK, and of charity schools, was Henry Newman, from a Puritan family in New England, who had settled in London in 1708 and acted as the Society's secretary. As Tate recorded dramatically in his poem, Queen Anne was dying, so that the following year, 1714, it was the Hanoverian King, George I, who attended the thanksgiving with his son, the future George II. Newman recorded in his diary:

> The charity children made a goodly appearance in St Paul's Churchyard, which the King and Prince were extremely pleased with, so that His Highness said he never saw anything so fine, and that he only wished he had his own with him to see them at the same time.[5]

Ironically, the Hanoverians were distinguished by the bad relations between father and son.

In fact, this was the only time that George I attended the service, and thereafter he and his heirs kept away. The Society was viewed with a certain amount of suspicion by the establishment and was nicknamed the Presbyterian Club. Nevertheless, the participating role of the London charity children was now part of the calendar, becoming an annual event held on Ascension Day, and known as Holy Thursday. Children from the schools in their various coloured uniforms would march in procession to a church for a service. Such was the number of children, and of crowds coming to see them, that the churches were soon overflowing. Sir Christopher Wren had vetoed the idea that St Paul's Cathedral should supply a suitable venue, and it was only in 1782 that wooden galleries were erected for them under the dome.

William Blake in his *Songs of Innocence*, published in 1789, described their annual gathering in the poem 'Holy Thursday':

Twas on a Holy Thursday, their innocent faces clean,
The children walking two and two, in red and blue and green,
Grey-headed beadles walk'd before, with wands as white as snow,
Till into the high dome of Paul's they like Thames' water flow

O what a multitude they seemed these flowers of London town
Seated in companies they sit with radiance all their own
The hum of multitudes was there but multitudes of lambs
Thousands of little boys & girls raising their innocent hands

Now like a mighty wind they raise to heaven the voice of song
Or like harmonious thunderings the seats of Heaven among
Beneath them sit the aged men wise guardians of the poor
Then cherish pity, lest you drive an angel from your door.

If the powers that be had regarded the SPCK as evangelical and radical, the view of Blake was yet more so, questioning why such children were living in poverty in one of the most prosperous nations in the world. His view was that the destitute existence of so many impoverishes that nation.

Along with Holy Thursdays, national events continued to be celebrated at St Paul's, albeit without the presence of the royal family. The defeat of Charles Stuart, the Young Pretender, at Culloden was marked in 1745, and three years later the Peace of Aix La Chapelle at the end of the War of the Austrian Succession. Royal association returned when George Pretyman, former Private Secretary to the Prime Minister, William Pitt the Younger, became Dean. Only 37 at the time of his appointment, Pretyman held the post from 1787 to 1820, covering the period that Britain was struggling against France. It was the combination of Pitt and Pretyman that meant that the cathedral of St Paul's, rather than the abbey at Westminster, was the theatre for public celebrations, giving it 'a place in national life unknown since Stuart times'.[6]

The service that brought George III to St Paul's on St George's Day 1789 was a celebration of his recovery from a bout of insanity. Symptoms of mental disturbance had started to manifest themselves in the autumn of 1788, but within months he was recovering. On 23 April, accompanied by Queen Charlotte, he rode in a carriage through the streets of London.

Three years earlier Margaret Nicholson, the daughter of a barber from Stockton-on-Tees, had attempted to assassinate him in the demented belief that the Crown was hers by right, and that if denied her, England would be deluged with blood. The King had been quick to intervene when the surrounding crowd had threatened to set upon her, telling them not to hurt her, for she was mad, a nice irony as it transpired. Security was therefore tight when George and Charlotte made their way to the cathedral, but the crowds were wildly enthusiastic, with crowns decorating public buildings, and candles illuminating windows along the route. When the royal party reached St Paul's shortly before noon, a rocket was fired from the statue of Queen Anne as a signal for the firing of the guns in salute at the Tower of London. Once inside the cathedral, the King was welcomed by a choir of 6,000 children singing part of the Hundredth Psalm.

George III returned in December 1797 for more celebrations as naval victories were secured against the French and Spanish fleets. Revolutionary state festivals had been held in France, organised by the artist Jacques-Louis David, to celebrate their gains, but the printing presses of the Churchyard and the surrounding neighbourhood pointedly noted that the British were thanking the Lord for theirs. A 'Cheap Repository Tract' produced by the printer John Marshall from his shop in St Mary Aldermary churchyard and sold through street hawkers reminded Londoners of this difference in attitude:

> Remember that we meet to celebrate not our own praises, but the praises of that God who hath delivered us. In France, indeed where they speak not of God in their public festivals, nor pretend to honour Him by them, it is natural to expect that a spirit of national pride only will be cultivated. . . . We also have our heroes whom we would thank, but we will not make Gods of them.[7]

On this occasion, French, Spanish and Dutch flags captured during naval battles were carried aloft through the streets and into the cathedral. This service was innovative, raising eyebrows by according ordinary seamen a place of honour.

The British may not have made gods of their heroes, but they were certainly prepared to honour them in style. Westminster Abbey had for centuries been the scene for coronations, and St George's Chapel in Windsor Castle for royal funerals, but in the eighteenth century St Paul's Cathedral became the resting place for illustrious Britons. This custom was strongly urged by the painter Sir Joshua Reynolds, President of the Royal Academy of Arts. The Churchyard thus became the theatre for pageantry, above all for the funeral processions of Admiral Nelson in 1806, and of the Duke of Wellington in 1852.

Admiral Nelson was killed on 21 October 1805 on the foredeck of his ship, *HMS Victory*, at the peak of the Battle of Trafalgar against combined French and Spanish fleets. Just half an hour after his death, the great victory that broke Napoleon's naval power and established the maritime supremacy of the British had been secured. Arriving in Gibraltar, Nelson's men insisted that his body should be brought home, and he was put into a cask of spirits and conveyed to the Royal Greenwich Hospital where he lay in state for three days in the Painted Hall. The pressure to view him was so great that arrangements almost collapsed, and the same huge upswell in emotion continued when Nelson was carried up the Thames to Whitehall Stairs. On 9 January 1806 the funeral procession, led by the Prince of Wales, left the Admiralty and made its way eastwards to St Paul's. According to the report in *The Times*, the tail end of the procession had not left Whitehall when the carriage bearing the catafalque arrived in the Churchyard.

An aquatint by Merigot and Augustus Pugin shows the moment of arrival, with thousands of people massed in the Churchyard, others on rooftops and at the windows of the houses. Soldiers are drawn up all around, but it was the seamen of *Victory* carrying her battle ensigns that apparently moved the crowds (Plate 15). When Nelson's coffin was taken for burial in the cathedral crypt, the men did not fold the colours and lay them on top, instead tearing them up to save as memorials. An elaborate structure was erected over his grave, featuring a casket in black marble, made three centuries earlier as part of the grand funerary monument that Cardinal Wolsey commissioned for himself from the Italian artist Benedetto da Rovezzano. At Wolsey's fall, it was commandeered by Henry VIII for his tomb, but never used: a nice touch that the diminutive man from Norfolk should now have it as his monument.

When Nelson left for Trafalgar, he was heard to say, 'Victory or Westminster Abbey?' But a nineteenth-century book argues that it was a higher distinction to have made the cathedral his final resting place: 'Of what do the millions of London think in connexion with St Paul's crypt but Wellington and Nelson?'[8] Contemporary accounts of visits to the cathedral and to the Churchyard comment on the number of sailors and their families who made the pilgrimage to pay their respects to the fallen admiral, although not always soberly. One traveller from Danzig, Johanna Schopenhauer, visited in 1816. She made the customary climb up to the dome for the view over London, remarking of course on the coal smoke from innumerable chimneys obscuring the view. The pending arrival of a boisterous group of sailors caused the departure of her party. But as they made their way down Ludgate Hill they noticed:

all the pedestrians standing still gazing anxiously at the cross on the top of St Paul's. . . . With the help of binoculars, we were able to discern one of the sailors whom we had encountered in the church. He had contrived to get himself onto the cross and at that horrible height was delighting in taking up some breath-taking positions, waving his cap, standing on one leg, driving the spectators into a state of terrified admiration. Of course a man like him, accustomed to standing high on the rocking mast of his ship, in the midst of the wild ocean, had long since lost any feeling of dizziness and probably found this firm, motionless spot quite safe in spite of the great height, whereas all of us below remained frozen with terror at the mere sight.[9]

Nelson's resting place continued to attract many visitors to the cathedral and the Churchyard. In 1837 the Home Secretary, Lord John Russell, with the backing of Queen Victoria, invited the dean and chapter to improve existing arrangements. Entrance fees to climb up to the Whispering Gallery and dome, to view Wren's Great Model and to visit the library, had always been relatively expensive, usually sixpence for each part of the building. Now it was suggested that a fee of twopence should be charged to view the interior, except for set times for services. The chapter resisted, but the pressure of visitors was making some kind of compromise necessary. In 1841 one of the canons, R.C. Packman, estimated that between two and three thousand visitors entered the cathedral during barrier-free Sundays. These were primarily London artisanal families, many of whom wished to visit the crypt. Weekday tourists tended to be 'out of towners'. An interesting debate ensued, reflecting social attitudes. One virger accused the London crowd of smoking, snacking and soliciting in the crossing under the dome, defacing monuments and relieving themselves in pews and dark corners. But Packman thought that the poorer classes 'if they are spoken to . . . behave better than a great many who style themselves gentlemen'. In contrast, he pointed to 'gentlewomen with plumes of feathers, not of a bad character, but strings of persons walking up and down, looking at each other, and lounging about'. This is uncannily reminiscent of the complaints made in the early seventeenth century, when the people of the Churchyard invaded the medieval cathedral and occupied the Middle Aisle, as described in Chapter 6.[10]

Almost half a century after Nelson's burial, when it came to the question of where the Duke of Wellington should be interred, Queen Victoria, the Prince Consort and the Prime Minister, the Earl of Derby, decided on St Paul's Cathedral. Their decision was influenced by consciousness of the precedent of Nelson, so that 'the greatest military [might rest] by the side of the greatest naval chief who ever reflected lustre on the annals of England'.[11] The funeral, which took place on 18 November 1852, has been described as probably one of the most ornate and spectacular ever staged. The press estimated that a million and a half people watched the procession as it made its way from the lying-in-state at Chelsea Hospital, via Horse Guards and on to St Paul's.

It is interesting to compare the depiction of St Paul's Churchyard for the two funerals. In the 40 years or so, the houses have been rebuilt, and are much taller and grander. The Duke's catafalque, described by the Poet Laureate Alfred Lord Tennyson in his long funeral ode as 'the towerwing [sic] car, the sable steeds', is floridly opulent compared to the restrained classicism of Nelson's funeral carriage. But the great size of the crowds is the same, flocking to the Churchyard to witness the passing of one of the nation's heroes. Wellington's tomb is just yards away from that of Nelson in the cathedral crypt, with old soldiers attending the actual interment, just as Nelson's sailors had done half a century earlier (Plate 16).

St Paul's Churchyard not only provided a stage for these solemn occasions, but also for protests, another centuries-old tradition. These took a variety of forms. In the summer of 1780, when Parliament was preparing to repeal legislation against Roman Catholics, a protest march was organised by Lord George Gordon, an MP and leader of the Protestant Association. He lost control, however, both of his followers and of the situation, which degenerated into a campaign of general destruction. Newgate Gaol was attacked, the prisoners released and the buildings set on fire. When the rioters then turned their attention to the Churchyard, threatening to destroy the deanery, the King sent a guard for the protection of St Paul's and its neighbourhood. One of the resident canons, John Douglas, claimed:

> I came up to London in June. Was at St Paul's when the riots began, and I got some credit, and I hope did some good, by my activity on that occasion. By getting a Detachment of soldiers posted in St Paul's churchyard, I saved our part of the Town which otherwise was in great danger. I entertained the whole party, officers and privates, the first day, at my own expense.[12]

The combination of Dean Pretyman and Prime Minister William Pitt had brought some very popular events to the Churchyard. However, Pitt's popularity was to seesaw wildly with the turbulent political climate of the 1790s. High prices and heavy taxation, combined with weariness at the length of the war with France, all took their toll. His repressive measures against what he saw as sedition alienated the radical members of the bookselling and publishing industries, with booksellers such as Joseph Johnson prosecuted and sent to gaol, as seen in the previous chapter. On one occasion in 1797 Pitt's coach was pelted as he passed through the Churchyard.

A protest of a rather different kind took place in 1820, following the death of George III. His son, who succeeded to the throne as George IV, was determined that his estranged wife, Caroline of Brunswick, should never become queen, and had tried unsuccessfully to obtain a divorce. When news of his succession reached Europe, Caroline returned to London to claim her position as Queen. She was hugely popular both with the radical press and with the British populace, while the new King's outrageously immoral behaviour

Queen Caroline's Procession to St. Paul's, November 29, 1820.
To return thanks for her Triumph over the Bill of Pains and Penalties.
Published by T. Batchelar, 115, Long Alley, Crown Street, Finsbury.

24. Queen Caroline being greeted by huge crowds as she made her way to St Paul's Cathedral in 1820.

attracted contempt. An archaic piece of legislation, the Pains and Penalties Bill, was introduced to Parliament in a move to secure a divorce, but Caroline's brilliant Attorney General, Henry Brougham, led her defence in the House of Lords. His speech, lasting two days, ridiculed the evidence against her and so powerful was his appeal to the consciences of their lordships that one rushed out of the chamber in tears. After 11 weeks of what amounted to Caroline's trial for adultery, the bill was withdrawn when the Prime Minister, Lord Liverpool, bowed to popular sentiment. There followed widespread rejoicing with London illuminated for three days.

Caroline was given support by the lord mayor and several prominent members of the corporation, including Alderman Wood, who suggested that there should be a solemn service of thanksgiving in St Paul's Cathedral for the deliverance of the Queen from her enemies. On 29 November she made her way in triumph through the streets of London to the Churchyard, with thousands cheering her on. In strong contrast, once she entered the cathedral, it was half empty, for the dean and chapter took a very different view from the leading members of the City. Caroline may not have appreciated that St Paul's Churchyard had staged many protests in the past, but her supporters knew very well. Popular engravings produced by some of the aldermen who were printers show the procession and call upon Britons to behold their Queen. Caroline's triumph was short-lived, however, for on the orders of her husband she was barred from the coronation that took place in July 1821. Falling ill in London, she died three weeks later and her funeral procession took her through the capital on its way to her native Brunswick for burial.

Half a century later, an interesting combination of a religious and secular protest took place in February 1887, when a Socialist rally stormed the cathedral. Forewarned, the dean and chapter decided to organise a popular service, including an invitation to the lord mayor and corporation. As reported by *The Times* the following day, this 'kindly feeling' was not reciprocated by the Socialist leaders who said:

> we have not the slightest hope that the Anglicans or any other Christian sect will ever declare against 'the rights of property' or take the side of the people against the plunderers. Modern Christianity is essentially a middle-class creed, with a capitalist paradise here.

Draping their banners of red, black and white on the railings around the statue of Queen Anne, some of the protesters joined the service inside the cathedral, barracking the Archdeacon of London, Dr Gifford, when he tried to deliver a message that rich and poor must meet together, for 'the Lord is the Maker of them All'. Others persuaded one of the canons, Robert Gregory, to hold an impromptu service outside. According to the newspaper report, 'the whole of the great space from the steps of the Cathedral to the bottom of Ludgate-hill was thronged with people presenting a sea of upturned faces'.[13] Despite the huge scale of the demonstration, at the end of the two services, the marchers dispersed peaceably.

The concept of a capitalist paradise brought another large-scale demonstration to St Paul's. In late 1905, at a time of rising unemployment in Britain, news was arriving of strikes in Russia, including one organised by a soviet, or council, in St Petersburg. On 17 December a service was held at St Paul's Cathedral. Reports, under the headline ' "Out-of-Works" at St Paul's', in a Scottish newspaper the following day presented two slightly different scenarios. The first described contingents of about a thousand unemployed marching to the cathedral to attend a service, where they were addressed by Canon Newbolt who remarked that 'the existing destitution, hunger and want did not brook delay, and must be attended to at once'. This was met with enthusiastic applause, but when one of the demonstrators attempted to deliver a speech on the steps of St Paul's, the police intervened, so the men marched away, singing the 'Marseillaise'. The second report put the number at 2,000 and claimed that

> when the service was about half completed, a large contingent of the unemployed left the cathedral and remained on the steps at the main entrance, singing the songs of the unemployed, raising cheers for their leadership and hooting the names of John Burns, Mr Balfour, and 'C.B.' [Campbell Bannerman] and others.[14]

Whichever of these reports was the more accurate, it echoes yet again how the Churchyard was recognised as a place of protest. Arthur Balfour was the Conservative Prime Minister who was offering little to the party's working-class voters. Henry Campbell-Bannerman, the leader of the Liberals, was concerned about the plight of the poor, but struggling to hold together the disparate groups within his party. John Burns was a trade unionist Liberal MP, unpopular for his stance on the subject of help for the unemployed, opposing any idea of provision of outdoor relief. In the speech on the cathedral steps, Burns was challenged to 'dare to be a Daniel'. Only weeks after this protest, in early 1906, the Liberals won a landslide victory at the general election and were able to bring in a series of social reforms.

While Queen Anne had favoured St Paul's Cathedral with her presence, Victoria did not do so. In fact, after the death of Prince Albert in 1861, the Queen was rarely in London at all, and was dubbed the Widow of Windsor. However, in the December of 1871 her son and heir, Prince Albert Edward fell dangerously ill with typhoid, the very disease that had killed her beloved husband. The Prince's recovery seemed close to miraculous, and it was agreed to hold a thanksgiving service at St Paul's on 27 February. The royal party received a thunderous welcome from the very people who had criticised the Queen for her stubborn regime of seclusion.

The Churchyard was not to witness the presence of the Queen again for another quarter of a century. In a private letter she described how at the thanksgiving service of 1872 she had found the interior of the cathedral 'dull, cold and dreary and dingy'.[15] Therefore, when plans were being prepared for Victoria's Diamond Jubilee in June 1897, it was agreed that she should not attend a service within St Paul's, but instead a service would be held on the steps leading up to the west doors. One of those responsible for masterminding the celebrations was Reginald Brett, Lord Esher. Aware of the dramatic potential of grand royal occasions, he was later to be responsible for widening the Mall with Queen Victoria's Memorial at the Buckingham Palace end and the Admiralty Arch by Trafalgar Square to provide a generous procession route. In 1897 the Queen was nearly 80 years old and would have had difficulty climbing the steps. This, added to her dislike of the interior of St Paul's, made it a masterstroke to hold an outside service, which could be watched by thousands.

In 1876 Prime Minister Benjamin Disraeli had engineered the bill which made Victoria Empress of India. The imperial theme was to dominate the next quarter of a century, with St Paul's Cathedral being described by Canon Sidney Alexander during the First World War as the 'parish church of the British Empire'. While heads of foreign states and their representatives had been the principal guests at the Queen's Golden Jubilee, now, 10 years on, it was decided that the celebrations should emphasise the Empire. A painting by Andrew Carrick Brown shows the arrival of the Queen's carriage. Just to the left, part of Queen Anne's statue group can just be glimpsed. When that group was unveiled in 1712, the British Empire was symbolised by 'America', along with Britain, Ireland and France. A large part of 'America' had been lost with the War of Independence, and the claim to the French Crown was finally ceded by the Treaty of Amiens in 1802. Huge swathes of the world, however, were now part of the British Empire.

While the Golden Jubilee had gathered all the crowned heads of Europe, the majority of whom were relations of the Queen, to ride in the procession to Westminster Abbey, the make-up for the Diamond Jubilee was quite different. Crowned heads were replaced by colonial premiers, and troops from British colonies all over the world marched in the procession. The service, held on 22 June 1897, lasted just 20 minutes, with a *Te Deum* performed by 650 voices and 200 instruments, prayers, a benediction and the 'Old Hundredth'. One of the choristers noted how a cheer went up when the Queen arrived, 'a more exciting moment I have or shall never live'.[16] St Paul's Churchyard had indeed become the theatre for the Empire.

Unlike Victoria, her eldest son and successor, Edward VII, was enthusiastic about the cathedral as a venue for public ceremonial. In June 1902 a service was held to celebrate the end of the Boer War and peace returning to South Africa, and the King returned a few months later to give thanks for his recovery, yet again, from serious illness. His son, George V, was likewise keen on using St Paul's and its Churchyard in a national role, all too necessary with the outbreak of the First World War. The idea of the open-air service on the steps of the cathedral that had been so successful for Queen Victoria's Diamond Jubilee was repeated in the summer of 1915. Bishop Winnington-Ingram conducted a service from the steps to a congregation clad in khaki, ending with an address on 'The Soul of the Nation'. In contrast to this very masculine occasion, a memorial service was held in October of the same year in memory of Edith Cavell, the British nurse executed by the Germans for helping Allied soldiers escape from occupied Belgium. This service was attended by the Queen Dowager, Alexandra, along with many contingents of nurses. It was hailed as 'a great tribute paid by women to heroic womanhood', all too rare an event during the war, and indeed in the long history of the Churchyard.[17]

With the return of peace to a world torn apart by war, the official national thanksgiving service was held on 6 July 1919, with George V and Queen Mary, along with the two archbishops, representatives of the various churches, the lord mayor and sheriffs, coming out of the cathedral to stand at the top of the steps. The artist Frank Salisbury had been commissioned to paint a picture for the Royal Exchange. In his autobiography he described how by chance he was at the bottom of the steps as the dignitaries emerged and was able to make a sketch, surrounded by the huge crowd in the Churchyard singing the 'Old Hundredth'.

Only two decades later St Paul's was occupying a special place yet again in the national consciousness as Britain entered the Second World War. In response to the threat of German bombing, Prime Minister Winston Churchill issued a message that 'St Paul's must be saved at all costs'. On 30 December 1940 this was miraculously achieved despite bad damage to the east end, north transept and to the Chapter House. The Churchyard, however, was devastated, as will be seen in the next chapter. Subsequent services of thanksgiving took place in surroundings that looked very different. So, when it came to the funeral of Winston Churchill himself, the scenario stood in complete contrast to those of Admiral Nelson and the Duke of Wellington in the previous century.

Following Churchill's stroke in 1953 plans had been made for such an event, given the title 'Operation Hope Not'. Two days after his death on 24 January 1965, by decree of Queen Elizabeth II, his body lay in state at Westminster Hall before being conveyed to St Paul's Cathedral. In a break with protocol the Queen was in attendance at the funeral service, and once more St Paul's Churchyard witnessed huge crowds. This time the funeral service was watched by thousands and broadcast all over the world, to an estimated 350 million. After the funeral, Churchill's body was taken by river to Waterloo Station ready for the final journey to the churchyard of St Martin's at Bladon in Oxfordshire. In tribute, the dockers on the Thames lowered their cranes.

Frank Salisbury not only painted the scene in the Churchyard of the national thanksgiving service in 1919, but in another picture featured the interior of the cathedral at the Silver Jubilee service for George V and Queen Mary in May 1935. This was entitled 'The Heart of the Empire'.[18] However, just as the physical fabric of the Churchyard had been completely transformed by the bombing in the Second World War, so in the 1940s the concept of the British Empire was radically changing, with Indian independence coming in 1947, followed over the years by that of colony after colony. So the idea of St Paul's and its surroundings as an imperial theatre was ending, although it remains the platform for London and for national events.

CHAPTER 12

LENGTHENING SHADOWS

In the summer of 1856, when the novelist Elizabeth Gaskell paid a visit to Paternoster Row, she summoned up a rather sad scene. She described

> a narrow flagged street, lying under the shadow of St Paul's. The dull ware-houses on each side are mostly occupied at present by wholesale book-sellers; if they be publishers' shops they show no attractive front to the dark and narrow street.[1]

At the time, she was writing her famous biography of Charlotte Brontë, and wanted to see the Chapter Coffee House,

> the tavern frequented by university men and country clergymen, who were up in London for a few days and, having no private friends or access to society, were glad to learn what was going on in the world of letters.

Charlotte's father, Patrick, would use it during his time as a student at Cambridge and as a curate in Essex. In February 1842 Patrick took Charlotte and her sister Emily to stay at the coffee house en route to Brussels where they were to study languages, and she later drew upon the experience in her novel, *Villette*. When her heroine, Lucy Snowe, spent her first night in London:

> I had just extinguished my candle and lain down, when a deep, low, mighty tone swung through the night. At first I knew it not; but it was uttered twelve times, and at the twelfth colossal hum and trembling knell, I said – 'I lie in the shadow of St Paul's'.[2]

Thus, naturally, the Chapter Coffee House was the place to which Charlotte and Anne Brontë came in 1848 when they travelled from Haworth to London. The two sisters had published novels, *Jane Eyre* by Charlotte under the pseudonym of Currer Bell, *The Tenant of Wildfell Hall* by Anne as Acton Bell. Now they wanted to prove their identities to their publisher, Smith, Elder & Co. Mrs Gaskell related how an old waiter, touched by the arrival of the two women in such a 'strange and desolate place', sought to make them comfortable in the 'long, low, dingy room, up-stairs where the meetings of the [book] Trade were held'. By the time Mrs Gaskell arrived it was unoccupied, with

the appearance of a dwelling-house, two hundred years old or so, such as one sometimes sees in ancient country towns; the ceilings of the small rooms were low, and had heavy beams running across them, the walls were wainscoted breast high; the staircase was shallow, broad and dark, taking up much space in the centre of the house.

To this careful physical description, she added, with her novelist's instinct, a note of melancholic nostalgia:

This then was the Chapter Coffee House, which a century ago, was the resort of all booksellers and publishers; and where the literary hacks, the critics and even the wits, used to go in search of ideas and employment. This is the place about which Chatterton wrote, in those delusive letters he sent to his mother in Bristol, while he was starving in London. 'I am quite familiar at the Chapter Coffee House and know all the geniuses there'. Here he heard of chances of employment; here his letters were to be sent.[3]

In the first half of the nineteenth century, the character of the Churchyard and the surrounding area was moving from an exceptional lay community into yet another commercial part of the metropolis. In 1800 the City was still a residential district of nearly 130,000 people, with most businesses run by those 'living above the shop'. Thus Joseph Johnson, for example, was entertaining his authors to dinners in No. 72 St Paul's Churchyard, and meeting with writers and other publishers in the coffee houses and taverns to enact business and exchange ideas, as described in Chapter 10. His great-nephew,

Rowland Hunter, continued the tradition of entertainment when he inherited the business. The essayist and journalist James Leigh Hunt in his autobiography described how his acquaintances

> used to assemble on Fridays at the hospitable table of Mr Hunter, the bookseller, in St Paul's Churchyard. They were the survivors of the literary party that were accustomed to dine with his predecessor, Mr Johnson. The most regular were Fuseli and Bonnycastle [John Bonnycastle, mathematician and close friend of Leigh Hunt]. Now and then Godwin was present.[4]

This, however, would seem to have been the last literary salon in the Churchyard.

Rowland Hunter's house also probably had a roof garden belonging to his step daughter, Elizabeth Kent. For intensely built-up areas of the City, such gardens were cherished. Thomas Fairchild in his *City Gardener*, published in 1722, focused on plants that 'thrive best in the London gardens', advising that currant trees in particular could cope with the city smoke. He assured his readers that with gentle and regular watering, they would survive. Leigh Hunt married Marianne Kent, Elizabeth's sister in 1809. However, such was his fondness for Elizabeth that their domestic arrangements were the subject of contemporary speculation. In 1813, despite the best efforts of the barrister Henry Brougham, Hunt was confined in Surrey Gaol in Southwark for libelling the Prince Regent in his journal, *The Examiner*, and was joined there by his wife. When it was realised that their son was not thriving in the environment, Elizabeth replaced her sister as his companion. By then Hunt was quartered in the former infirmary, where he created both a flowery bower indoors, and landscaped a piece of the garden.[5]

After Hunt's release, Elizabeth continued to act both as his confidante and his agent in dealing with booksellers. A mutual interest in botany prompted him to encourage her writing of *Flora Domestica, or, the Portable Flower-Garden*, which was published anonymously in 1823. She wrote of how after watching her plants 'die one after the other, rather from attention ill-directed than from the want of it', she managed to grow flowers, shrubs and small trees in pots and tubs. She may well have inspired Charles Dickens to introduce two roof gardens in his writings. First, he had Mr Riah, a Jewish moneylender 'of noble and generous nature' in *Our Mutual Friend* provide shelter for Jenny Wren and Lizzie Hexam. They would sit on Mr Riah's rooftop, leaning against a 'blackened chimney-stack over which some humble creeper had been trained . . . . A few boxes of humble flowers and evergreens completed the garden; and the encompassing wilderness of dowager old chimneys twirled their cowls and fluttered their smoke.' A second reference comes in a short story, 'The Country Cousin', where Hetty grows tulips 'which flourished wonderfully between sloping roofs in a nook where the chimneys luckily stood aside, as if to let the sun across many obstacles upon the garden'. Hetty's father was a bookseller, reinforcing the connection with Elizabeth Kent.[6] Charles Dickens was to make Leigh Hunt the model for Harold Skimpole in *Bleak House*.

In 1839 John Tallis, a printer based near St John's Gate in Clerkenwell, published a pamphlet with a panorama of St Paul's Churchyard. This formed part of a series that he produced from 1838 into the 1840s as 'a complete stranger's guide through London'. Each part of his *London Street Views* consisted of four pages of adverts and text with a double-page engraved elevation of a street. Not only the style of the buildings can be seen, but also in many cases Tallis has included the names of the proprietors and nature of their businesses, for which he charged a fee.

From Tallis's views we can take a 'virtual' perambulation to browse around the Churchyard at the very outset of the reign of Queen Victoria. No. 1, on the south corner with Ludgate Street, facing the west end of the cathedral, was the premises of Dakin & Co., tea merchants; their neighbours were warehousemen, a wine merchant and a bookseller. Moving eastwards, a wide range of businesses are listed: Houston & Thomas selling shawls; Allsup offering china and glass; C. & G. Roberts, purveyors of silk, ribbon, millinery and artificial flowers; Hardy & Sons, playing card manufacturers. When Tallis drew up his street view, J.F. Pawson & Co., a wholesale silk warehouse at No. 9, was just seven years old. Longer established was the wholesale linen drapers Cook & Gladstone, that occupied extensive premises from Nos 21 to 25. William Cook, the son of a Norfolk farmer, had arrived here as a young man in the first decade of the nineteenth century, after being rejected by banking houses because of his poor handwriting. His business rapidly expanded, so that he was able to open a further establishment in Clerkenwell and a warehouse in

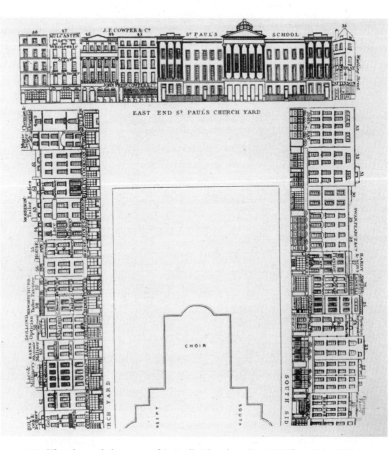

25. The plan and elevations of St Paul's Churchyard in 1839 from John Tallis's *London Street Views*.

Cheapside, as well as becoming a member of the wealthy Drapers' Company. It became, along with Pawson's, one of the most prestigious haberdashery establishments in London.

The south side of the Churchyard was still part of the main shopping thoroughfare for London, so that carriages swept through it from Cheapside to Ludgate Hill, Fleet Street and the Strand. For those requiring refreshment and respite during their shopping, the Royal City Divan was on hand at No. 16.

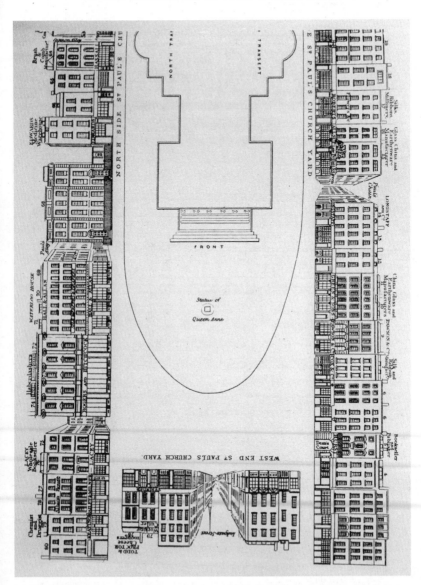

25 continued

A trade card dating from 1831 offered a reading room with an annual subscription of one guinea, providing 'the English and Foreign Papers, and other publications of the day'. Coffee and the best cigars were available, with a reduced price for subscribers.

Dominating the terrace at the east end of the Churchyard was St Paul's School. The building erected after the Great Fire had been replaced in 1822 by a grand establishment with an imposing classical facade designed by George Smith, the architect for the Mercers' Company. It was similar in style to the National Gallery in Trafalgar Square, built a decade later by William Wilkins, featuring a central pedimented portico surmounted by a low dome, and two flanking pavilions in the Italianate style.

One of the neighbours of the school was the wholesale medicine warehouse of Francis Newbery & Son. The son of John Newbery had quarrelled and parted company with his stepbrother, Thomas Carnan, and thus with children's publications, but had inherited the patent for Dr James's fever powder. When Oliver Goldsmith died from a suspected overdose of the powder in 1774, Francis issued a lengthy statement in defence of the medicine, and concentrated on its sale, a business continued by his heirs. They also ran a state lottery office, offering cash prizes rising up to £20,000. The Churchyard had long been associated with lottery schemes. Thomas Rowlandson made the connection with a cartoon in a series, *Characteristic Sketches of the Lower Orders*, published in 1820. This showed a gentleman attracted by a placard announcing that two prizes of £30,000 would be drawn the next day. While he was enthralled by the prospect of such huge prizes, another figure was picking his pocket. The dome of St Paul's rose up in the background.

At the corner of this row, 'one door from Cheapside', was the Cathedral Hotel, 'at the very centre of the Metropolis' as proclaimed in an advertisement. Here soup, fish, joints and poultry could be had from 1 p.m. to 7 p.m. at one shilling and sixpence or two shillings and sixpence, while a bed, 'including attendance', would cost two shillings. The advertisement also points out that 'Omnibuses pass the Door from all parts of the Metropolis, Suburbs, and Railway Stations every five minutes – Charge 3d and 6d'. This is a reminder that modes of transport were changing. A suggestion that a bridge should be built across the Thames, running up to the cathedral's east end, was considered, but never materialised. But an obtrusive bridge was to be

26. 'Placard' by Thomas Rowlandson satirising the sale of lotteries in the Churchyard.

built across Ludgate Hill in 1863–5 for the London, Chatham and Dover Railway, despite public protests at the time. The view up to the cathedral from the west that so exercised Sir Christopher Wren was now blighted: the last vestige of the bridge was removed only in 1990.

Crossing the beginning of Cheapside, the browser would have reached the premises of D. Nicholson, listed by Tallis as a shawl warehouse. In 1843 the company expanded to take over Nos 50 to 54 St Paul's Churchyard and to describe themselves as 'Silk, Woollen, and Manchester Warehousemen'. The term 'Manchester goods' referred to household textiles and all kinds of cottons. An advertisement shows that this included mantles, shawls and juvenile clothing, gloves, lace, hosiery and ribbons, along with parasols and furs (Plate 13).

27. An advertisement for the Cathedral Hotel presenting the many advantages
of its location.

Turning eastward to inspect the businesses on the north side of the Churchyard, shoppers would have found themselves in more peaceful surroundings, for the main traffic wound its way up Cheapside. A drawing dating from 1822 shows a barrier across the road, closing it to wheeled traffic. In 1839, No. 57 was the premises of Chubb's, the locksmith. The firm had begun in Portsea when Charles Chubb, a trained blacksmith, set up a hardware business. He was joined at some point by his brother Jeremiah who invented the detector lock, probably for the Admiralty in order to stop pilfering in the docks and to provide greater security on the nearby prison hulks. Having patented the detector in 1818, the Chubb brothers moved its manufacture to Wolverhampton, the centre of English lock-making. After some uneasy years, Charles succeeded in persuading the admiral of the fleet of

28. An early nineteenth-century engraving of the north part of St Paul's
Churchyard with bollards erected to prevent access to wheeled traffic.

the superiority of his lock, and moved to St Paul's Churchyard. Customers
included the Bank of England, the King and the Duke of Wellington, who
called upon the locksmiths to open his front door at Apsley House, at Hyde
Park Corner, known as No. 1 London, and to supply him with new locks.

Right by Chubb's was the premises of P. & J. Dollond (see p. 191). In 1805,
following the death of his brother John, Peter Dollond took into partnership the
son of his niece, George Huggins, who then changed his name by licence. Like
Peter, George Dollond was highly inventive and made instruments for expeditions, such as one to the Arctic in 1821 and for surveys of Australasia. He was the
author of many papers published in the *Philosophical Transactions*, and Fellows of
the Royal Society would have made their way to his shop at No. 59 St Paul's
Churchyard, an echo of such visits to the bookshop of James Allestree two centuries earlier (p. 154). Two years after Tallis drew his panorama, George Dollond
was appointed optician to Queen Victoria. At the Great Exhibition of 1851 he
was awarded a medal for his invention of a type of weather station where instruments measuring variations in air pressure, temperature, humidity, rainfall, and
the force and direction of the wind could be recorded on a roll of paper.

The style of the shop next door to P. & J. Dollond presented a complete contrast. A card issued in 1835 by the Central City Emporium at 60 St Paul's Churchyard proudly announced that

> the Proprietors have just completed conjunctively with many British and Foreign Manufactures, arrangement upon an extended scale for a succession 'monthly,' of the most *Elegant, Novel*, and *indisputably Cheap Goods*, in *Ribbons, Blonds, Chantilly and Bobbin Lace Veils, Foreign Flowers, Wreaths, &c. Gloves, Lace, Silk Hosiery, Silks, Shawls, Linens, Furs, Merinoes, Indianas, Cashmeres, Cambrics, Hollands, Lawns, Diapers, Sheetings, Table Linen, Quilts and Counterpanes*, besides a doubtless multiplicity of *Novel Fancy Articles*.

The card ends with '*Royal Opera, Riding*, and *Promenading Cloaks* of the *Richest Material*, and sumptuously Trimmed with costly Furs of every clime'. A postscript adds that there was also 'a large Stock of Articles for *Charitable Purposes*'. This presents a vivid picture of the bewildering variety of haberdashery on offer to discerning ladies in fashionable London shops in the mid-nineteenth century.

The publishing family of the Rivingtons remained in their Churchyard premises at No. 62. In 1839 the firm was in the hands of John, George and Francis Rivington of the fourth generation, and John of the fifth. Back in the eighteenth century, John Rivington had been noted for his attendance at early morning services in the cathedral, sometimes completing his toilet there (p. 205). Now, however, the Rivingtons no longer lived over the shop, having moved out to Waterloo Place, just below Pall Mall. But the family's reputation for High Anglicanism was retained, with Francis Rivington becoming involved in the Oxford or Tractarian movement that was causing so much controversy within the Church of England. The leaders of the movement, associated particularly with Oxford University, argued for the reinstatement of some of the traditions of faith of the early Church and for their inclusion into Anglican liturgy and theology. The ideas of John Henry Newman, John Keble and Edward Pusey were set out in pamphlets entitled *Tracts for the Times* which from 1834 were printed, published and distributed by the firm. Henry Curwen in his book about booksellers noted how 'the publication of these

"Tracts" still further strengthened the Rivingtons in their position of High Church publishers, and their business benefited considerably by the great increase of the High Church party'.[7]

This development, however, came at a price, for as the religious controversy mounted, the Society for the Promotion of Christian Knowledge, evangelical in outlook, severed connection with the Rivingtons, publishing for itself in direct competition. A serious blow came when in 1845 John Newman and many of his associates moved to the Church of Rome, awakening the fear that the real object of the Tractarians was to reconcile England with the Vatican. As one member of the Rivington family wrote:

> Here was the publishing firm left high and dry – some of its friends gone over to the Church of Rome, others looking askance at them on account of their former connection, the Broad Church party going to other publishers, the Evangelical of course avoiding the name of Rivington, and the Rivingtons themselves deeply affected, personally, by the shock of events.[8]

It is ironical, therefore, that their near neighbour in the Churchyard should be the Religious Tract Society, with premises at No. 65. This had been founded in 1799 not only in the Churchyard, but also in Paternoster Row and in Piccadilly, producing literature of an evangelical nature, aimed particularly at children, women and the poor. As the name suggests, the society began by producing tracts, but in time developed into the publisher of books and periodicals, most notably the *Boy's Own Paper*. The first issue of the paper appeared in 1879, with weekly editions thereafter, which were also bound up and sold as annuals. The mainstay of the content was adventure stories, with notes on nature study, sports and games, and an enthusiastic promotion of the concept of the British Empire.

The north-west section of the Churchyard was dominated in 1839 by the premises of two firms of linen drapers, Allan, Son and Co at Nos 69 to 71, and next door, Hitchcock and Co at Nos 72 to 74. Hitchcock's not only took over the former home of the booksellers Joseph Johnson and Rowland Hunter, but also the Chapter Coffee House leading off Paternoster Row. In place of the Georgian houses depicted in the aquatint of Nelson's funeral procession,

the drapers' premises are shown as grander retail buildings in Tallis's panorama, and in the engraving of Wellington's funeral in 1852. Strikingly, the
ground floor of Hitchcock & Co. boasts high glass windows, with a grand
series of Corinthian pilasters adorning the upper storeys.

In 1851 the publisher and author Charles Knight wrote in his survey of
London:

> To whatever part . . . we direct our steps, we shall find that the drapers'
> shops – including in this term those which sell cotton, linen, silk, and
> worsted goods – are among the handsomest. . . . When we arrive at St
> Paul's Churchyard we come to the very world of show.

He then describes the premises of Hitchcock & Co:

> Here we find a shop whose front presents an uninterrupted mass of glass
> from the ceiling to the ground; no horizontal sash bars being seen, and the
> vertical ones made of brass. Here, too, we see on a winter's evening a mode
> of light recently introduced, by which the products of combustion are
> given off in the street, instead of being left to soil the goods in the window;
> the lamps are fixed outside the shop, with a reflector so placed as to throw
> a strong light upon the commodities in the window.[9]

A portrait of the firm of Hitchcock & Co. in the mid-nineteenth century
is given in a biography of one of its partners, George Williams:

> So quick was the growth of the business that ten years after it had
> been established, it was found necessary to employ a staff of about
> 140 assistants. . . . The hours were from seven to nine in the summer
> months and from seven to eight in winter, shorter hours than in any
> other houses. . . . All young men in the establishment wore black
> broadcloth coats and a white tie was essential, while a moustache, if it was
> not as in most similar establishments a sin 'beyond the imagination of the
> wildest youngster' was at least so uncommon that the sole assistant allowed
> the privilege was quite noted throughout the City as 'Hitchcock's
> Frenchman'.[10]

His evangelical beliefs led George Williams to support efforts at ameliora-
tion of the working conditions of London's shop assistants. First, he inaugu-
rated the push to secure early closing legislation, holding an initial meeting in
1842 in a room in his store. Two years later he was the prime mover in the
foundation of the Young Men's Christian Association (YMCA), concerned by
the poor working conditions for men in the capital. The association's first
meeting, supported by 11 other City drapers, was also held in the room,
which thereafter was kept as a memorial to its creation.

Moving westwards, the browsing walker would have found at the corner of
the Churchyard according to Tallis's view, the shop of Wingrave, an Italian
warehouse, the Victorian equivalent of a delicatessen, specialising in food-
stuffs such as olive oil, preserves and pasta. Next door was Todd & Procter,
cheesemongers. The very last shop carried a Ludgate Street address rather than
that of the Churchyard: the premises of John Harris, publisher and bookseller
specialising in children's books. Harris had worked for the Newbery firm,
which had passed at John's death in 1767 first to his son Francis and his stepbrother, Thomas Carnan, and then to his nephew, another Francis, and his
wife Elizabeth. When Elizabeth retired in 1802, Harris bought the business
from her on condition of paying her an annuity.

In the next 40 years John Harris produced a whole series of books in his
Juvenile Library. Observing that John Newbery's more playful books, such as
Mother Goose's Melody, full of nursery rhymes, sold better than didactic publications, he focused on titles such as *The Comic Adventures of Old Mother
Hubbard and Her Dog*, issued in 1805. He also diverged from Newbery's style
by including engravings on every page, and in copper plate rather than woodcuts. One of his most successful ventures was a poem by William Roscoe, *The
Butterfly's Ball*, illustrated by William Mulready and published in 1807. In the
same year he began to produce a series of attractive picture books in a square
format, *Harris's Cabinet of Amusements and Instruction*, and quickly built up a
considerable list.

Fairy tales had been slow to catch on in England, with the religious and
educational establishments regarding with disapproval what were characterised as bawdy ballads and feigned fantasies. Charles Perrault's famous *Histoires
ou contes du temps passé*, as told by Mother Goose, were translated by Robert
Samber and published in London in 1729. However, it took many years for

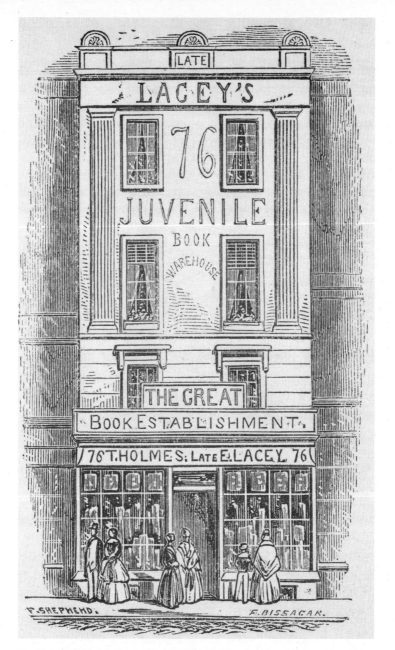

29. Thomas Holmes's shop at No. 76 St Paul's Churchyard continuing the tradition of providing books for children established by John Newbery.

these tales, that included 'Cinderella' and 'Little Red Riding Hood', to catch popular attention. In 1819 John Harris was joined in the firm by his son, also John, and in the following year published Perrault's tales in *The Court of Oberon; or The Temple of Fairie*, along with another famous collection of tales from late seventeenth-century France, the tales of Madame D'Aulnoy, anglicised as Madame Bunch. These had titles like 'The White Cat' and 'The Yellow Dwarf', adapting easily to the English market because they concentrated on incident and characterisation rather than locality. A third element in *The Court of Oberon* were stories from *The Arabian Nights*, marking a milestone in children's literature in the English language.

John Harris's establishment is one of only five booksellers listed in the Churchyard by Tallis: a hundred years earlier, 23 had been recorded. The five mentioned, moreover, were the publishers' business premises rather than their homes, which were often now in the leafy suburbs. The Robinson family, for example, held their soirées at their house in Streatham. Some had more spacious premises in the West End rather than the overcrowded City. Thus the son of John Murray I, who had attended Joseph Johnson's literary dinners at 72 St Paul's Churchyard, held evening entertainments for such distinguished authors as Walter Scott and Lord Byron at his house in Albemarle Street in Piccadilly.

Interest in the history of the Churchyard and the surrounding area was developing, in tune with the romantic style of the time. William Harrison Ainsworth was both a publisher and a writer, specialising in dramatic historical fiction. He began with a romantic account of the career of Dick Turpin in *Rookwood*, published in 1834, followed by that of another highwayman, Jack Sheppard, whose spectacular escapes from Newgate Prison had captured the early eighteenth-century popular imagination. Ainsworth's so-called Newgate novels proved equally popular, but also earned disapproval from contemporary writers such as Thackeray for glamorising crime. Disapproval sharply intensified in 1840 when Lord William Russell, uncle of the leader of the Whig party, John Russell, was murdered by his valet, who boasted in Newgate's condemned cell that he had been inspired by Ainsworth's *Jack Sheppard*.

The novelist, maintaining a dignified silence, turned to safer themes, including a romance set in Old St Paul's during the year of the Great Plague in 1665, which was published in serial form in 1841. The Churchyard he characterised as 'the great mart for booksellers' who 'fixed their shops against the massive pillars of its nave. Besides booksellers, there were seamstresses, tobacco-merchants, vendors of fruit and provisions, and Jews – making preparations for the business of the day.'[11] Turning to the visitors congregating on Paul's Walk he quoted verbatim the description given 'of the whole world's map' by the seventeenth-century satirist, John Earle (p. 116).

Charles Dickens also drew upon the history of the area, although avoiding plagiarism and glamorisation of crime. A visit to Newgate forms one of the *Sketches of Boz*, and Dickens described how it had been burned during the Gordon Riots in his historical novel *Barnaby Rudge*. In 1831, at the age of 18, having taken a course in shorthand, he had occupied rooms in Bell Yard off Carter Lane, just to the south of the cathedral. He was working as a freelance reporter in Doctors' Commons, which by this time had become a rather quaint institution, in its final years of existence. In his semi-autobiographical novel *David Copperfield* he was to describe it as a 'cozy, dozy, old-fashioned, time-forgotten, sleepy-headed little family party'.[12] Close by was the Horn Coffee House, which Dickens brought into *The Pickwick Papers.* While Mr Pickwick was in the Fleet Prison, his friends Winkle, Snodgrass and Tupman paid him a visit. After a meal cooked in the prison kitchen, a couple of bottles of very good wine was sought from the Horn: 'The bottle or two, indeed, might be more properly described as a bottle or six; for by the time it was drunk, the bell began to ring for strangers to withdraw'.[13]

Dickens, like Elizabeth Gaskell, noted how the City was rapidly changing, and expressed some regret at what was passing. This sentiment was shared by several writers who focused on the history of the bookselling trade. William West, for example, came to London in 1784, inspired by reading of the death of Samuel Johnson. In his memoirs, written 50 years later, he described how he first approached Paternoster Row through 'a dark and narrow entry (London House Yard)', adding that his 'mind was pervaded with a kind of awe at the gloomy appearance of the stores of literature before me'.[14] In 1865 Charles Knight published his *Shadows of the Old Booksellers*, in which he traced the trade from the time of William Caxton, but a large part of the book concentrated on the eighteenth century and the men who gathered in the Chapter Coffee House to discuss business and to socialise. He described these meetings as the 'parliament of old booksellers'.[15]

Although these businesses no longer dominated in the Churchyard, they were packed into the streets beyond. A pen portrait of Paternoster Row published in 1857 estimated that there were around 50 publishers in the street, and streets leading off from it. The Row was not a grand thoroughfare, but rather 'a foot pavement scarcely wide enough for two individuals to pass each other, and a roadway through a good part of which vehicles can pass only in a single file' (Plate 14).[16] The Paternoster Row publishers produced magazines and journals as well as books, and some of those books, such as the novels of Ainsworth and Dickens, were produced in serial form.

The first Thomas Longman established his business in the Row in 1724 at the Sign of the Ship. This sign was to be proudly displayed over the centuries both over the door of Nos 39–41 and on the title pages of the books. Thomas Longman of the second generation died in 1797, leaving a large family who intermarried with others in the publishing community, so that their enterprise was known as the Leviathan. Owen Rees, from a Welsh dissenting family, joined the firm, and as a result one of the main manifestoes of the Romantic movement, the *Lyrical Ballads* of Wordsworth and Coleridge, appeared under the Longmans imprint in 1798. A procession of partners from outside the family followed, so that at one stage the company was known as Longman, Hurst, Rees, Orme and Green. A wide literary range was produced, and with the acquisition of the equally venerable publishing house of Rivington in 1890 a wide Church was also represented. Sir George Otto Trevelyan wrote that Longmans was not 'a creature of the State, nor of the Church, nor of the Universities, nor of any corporate body'. The house stood both for 'self-help and the effort of the individual' and for 'family tradition, for ideals of public usefulness and assistance to the cause of literature and science, handed on from generation to generation'.[17]

Details of the layout of Longmans' premises have survived. As the firm occupied virtually a corner site, these were more spacious than those of most publishers, who were squashed into narrow sites. Longmans had front and back shops on the ground floor, one dealing with new books, the other with second-hand titles. There was also a warehouse, divided into foreign and country departments, a kitchen and wash house. Originally living quarters occupied the upper floors, with a small parlour and dining room and bedrooms for the family, and at the very top, accommodation for apprentices and servants. However, in 1798, Thomas Longman III moved out to Hampstead and the Paternoster Row building was gradually turned over to offices. Until the First World War, a library was available to the staff to borrow books. Oral history relates that these were presided over by Joseph Ridgewell, the head porter, resplendent in a frock coat. 'He not only saw visitors on and off the premises, but also served the partners by daily bringing a menu from a nearby restaurant.'[18]

One of Longmans' neighbours was the London office of the Edinburgh publishers, Blackwood & Son, squeezed into a corner on Ave Maria Lane. They were not the only Scottish house to have an office in Paternoster Row. W. & R. Chambers and Thomas Nelson, both from Edinburgh, and Blackie & Son from Glasgow all acquired premises here, for this was the Mecca of the book world. But the area was far from conducive to elevated literary thoughts. Just to the north was Newgate Market, which became the main meat market for London after the Great Fire, with large numbers of sheep and cattle slaughtered daily. A by-product of the market was the rendering of animal fat to make tallow, an extremely noxious activity. One tallow chandler, Knight & Son, caused a serious fire in 1861 that destroyed much of Longmans' stock. The chandlers departed, no doubt to the relief of their neighbours, and in 1869 the market itself was closed, moving still further north to Smithfield. One of the detailed fire insurance maps compiled by Charles Goad that began to be kept from 1886 shows how the quadrangular site of the former market was developed, with buildings in the centre, and around the edges. Paternoster Square, as it was renamed, was quickly taken over by the manufactories of books and journals: publishing houses, wholesale stationers, steam press printers and binders, and paper warehouses.[19]

A vivid description of Paternoster Row was written by Charles Mumby Smith in his sketchbook of London scenes in 1857, published by Arthur Hall, Virtue & Co., whose establishment was at No. 25, so local knowledge was guaranteed. Smith described the street as generally a quiet place, with 'a good deal of gossiping in the shops among clerical-looking gentlemen in white ties, and much lounging and reading of newspapers and magazines over the counter among clerics and shopmen'. But this sea of calm was disrupted once a week when the publishers fulfilled orders to their country customers.

By post-time on Friday, the weekly papers march off in sacks, bags and parcels to the post-office, and of these the Row furnishes a liberal quota. The procuring of papers from the publishers of each, which is often attended with no small amount of squabbling and delay – the packing for agents – the addressing to private customers – the invoicing and final bundling off on the back of the boy to the post-office – all together put the whole force of the publisher on their mettle. . . .

This, however, was nothing compared to Magazine Day, which occurred on the last day of every month, when the Row was 'as much alive as an Egyptian pot of vipers'. The proceedings started the night before, receiving the orders from country booksellers, with regular customers having allotted pigeon-holes:

because, in a case where a man has to supply in one day the monthly parcel of a hundred or more country booksellers, each of whom would think there was a design to ruin him if his parcel did not arrive on the first of the month, he cannot afford the risk of a moment's avoidable delay.

Here enters the 'collector',

for the most part, neither man nor boy, but in that transition period of existence known as hobbledehoyhood . . . he wears a seedy suit, surmounted by a cloth cap or crushed hat; and he carries on his shoulders a dust-coloured canvas-bag . . . his voice is loud, his bearing independent, and his speech sharp, rapid, and abbreviated . . . A specific sort of knowledge he has in perfection – a knowledge of little books and low-priced publications, and who their publishers are, and where they may be got.

A sample of the kind of banter is provided, as the 'collectors' jostled and haggled for their trove, cheap books, particularly of a religious subject:

'Pots of manna, six and phials of wrath, thirteen as twelve' . . . 'Coming struggles, twenty-six as twenty-four; two devices of Satan; and one little Tommy Tubbs' . . . 'Do you keep the pious pieman?' . . . 'No,' says the shopman, 'over the way for the pious pieman' . . . 'Well, give us a dozen blaspheming blacksmiths – thirteen you know'. . . . 'Nine broken pitchers and Jacob's well' . . . 'Ten garments of faith, and fifty bands of hope.'

Some of these must have been collected from the Warehouse of Pious Tracts that was also situated in the Row.

This veritable Tower of Babel contrasts with the traffic in more expensive books and magazines, which was apparently conducted with some decorum. But all the parcels had to be packed up and ready for collection by 6 p.m., when the carts and vehicles performing the task of delivering them to the carriers' depots entered the Row from the west end and moved in line towards Cheapside. Then peace returned to the street as publishers' clerks and shopmen left for 'a late dinner; chops, steaks, and cups of coffee'.[20]

In his history published in 1873, Henry Curwen wrote of how the first half of the nineteenth century witnessed a new phase in bookselling:

The schoolmaster . . . was abroad; the repressive taxes on knowledge either were, or were about to be removed; learning, or a smattering of learning, was within the reach of most. . . . The public writer henceforth was to occupy the preacher's pulpit, and his congregation, far above the limits of any St. Peter's or St. Paul's, was to be told only by millions. Books were to be no longer the curious luxuries of the rich man's library, or the hoarded and hardly-earned treasures of the student's closet, but were to be fairly placed at the disposal of the many.[21]

The development of the rotary press powered by steam made books cheaper to produce and hugely increased output. Curwen identified three men in particular who brought about this revolution in publishing: Charles Knight, Robert Chambers and John Cassell.

Charles Knight was a publisher and writer whose idea for a 'National Library' in print, with good content at a cheap price, caught the attention of the eminent lawyer Henry Brougham. As a utilitarian, Brougham believed that the imparting of elements of scientific knowledge through classes, lectures and libraries would make for better workers and, by strengthening religious belief, ideas of revolution would be held in check. In 1826, therefore, he founded the Society for the Diffusion of Useful Knowledge. Knight became the editor of the Society's publications, producing a series of books and journals, including the *Working Man's Companion,* the *Quarterly Journal of Education*, the *Penny Magazine* and most bravely the *Penny Encyclopaedia*. In the last venture, launched in 1833, Knight included many illustrations that made use of the latest printing techniques for steel engravings and lithography. His good intentions, however, imperilled finances, and in 1846 he became bankrupt, along with the Society.

The concept of the *Penny Encyclopaedia* was continued by the Chambers brothers, William and Robert. In 1860 Robert left his brother in Edinburgh to open an office of their publishing business at 47 Paternoster Row, and to make use of the resources of the British Museum Reading Room for his research on projects. The speciality of the firm was encyclopaedias, the most ambitious being *Chambers' Encyclopaedia of Universal Knowledge for the People*. The first edition appeared between 1859 and 1868, in weekly parts, priced at three half-pence apiece, ultimately totalling ten volumes in octavo articles from over a hundred authors. This massive venture continued to be published through to the 1960s.

Chambers and Knight were both from middle-class families, determined to improve the lot of the common man. The third of Curwen's trinity, John Cassell, however, had been a child labourer in a local cotton mill in Manchester before being apprenticed to a Salford joiner. There are many legends about how he came to London and into the publishing industry, but perhaps the most likely was that, having taken to drink, he signed the temperance pledge and came south to lecture on the sins of alcohol. His wife's patrimony enabled him to set up business, first selling shilling bags of tea and coffee. Using a small press that printed the labels for his beverages, he began his publishing career with *Teetotal Times*. Appearing before a select committee in 1851, he explained: 'I entered into the publishing trade for the purpose of issuing a series of publications which I believed were calculated to advance the moral and social well-being of the working classes'.[22]

John Cassell moved into part of the Belle Sauvage, off Ludgate Hill. This coaching inn, which over the centuries had provided substantial accommodation in the galleries around the courtyard, and stabling for hundreds of horses, was losing out to the developing railway system. With the prospect of large numbers of visitors to London for the Great Exhibition of 1851, an entrepreneur, John Thorburn, had leased the other part to turn into a hotel. This idea was short-lived, for when Cassell introduced printing presses, the building shook and the noise was so great that guests would not stay. Thorburn thankfully ceded his interest to Cassell, and in the years that followed the site was developed into his publishing house. Here he produced he *Working Man's Friend*, *Cassell's Illustrated Family Paper*, *Cassell's Magazine* and *Cassell's Popular Educator*.

Although the development of the railway may have spelt the end for coaching inns like the Belle Sauvage, it offered a profitable opportunity for the book trade. From 1848 the publisher George Routledge began to produce novels priced at one shilling in what he called his Railway Library. He was able to do this by evading the laws of copyright and reprinting American titles, beginning with James Fenimore Cooper's sea yarn, *The Pilot*. Successful novels, both American and English, followed, but his real coup was Harriet Beecher Stowe's *Uncle Tom's Cabin*. Following a highly favourable review in *The Times* in 1852, one witness reported 'flaring placards were to be seen in the booksellers' windows announcing its publication in various forms, sizes and prices. No collector in the trade at this time will forget the scramble there was to obtain copies'.[23] In total, Routledge sold over half a million copies. In 1889, the year after George's death, the family firm moved a small distance from the Broadway, Ludgate, into offices south of the Churchyard on Carter Lane. In his map, Goad shows their premises, ready for their arrival, with specially reinforced floors to take the weight of the book stock. Around them was a cluster of book-related industries, such as wholesale paper and binders.

By the end of the nineteenth century, the whole area around St Paul's had been developed and, with the increasing value of the land, new buildings were provided with extra storeys. A photograph of Paternoster Row taken in 1912 shows the effect of this. The feel of the street must have been like that of Bow Lane today. Running from Cheapside down to Watling Street, Bow Lane is pedestrianised, flanked by tall buildings, with courts and yards leading off. Little wonder that the darkness of Paternoster Row was frequently remarked upon. The publishers Hodder & Stoughton moved into No. 27 in 1868, displaying their books in the windows of the ground-floor shop but, despite frequent dusting and new displays, the dim light and London dust gave potential customers little idea of their output.[24]

Close by in the Row was the publishing house and shop of Bagster. The firm had been founded by Samuel Bagster, a scholar particularly interested in biblical texts. Noting that the patent for printing bibles did not apply when notes were attached, he produced a nineteenth-century version of the Polyglot Bible (see pp. 150–1). First published in 1816, this contained Hebrew, Samaritan, Greek, Latin and Syriac texts along with English, French, German, Italian and Spanish, beautifully printed and bound in octavo foolscap. The venture proved enormously successful, particularly in the United States. It was noted that 'the house of every substantial farmer in the days following the Revolution had three ornaments – a polyglot Bible, a tin reflector and a wooden clock', but many of the bibles, sold by travelling pedlars, were pirate editions and far from genuine.[25] The firm continued to produce bibles, including the 'Bible of every land' with over 270 languages and versions. Particularly redolent of the history of St Paul's Churchyard was Bagster's 'English Hexapla', reproducing the Scriptures associated with John Wycliffe, William Tyndale, Thomas Cranmer, and the Geneva, Anglo-Rhenish and King James Bibles.

The importance of religious texts in Victorian life is shown by the publication of the Revised New Testament by the Oxford University Press (OUP) in 1881. The publishing concept, masterminded by Henry Frowde, was to adapt the King James version into modern language without changing the idiom. He expanded OUP's presence in London by opening a bindery in Aldersgate Street, renewing the lease on a bible warehouse at 7 Paternoster Row and establishing an office at Amen Corner. On 17 May one million copies of the Revised New Testament were sold. Special arrangements had been organised in advance with the railway companies for delivery to towns and villages, and as St Paul's struck midnight, the doors of 7 Paternoster Row were opened to begin the trade within the capital. Extra police were called in to control both the traffic and the public, who were scrambling for copies, according to the journal *The Leisure Hour*.[26]

While the book trade crammed itself into the streets leading off the Churchyard, the shops immediately around the cathedral enjoyed more spacious surroundings, many of them rebuilt in grand style. Thus Cook & Gladstone, who had become Cook & Son, had their linen drapers' shop on the south side of the Churchyard rebuilt in the Italian manner designed by James Knowles in 1853. Francis Cook combined his profession as a merchant with a passion for art, and some of his collection was hung in these appropriate surroundings. Whether the 'Madonna and Child with Saints' by Jacopo da Pontormo or 'A Homeric Legend' by Angelica Kauffmann watched over customers as they purchased their linen goods, as opposed to hanging in offices, is not known. Whatever the location, Francis Cook clearly had to have some of his collection wherever he spent his days.[27]

The Goad maps show that by the late nineteenth century, St Paul's Churchyard had become the 'citadel' of the drapery trade in the words of the shopping historian, Alison Adburgham. Nicholson's, in the north-eastern corner, was appointed silk mercers to the Queen, with established premises in Paternoster Row and, famously, the Argyll Mourning Warehouse at Oxford Circus. Despite Oxford Street becoming the venue for West End shopping, Nicholson's always retained their identity 'of St Paul's'. In 1887 they produced their Jubilee Sale catalogue, in which they offered all kinds of garments in the knitted stitch known as stockinette which made it very flexible: 'New jersey jacket in Stockinette; the Habit Jersey in Stockinette; richly braided or beaded jackets in firm Stockinette. Also the Garibaldi Jaquette in fashionable striped Jersey Cloth, with silk collar, cuffs, suitable for boating, tennis, etc.' A catalogue published in 1910 offered not only outfits for skating, but also 'The Bodyskirt', an 'all-in-one undergarment', available ready-made for drapers all over the country to sell. A far cry from the crinolines that had been the fashion half a century earlier.[28]

The grand classical building created for St Paul's School proved all too short-lived. After just six decades it was vacated and demolished in 1884 when the decision was made to move the boys out to a new site in Hammersmith. A plan for two Manchester wholesale warehousemen to take the site with a single coherent elevation was put on hold while a petition was delivered to the Corporation of London by the President of the Royal Institute of British Architects to ask that the view opened up to the cathedral should be protected. However, real estate was too precious, and the building was duly constructed. Nevertheless the Corporation did ensure a better view of St Paul's at the south-east end by the creation of Cannon Street West.

When the Churchyard was a centre of the drapery trade in the seventeenth and eighteenth centuries, apprentices would live in the household, either sleeping in the attics or under the counter in the shop. With the expanding

30. A photolithograph of 1886 showing textile emporia known as warehouses built at the east end of the Churchyard, with the church of St Augustine, Watling Street.

businesses moving into the Churchyard in the nineteenth and twentieth centuries, living quarters had to be found for the considerable workforces. In some of the buildings, a dormitory storey was provided, but this was not always sufficient, and for the new premises by Cannon Street a gallery was installed in the church of St Augustine's Watling Street to provide additional accommodation. At the other end of the Churchyard, at the top of Ludgate Hill, the textile warehouse built in 1896–7 for Pawson & Leaf provided three storeys of living accommodation for their staff, including dining and sitting rooms.

The assistants who worked in these large-scale premises represented the last of a series of lay residential communities of the Churchyard that stretched back through the centuries. In 1923 Hitchcock & Co. closed its retail outlet and under the name of Hitchcock & Williams concentrated on providing wholesale for the textile trade. A photograph of one of their departments shows the considerable scale of the enterprise. Some of the workers, like those of Pawson & Leaf, lived on the premises, at No. 80 the Churchyard. This number increased in 1939 with the increasing threat of another war, and in particular the anticipation of aerial bombing raids. As the threat of another war grew, so did preparations. The account of the firm written in 1946 gives us a good picture of the social life of Hitchcock & Williams in the time of war, which was replicated by the other textile stores nearby. A darts tournament, for example, was held among the warehouses, and a photograph shows a quoits competition taking place on the roof, with the western clock towers of the cathedral in the background.

There were various alarums throughout 1940, as bombing raids were made over the City. Churchill, recognising that the cathedral represented such an important national icon, had urged for it to be protected at all costs, and the 'keymen' of the textile warehouses played their part in fighting the fires that resulted from the raids, along with choristers stationed at the top of St Paul's. Then, on 29 December 1940, on a clear night, the most devastating German raid took place, with hundreds of incendiary and high-explosive bombs dropped around St Paul's. At the height of the raid, Hitchcock's had over one hundred staff fighting numerous blazes. Nos 69–70 in the Churchyard caught fire, and the police eventually persuaded the firefighters to leave, dragged out of the burning building by their manager. One man later wrote how

> Narrow thoroughfares, old familiar places and historic landmarks, were obliterated . . . It was an awe-inspiring and wonderful sight for those of us who witnessed it. St. Paul's Cathedral, ringed by raging fires and falling masonry, its great dome superimposed and reddened all night by the reflected flames, seemed to take upon itself an even greater dignity.[29]

In Paternoster Row, just behind, 17 publishing houses were destroyed, along with the leading wholesaler, Simpkin Marshall, and an estimated 20 million books. Even this disaster brought out a certain black humour: George Bernard Shaw remarked how 'the Germans have done what Constable's never succeeded in doing. They have disposed of 86,701 sheets of my work in less than twenty-four hours.'

Just as Samuel Pepys and John Evelyn provided obituaries at the destruction of the Churchyard in the Great Fire of 1666, so a moving tribute was provided for this second 'Great Fire'. The City bookseller Hubert Wilson, under the pseudonym of Petrel, wrote in the *Bookseller*:

It is the eve of the new year – and the hub of the English book trade lies in smoking ruins. Such a scene of destruction I have never seen or imagined. . . . With many others Simpkins, Whitaker's, Longman's, Nelson's, Hutchinson's, and, further afield Collins and Eyre & Spottiswoode, are gutted shells. . . . As I picked my way gingerly across from brick to brick, hot gouts of sulphurous fumes from buried fires seeped up between my feet: desultory flames played in the remains of a rafter here or a floor joist there, and on either side of the smoking causeway fell sharply into cavernous glowing holes, once basements full of stock, now the crematories of the City's book world.[30]

EPILOGUE

Photographs of the destruction wrought in St Paul's Churchyard following the night raid of 29 December 1940 still have the power to shock (Plates 19 and 20). The Prime Minister Winston Churchill had declared that the cathedral should be saved at all costs, and valiant defence work, along with a large amount of luck, did ensure that it did not suffer fundamental damage. Amid the total devastation there were scattered survivors. 'Stationers' Hall, rebuilt after the Great Fire, this time also survived, along the neighbouring seventeenth-century houses in Amen Corner, and the ground floor of Wren's Chapter House on the north side of the Churchyard.

On the south side, where the damage was not so great, the deanery built by Wren survived, along with St Paul's Choir School on Carter Lane. This last was to be described by the architectural historian Nikolaus Pevsner as in 'the South Kensington style, that is with Renaissance sgraffito decoration, Venetian windows, and a general air of say Bergamo or Brescia'. The striking building, opened in 1875, owed much to the lifelong efforts of the philanthropist Maria Hackett to improve the living conditions of the cathedral's choristers. In a distinct echo of the Children of Paul's in the Tudor period, she had found that they did not receive proper housing, education or supervision, often being hired out at public events with little thought for their safety or moral welfare. At the age of 90 she had been taken to see the new school.[1]

The lighter damage to the south side of the cathedral meant that the trades of drapery and publishing that had dominated the Churchyard over the centuries were able to survive in diminished form. Thus Cook, Son & Co. continued to do business at 21–26 St Paul's Churchyard. A book produced for

269

the Festival of Britain in 1951 presented 'stories of institutions and business organisation by virtue of their contributions towards making London the gateway to world trade'.[2] The optical instrument makers, Dollond, and the manufacturer of locks, Chubb, both appeared in the book, but they had departed from the Churchyard by the twentieth century. The sole representative therefore was Cook's under the title of 'In the Shadow of St Paul's'.

In the nineteenth century Francis Cook had developed the idea of employing commercial sales representatives to travel by rail to various locations, carrying samples of the company's merchandise. Thus Cook's, like its neighbour, Hitchcock & Williams on the north side of the Churchyard, had become a warehouse and distribution centre rather than a retail establishment. A fundamental reorganisation had taken place in 1947, with the ground and first floors given over to displays of the range of stock. In the fashion showroom, mannequins modelled cloths for buyers, with textile fairs held twice a week in June and November. The brand name of 'Cook of St Paul's' was adopted, with wide advertising in the press and on the Underground and buses. This all came to an end in the 1960s when the grand Italianate building was demolished. On the north-west side of the Churchyard Hitchcock & Williams had rebuilt their premises and also continued trading. The recession of the 1960s, however, damaged the business and the company closed in 1984, marking the end of the long connection between the Churchyard and the textile trade.

Representatives of the book trade likewise held on for a time. Cassells, housed in the venerable Belle Sauvage Inn, survived the Blitz in 1940, but was destroyed the following May when a V2 laid waste the whole area around Ludgate Hill, leaving only the railway bridge across the road. In 1966 Oxford University Press left their premises at Amen House in Warwick Square, so that the one reminder of the extensive publishing industry that had represented such an important element of the Churchyard was the firm of Routledge & Kegan Paul. They in turn left their Carter Lane offices in 1976, driven out not by bombs, but by a tenfold increase in their rent. St Paul's Churchyard was now too expensive for the business of books, and Routledge moved to Store Street, joining the vibrant community of publishers based in Bloomsbury.

Not only had the bomb damage destroyed large areas of the Churchyard, but it had also shattered its architectural integrity, and this was the challenge in rebuilding the area. As Nikolaus Pevsner was to point out:

The planning problem was how to treat the immediate surroundings of a monument of the size and scale of St Paul's. Victorian London had instinctively made a good job of it. . . . On the S[outh] especially the even walls of the warehouses, subdued in their motifs yet not wholly utilitarian, and in height almost a match to the walls of the cathedral, were a blessing. The sides of St Paul's were not designed to be seen full on and at a distance.[3]

Pevsner was echoing the desire that Sir Christopher Wren had cherished back in the seventeenth century to set his new cathedral within a formal cloistered piazza with houses five storeys high (p. 223). This had proved an impossible vision because of the necessity to rebuild swiftly after the Great Fire. Now, three centuries later, the debate began again, and raged fiercely. The first plan to be put forward came from the Royal Academy Planning Committee, chaired by Sir Edwin Lutyens, developed between 1942 and 1944. An exercise in monumental classicism, it included aesthetic considerations, such as duplicating the surviving seventeenth-century deanery and chapter house.

A second plan also appeared from the City Engineer, F.J. Forty, with generous open spaces to the east, west and south of the Churchyard, defined by a uniform skyline. This was, however, judged lacking in imagination, and its emphasis on high density of office accommodation was contrary to the ethic of the time. A third proposal followed from the progressive architects associated with the *Architectural Review*. This has been defined by the architectural historian Simon Bradley as 'developing a new reconstruction aesthetic based on slabs and towers deployed with picturesque asymmetry meant to evoke a distinctively English tradition of place-making'.[4]

To concerns about architectural style and setting – traditional or modern – and costs and financial returns, was added the question of the skyline. Back in 1934, an article entitled 'What Would Wren Have Built Today?' had declared:

We must give up the building rule which restricts the height of buildings, and we must not only do that, but we must build office blocks twice as high as St Paul's, and have green spaces and wide roads in between the blocks. . . . Two dozen skyscrapers, though they would obviously dwarf

St Paul's, would not take away from its beauty if they were beautiful themselves. They would alter the skyline, certainly, yet we should not sacrifice health, time and comfort to one skyline because we have not the courage to create another.

This startlingly radical view was put forward by none other than John Betjeman, later to become known as a leading conservationist.[5] At the time of writing, he could have no idea that London would suffer the wholesale bombing of the Second World War. His idea, moreover, of what constituted beautiful buildings would no doubt be rather different from that held by the man who is so often described as his diametric opposite, Nikolaus Pevsner.

In the late 1950s a scheme for rebuilding the northern side of the Churchyard was at last taking shape. In 1950 the writer Rose Macaulay had painted a vivid picture of the area around St Paul's Cathedral:

a wilderness of little streets, caves and cellars, the foundations of a wrecked merchant city, grown over by green and golden fennel and ragwort, coltsfoot, purple loosestrife, rosebay willow herb, bracken, bramble and tall nettles, among which rabbits burrowed and wild cats crept and hens laid eggs.[6]

Another observer described Paternoster Row as a 'a narrow country lane bordered by weeds and bushes and wild flowers'.[7]

Pevsner thoroughly commended the scheme, describing it as 'outstandingly well conceived . . . sensible and unobtrusive, i.e. not competing with the cathedral'. He concluded, 'With its flower-boxes, its shops, restaurants and cafes, the whole area looks inviting to local employees as well as to the tourists'.[8] But his opinion on the Holford scheme was not shared by many: the general consensus was that it was disappointing and it was very short-lived. Following the decision to undertake a second rebuilding, more arguments ensued. Modernist schemes submitted by Arup Associates and by Richard Rogers proved controversial, with the Prince of Wales complaining that planners, developers and architects had 'wrecked the London skyline and desecrated the dome of St Paul's with a jostling scrum of office buildings'. New plans were therefore drawn up by neo-classicist architects, Terry Farrell and Thomas Beeby. As Simon Bradley vividly notes, 'by contrast with the suicidally uncommunicative work-in-progress images put out by Arups: watercolours showed sunny spaces alive with workers, tourists and well-behaved children'.[9]

The new precinct was finally opened to the public in the autumn of 2003. Reminders of the history of the area could be enjoyed by those workers, tourists and well-behaved children. Elisabeth Frink's sculpture 'Paternoster – Shepherd and Sheep' paid tribute to the many animals who had been brought here over the centuries to the meat market. An amalgam of a fountain and seats for visitors had a Corinthian column recalling the west portico of the cathedral built in the 1630s by Inigo Jones, supporting a copy of the flames that top the Monument to the Great Fire by Robert Hooke. Entry from Paternoster Square into the Churchyard itself is now through Temple Bar. This was the gatehouse that originally marked the western limit of the City, standing astride Fleet Street. Rebuilt in the early 1670s by Christopher Wren, it spent a century in Theobalds Park in Hertfordshire before being erected as the final part of the square.

The long shadow of St Paul's can be glimpsed from various angles in the new precinct. Perhaps one of the most striking views of the cathedral is gained by walking through Queen's Head Passage from Newgate Street. The dome and north facade resemble the iconic view of the temple at Petra seen through a narrow canyon.

The eastern and southern parts of the Churchyard present a very different landscape. On New Change are the modern blocks of the cathedral school that succeeded the Carter Lane building, along with the tower of St Augustine Church, Watling Street. Surrounding the east end of the cathedral are gardens enclosed by the early eighteenth-century cast iron railings. Engravings and photographs from the nineteenth and early twentieth centuries show that there were well-established trees. When the original planting took place is not certain, but it is possible that some trees were put here before the railings were installed in 1714. Therefore it is further possible that some were of exotic origin, introduced by Bishop Henry Compton, a renowned horticulturalist who had a particularly famous garden at Fulham Palace, with many plants from North America, at that time part of his see. Today there are several fine examples of exotic trees in the Churchyard, especially in the north-eastern part, where there is also a replacement Paul's Cross, erected in 1910 to 'recall and to renew the ancient memories'.[10] One of the trees nearby is *Liquidambar*

Styraciflua, American sweetgum, which was traditionally used as a veneer or satinwood in furniture: possibly a reminder of the distinguished furniture establishments that ran along the south side of the Churchyard in the eighteenth century. Other trees in the Churchyard have dyeing and medicinal properties, and some have biblical connections.

In 1878 the open spaces around the eastern end of the cathedral, some of which had been used as burial grounds, were handed over by the dean and chapter to the Corporation of London to create and manage the gardens. In the southern part, the vista is more open. A recalling of ancient memories, albeit in very twentieth-century form, is a recumbent statue of St Thomas Becket by Edward Bainbridge Copnall. Created in 1970 on the anniversary of his murder in Canterbury Cathedral, it shows the martyred figure gazing heavenwards. In addition to gardens enclosed by the railings, there is also an area that was formally laid out to celebrate the Festival of Britain in 1951, with pleached lime hedges and water features. Just by this is a bust of John Donne, the seventeenth-century Dean of St Paul's, his gaze fixed upon the busy traffic route from Cheapside through to Fleet Street with its red London buses. Some of these bus passengers are no doubt mystified as to why one of the stops is described as St Paul's Churchyard for, as Pevsner pointed out, this is no longer an architecturally integrated space.

Moving westwards, the modern visitor can see laid out on the south side of the cathedral a recreated footprint of the fifteenth-century Chapter House with its many buttresses, which was originally enclosed by a cloister (Plate 8). The only part that could be called cohesive, and a reminder of how the Churchyard was laid out over the centuries, is to be found further to the west, beyond the main entrance to the cathedral. Originally overlooking the Atrium, numbers 5 to 13 St Paul's Churchyard were built by Herbert Ford at the very end of the nineteenth century. Answering on the north side is a curved arcade that replaced the premises of Hitchcock & Williams at the end of the twentieth century.

Along with the loss of architectural integrity there is no longer a secular residential community. From the early nineteenth century the residential population of the City began to decline, so that the last workers who actually lived in the Churchyard were the employees of the textile warehouses. Now, by day the area is populated by office workers and tourists, while the one community that remains is that of the clergy connected to the cathedral who discreetly reside in the houses of Amen Court.

There are, however, reminders of the traditions of the Churchyard. Ceremonial occasions continue to take place, such as the annual greeting of the newly appointed lord mayor by the Dean of St Paul's during the Lord Mayor's Show. And the Churchyard still represents a theatre for opposition and protest. The largest and most central of the buildings in Paternoster Square is the London Stock Exchange. It is this building's presence that drew the Occupy Movement to the square in October 2011. Originating with Occupy Wall Street in New York earlier in that year, the movement called for alternatives to a global financial system that the members defined as unjust and undemocratic. Their initial intention was to camp outside the Stock Exchange, but as Paternoster Square is a privately owned space, the police blocked access, enforcing a High Court injunction. Instead, the protesters, some 2,500 to 3,000 strong, gathered in the Churchyard outside the west doors of the cathedral. Around 250 of them set up camp to sleep overnight.

On the Sunday morning, 16 October, Giles Fraser, the Canon Chancellor of St Paul's, asked the police to leave the cathedral steps, assuring them that he was happy for the people to exercise their right to protest peacefully. In their discussions with him, the leaders of the movement made it clear that they were aware of the tradition of the Churchyard as a theatre of protest.[11] Five days later the Dean, Graeme Knowles, announced that the cathedral would close until further notice, but another five days later rescinded this decision following the resolution of health and safety concerns. The event, however, had brought about the resignation of Giles Fraser, disagreeing about the handling of the protesters, saying that he believed the chapter was set on a course of action that could result in violence in the name of the Church.[12] The Dean's resignation shortly followed. The protesters' camp remained outside the cathedral until the end of January 2012, when the occupants were evicted as a result of a High Court ruling in favour of the City of London Corporation.

To get some feeling of the old Churchyard area and the communities who used to live here, and who thronged the streets, the coffee houses and taverns, the visitor should go down to Carter Lane, running east to west in parallel with the Churchyard. Overshadowed by the dome of St Paul's, here are smaller dwellings in a narrow street, with courts and alleys leading off, including one described as the Royal Wardrobe. As the bell of the cathedral tolls the hours, it seems possible here also to catch the voices of the craftsmen, sermon gadders and protesters, booksellers and other traders, their customers and tourists: precious reminders of one of the most fascinating parts of London.

NOTES

Chapter 1 Setting the Scene

1. Stephen Inwood, *A History of London*, Macmillan, 1998, p. 29.
2. John Stow, *Survey of London*, ed. C.L. Kingsford, 2 vols, Clarendon Press, 1908, I, p. 194; II, p. 125.
3. Bede, *A History of the English Church and People,* trans Leo Sherley-Price, Penguin Classics, 1955, p. 103.
4. Stow, *Survey of London*, vol. I, p. 333.
5. Derek Keene and Pamela Taylor, 'Foundation and Endowment: St Paul's and the English Kingdoms, 604–1087', in Derek Keene, Arthur Burns and Andrew Saint (eds), *St Paul's: The Cathedral Church of London, 604–2004*, Yale University Press, 2004, p. 11.
6. Along with Chichester, Exeter, Hereford, Lichfield, Lincoln, Salisbury, Wells and York.
7. Edward III, 1345. Letter Book F, fol. cxi, Guildhall, quoted in H.T. Riley (ed.), *Memorials of London and London Life*, Longman and Sons, 1868, pp. 228–9.
8. The so-called *Leges Edwardi Confessoris,* in Felix Liebermann, *Die Gesetze der Angelsachsen*, Niemeyer, 1903, vol. I, p. 655.
9. Quoted in Christopher Brooke and Gillian Keir, *London 800–1216: The Shaping of a City*, University of California Press, 1975, p. 116.
10. Bede, *A History*, pp. 102–3.

Chapter 2 The Times Newspaper of the Middle Ages

1. W.C. Sellars and R.J. Yeatman, *1066 and All That*, Methuen, 1936, p. 24.
2. Translated by Catherine Hanley, *Louis: the French Prince who Invaded England*, Yale University Press, 2016, p. 58.
3. M. Tyson, 'The Annals of Southwark and Merton', Surrey Archaeological Collections, vol. xxxvi, 1925, pp. 50–1.
4. On the death of Philip Augustus in 1225, the Prince succeeded to the throne as Louis VIII.
5. Thomas Carlyle, *Cromwell's Letters and Speeches: vol 1*, in *Complete Works*, 30 vols, Chapman & Hall, 1870, vol. 14, pp. 65–6; H. Gareth Owen, 'Paul's Cross: The Broadcasting House of Elizabethan London', *History Today*, 9, 1961, 836–42.
6. John Stow, *Survey of London*, ed. C.L. Kingsford, 2 vols, Clarendon Press, 1908, I, p. 331.
7. Arnold fitz Thedmar in *Liber de Antiquis Legibus*, now at the London Metropolitan Archives, (CLA/C5/01/001/001).
8. Gwyn A. Williams, *Medieval London: From Commune to Capital*, Athlone Press, 1963, Appendix C.

9. Stow, *Survey of London*, I, p. 167.

10. T.P. Dolan, 'English and Latin Versions of FitzRalph's Sermons', in A.J. Minnis, ed., *Latin and Vernacular Studies in Late-Medieval Texts and Manuscripts,* Brewer, 1989.

11. Stow, *Survey of London*, I, pp. 333–5.

12. See Marion Turner, 'Conflict', in Paul Strohm, ed., *Middle English*, Oxford University Press, 2007, p. 306.

13. Thomas Walsingham, *Historia Anglicanum,* ed. H.T. Riley, Rolls Series 1863–4, ii, pp. 157–9.

14. *St Albans Chronicle*, pp. 1–2. A copy of Taylor's sermon is in the Bodleian Library, Ms Douce 53, and reproduced in Anne Hudson, *Two Wycliffite Texts,* Early English Text Society, Oxford University Press, 1993.

15. Arundel's letter and the passage from the continuator of the Chronicle of Henry Knighton are both quoted in David Daniell, *The Bible in English,* Yale University Press, 2003, p. 67.

16. Daniell, p. 76.

17. Corinne Saunders, *Magic and the Supernatural in Medieval English Romance*, Brewer, 2010, p. 75.

18. For the tangled web of Pecock's career, see Wendy Scase in the *Oxford Dictionary of National Biography*, 2004.

19. Antony Goodman, *The Wars of the Roses: The Soldiers' Experience,* Tempus, 2005, p. 198.

20. A. Hinds and Public Record Office, 1912, *Calendar of State Papers and Manuscripts Existing in the Archives and Collections of Milan, 1460*, HMSO, 1912, item 37.

21. Edward IV was tall and fair, while the rest of the family were small and dark, so the suggestion has been put forward that Cecily Neville had borne the child of an archer in the Yorkist entourage.

22. *Richard III*, Act III, Scene VII; A.H. Thomas and I.D. Thornley, eds, *The Great Chronicle of London*, G.W. Jones, 1938, p. 233; St Thomas More, *The History of King Richard III*, ed. R.S. Sylvester, 1976, vol. 2 of *The Yale Edition of the Complete Works of St Thomas More*, pp. 55–6.

Chapter 3 The Centre of the Book World

1. Wörth was suggested by James Moran, *Wynkyn de Worde: Father of Fleet Street,* Wynkyn de Worde Society, revised edition, 1976; Woerden by Lotte Hellinga, 'Wynkyn de Worde's Native Land', in Richard Beadle and A.J. Piper, eds, *New Science out of Old Books: Studies in Manuscripts and Early Printed Books in Honour of A.J. Doyle*, Scolar Press, 1995, pp. 342–59.

2. Peter Blayney, *The Stationers' Company and the Printers of London, 1501–1557,* Cambridge University Press, 2013, vol. 1, p. 69.

3. C.P. Christianson, *A Directory of London Stationers and Book Artisans, 1300–1500*, Bibliographical Society of America, 1990, p. 31, quoted in James Raven, 'St Paul's Precinct and the Book Trade to *c.* 1800', in D. Keene, A. Burns and A. Saint, eds, *St Paul's: The Cathedral Church 604–2004*, Yale University Press, pp. 430–1.

4. A 'misterie' was a trade or skill – hence the Mystery Plays still staged in York, for example, which were originally enacted by local guilds.

5. John Rastell, *The Four Elements*, ed. Roger Coleman, Cambridge University Press, 1971, p. 7.

6. Blayney, *The Stationers' Company and the Printers of London, 1501–1557*, Cambridge University Press, 2013, vol. 2, pp. 983–1002.

7. David Daniell, *The Bible in English*, Yale University Press, 2003, p. 206.

8. Daniell, pp. 129–30. The figures he quotes for sale of bibles in Elizabethan and Jacobean England are spectacular: 'Estimating 2,000 printed for each English Bible in Shakespeare's lifetime makes 422,000 Bibles bought, just under half a million . . . out of a population of about six million.'

9. Quoted in David Hall's introduction to *A History of the Book in America*, Cambridge University Press, 2000, vol. 1, p. 3.

10. Richard Smyth and Stephen Gardiner, see Chapter 4.

11. Peter Blayney, *The Bookshops in Paul's Cross Churchyard*, Occasional Papers of the Bibliographical Society, No. 5, 1990, p. 19.

12. The registers of the Company were rescued during the Great Fire of London, and remain one of the great treasures of the Company.

13. Parker's letter, British Library, MS Lansdowne 15/50; the lease, Guildhall Library, MS 25, 630/2, fols 405r–406r. Peter Blayney, in 'John Day and the Bookshop That Never Was', in Lena Cowen Orlin, ed., *Material London, ca. 1600*, University of Pennsylvania Press, 2000, chapter 16.

14. Translated from Latin by Graham Pollard in Graham Pollard and Albert Ehrman, eds, *The Distribution of Books by Catalogue From the Invention of Printing to AD 1800*, Cambridge University Press, 1965, p. 47.

15. Andrew Maunsell, *The Catalogue of English Printed Bookes*, 2 parts, London 1595; photographic reprint, Gregg Press, 1965, preface.

16. Translated from Latin by Graham Pollard in *The Distribution of Books*, p. 75.

17. See Julian Roberts, 'The Latin Trade' in J. Barnard and D.F. McKenzie, eds, *The Cambridge History of the Book in Britain, Vol IV, 1557–1695*, Cambridge University Press, 2002, pp. 141–73.

18. See Kirk Melnikoff's 'Isabella Whitney Amongst the Stalls of Richard Jones' in Valerie Wayne, ed., *Women's Labour and the History of the Book in Early Modern England*, Arden Shakespeare, 2020, pp. 145–61.

19. The journals are in the Folger Shakespeare Library in Washington DC, MS V.a. 459–61.

20. There are two, almost identical, copies of the inventory, TNA E159/421/435 and TNA E178/2980.

21. His life and details of his books are described in Jason Scott-Warren, *Shakespeare's First Reader: The Paper Trails of Richard Stonley*, University of Pennsylvania Press, 2019.

22. Devonshire Mss. CHA, Hardwick Mss, 10A, Book of Accounts for 1597–1601. See Margaret Willes, *Reading Matters: Five Centuries of Discovering Books*, Yale University Press, 2008, pp. 244 and ff.

23. *The Letters of John Chamberlain*, ed. Norman Egbert McClure, 2 vols, The American Philosophical Society, 1939, I, p. 157.

24. Queen Square in Holborn was originally called Devonshire Square, which suggests that William Cavendish's house may have stood here.

25. Daniell, *The Bible in English*, p. 772.

26. Daniell, p. 439.

27. Patrick Collinson, Arnold Hunt and Alexandra Walsham, 'Religious Publishing in England 1557–1640', in *The Cambridge History of the Book, Vol IV*, p. 29.

28. Margaret Spufford, 'Books of the Common Sort', in *The Cambridge History of Libraries*, Cambridge University Press, vol. I, p. 523.

Chapter 4 The Fires of Reformation

1. *The Journals of Two Travellers in Elizabeth and Early Stuart England: Thomas Platter and Horatio Busino*, ed. Peter Razzell, Caliban Books, 1995, pp. 39–40.

2. Cecilia Hatt introducing Fisher's sermon, in T. Kirby, P.G. Stanwood, M. Morrissey and J.N. King, eds, *Sermons at Paul's Cross, 1521–1642*, Oxford University Press, 2017, p. 4. The text of the sermon is given in full, pp.12–31.

3. Mary Morrissey, *Politics and the Paul's Cross Sermons, 1558–1642*, Oxford University Press, 2011, p. xi. A register was originally compiled by Millar MacLure as an appendix in *The Paul's Cross Sermons, 1534–1642*, University of Toronto Press, 1958, revised and published separately by Peter Pauls & J.C. Boswell, 1989.

4. William Tyndale, *Doctrinal Treatises*, Parker Society, Cambridge University Press, 1848, p. 221.
5. MacLure, *The Paul's Cross Sermons*, p. 4.
6. The sermon was printed by Thomas Godfray in 1536. Only one copy survives, in Lincoln Cathedral. The text is reproduced in *Sermons at Paul's Cross, 1521–1642*, pp. 36–49
7. Andreas Löwe, *Richard Smyth and the Language of Orthodoxy*, Brill, 2003, p. 35; 'A Godly and Faythfull Retraction Made and Published at Paules Crosse 1547', published by Reyner Wolfe. The text is reproduced in *Sermons at Paul's Cross, 1521–1642*, pp. 93–100.
8. *Foxe's Book of Martyrs*, 1563 edition, iv, p. 795.
9. Charles Wriothesley, *A Chronicle of England During the Reign of the Tudors from ad 1485 to 1559*, ed. W.D. Hamilton, 2 vols, Camden Society, 1875, vol. 1, p. 90; *Foxe's Book of Martyrs*, 1570 edition, p. 1398.
10. Wriothesley, p. 90.
11. 'The Sermon on the Ploughers' was printed by John Day and William Seres. The text is reproduced in *Sermons at Paul's Cross, 1521–1642*, pp. 104–17.
12. *A Sermon very Notable, Fruictefull and Godlie . . .*, printed by Robert Caly 'within the late dissolved house of the Graie Friars', 1533.
13. David Daniell, *The Bible in English*, Yale University Press, 2003, p. 131.
14. Torrance Kirby in *Sermons at Paul's Cross, 1521–1642*, p. 226. The text of the sermon follows, pp. 231–59.
15. Stonley's journal, Folger Shakespeare Library, 22 April 1582.
16. Richard Andrews, 'Dirae', mid-1620s, BL Harleian MS 4955, f. 157. Maister Gowge was William Gouge, a highly considered preacher, Arnold Hunt, *The Art of Hearing: English P reachers and Their Audiences, 1590–1640*, Cambridge University Press, 2010, p. 214.
17. 26 November 1559; 3 March 1560, *The Diary of Henry Machyn, Citizen and Merchant-taylor of London from A.D. 1550 to A.D. 1563*, ed. John Gough Nicols, 1848.
18. Machyn, 13 August 1553.
19. Stow, *Annales*, 1632, p. 624; Machyn, 23 November 1561.
20. Hunt, *The Art of Hearing*, p. 330; Aylmer to Sir James Harvey, 1 March 1581–2, *Memoirs of the Life and Times of Sir Christopher Hatton*, ed. Sir Harris Nicholas, Richard Bentley, 1847, pp. 236–8.
21. *Sermon Preached at Paule's Crosse, 1580*, printed by Thomas Woodcocke, 1581, sig. D4v. The sermon is reproduced in *Sermons at Paul's Cross, 1521–1642*, pp. 262–82.
22. John Strype, *The Life and Acts of Matthew Parker*, John Wyat, 1711, vol. 1, pp. 318–19.
23. 'A Sermon preached at Paul's Cross, the 9 of Februarie 1588', printed for I.I[ackson] for Gregorie Seton, sig. B3r-v. The text of the sermon is reproduced in *Sermons at Paul's Cross, 1521–1642*, pp. 338–80.
24. Thomas Platter, *The Journals of Two Travellers*, p. 40.
25. Stow, *Annales*, p. 750.
26. Mervyn James, 'At the Crossroads of the Political Culture: the Essex Revolt, 1601', in *Society, Politics and Culture: Studies in Early Modern England*, Cambridge University Press, 1986.
27. Lambeth Palace Library, MS 2872, fols 57r–58r.
28. The sermon was printed by Matthew Law. Its text is reproduced in *Sermons at Paul's Cross, 1521–1642*, pp. 385–406.
29. Morrissey, *Politics and the Paul's Cross Sermons*, p. 78.

Chapter 5 The Children of Paul's

1. Privy Council Register, Elizabeth, II, 408, 3 December 1575.
2. *Thomas Tusser: Five Hundred Points of Good Husbandry, 1557*, ed. Geoffrey Grigson, Oxford University Press, 1984, p. 203.

3. Quoted in Samuel Knight, *The Life of John Colet, Founder of St Paul's School*, J. Downing, 1724, pp. 100–1.

4. *The Merry Wives of Windsor*, Act IV, Scene I.

5. See note 2.

6. The indenture of Thomas Gyles, 1584, quoted in Reavley Gair, *The Children of Paul's: The Story of a Theatre Company, 1553–1608*, Cambridge University Press, 1982, pp. 37, 38. Gair has set out the complete document in 'The Conditions of Appointment for Masters of Choristers at Paul's (1553–1613)', *Notes and Queries*, ns 27, 1980, pp. 116–24.

7. Quoted and analysed in Gair, p. 81; see also Albert Feuillerat, *Documents Relating to the Office of the Revels*, Uystpruyst, 1908, p. xiv.

8. Feuillerat, pp. 218–19.

9. 14 Eliz.I.c.5.

10. Gair, *The Children of Paul's*, pp. 44 and ff.

11. Roger Bowers, 'The Playhouse of the Choristers of Paul's, *c.*1575–1608', *Theatre Notebook*, 54, 2000, pp. 70–85; See also Herbert Berry, 'Where was the Playhouse in which the Boy Choristers of St Paul's Cathedral performed Plays?', *Medieval and Renaissance Drama in England*, 13, 2001, pp. 109–13.

12. Warrant printed in T.H. Vail Motter, *The School Drama in England*, Longmans, Green, 1929, p. 144n.

13. The story of Thomas Clifton was told by Katherine Rundell in a BBC TV programme, *Abducted*, broadcast on 6 August 2018. The quotations of the court proceedings appeared in an article by Katherine Rundell in *The Times*, 30 July 2018.

14. My thanks to Bruce Alexander and his website www.namedbyshakespeare.com; *Hamlet*, Act II, scene 2, lines 317–24.

15. *Ben Jonson's Works*, ed. C.H. Herford and Percy Simpson, Clarendon Press, 1947, VIII, p. 77. The tradition of a boys' company continues today with Edwards' Boys from Stratford upon Avon. The author, watching them perform some of the plays originally written for the boys of Paul's and Blackfriars, found they demonstrated great skill and emotional depth in their scenes, whether playing men or women.

16. The details of this dispute come from *The Visitation Report of Bishop Bancroft*, LMA MS.9537/9. They are also enumerated in Gair, *The Children of Paul's*, pp. 113–15.

17. Bancroft's Visitation Report, LMA MS.9537/9, fols 42v–61.

18. *Selected Plays of John Marston*, ed. MacDonald P. Jackson and Michael Neill, Cambridge University Press, 1986: *Antonio and Mellida*, Act V, Scene II, p. 83; *Endymion, or the Man in the Moon*, Induction, p. 202.

19. William Percy, quoted in G.G. Reynolds, 'William Percy and his Plays, with a Summary of the Customs of Elizabethan Staging', *Modern Philology*, 12, 1914–15, p. 259.

20. Darrell's accounts are printed in H. Hall, *Society in the Elizabethan Age*, Sonnenschein & Co., 1888, pp. 101, 206–33.

21. *The Sermon Preached at the Crosse, Feb. xiii 1607*[o/s], W. Crawshawe, 'sold at the great Northgate of S. Paules', 1608, pp. 170–1.

Chapter 6 The Twilight of Old St Paul's

1. These exceptions were perceived Catholic traitors such as John Felton, executed at the Ludgate end of the Churchyard for pinning to the door of the bishop's palace a copy of the papal bull excommunicating Elizabeth I in 1570. Also executed on this site in February 1592 was Thomas Portmort, a Roman Catholic priest, who at his trial for treason had accused the Queen's torturer and interrogator, the notorious Richard Topcliffe, of salacious acts: Topcliffe used rape as a means of acquiring information. As he stood on the steps of the gallows Portmort was harangued for two hours by Topcliffe in an attempt to secure a retraction of these accusations.

2. Gorges to Salisbury, 29 January 1606, HMC, *Salisbury*, vol. 18, pp. 36–7.
3. *A Sermon Preached at Pauls Cross the 5th of November 1614. By Doctor Goodwyn, then Vice Chancellor of Oxford*, folios 14v and 15r. This sermon was circulated as a manuscript rather than published in printed form. Its text is reproduced in T. Kirby, P.G. Stanwood, M. Morrissey and J.N. King, eds, *Sermons at Paul's Cross, 1521–1642*, Oxford University Press, pp. 436–53.
4. L. Grenade's description of *The Singularities of London, 1578*, translated from the French, and reproduced by the London Topographical Society, 2014, folios 70r–v.
5. The inclusion of the representation of a rhinoceros is intriguing. At the time the Grocers' Company included apothecaries, but in 1617 they broke away to form their own company, and chose as their emblem the rhinoceros because of the medicinal properties associated with the animal's horn.
6. The route is shown on the Map of Early Modern London website, http://mapoflondon.uvic.ca.
7. The drawings are now in the Guildhall Library.
8. *Thomas Coriate, Travellere for the English Wits: Greeting*, W. Jaggard and Henry Featherston, 1616, p. 37.
9. *Walton's Lives of Dr. John Donne, Sir Henry Wotton* et al, George Bell & Sons, 1884, p. 38; *The Diary of Thomas Crosfield*, ed. F.S. Boas, Oxford University Press, 1935, p. 30.
10. *Walton's Lives*, p. 47.
11. *Letters of John Chamberlain*, ed. Norman Egbert McClure, 2 vols, American Philosophical Society, 1939, vol II, pp. 407–8.
12. Chamberlain, vol. II, p. 451.
13. The manuscript version was found in the British Library by Jeanne Shami and published as *John Donne's 1622 Gunpowder Plot: A Parallel-text Edition*, Duquesne University Press, 1996. John Wall of North Carolina State University has created a project reconstructing the Cross Churchyard in the 1620s as context for his study of the sermons of Donne and other early seventeenth-century preachers. I am very grateful to Professor Wall for clarifying the complex process. The Virtual Paul's Cross project can be seen at http://vpcp.chass.ncsu.edu.
14. Both quoted by Henry Hart Milman, *Annals of St Paul's Cathedral*, John Murray, 1868, pp. 284–5.
15. Bishop Bancroft's visitations of 1598 and subsequent visitations are in the Guildhall Library MS. 9537/9.
16. Visitation, fol. 57.
17. Donne, *Sermons*, vol. 7, 10 January 1627, p. 318.
18. John Earle, *Microcosmography*, first published in 1628, 1811 edition, ed. S.T. Irwin, Simpkin Marshall, pp. 104–5.
19. Francis Osborne, *Traditionall Memoyres on the Raigne of King James*, 1658, pp. 64–5.
20. Thomas Dekker, *The Gull's Horne Book,* 1609, pp. 39–40.
21. This dialogue is shown in detail in Roze Hentschell, *St Paul's Precinct in Early Modern Literature and Culture*, Oxford University Press, 2020.
22. *Letters of John Chamberlain*, vol. I, p. 288, 28.2.1618; p. 171, 19.11.1602.
23. The Butter family had earlier published accounts of current events. His father, Thomas, for example, had published in 1585 an account of a sea battle between Spain and England in a pamphlet, and his mother Joan continued in this genre after Thomas's death and her marriage to another bookseller, John Newbery. See Sarah Neville, 'Stationers and their Second-Plus Husbands', in Valerie Wayne, ed., *Women's Labour and the History of the Book in Early Modern England*, Arden Shakespeare, 2020.
24. Thomas Dekker, *The Dead Tearme*, 1608, p. 40.
25. TNA SP/14/15, no. 28, quoted in William Dugdale, *History of St Paul's Cathedral*, Lockington, Hughes, 1818, p. 101.

26. The drawing is now in Worcester College, Oxford.
27. *Letters of John Chamberlain*, letter 350, p. 297.
28. The diptych is now in the collection of the Society of Antiquaries. A detailed analysis of the paintings is given by Pamela Tudor-Craig in *Old St Paul's: The Society of Antiquaries' Diptych, 1616*, London Topographical Society and The Society of Antiquaries of London, 2004.
29. *Letters of John Chamberlain*, letter 351, p. 299.
30. Chamberlain, letter 409, 22.6.1622; letter 351, p. 300; letter 358, 4.8.1620, p. 315.
31. John Stubbs, *Donne, The Reformed Soul*, Penguin Books, 2007, p. 373.
32. See H.R. Plomer, 'St Paul's Cathedral and its Bookselling Tenants', *The Library*, NS III, 1902, pp. 261 and ff.
33. Chamberlain, letter 32, 10.10.1600, p. 107.
34. Chamberlain, letter 133, 12.2.1612, vol. I, p. 334.
35. Donne, *Sermons*, vol. 10, no. 11, 25 Feb 1631, p. 233.
36. *Walton's Lives*, p. 75.
37. Quoted in Timothy Harris, *London Crowds in the Reign of Charles II*, Cambridge University Press, 1987, p. 45.
38. *The Diary of John Evelyn*, ed. E.S. De Beer, Clarendon Press, rev. edn 2000, 29 May 1660, vol. iii, p. 246.
39. *The Diary of John Evelyn*, 27 August 1666, vol. iii, p. 449.

Chapter 7 Resetting the Scene

1. *The Autobiography and Anecdotes of William Taswell (1652–82)*, reprinted in Camden Miscellany, Camden Society, 1853, vol. II, p.11; *Reliquiae Baxterianaae; or Mr. Richard Baxter's Narrative of the Most Memorable Passages of His Life and Times*, ed. M. Sylvester, published by T. Parkhurst, J. Robinson, J. Lawrence and J. Dunton, 1696, Part 3, p. 16; Locke quoted in J. Bedford, *London's Burning*, Abelard Schuman, 1966, p. 24.
2. *The Diary of Samuel Pepys*, ed. R. Latham and W. Matthews, Bell & Hyman, 1970–83, vol. vii, p. 279, 7 September 1666; *The Diary of John Evelyn*, ed. E.S. De Beer, Clarendon Press, rev. edn 2000, vol. iii, p. 459, 7 September 1666.
3. *Autobiography and Anecdotes of William Taswell*, p. 13.
4. John Evelyn, *Fumifugium*, 1661, p. 3; *London Revived*, ed. E.S. De Beer, Clarendon Press, 1938, pp. 48–9.
5. *The Diary of John Milward Esq*, ed. Caroline Robbins, Cambridge University Press, 1938, p. 9, entry for 27 September 1666.
6. BL Add. Ms 78333, f. 5.
7. The First Rebuilding Act of February 1667, 19 Caroli, II.
8. See Jacob Field, *London, Londoners and the Great Fire of 1666: Disaster and Recovery*, Routledge, 2018, p. 73.
9. Lydia Soo, *Wren's Tracts on Architecture and Other Writings*, Cambridge University Press, 1998, p. 115.
10. Wren Society, vol. XIII, p. 26.
11. Ibid.
12. Nikolai Karamazin, *Letters of a Russian Traveller*, trans. and ed. Andrew Kahn, Voltaire Foundation, Oxford, 2003, p. 404.
13. Karamazin, *Letters of a Russian Traveller*, p. 31.
14. Christopher Wren, *Parentalia*, 1750, pp. 282–3.
15. *The Diary of Samuel Pepys*, vol. ix, p. 305, 14 September 1668; pp. 307–8, 16 September.
16. The Convocation House was demolished in 1684 to make way for part of the nave.
17. See Lucy Inglis, *Georgian London: Into the Streets*, Penguin, 2013, p. 17.
18. Wren, *Parentalia*, pp. 266–7; John Strype, *A Survey of the Cities of London and Westminster*, 1720, vol. II, p. 692.

19. Memorandum book, BL Sloane MS 958 fols 105r–142r. Public display of the finds was noted in the *Athenian Mercury*, vol V. no. 16, 21 November 1691.
20. Wren, *Parentalia*, p. 292.
21. Leo Hollis, *The Phoenix: St Paul's Cathedral and the Men who Made Modern London*, Weidenfeld & Nicolson, 2008, p. 224.
22. *Diary of Robert Hooke, 1672–1680*, ed. H.W. Robinson and Walter Adams, Taylor and Francis, 1935, e.g. 21.7.1677, p. 303; 13.10.1677, p. 320.
23. *The Diary of John Evelyn*, vol. v, pp. 278–9.
24. Dedicated to 'An Account of Architects and Architecture', in John Evelyn, *A Parallel of the Antient Architecture with the Modern* (1707 edition). The dedication is dated 21 February 1698. His letter to Wren, dated 21 February 1697, pp. 36–7, Wren Society XIII.
25. *Phoenix Paulina, a Poem on the New Fabrick of St. Paul's Cathedral by James Wright, Barrister at Law*, Arthur Collins, 1709, p. 9, verse 22.
26. The railings are said to have cost £11,200, about 1.5% of the total cost of the cathedral.
27. *Fact Against Scandal, or a Collection of Testimonials, Affidavits, and other Authentick Proofs in Vindication of Mr Richard Jenings, Carpenter . . .*, John Morphew, 1713.
28. *Bleak House*, chapter 19.

Chapter 8 Resurgam

1. *The Diary of Samuel Pepys*, ed. R. Latham and W. Matthews, Bell & Hyman, 1970–83, vol. viii, p. 526, 11 November 1667.
2. 'In a profession that was predominantly bourgeois and Whig, he was a totally unreconstructed Cavalier aristocrat, with a violent and unrelenting hatred of Dissenters, Whigs and Trimmers', T.A. Birrell, 'Sir Roger L'Estrange: The Journalism of Orality', in John Barnard and D.F. McKenzie, eds, *Cambridge History of the Book in Britain, Vol. IV, 1557–1695*, Cambridge University Press, 2002, p. 657.
3. *The Diary of Samuel Pepys*, vol. iv, p. 297, 4 September 1663; vol. vi, p. 305, 22 November 1665.
4. G.K. Fortescue, ed., *Catalogue of the Pamphlets, Books, Newspapers, and Manuscripts Relating to the Civil War, the Commonwealth, and Restoration, Collected by George Thomason, 1640–1661*, The Trustees of the British Museum, 2 vols, 1908, vol. 1, p. v.
5. *The Diary of Samuel Pepys*, vol. vi, p. 2, 2 January 1665; p. 17, 20 January 1665; vol. vii, p. 226, 29 July 1666.
6. The letter is in Museum Plantin-Moretus, Antwerp, Archives 649, ff. 689–90. The date is Old Style (English)/New Style (Continental), 10/20 September 1666. The translation from the original French is by Giles Mandelbrote, as reproduced in 'Workplaces and Living Spaces: London Book Trade Inventories of the Late Seventeenth Century', in Robin Myers, Giles Mandelbrote and Michael Harris, eds, *The London Book Trade, Topographies of Print*, Oak Knoll Press and the British Library, 2003, pp. 21–43.
7. *The Diary of Samuel Pepys*, vol. ix, p. 161, 10 April 1668, p. 335, 23 October 1668.
8. Washington Irving, *The Sketch Book*, 'Little Britain', 1819–20.
9. *The Diary of Samuel Pepys*, vol. ix, p. 23, 14 January 1668.
10. The concept of the English stock was dissolved only in the 1960s. Some of the money of the jointstock was invested in financing expeditions to America, see Paul Wilson, *Pilgrims, Profit and Print: The Stationers of London and the English Settlement of North America*, Phillimore Book Publishing, 2019. Although there were also Latin and Irish stocks, the former was dissolved in 1627 and the second hardly functioned. A fourth scheme, Ulster stock, was a joint venture between the Stationers' and the Skinners' Company to invest in plantations in Ireland.
11. Stationers' Company Archive TSC/1/E/English Stock/D/01, Books in the Treasurer's warehouse 1663–1723. I am very grateful to Dr Frendo, the company's archivist, for pointing

this out to me. The relationship between the universities and the Stationers is explained in Cyprian Blagden, *The Stationers' Company, A History 1403–1959*, George Allen & Unwin, 1960, pp. 101–4.

12. *The Diary of Robert Hooke, 1672–1680*, ed. Henry Robinson and Walter Adams, Taylor and Francis, 1935, 4 June 1673.

13. Quoted in J.E. Hodgson, 'Romance and Humour of the Auction Room', *Connoisseur*, June 1939.

14. *Letters and the Second Diary of Samuel Pepys*, ed. R.G. Howarth, J.M. Dent and Sons, 1932, p. 266, letter 249, 16 March 1697. The book in question was *Stobaei Sententiae*.

15. *The London Gazette*, 2554, 5 May 1690.

16. Ned Ward, *A Fair Step to Stir-Bitch-Fair: With Remarks upon the University of Cambridge*, 1704.

17. 'An Elegy on the Death of Mr Edward Millington, the Famous Auctioneer', in Thomas Brown, *Serious and Comical Essays*, 1709.

18. The dispute between Clavell and Starkey, with interventions from other booksellers, is detailed by Graham Pollard in Graham Pollard and Albert Ehrman, eds, *The Distribution of Books by Catalogue: From the Invention of Printing to AD 1800*, Roxburghe Club, 1965, pp. 129–31.

19. See Peter Beal, 'Books are the Great Joy of My Life, Sir William Boothby, 17th-century Bibliophile', *Book Collector*, 46, 3, 1997. Boothby's four letterbooks are in the British Library, Add Mss 71689–71692. The quote is in a letter to Charles Cotton, 21.7.1685.

20. Ned Ward, *The London Spy*, ed. Paul Hyland from the 4th edition of 1709, East Lansing Colleagues Press, 1993, part IV, p. 78; part V, p. 81.

21. John Dunton, *The Life and Errors of John Dunton*, 1709, pp. 280, 221–2; 210–1.

22. Maureen Bell, 'Women in the English Book Trade, 1557–1700', *Leipziger Jahrbuch zur Buchgeschichte*, 6, 1996, pp. 13–45.

23. Dunton, *The Life and Errors*, pp. 253–3.

24. The portrait hangs in the National Portrait Gallery. For a detailed examination of Elinor James and of other female printers and booksellers, see Paula McDowell, *The Women of Grub Street: Press, Politics and Gender in the London Literary Marketplace*, Clarendon Press, 1998.

25. TNA C.5 538/15.

26. Dunton, *The Life and Errors*, p. 233.

27. *London in 1710, from the Travels of Zacharias Conrad von Uffenbach*, ed. and trans. W.H. Quarrell and Margaret Mare, Faber & Faber, 1934, pp. 18–19, 52.

28. James Raven, James Raven, 'St Paul's Precinct and the Book Trade to *c.* 1800', in D. Keene, A. Burns and A. Saint, eds, *St Paul's: The Cathedral Church 604–2004*, Yale University Press, p. 435.

Chapter 9 A Place to be Seen

1. *The Diary of Samuel Pepys*, ed. R. Latham and W. Matthews, Bell & Hyman, 1970–83, vol. vii, pp. 367–8, 12 November 1666.

2. *Letters of John Chamberlain*, ed. Norman Egbert McClure, 2 vols, American Philosophical Society, 1939, vol. I, p. 91, Letter to Dudley Carleton, 5 March 1600.

3. Today Erconwald is remembered in a street name, along with other figures from the early history of St Paul's such as Mellitus and Braybrooke, in the unlikely purlieus of the underground station at East Acton.

4. *Letters of John Chamberlain*, vol. 1, p. 118, Letter of 3 February 1601.

5. *The Journals of Two Travellers in Elizabethan and Early Stuart England: Thomas Platter and Horatio Busino*, ed. Peter Razzell, Caliban Books, 1995, p. 38.

6. Edmund Howes's enlargement of Stow's *Annales or Generall Chronicle of England*, 1615, p. 886.

7. Thomas Dekker, *The Gull's Horne Book*, 1609, p. 21.
8. John Aubrey, *Brief Lives*, ed. Oliver Lawson Dick, Nonpareil Books, 1999, p. 70.
9. *London in 1710, from the Travels of Zacharias Conrad von Uffenbach*, ed. and trans. W.H. Quarrell and Margaret Mare, Faber & Faber, 1934, pp. 31–3.
10. See Ralph Hyde, 'Images of St Paul's', in D. Keene, A. Burns and A. Saint, eds, *St Paul's: The Cathedral Church of London, 604–2004*, Yale University Press, 2004, pp. 317–34.
11. *The Diary of Dudley Ryder, 1715–16*, ed. William Matthews, Methuen, 1939, pp. 306–7. Ryder went on to become Lord Chief Justice.
12. *Lichtenberg's Visits to England, as Described in his Letters and Diaries,* trans. and ed. Margaret Mare and W.H. Quarrell, Clarendon Press, 1938, p. 54. The 'first place of worship' was probably St Peter's in Rome; the three bridges were London, Blackfriars and Westminster.
13. *Nikolai Karamazin: Letters of a Russian Traveller*, trans. and ed. Andrew Kahn, Voltaire Foundation, 2003, Letter 141, July 1790.
14. Robert Hubert, *A Catalogue of Natural Rarities*, 1664, pp. 1–2, 60; p. 5.
15. Ned Ward, *The London Spy*, ed. Paul Hyland from the 4th edition of 1708, East Lansing Colleagues Press, 1993, Part V, p. 81.
16. *The Pleasant Musical Companion: Being a Choice Collection of Catches for Three or Four Voices. Compos'd by Dr. John Blow, the late Mr. Henry Purcell, and other Eminent Masters*, printed by William Pearson and sold by John Young, Musical-Instrument-Maker at the Dolphin and Crown at the West End of St Paul's Church, London, 1726. The catch, p. 89, is attributed to Dr Caesar. John Young's trade card of *c.* 1700 is in the Heal collection in the British Museum.
17. *A New Guide to London, or Directions to Strangers*, 2nd edition, 1726, pp. 33, 37.
18. Thomas Dekker, *The Gull's Horne Book*, 1609, p. 20.
19. Meriton Latroon, *The English Rogue*, 1665, vol. II, p. 163.
20. Ned Ward, *The London Spy*, Part V, pp. 86–7.
21. *Diary of Samuel Pepys*, vol. i, p. 298, 21 November 1660; vol. iv, p. 199, 25 June 1663; vol. v, p. 302, 21 October 1664; vol. vii, p. 7, 8 January 1666.
22. John Strype, *A Survey of the Cities of London and Westminster*, 1720, Book III, p. 195.
23. See Marion Turner, *Chaucer: A European Life*, Princeton University Press, 2019, p. 11. In the Miller's Tale in *The Canterbury Tales*, Chaucer introduced the parish clerk 'With Poules window corven on his shoos', l. 3318.
24. These collections, with other trade cards, are held in the Prints and Drawings Collection in the British Museum. More cards are to be found in the John Johnson Collection of ephemera in the Bodleian Library in Oxford, and in the London Metropolitan Archives.
25. *The Purefoy Letters, 1735–1753*, ed. G. Eland, Sidgwick and Jackson, 1931, vol. 1, pp. 107–8, 111.
26. Ibid, pp. 113, 69.
27. An exhibition, 'City Women in the 18th Century' was held in the area from St Paul's to the Royal Exchange during the autumn of 2019, and can be viewed online at www.cam.ac.uk/citywomen. I am grateful to Amy Erickson and Sheila O'Connell for their help and advice on details of these women traders.
28. Fanny Burney, *Evelina,* 1778, Letter X, Evelina to Rev. Mr Villars.
29. *Lichtenberg's Visits to England*, pp. 63–4. The letter quoted was to Professor Baldinger at Gottingen, 10 January 1775.

Chapter 10 Literary Circles

1. Different dates are given for this incident. Griffiths' biographer, Antonia Forster, in the *Oxford Dictionary of National Biography* puts it in 1749 when *Fanny Hill* was first published. James Raven, who has made a close study of the locations of bookshops, suggests some time between 1754 and 1759 when Griffiths is known to have had a shop in Paternoster Row.

Griffiths is now known as 'Dr' after being given an honorary degree in 1790 by Dartmouth College in the United States.

2. James Raven, 'St Paul's Precinct and the Book Trade to *c.* 1800', in D. Keene, A. Burns and A. Saint, eds, *St Paul's: The Cathedral Church of London 604–2004*, Yale University Press, 2004, p. 433.

3. Quoted in G.M. Trevelyan, *England Under Queen Anne, vol. 3, The Peace and the Protestant Succession*, Longman Green, 1934, p. 42.

4. Henry Sacheverell, *The Perils of False Brethren, Both in Church and State*, 1709, p. 25.

5. Quoted by Jeremy Gregory, 'Preaching Anglicanism at St Paul's, 1688–1800', in Keene et al., *St Paul's*, p. 344.

6. The bookseller William West in H. Curwen, *A History of Booksellers, the Old and the New*, Chatto & Windus, 1873, p. 302.

7. Rivingtons was bought by Longmans in 1890, and the Pearson Group bought Longmans in 1968.

8. Henry Dell, *The Booksellers: A Poem*, 1766. Reproduced in Terry Belanger, 'A Directory of the English Book Trade, 1766', *Publishing History*, 1, 1977, p. 19.

9. 'The True Domestick Intelligence, or News both from City and Country', 31 October 1679. The review is reproduced in the Appendix to Margaret Willes, *The Curious World of Samuel Pepys and John Evelyn*, Yale University Press, 2017.

10. The engraving, dating from the 1740s, shows Wright's Circulating Library in Exeter Court, the Strand. It is reproduced in Margaret Willes, *Reading Matters: Five Centuries of Discovering Books*, Yale University Press, 2008, p. 142.

11. *Dr Campbell's Diary of a Visit to England in 1775*, ed. James L. Clifford, Cambridge University Press, 1947, p. 58.

12. Robert Wodrow, *Analect, or Materials for a History of Remarkable Providences Mostly Relating to Scotch Ministers and Christians,* first published in 1728, reprinted for the Maitland Club, Edinburgh, 1843, vol. 3, p. 515; Joseph Cradock, *Village Memoirs in a Series of Letters Between a Clergyman and his Family*, 3rd edn, 1776, p. 48.

13. Reproduced in Iona and Robert Opie and Brian Alderson, *The Treasures of Childhood*, Pavilion Books, 1989, p. 47.

14. Wilbur Macey Stone, *The Gigantick Histories of Thomas Boreman*, Southworth Press, 1933, p. 17.

15. Dell, *The Booksellers*, p. 19.

16. Samuel Johnson, *The Idler*, no. 19, 19 August 1758.

17. Oliver Goldsmith, *The Vicar of Wakefield*, 1766, Chapter 18.

18. See Vernon W. Crane, 'The Club of Honest Whigs: Friends of Science and Liberty', *William and Mary Quarterly*, 23, April 1966, pp. 210–33.

19. Frank Brady and Frederick A. Pottle, eds, *Boswell in Search of a Wife, 1766–1769*, Heinemann, 1957, p. 26.

20. Quoted in Henry Curwen, *A History of Booksellers, the Old and the New*, Chatto & Windus, 1873, p. 67.

21. The minutes of the Society are held as MS Gunther 4 in the Museum of Science in Oxford. See T.H. Levere and G.L'E Turner, *Discussing Chemistry and Steam: The Minutes of a Coffee House Philosophical Society, 1780–7*, Oxford University Press, 2002.

22. These figures are cited in John Brewer, *The Pleasures of the Imagination: English Culture in the Eighteenth Century*, Harper Collins, 1997, p. 135.

23. Exception seems to be made for the niece of the printer John Boydell. She is described as conferring a sham knighthood satirising the pomposity of the City on a wax chandler during a meeting of a club called the Free and Easy under the Rose in the Queen's Arms in the Churchyard.

24. *The Monthly Review,* vol. XXVII, December 1798, p. 422.

25. William West, *Fifty Years' Recollections of a Bookseller*, 1837, pp. 92–3.

26. William West, 'Annals of Authors, Artists,. Books, and Booksellers, Letter XI', *Aldine Magazine*, 1839, p. 205.
27. Campbell's letter quoted by M. Macgregor, 'Amelia Alderson Opie: Worldling and Friend', Smith College, 1933, p. 36; Marilyn Gaull, 'Joseph Johnson: Literary Alchemist', *European Romantic Review*, 10.3, 1999, p. 266.
28. Godwin's diary, Ms. Abinger e.4, fol. 5v, 13 November 1791, Bodleian Library, Oxford.
29. *The Monthly Review,* September 1796, p. 89.
30. John Bugg, ed., *The Joseph Johnson Letterbook,* Oxford University Press, 2016, p. xix.
31. *Pinnock's Guide to Knowledge*, 1834, p. 278.

Chapter 11 Theatre for London, Britain and the Empire

1. *The London Diaries of William Nicolson, Bishop of Carlisle, 1702–18,* ed. Clive Jones and Geoff Holmes, Oxford University Press, 1985, p. 406.
2. Quoted in W.R. Matthews and W.M. Atkins, eds, *A History of St Paul's Cathedral*, Phoenix House, 1957, p. 208.
3. Nigel Aston, 'St Paul's and the Public Culture of Eighteenth-century Britain', in D. Keene, A. Burns and A. Saint, *St Paul's: The Cathedral Church of London, 604–2004,* Yale University Press, 2004, p. 363.
4. Quoted in Matthews and Atkins, *A History of St Paul's Cathedral*, p. 210.
5. Letter to Mr Hales in Hanover, 24 September 1714, in *Henry Newman, An American in London, 1708–43*, ed. Leonard Cowie, SPCK, 1956, p. 86.
6. Aston, 'St Paul's and the Public Culture', p. 367.
7. *Thanksgiving Day: An Address to All Persons, Especially to our Brave Sailors, . . . Showing what Great Reason we have for a NATIONAL THANKSGIVING, and how the Day Ought to be Kept by All Good Christians. To which is Added an Account of the Procession to St Paul's*, 1797, p. 6. Cheap Repository Tracts were initially produced by Hannah More and printed by Samuel Hazard in Bath and John Marshall in London. After 1798 the copyright of official tracts was sold, and later collected editions were published by the Rivingtons for the SPCK.
8. 'Aleph', *London Scenes and People*, reprints from City Press, 1863, p. 7.
9. *A Lady Travels: Journeys in England and Scotland from the Diaries of Johanna Schopenhauer*, trans. Ruth Michaelis-Jena and Willy Merson, Routledge, 1988, pp. 211–12.
10. For the debate, see Arthur Burns, 'From 1830 to the present', in Keene et al., *St Paul's*, pp. 87–8.
11. Quoted in John Wolffe, 'National Occasions at St Paul's since 1800', in Keene et al., *St Paul's*, p. 384.
12. Quoted in Matthews and Atkins, *A History*, p. 235.
13. *The Times,* 28 February 1887.
14. *Edinburgh Evening News*, 18 December 1905.
15. George Earle Buckle, ed., *The Letters of Queen Victoria*, John Murray, 1926, vol. ii, p. 195.
16. From the diary of F.S. Girdlestone, quoted by John Wolffe, 'National Occasions at St Paul's', p. 386.
17. St Paul's Cathedral Library, Newbolt scrapbooks, vol. x, 45–8.
18. The study for the national thanksgiving and the painting of the 'Heart of the Empire' are both in the Royal Collection.

Chapter 12 Lengthening Shadows

1. Elizabeth Gaskell, *The Life of Charlotte Brontë*, Smith, Elder & Co., 1857, p. 273.
2. Charlotte Brontë, *Villette*, Smith, Elder & Co., 1853, Chapter 5.
3. Gaskell, *Life of Charlotte Brontë*, p. 273.
4. James Leigh Hunt, *Table Talk*, Smith, Elder & Co., 1851, p. 188.

5. The relationship between Leigh Hunt and Elizabeth Kent is analysed in Daisy Hay, *The Young Romantics: The Shelleys, Byron and Other Tangled Lives*, Bloomsbury, 2010, pp. 15ff.

6. Elizabeth Kent, *Flora Domestica*, Taylor and Hessey, 1823, p. xiii; Charles Dickens, *Our Mutual Friend*, Book II, Chapter IV; 'The Country Cousin' in *All the Year Round*, 16 and 23 May 1874.

7. Henry Curwen, *A History of Booksellers, the Old and the New*, Chatto & Windus, 1873, p. 311.

8. Septimus Rivington, *The Publishing Family of Rivington*, Rivingtons, 1919, p. 142.

9. *Charles Knight's Cyclopaedia of London*, 1851, p. 761.

10. J.E. Hodder Williams, *The Life of Sir George Williams*, Hodder & Stoughton, 1906, quoted in H.A. Walden, '*Operation Textiles': A City Warehouse in War-time*, Thos. Reed, n.d. (1946), pp. ii–iii.

11. William Harrison Ainsworth, *Old St Paul's*, Hugh Cunningham, 1841, p. 143.

12. Charles Dickens, *David Copperfield*, 1849, Chapter 23. Doctors' Commons was dissolved in 1857.

13. Charles Dickens, *The Pickwick Papers*, Chapter 44. The public house is now called the Centre Page.

14. William West, *Fifty Years' Recollections of an Old Bookseller*, 1837 edn, p. 44.

15. Charles Knight, *Shadows of the Old Booksellers*, Bell and Daldy, 1865, p. 261.

16. Charles Mumby Smith, *The Little World of London*, Arthur Hall, Virtue & Co., 1857, p. 40.

17. Harold Cox and John E. Chandler, *The House of Longman: A Record of their Bi-centenary Celebrations*, Longman Green & Co., 1925, p. 56.

18. Asa Briggs, *A History of Longmans and Their Books, 1724–1990*, British Library, 2008, quoted p. 373.

19. The Goad insurance maps are to be seen in the London Metropolitan Archives, SC/GL/GOA/1/1886.

20. Mumby Smith, 'Paternoster Row and Magazine-Day', in *The Little World of London*, pp. 41–8.

21. Curwen, *A History of Booksellers*, pp. 234–5. The reference to the schoolmaster came from a speech made by Henry Brougham on 20 January 1828. Thomas Love Peacock described the Society for the Diffusion of Useful Knowledge as the 'Steam Intellect Society'.

22. Simon Nowell-Smith, *The House of Cassell, 1848–1958*, Cassell & Company, 1958, p. 22.

23. Quoted by F.A. Mumby, *The House of Routledge: 1834–1934*, G. Routledge and Sons, 1934, p. 53.

24. John Attenborough, *A Living Memory*, Hodder & Stoughton, 1975, p. 20. Matthew Hodder was a great friend of George Williams at Hitchcock's and became involved in the YMCA. The two families intermarried so that the Hodder-Williams family became an important part of the publishing company.

25. Quoted in David Daniel, *The Bible in English*, Yale University Press, 2003, p. 640.

26. Peter Sutcliffe, *The Oxford University Press: An Informal History*, Oxford University Press, 1978, p. 51.

27. Nine of the collection are listed as in St Paul's Churchyard in *A Catalogue of the Paintings in the Collection of Sir Frederick Cook Bt, Visconde de Monserrate*, 3 vols., London 1913–15. I am grateful to Charles Sebag-Montefiore for this information.

28. Quoted in Alison Adburgham, *Shops and Shopping, 1800–1914*, Allen & Unwin, 1981, pp. 193, 263. Nicholson's was taken over by Debenham's after the Second World War.

29. Walden, '*Operation Textiles*' p. 37.

30. Shaw's quip, from Ian Norrie, *Mumby's Publishing and Bookselling in the Twentieth Century*, Bell & Hyman, 1982, p. 87. The account from the *Bookseller* is quoted on pp. 87–8.

Epilogue

1. Nikolaus Pevsner, *Buildings of England: The City of London*, 3rd edn, 1973, Penguin, p. 225. This building is currently providing shelter for homeless people.
2. Alexander Howard and Ernest Newman, *London Business Cavalcade*, Lincolns-Prager, 1951, p. iv.
3. Pevsner, *The City of London*, pp. 284–5.
4. Simon Bradley, 'The Precinct and Setting of St Paul's from the Nineteenth Century', in *St Paul's: The Cathedral Church of London 604-2004,* ed. D. Keene, A. Burns and A. Saint, Yale University Press, 2004, p. 444.
5. Quoted by David Kynaston in *A World to Build: Austerity Britain 1945-48*, Bloomsbury, 2005, p. 29.
6. Rose Macaulay, *The World My Wilderness*, Virago Modern Classics, 1983, p. 46.
7. Quoted by Bradley, 'The Precinct and Setting of St Paul's', p. 444.
8. Pevsner, *The City of London*, pp. 285–6.
9. Bradley, 'The Precinct and Setting of St Paul's', p. 448.
10. Bradley, p. 443. The Cross was designed by Reginal Blomfield, with sculpture by Bertram Mackenna.
11. Confirmed in an email to the author.
12. Sarah Rainey, 'Dr Giles Fraser Resigns from St Paul's', *Daily Telegraph*, 27 October 2011.

BIBLIOGRAPHY

Primary Manuscript Sources

The Visitation Report of Bishop Bancroft, 1598, Guildhall MS. 9537/9.

Household Accounts of William Cavendish, Chatsworth Ms 10A-E.

Memorandum book of John Conyers, BL Sloane MS 958.

Diaries of Richard Stonley, Folger Shakespeare Library, MS V.a.459-61. Online transcription by Alan Nelson, https://folgerpedia.folger.edu/Diaries_of_Richard_Stonley,_1581–1598,_V.a.459-V.a.461.

Stationers' Company Archive, TSC/1/E/English Stock/D/01.

Printed Primary Sources

'Aleph', *London Scenes and People*, reprints from City Press, 1863.

Bede, *A History of the English Church and People*, trans Leo Sherley-Price, Penguin Classics, 1955.

The Letters of John Chamberlain, ed. Norman Egbert McClure, 2 vols, The American Philosophical Society, 1939.

Curwen, Henry, *A History of Booksellers, the Old and the New*, Chatto & Windus, 1873.

John Dunton, *The Life and Errors of John Dunton*, 1709.

The Diary of John Evelyn, ed. E.S. De Beer, 6 vols, Clarendon Press, 1955, revised edn, 2000.

Feuillerat, Albert, *Documents Relating to the Office of the Revels*, Uystpruyst, 1908.

Foxe, John, *Actes and Monuments (Foxe's Book of Martyrs)*, 1563.

Diary of Robert Hooke, ed H.W. Robinson and Walter Adams, Taylor and Francis, 1935.

The Joseph Johnson Letterbook, ed. John Bugg, Oxford University Press, 2016.

Karamazin, Nikolai, *Letters of a Russian Traveller*, trans. and ed. Andrew Kahn, Voltaire Foundation, 2003.

Lichtenberg's Visits to England, as Described in his Letters and Diaries, trans. and ed. Margaret Mare and W.H. Quarrell, Clarendon Press, 1938.

The Diary of Henry Machyn, Citizen and Merchant-taylor of London from A.D. 1550 to A.D. 1563, ed. John Gough Nicols, 1848.

Maunsell, Andrew, *The Catalogue of English Printed Bookes*, 2 parts, London 1595, photographic reprint, Gregg Press, 1965.

The Diary of John Milward Esq, ed Caroline Robbins, Cambridge University Press, 1938.

Mumby Smith, Charles, *The Little World of London*, Arthur Hall, Virtue & Co., 1857.

Henry Newman, An American in London, 1708–43, ed. Leonard Cowie, SPCK, 1956.

The London Diaries of William Nicolson, Bishop of Carlisle, 1702–18, ed. Clive Jones and Geoff Holms, Oxford University Press, 1985.

The Diary of Samuel Pepys, ed. Robert Latham and William Matthews, 11 vols, Bell & Hyman, 1970–83.

Letters and Second Diary of Samuel Pepys, ed. R.G. Howarth, J.M. Dent and Sons, 1932.

The Journals of Two Travellers in Elizabethan and Early Stuart England: Thomas Platter and Horatio Busino, ed. Peter Razzell, Caliban Books, 1995.

The Purefoy Letters, 1735–1753, ed. G. Eland, 2 vols, Sidgwick & Jackson, 1931.

Rastell, John, *The Four Elements*, ed. Roger Coleman, Cambridge University Press, 1971.

The Diary of Dudley Ryder, 1715–16, ed. William Matthews, Methuen, 1939.

A Lady Travels: Journeys in England and Scotland from the Diaries of Johanna Schopenhaeur, trans. Ruth Michaelis-Jena and Willy Merson, Routledge, 1988.

Stow, John, *Survey of London*, ed. C.L. Kingsford, Oxford University Press, 1908.

Stow, John, *Annales, or a Generall Chronicle of England*, 1632.

Strype, John, *A Survey of the Cities of London and Westminster*, 2 vols, 1720.

Tallis, John, *London Street Views*, London Topographical Society, 2002.

Taswell, William, *Autobiography and Anecdotes*, Camden Society Old Series, vol. 55, 1853.

Catalogue of the Pamphlets, Books, Newspapers and Manuscripts Relating to the Civil War, the Commonwealth, and Restoration, Collected by George Thomason, 1640–1661, 2 vols, ed. G.K. Fortescue, The Trustees of the British Museum, 1908.

von Uffenbach, Zacharias Conrad, *London in 1710, from the Travels of Zacharias Conrad von Uffenbach*, ed. and trans. W.H. Quarrell and Margaret Mare, Faber & Faber, 1934.

Walden, H.A., *'Operation Textiles': A City Warehouse in War-time*, Thos. Reed, n.d. [1946].

Ward, Ned, *A Fair Step to Stir-Bitch-Fair: With Remarks upon the University of Cambridge*, 1704.

Ward, Ned, *The London Spy*, 4th edn, ed. Peter Hyland, East Lansing Colleagues Press, 1993.

West, William, *Fifty Years' Recollections of an Old Bookseller*, 1837.

Wren, Christopher, *Parentalia*, 1750.

Wriothesley, Charles, *A Chronicle of England During the Reign of the Tudors from AD 1485 to 1559*, ed. W.D. Hamilton, 2 vols, Camden Society, 1875.

Secondary Sources

Adburgham, Alison, *Shops and Shopping, 1800–1914*, George Allen & Unwin, 2nd edn, 1981.

Ambler, Sophie Therese, *The Song of Simon de Montfort: England's First Revolutionary and the Death of Chivalry*, Picador, 2019.

Attenborough, John, *A Living Memory*, Hodder & Stoughton, 1975.

Barnard, John, and D.F. McKenzie, eds, *The Cambridge History of the Book in Britain, Vol. IV, 1557–1695*, Cambridge University Press, 2002.

Barron, Caroline M., *London in the Later Middle Ages, Government and People, 1200–1500*, Oxford University Press, 2004.

Berry, Herbert, 'Where was the Playhouse in Which the Boy Choristers of St Paul's Cathedral Performed Plays?', *Medieval and Renaissance Drama in England*, 13, 2001, pp. 109–13.

Blagden, Cyprian, *The Stationers' Company, A History 1403–1959*, George Allen & Unwin, 1960.

Blayney, Peter W.M., *The Bookshops in Paul's Cross Churchyard*, Occasional Papers of the Bibliographical Society, No. 5, 1990.

Blayney, Peter W.M, 'John Day and the Bookshop That Never Was', in Lena Cowen Orlin, *Material London, ca. 1600*, University of Pennsylvania Press, 2000, chapter 16.

Blayney, Peter W.M., *The Stationers' Company and the Printers of London, 1501–1557*, 2 vols, Cambridge University Press, 2013.

Bowers, Roger, 'The Playhouse of the Choristers of Paul's, *c.*1575–1608', *Theatre Notebook*, 54, 2, 2000, pp. 70–85.

Briggs, Asa, *A History of Longmans and Their Books, 1724–1990*, British Library, 2008.

Brooke, Christopher N.L., and Keir, Gillian, *London 800–1216: The Shaping of a City*, Secker & Warburg, 1975.

Christianson, C.P., *A Directory of London Stationers and Book Artisans, 1300–1500*, The Bibliographical Society of America, 1990.

Cox, Harold, and Chandler, John E., *The House of Longmans, A Record of Their Bi-centenary Celebrations*, Longman Green & Co., 1925.

Cox, Nancy, *The Complete Tradesman: A Study of Retailing, 1550–1820*, Ashgate, 2000.

Cressy, David, 'Book Burning in Tudor & Stuart England', *Sixteenth Century Journal*, 36, 2, 2005, pp. 359–74.

Curwen, H., *A History of Booksellers: The Old and the New*, Chatto & Windus, 1873.

Daniell, David, *The Bible in English*, Yale University Press, 2003.

Davis, Dorothy, *A History of Shopping*, Routledge & Kegan Paul, 1966.

Duffy, Eamonn, *The Fires of Faith: Catholic England Under Mary Tudor*, Yale University Press, 2010.

Field, Jacob, *London, Londoners and the Great Fire of 1666: Disaster and Recovery*, Routledge & Kegan Paul, 2018.

Franklin, Norman, *Routledge & Kegan Paul, 150 Years of Great Publishing*, Routledge & Kegan Paul, 1986.

Gair, Reavley, *The Children of Paul's: The Story of a Theatre Company, 1553–1608*, Cambridge University Press, 1982.

Gomme, G.L., *Primitive Folk Moots, Open Air Assemblies in Britain*, Sampson Lowe, 1880.

Goodwin, George, *Fatal Colours: Towton 1461*, Weidenfeld & Nicolson, 2011.

Hanley, Catherine, *Louis: The French Prince who Invaded England*, Yale University Press, 2016.

Hentschell, Roze, *St Paul's Cathedral Precinct in Early Modern Literature and Culture*, Oxford University Press, 2020.

Hill, Tracey, *Pageantry and Power: A Cultural History of the Early Modern Lord Mayor's Show 1585–1639*, Manchester University Press, 2011.

Hodder Williams, J.E., *The Life of Sir George Williams*, Hodder & Stoughton, 1906.

Hollis, Leo, *Phoenix: St Paul's Cathedral and the Men Who Made Modern London*, Weidenfeld & Nicolson, 2008.

Hone, Joseph, *The Paper Chase: The Printer, the Spymaster & the Hunt for the Rebel Pamphleteers*, Chatto & Windus, 2020.

Hudson, Anne, *Lollards and Their Books*, The Hambledon Press, 1985.

Hunt, Arnold, *The Art of Hearing: English Preachers and Their Audience, 1590–1640*, Cambridge University Press, 2010.

Inglis, Lucy, *Georgian London: Into the Streets*, Penguin, 2013.

Inwood, Stephen, *A History of London*, Macmillan, 1998.

Keene, Derek, Burns, Arthur and Saint, Andrew, eds, *St Paul's: The Cathedral Church of London 604–2004*, Yale University Press, 2004.

Kirby, Torrance, Stanwood, P.G., Morrissey, Mary and King, John N., eds, *Sermons at Paul's Cross, 1521–1642*, Oxford University Press, 2017.

Charles Knight's Cyclopaedia of London, 1851.

Knight, Charles, *Shadows of the Old Booksellers*, 1865.

Lang, Jane, *Rebuilding St Paul's After the Great Fire of London*, Oxford University Press, 1956.

Leedham-Green, Elisabeth and Webber, Teresa, eds, *The Cambridge History of Libraries, vol. 1 to 1640*, Cambridge University Press, 2006.

Levere, T.H., and Turner, G.L'E, *Discussing Chemistry and Steam: The Minutes of a Coffee House Philosophical Society 1780–87*, Oxford University Press, 2002.

MacCulloch, Diarmaid, *Thomas Cromwell*, Allen Lane, 2018.

Macleod, Roderick, *The Topography of St Paul's Precinct, 1200–1500*, London Topographical Record, 1990, vol. xxvi.

Maddicott, John, *Simon de Montfort*, Cambridge University Press, 1994.

Matthews, W.R., and Atkins, W.M., eds, *A History of St Paul's Cathedral, and the Men Associated with it*, Phoenix House, 1957.

McDonnell, Michael, *The Annals of St Paul's School*, St Paul's School, 1959.

McDowell, Paula, *The Women of Grub Street: Press, Politics and Gender in the London Literary Marketplace*, Clarendon Press, 1998.

Milman, Henry Hart, *Annals of St Paul's Cathedral*, John Murray, 1868.

Moran, James, *Wynkyn de Worde: Father of Fleet Street*, Wynkyn de Worde Society, revised edn, 2003.

Morrissey, Mary, *Politics and the Paul's Cross Sermons, 1558–1642*, Oxford University Press, 2011.

Mumby, F.A., *The House of Routledge: 1834–1934*, G. Routledge & Sons, 1934.

Myers, Robin, Mandelbrote, Giles and Harris, Michael, eds, *The London Book Trade, Topographies of Print*, British Library, 2003.

Naismith, Rory, *Citadel of the Saxons: The Rise of Early London*, I.B. Tauris, 2019.

Nowell-Smith, *The House of Cassell, 1848–1958*, Cassell & Co., 1958.

Plomer, H.R., 'St Paul's Cathedral and its Bookselling Tenants', *The Library*, NS III, 1902.

Pollard, Graham, and Ehrman, Albert, *The Distribution of Books by Catalogues from the Invention of Printing to AD 1800, Based on Material in the Broxbourne Library*, Roxburghe Club, 1965.

Raven, James, *The Business of Books: Booksellers and the English Book Trade*, Yale University Press, 2007.

Raven, James, *Bookscape: Geographies of Printing and Publishing in London before 1800*, British Library, 2014.

Reddaway, T.F., *Rebuilding of London After the Great Fire*, Jonathan Cape, 1940.

Schofield, John, *St Paul's Cathedral Before Wren*, English Heritage, 2011.

Scott-Warren, Jason, *Shakespeare's First Reader: The Paper Trails of Richard Stonley*, University of Philadelphia Press, 2019.

Stone, Ian, 'The Rebel Barons of 1264 and the Commune of London: An Oath of Mutual Aid', *English Historical Review*, 129, 2014, pp. 1–18.

Stubbs, John, *Donne, The Reformed Soul*, Viking, 2006.

Sutcliffe, Peter, *The Oxford University Press: An Informal History*, Oxford University Press, 1978.

Tinniswood, Adrian, *His Invention so Fertile: A life of Christopher Wren*, Cape, 2001.

Tomalin, Claire, *The Life and Death of Mary Wollstonecraft*, Weidenfeld & Nicolson, 1974.

Walton, Isaak, *The Lives of John Donne, Sir Henry Wotton, Richard Hooker & Robert Sanderson*, 1670, reprint Oxford University Press, 1927.

Wayne, Valerie, ed, *Women's Labour and the History of the Book in Early Modern England*, The Arden Shakespeare, 2020.

Weinreb, Ben, and Hibbert, Christopher, eds, *The London Encyclopaedia*, Macmillan, 1995.

Williams, Gwyn A., *Medieval London: From Commune to Capital*, Athlone Press, 1963.

INDEX

Page numbers in italic refer to illustrations

Abbott, George, Archbishop of Canterbury, 111
Aethelred II, King of England, 9, 15
Ainsworth, William Harrison, 256–7
Aldersgate, 42, 47, 53, 90, 171
Allestree, James, 133, 154–5, 157–8, 200
Allestree, Richard, 158, 200–1
Anne, Queen of Great Britain, 147, 201, 204–5, 224–7, *226*, 228, 236
Arundel, Thomas, Archbishop of Canterbury, 30, 31
Aubrey, John 140, 161, 177
Ave Maria Lane 133, 157, 158, 163

Bagster, Samuel, 264
Bainham, James, 66, *67*, 76
Bancroft, Richard, Bishop of London, 59, 82, 84, 98, 115–16
Barker, Robert, 59, *Plate 6*
Barlow, William, 85
Becket family, 12, 72, 175, 274
Bede, the Venerable, 8, 18
Belle Sauvage Inn, 92, 144, 167, 181, 262–3, 270
Betjeman, John, 271–2
bibles: Geneva, 58; Great Bible, 44, 46, 58, *Plate 5*; King James, 58–9, *Plate 7*; Lollard, 30; Matthew, 43; Bishops', 58; Polyglot, 42, 150–2, 160, 264
Birckmann family, 50
Bird, Francis, 147, 225, *226*
Bisse, James, 80–1
Blackfriars, 91, 93, 95–6, 100, 103, 104
Blake, William, 220, 221, 229

Bonner, Edmund, Bishop of London, 76
Boothby, Sir William, 166–7, 168
Bowles, Thomas, 179, 182–3
Braybrooke, Robert, Bishop of London, 27, 29, 174, 177
Brontë family, 241–2
Brougham, Henry, 235, 243, 261–2
Burney, Fanny, 194–6, *194*

Cambridge University, 159, 162, 163
Camden, William, 8, 55, 140
Canute, King of England and Denmark, 9, 18
Carlyle, Thomas, 2, 22, 36
Carnan, Thomas, 218, 247
Caroline of Brunswick, Queen, 234–6, *235*
Carter Lane, 114, 263, 269, 275–6
Cassell, John, 261–3, 270
catalogues, 48–50, 56
Cavendish, William, 55–7
Caxton, William, 37–8
Cecil, Robert, Earl of Salisbury, 84–5, 105, 119, 186
Cecil, William, Lord Burghley, 47, 60, 161
Chamberlain, John, 4, 111, 113, 118, 121, 123, 166, 174, 175
Chambers, Robert, 261–2
Chapman, George, 102–3, 104
Chapter Coffee-house, 143, 165, 173, 210, 215–17, 220, 241–2, 252, 257, 267
Chapter House (Convocation House), 11, 93, 174, 177, *Plate 8*
Charles I, King of England, 109, 116, 120–2, 124–5, 127, 153, 181, 184, 200

Charles II, King of England, 124, 127, 130–2, 136, 138, 143, 152, 153, 154, 161, 163, 171, 181, 202, 223

Chaucer, Geoffrey, 87, 150, 286 n23

Cheapside, 4, 13, 25, 27, 31, 40, 51, 64, 74, 107, 183–4, 189, 248

Chiswell, Richard, 166, 168, 205

Christchurch, Newgate Street, 102, 129, 134, 156

Chubb, Charles, 249–50, 270

Churchill, John, Duke of Marlborough, 147, 179, 224

Churchill, Sarah, Duchess of Marlborough, 201, 205, 224

Churchill, Winston, 240, 267, 269

Clavell, Robert, 162, 165–6

Cleland, John, 198, 208

Cloister Churchyard, 11, 72, 93

coffee-houses, 4, 142–3, 162, 163, 165, 167, 204, 210, 215–17, see also Chapter Coffee-house

Colet, John, Dean of St Paul's, 87–8, 177, 227

Compton, Henry, Bishop of London, 145–6, 147, 273

Conyers, John, 141–2

Cook & Gladstone, 247, 164–5, 269–70

Coppini, Bishop Francesco, papal legate, 33–4

copyright, 198–200, 205, 217

Courtenay, William, Bishop of London, 28

Coxed and Woster, 186–7, 192

Cranmer, Thomas, Archbishop of Canterbury, 41, 43–4, 45, 58, 76, 264, Plates 3, 4, 5

Cromwell, Oliver, 127, 152

Cromwell, Thomas, 41, 43–4, 68, 70, 71, Plates 3, 5

Cross Churchyard, 2, 40, 47, 115, 123

Cutpurse, Moll, 123, 124

Day, John, 42, 44–8, 45, 76, 77

De Burgh, Hugh, 22

Defoe, Daniel, 207, 214

Dekker, Thomas, 100, 117, 118, 123, 177, 183

De Montfort, Simon, Earl of Leicester, 22–4

De Worde, Wynkyn, 37–8, 38, 41, 65, 157

Devereux, Robert, Earl of Essex, 84, 109

Dickens, Charles, 149, 197, 243–4, 257

Doctors' Commons 102, 134, 214, 216, 257, Plate 17

Dollond family, 191, 250, 270

Dolly's Chophouse, 214

Donaldson, Alexander, 217

Donne, John, Dean of St Paul's, 85, 109, 114, 116, 125, 126, 127, 274

Duck Lane, 133, 157

Dudley, Robert, Earl of Leicester, 47, 92

Dugdale, William, 10, 150, 152, 160

Dunton, John, 168–71, 172, 208

Earle, John, Bishop of Salisbury, 116

Edgeworth, Maria, 220–1

Edmund Ironside, King of England, 9

Edward I, King of England, 23

Edward II, King of England, 26–7

Edward III, King of England, 25, 27

Edward IV, King of England, 35–6, 37

Edward VI, King of England, 15, 25, 44, 69–70, 71, 74, 75, 111, 175, Plate 2

Edward VII, 237, 239

Elizabeth I, Queen of England, 46–7, 49, 54, 70, 74, 77–83, 86, 90–2, 105, 114–15, 119, 123, 124, 143, 161, 186

Elizabeth II, Queen of Great Britain, 240

English stock, 158–9, 205

Erasmus, Desiderius, 43, 62, 88

Ethelbert, King of Kent, 8–9

Evans, Henry, 94–5, 99

Evelyn, John, 127–8, 130, 131, 144, 145–6, 154–5, 156, 208, 268

Farley, Henry, 119–20

Felton, John, 80, 143, 281 n1

Field, Nathan, 96, 123

Field, Richard, 53, 57

Fielding, Henry, 198, 208, 209, 213

Fisher, John, Bishop of Rochester, 62, 65–6, 68, Plate 3

Fitz Ailwin, Henry, 18

Fitz Osbert, William, 17–18

Fitzralph, Richard, 24–5

Fitzstephen, William, 11, 17

FitzWalter, Robert, 21

Fleet Street, 37–9, 130, 141, 158, 189, 196, 210

folk moot, 16–17, 22, 23

Foxe, John, 47, 53, 60, 66, 67, 74–6, Plates 3, 4

Franklin, Benjamin, 221

Gardiner, Stephen, Bishop of Winchester, 69, 74–6

Garnet, Father Henry, 106
Garthwaite, Timothy, 200–1
Gaskell, Elizabeth, 241–2
George I, King of Great Britain, 149, 225, 228
George II, King of Great Britain, 228
George III, King of Great Britain, 229–30
George IV, King of Great Britain, 234
George V, King of Great Britain, 239
Gerard, John, 57
Gibbons, Grinling, 144, 145
Gipkyn family, 42, 54–5, 64, 107, 120, Plate 1
Goad, Charles, 5, 259, 263–5
Godolphin, Henry, Dean of St Paul's, 147–8
Godwin, William, 219–20
Goldsmith, Oliver, 212–14, 216–17, 247
Goose and Gridiron Tavern, 140, 167, 181
Gresham College, 132, 140, 141, 154, 178
Griffiths, Ralph, 198, 209, 215, 219
Grindal, Edmund, Bishop of London, 78, 92
Guildhall, 16, 19, 107, 113
Gunpowder Plot, 105–6, 108
Gyles, Thomas, 93–4, 98

Hardel, William, 18, 21
Hare, Francis, 147–8
Harris, John, 254
Hawksmoor, Nicholas, 135, 179
Henry I, King of England, 16, 18, 21
Henry II, King of England, 15, 18
Henry III, King of England, 18, 21
Henry IV, King of England, 29, 31
Henry V, King of England, 30, 31, 117
Henry VI, King of England, 31–5
Henry VII, King of England, 35, 62
Henry VIII, King of England, 43, 62, 65, 69, 74, 75, Plates 3, 5
Hilsey, John, Bishop of Rochester, 68, 71
Hitchcock & Williams, 252–4, 267, 270, 274
Hogarth, William, 189, 197, 206, 211
Holinshed, Raphael, 53, 57
Hollar, Wenceslaus, 10, 11, 151, 152, 161
Hooke, Robert, 10, 132–3, 134, 135, 137, 139–40, 141, 154–5, 160, 162–3, 171, 273

James I, King of England, 58, 104, 105, 108–12, 119–21, 122, 124, 127, 176
James II, King of England, 143, 146, 167, 171, 181, 202, 204

James, Elinor, 169–71
Jerman, Edward, 134
Jewel, John, Bishop of Salisbury, 77
John, King of England, 18, 20–1
John of Gaunt, Duke of Lancaster, 13, 27–9
Johnson, Joseph, 219–22, 234, 242
Johnson, Samuel, 166, 206, 213–15, 217, 218
Jones, Inigo, 109, 119, 122, 127, 130, 136, 144, 153, 273
Jones, Richard, 52, 55
Jonson, Ben, 95–6, 99, 100, 104, 109, 111, 117, 118
journals, 154, 208–10, 219

Karamazin, Nikolai, 180
Kempe, Thomas, Bishop of London, 35
Kent, Elizabeth, 243
King, John, Bishop of London, 110
Kirton, Joshua, 150, 152, 166
Knight, Charles, 253, 257, 261–2
Knightrider Street, 57, 102, 134

Latimer, Hugh, Bishop of Worcester, 3, 71–4, 76, Plate 4
Laud, William, Bishop of London and Archbishop of Canterbury, 116, 122, 124, 136
Leigh Hunt, James, 243
L'Estrange, Sir Roger, 153, 166
Lichtenberg, Georg Christoph, 180, 196–7
Lily, William, 88, 160, 211
Little Britain, 151, 153, 156–7, 163, 169, 171, 173, 189
Littlebury, Robert, 163, 171
Lollards, 29–31, 33, 76
Longchamp, William, 20
Longman family, 205–6, 258–9, 268
lotteries 161–2, 247, 248
Louis, Prince, later Louis VIII, King of France, 20–1
Ludgate Hill, 6, 16, 191, 211, 223, 232, 248, 262
Luther, Martin, 29, 43, 62
Lyly, John, 80, 82, 88, 93–4, 96–7, 101

Machyn, Henry, 77–9
Magazine Day, 260–1
Margaret of Anjou, Queen, 32–4
Marlowe, Christopher, 50, 52, 54
Marprelate, Martin, 81–2, 96–7
Marshall, William, 21

Marston, John, 98–9, 100–1, 104, 175
Martin, James, 154–5, 158
Mary I, Queen of England, 45–6, 65, 70, 74–5, 114
Mary II, Queen of England, 144, 167, 224
Maunsell, Andrew, 49–50, 54, 56, 60
May, Hugh, 128, 132, 135
Mellitus, Bishop of London, 8
Middle Aisle, the (nave), 113–18
Middleton, Thomas, 103–4, 107–8, 117, 123
Millington, Edward, 164–5
Mills, Peter, 132
More, Thomas, 35–6, 40, 66, 109
Morocco, the wonder horse, 175, *176*
Mumby Smith, Charles, 259–61

Nashe, Thomas, 81, 96
Nelson, Admiral Horatio, 231–2, 252, *Plate 15*
Newbery, John, 212–14, *213,* 217, 218, 247, 253
newsbooks, 118, 153–4
Nicolson, William, Bishop of Carlisle, 224
Norton, John, 56–7, 166
Nowell, Alexander, Dean of St Paul's, 81, 83, 97–8

Occupy Movement, 275
Ogilby, John, 160–2
Oxford Arms, Warwick Lane, 167, *Plate 18*
Oxford University, 159, 163

Pardon Churchyard, 2, 12, 26, 72, 174
Paris, Matthew, 21
Parker, Matthew, Archbishop of Canterbury, 47–8, 58,
Paternoster Row, 5, 13, 39, 59, 92, 97–8, 114, 133, 134, 143, 156, 157–8, 164, 172–3, 184, 185–6, 198, 206, 207, 218–19, 257–61, 263–4, 267–8, 272–3
Paulesbyrig, 2, 10
Paul's Cross, 2–3, 22, 24–5, 31–4, 55, 61, 62–85, 93, 103, 106, 109, 111–13, 115, 117, 120, 123–4, 146, 150, 273
Paul's Alley, 93, 114
Paul's Walk (Pissing Alley), 115, 173, 183
Pearce, Edward, 98
Pecock, Reginald, Archbishop of St Asaph, 32–3

Pepys, Samuel, 4, 128, 130, 139, 150, 152, 153–4, 156, 157, 160, 163, 166, 168, 174, 177, 178, 185, 268
Petre, William, 53, 90, 92
Pevsner, Nikolaus, 269, 270–1, 272, 274
Philip Augustus, King of France, 20–1
Philip II, of Spain, 75–6, 114
Pitt, Moses, 171–2
Pitt, William (the Younger), 229, 234
Plantin, Christopher, 50–1, 150, 156
Platter, Thomas, 64, 83, 175
Pole, Reginald, Cardinal, 75
Pope, Alexander, 214, 217
Pratt, Roger, 128, 132, 135, 136
Pretyman, George, Dean of St Paul's, 229, 234
Purefoy family, 190–2
Pynson, Richard, 38–9, 41, 64

Rastell, John, 40–1, *40*
Redford, John, 86, 89–90
Restitutus, Bishop of London, 6
Richard I, King of England, 15, 17, 18
Richard II, King of England, 28–9, 108
Richard III, King of England, 35–6, 85
Richardson, Samuel, 206–8, 209, 213, 217
Ridley, Nicholas, Bishop of London, 74, 76, 114, *Plate 4*
Rivington family, 205–6, 208, 251–2
Robinson, George, 219
Rogers, John, 45, 58, 76
Routledge, George, 263, 270
Royal College of Physicians, 57, 134, 143, 214
Royal Society, the, 140–1, 143, 154–5, 171, 178, 214, 216
Ryder, Dudley, 179

Sacheverell, Henry, 202–5, *203*
St Alphege, Archbishop of Canterbury, 9
St Augustine's Church, Watling Street, 12, 13, 25, 118, 135, 266, *266*
St Erconwald, Bishop of the East Saxons, 8–9, 72, 174–5
St Faith's Chapel, 12, 78, 139, 156, 174
St Gregory's Church, St Paul's Churchyard, 12, 78, 97, 102, 134, 142
St Martin Church within Ludgate, 12, 134, 146
St Mary Colechurch, 12, 25, 26
St Mary Magdalene Church, Knightrider Street, 135

St Mary Spital pulpit, 24, 78
St Michael le Querne Church, 12
St Paul's Cathedral designs: dome, 146; First Model, 136; Great Model, 137; Greek Cross, 137; Warrant, 138, 146
St Paul's School, 87–9, 96, 98, 115, 130, 134, 211, 227, 265
St Peter's College, 13, 46–7, 59
St Peter's Church, Cornhill, 6, 25
St Thomas Becket, Archbishop of Canterbury, 12, 15, 17, 25, 26, 87, 175
St Vedast Church, Foster Lane, 12–13, 78
Sancroft, William, Dean of St Paul's, 135, 141, 147
Seymour, Edward, Duke of Somerset, 44, 69–70, 71–2, 175
Shaa, Canon Ralph, 35, 85
Shakespeare, William, 21, 31, 32, 35, 53–4, 57, 88, 95, 99, 100–1, 113, 150, 217
Sheldon, Gilbert, Archbishop of Canterbury, 135
Shore, Jane, 35–6
Shrewsbury, William, 157, 169
Smithfield, 2, 6, 18, 25, 108
Smollett, Tobias, 209
Smyth, Richard, 69–70, 76, *Plate 4*
Society for Promoting Christian Knowledge (SPCK), 252, 288 n7
Starkey, John, 165–6
Stationers' Company, 39–40, 41–2, 46–7, 49, 59, 129, 158–60, 169, 206
Stationers' Hall, 37, 123, 129, 134, 158, 160, *218*, 269, *Plate 11*
Stillingfleet, Edward, 140–1
Stonley, Richard, 3–4, 53–5, 78
Stow, John, 4, 6, 8, 10, 23, 24, 26, 72, 83, 140–1, 150, 176–7
Strong, Thomas, 142, 147
Sudbury, Simon, Archbishop of Canterbury, 28

Tallis, John, 5, 244–6, *245–6*, 248
Taswell, William, 129, 130
Temple Bar, 173, 273

Thomason, George, 153
Thornhill, James, 147, 179
Tijou, Jean, 144
Tokefield, George, 159, 160
Tunstall, Cuthbert, Bishop of London, 43, 65
Tusser, Thomas, 86–7, 89
Tyndale, William, 43, 57–8, 66, 264

Victoria, Queen of Great Britain, 232–3, 237–9
von Uffenbach, Zacharias Conrad, 172–3, 178

Walton, Brian, Bishop of Chester, 150, 152, 160
Walton, Izaak, 109–10, 125
Ward, Ned, 164, 168, 179, 181–2, 184–5, 196
Warwick Lane, 134, 143
Warwick, Richard Neville, Earl of, 34
Watts, Joseph, 167
Webster, John, 117
Wellesley, Arthur, Duke of Wellington, 231–3, 250, 253, *Plate 16*
Westcott, Sebastian, 86, 90, 93
Whitgift, John, Archbishop of Canterbury, 81, 84, 97
Whitney, Isabella, 3–4, 51–2
William III, King of England, 144–6, 167, 171, 178, 202, 223–4, 227
Wolfe, Reginald (Reyner), 41–2, *45*, 44–6, 49, 52, 70, 280 n7
Wollstonecraft, Mary, 220–1
Wolsey, Thomas, Cardinal, 62–4, 65, 68–9
Woodroffe, Edward, 133, 139
Wren, Christopher, 10, 128, 131, 132, 135–49, 154, 160, 171, 178–9, 188, 223, 269, 271, 273
Wriothesley, Charles, 70–1
Wycliffe, John, 27–9, 65, 76, 264

York, Richard, Duke of, 33–5
Young, John, 182